THE UNDEAD
AND THEOLOGY

THE UNDEAD
AND THEOLOGY

KIM PAFFENROTH AND JOHN W. MOREHEAD

◆PICKWICK *Publications* • Eugene, Oregon

THE UNDEAD AND THEOLOGY

Copyright © 2012 Wipf and Stock Publishers. All rights reserved. Except for brief quotations in critical publications or reviews, no part of this book may be reproduced in any manner without prior written permission from the publisher. Write: Permissions, Wipf and Stock Publishers, 199 W. 8th Ave., Suite 3, Eugene, OR 97401.

Pickwick Publications
An Imprint of Wipf and Stock Publishers
199 W. 8th Ave., Suite 3
Eugene, OR 97401

www.wipfandstock.com

ISBN 13: 978-1-61097-875-0

Cataloguing-in-Publication data:

The undead and theology / edited by Kim Paffenroth and John W. Morehead.

xx + 276 pp. ; 23 cm. Includes bibliographical references and index.

ISBN 13: 978-1-61097-875-0

1. Zombies. 2. Zombie films—History and criticism. 3. Vampires. 4. Christian theology. 5. Popular culture. I. Paffenroth, Kim, 1966–. II. Morehead, John W. III. Title.

BF1543 P34 2012

Manufactured in the U.S.A.

Contents

Acknowledgments · vii
Introduction · ix
Contributors · xvii

PART ONE: VAMPIRES

1. Vampires and Female Spiritual Transformation: Laurell K. Hamilton's *Anita Blake, Vampire Hunter*
—*Vicky Gilpin* · 3

2. Crossing the Spiritual Wasteland in *Priest*
—*Joseph Laycock* · 19

3. Vampires Are People, Too: Personalism in the Buffyverse
—*Jarrod Longbons* · 34

4. The Vampire that Haunts Highgate: Theological Evil, Hammer Horror, and the Highgate Vampire Panic in Britain, 1963–1974
—*W. Scott Poole* · 54

PART TWO: ZOMBIES

5. The Living Christ and *The Walking Dead*: Karl Barth and the Theological Zombie
—*Jessica DeCou* · 79

6. Zombie Walks, Zombie Jesus, and the Eschatology of Postmodern Flesh
—*John W. Morehead* · 101

Contents

7   When All Is Lost, Gather 'Round: Solidarity as Hope Resisting Despair in *The Walking Dead*
    —*Ashley Moyse* · 124

8   Apocalyptic Images and Prophetic Function in Zombie Films
    —*Kim Paffenroth* · 145

9   Negotiating (Non)Existence: Justifications of Violence in Robert Kirkman's *The Walking Dead*
    —*J. Ryan Parker* · 165

PART THREE: OTHER UNDEAD

10 When You're Undead, the Whole World Is Jewish
    —*Arnold T. Blumberg* · 195

11 "Eat of My Body and Drink of My Blood": Johannine Metaphor, Gothic Subculture, and the Undead
    —*Beth Stovell* · 209

12 Fire, Brimstone and PVC: Clive Barker's Cenobites as Agents of Hell
    —*Andrea Subissati* · 227

Bibliography · 241
Index · 257

Acknowledgments

Thanks go to Christian Amondson at Wipf and Stock, for making the editorial process go exceptionally smoothly.

Most of the cost of typesetting was financed by generous grants from Iona College (New Rochelle, New York) and St. Thomas University (Miami Gardens, Florida). The editors would like to thank these schools for their commitment to putting the academy in dialogue with the larger community, helping to show how popular culture is a vital and worthwhile object of scholarly analysis, while also demonstrating the relevance of scholarship to a wider audience outside the confines of academia. The remainder of the cost was raised through a Kickstarter campaign (www.kickstarter.com). Among the backers of that campaign, special thanks go to John Cozzoli, Jessica DeCou, Chris Dockins, Anthony Hogg, Robert P. Kennedy, William Lebeda, Vicente Melendrez, Mark Moroz, and Ursula K. Raphael.

Finally, we were assisted with the indexing by Savannah M. Lang, a student in the Iona College Honors Program.

Introduction

KIM PAFFENROTH AND JOHN W. MOREHEAD

In times past, various undead creatures were the stuff of folklore, later literature, and finally the silver screen and the small screen. But these monsters have not stayed within their narrative media. They have had a tendency to break out, and now vampires, zombies, and many other monsters can be found throughout popular culture. The academy has taken notice, and now it is possible to find any number of volumes that take a serious look at the meanings of our monsters beyond their entertainment value. Two monsters have been especially popular, and hence have received large measures of scholarly scrutiny. The vampire and the zombie are the focus of many academic studies from a variety of analytical perspectives, from media studies to sociology to political science to philosophy. But despite the increasing number of academic studies of the monstrous, those providing a theological or religious analysis have been relatively few. On the one hand this is curious because several scholars have noted the intimate connection between religion and monsters, and the Judeo-Christian tradition—the most influential in the Western world—is no exception to this phenomenon. But on the other hand, the hesitancy to connect theology to the monster is understandable, particularly among religious conservatives, who may have a tendency to sanitize their religious tradition, and put a wedge between their understanding of the divine and the darkness that the monstrous symbolizes and embodies. But it is the contention of this volume that keeping monsters at arms length means missing an important opportunity for theological reflection. Humanity has a long history of monstrous expression, many times intertwined with our religious traditions, and therefore something

Introduction

valuable can be gained by drawing upon various monsters and engaging them with critical theological reflection.

A few words are in order about the selection and arrangement of the material in this volume. We are familiar with the debates about definitions in regards to the term "undead," and while vampires are usually put under this categorization, zombies are questionable, with some preferring labels like "living dead" or other terms. In the pages that follow the reader will find discussions of vampires, zombies, as well as other "monstrous" creatures not usually considered under the common or traditional label of the "undead." Although we support precision in scholarly definitions, and recognize the importance of such considerations in various contexts, the intent of this volume is to cast a wide net so as to consider a broader meaning of undead, defined more by what these creatures have in common, rather than what separates them, and thereby to see how they function as objects and catalysts for theological reflection. In addition to this definitional consideration, this volume is arranged by the type of creature, beginning with the vampire, moving in turn to the zombie, and concluding with three other forms of monstrous expression. The essays within each section are presented in alphabetical order by the author's name.

Vicky Gilpin provides a consideration of the vampire through a popular literary take on the creature. An originator of the "urban fantasy" genre, Laurell K. Hamilton's *Anita Blake, Vampire Hunter* series encouraged new pop cultural interpretations of vampire existence and the effects vampires have on humans and other paranormal creatures, as well as vice versa. Through the mostly human protagonist's psychological, magical, and spiritual growth as a result of her paranormal circumstances, the works explore the question, "What is the definition of monsterhood?" A character with strong religious identification, Anita's increasingly sex-based powers and desires, as well as her ruthlessness in protecting those she considers her own, often cause her to question her spiritual standing. The depictions of religion and spirituality in the Anita Blake series, as well as the constant themes of sexual power, demonstrate the importance of a character's spiritual and reflective journey as another lens through which to view theology and the undead. Anita Blake's spiritual journey relied on not only her closeness to the monsters, but also her exploration of different types of spirituality, which allowed her to accept other modes of worship or belief; her journey also showed the importance of love and friendship as elements of spiritual transformation.

Introduction

The following chapter considers vampires in cinema. Joseph Laycock provides an analysis of the film *Priest* (2011), a vampire film that combines elements of the science fiction, Western, and martial arts genres. While theater audiences found this mix difficult to digest, *Priest* does succeed in manipulating audience expectations about vampires and their relationship to the sacred order. In *Priest*, the Church has the power to protect us from vampires, but it is also a totalitarian monster-state. Meanwhile, the vampires are utterly devoid of humanity, and yet they possess a sort of alien divinity. As Laycock demonstrates, the horror of *Priest* is not the vampires as a manifestation of demonic evil, but the possibility of an anomic world where the sacred order is undone, and good and evil are no longer meaningful categories. With the protagonist, the audience is left in a wasteland where our assumptions about the sacred appear to lie in ruins.

Jarrod Longbons continues the exploration of the vampire by interaction with a popular expression of the creature in television. In his essay, Longbons argues that the vampires of folklore express ancient anxieties about the body and the duality between good and evil. Contemporary postmodern vampires, however, such as those found in *Buffy the Vampire Slayer* (BtVS), reveal current secular anxieties, such as the threat of absurdity and the desire for belonging. An initial reading of BtVS might conclude that the contemporary vampire is simply a human, soulless body that has been possessed by a demon. But deeper readings reveal ambiguity over the "life" of the undead in the Buffyverse. This essay makes use of the theological personalism of both John Paul II and Benedict XVI to demonstrate the real distinction between humans and vampires in the Buffyverse: relationships founded on altruism. From this perspective, the difference is not merely the presence of a metaphysical soul, but personalism founded on a series of relations. The importance of a soul in BtVS is not its ontological status, but that it gives creatures the ability to be persons in relation. In the character arc of the vampire "Spike," one of the undead is capable of becoming a person as part of its redemption (and humans are capable of being less than persons in BtVS). In BtVS, this redemption is wholly immanent; Spike's highest good arrives when he lives in and for the community, but never for God.

The last essay in the vampire category takes a historical approach. W. Scott Poole's chapter examines how Hammer Studio films use of satanic metaphors in the late 60s and early 70s reflected an increased fascination with the devil as a new kind of horror film monster, as well as anxieties

Introduction

about "real" devil worship. His analysis includes the work of several significant evangelical and Pentecostal theologians whose work touched on the role of the demonic, such as Carl F. H. Henry, Gordon Fee, and John Christopher Thomas. The essay shows the links between moral panics, modern folklore, theology, and film audiences.

This volume continues by way of theological reflection on the undead through interactions with the zombie. Jessica DeCou devotes her chapter to zombies in a popular television series. The characters that inhabit the bleak world of AMC's *The Walking Dead* are confronted with a variety of ethical and theological questions concerning the nature of life and death, the meaning of hope, the intersection of faith and doubt, and one's rights and responsibilities in relation to the other (living or dead or otherwise). Subject to an incessant barrage of evidence against divine immanence and benevolence, those who struggle to live under the tyranny of the dead are stricken with a sense of spiritual abandonment so profound as to threaten their very humanity. DeCou's essay steps into this dark and dangerous world in an effort to explore these issues from a more systematic theological perspective. Using Karl Barth's theology as a starting point, this chapter considers the potential impact such a scenario might have on our understanding of fellow-humanity and the traditional Christian doctrine of bodily resurrection in the eschatological future. Ultimately, the central question underlying this fictional analysis is whether the struggle to survive in so grim and brutal a world could serve to reanimate, or only to destroy, eschatological hope.

The zombie in popular culture can now be found in a variety of manifestations, and John W. Morehead explores the Zombie Walk phenomenon. At some of these gatherings Zombie Jesus can be found, and Morehead suggests that the presence of a satirical religious figure at the walks hints that something more than entertainment is involved. He discusses how these events involve imaginative postmodern twists on Christian eschatology, including apocalyptic and resurrection narratives. But there is more. Drawing upon the work of Walter Kendrick and Linda Badley, he considers how horror and the zombie function as a means of expressing anxieties about death, as well as a means for experimentation with concepts of the body and the self. In the Zombie Walk, a satire of Christian resurrection is at play, but drawing upon Catherine Albanese and her analysis of American metaphysical religion and its enlightened body-self, a postmodern form of Christian eschatology combines with metaphysical ideas in popular culture, resulting in a new synthesis in

Introduction

body-self concepts. In the final section of the essay, Morehead offers suggestions for theologians who want to participate in self-reflection through engagement of the Zombie Walk in popular culture.

In another chapter examining *The Walking Dead*, John Ashley Moyse discusses the despair that tempts the many survivors in a world where the dead walk. Yet, hope may be found with someone, somewhere. This essay explores the themes of despair and hope as revealed in the television series, while also attempting to argue that hope, as embodied solidarity, has the potency and power to overcome despair. Friedrich Nietzsche serves to instruct on the theme of despair, which is the condition of the nihilist, overcome by the meaninglessness of life. Solidarity as hope is explored through the writings of Gabriel Marcel, Dietrich Bonhoeffer, and Karl Barth. Through these individuals, Moyse argues that authentic relationships encountered in the community of survivors may offer the survivors not only strength, but also hope during times of crisis. In this, nihilism is not negated, but hope is offered as an embodied counterweight that may overcome it as one chooses to live not only with, but also for the others tempted by despair.

Kim Paffenroth adds to the reflection on the zombie, tying it to biblical narratives. Paffenroth's essay shows how Romero's zombie films—especially *Dawn of the Dead* (1978) and *Land of the Dead* (2005)—build on two major biblical genres—apocalyptic and prophecy. While the imagery and the final outcome are more directly reminiscent of the horrors of Revelation and Ezekiel, the anti-racist, anti-capitalist message of the films continues the social critiques offered by the Hebrew prophets.

The final essay under the zombie category interacts with *The Walking Dead*, but does so by way of the graphic novel. J. Ryan Parker's chapter considers instances of violence between humans and zombies, and within and between communities of survivors in Robert Kirkman's comic book series, *The Walking Dead*. With violence plaguing Kirkman's world well before zombies stumbled on the scene, this chapter considers how this apocalyptic moment intensified violence between humans. Their violent tendencies explode in reaction to the zombie presence and further degrade their interactions with one another, proving that the humans themselves are a greater threat to their future survival than the zombies could ever be. Yet Kirkman also provides glimpses of pacifism in the zombie apocalypse that should give readers pause as characters briefly try out more peaceful ways of living in a violent world. Kirkman's narrative sheds light on our own violent condition and our justifications

Introduction

of it, reveals how we are more often than not our own greatest enemy, and suggests ways for nonviolently negotiating our own precarious existence. In the process, this chapter engages several recent scholarly texts on *The Walking Dead* and the zombie genre at large, as well as essays on moral justifications of violent behavior. Of special importance are studies of the series and genre that highlight the problems of violence and the ways in which, through violence, humans become something akin to zombies themselves.

As popular as vampires and zombies are in popular culture, they are not the only monsters lurking in the shadows. The concluding section of this book considers other "monstrous" figures, starting with the golem. In his essay, Arnold T. Blumberg asks, "When the subject of the living dead arises, where are the Jewish zombies?" Although it may not fit within the expected categories of its fellow undead, the mythical golem holds a unique position as an artificially constructed, supernaturally animated liminal being caught between life and death, neither and both at the same time. Jewish folklore often features these creatures in stories of injustice and vengeance. The automaton is impelled by belief in God, but is a possible danger to its creator as much as its intended victims. Tales of the golem provide a vital link between the more familiar legends of the living dead around the world and are often overlooked in our expanding exploration of their cultural impact. Blumberg makes a good argument that it is time for the golem to get a little respect.

Although not usually considered monsters, members of the Gothic subculture have a long history of interactions with death and the undead. Beth Stovell contributes an essay that examines inclusion and exclusion in the biblical Johannine literature, Gothic subculture, and modern "undead" literature, suggesting three critical ways that apocalyptic metaphors are used in these contexts: first as a reaction against mainstream culture; second, as a reaction against exploitation; and third, as a form of paradox and irony that subverts expectation. By creating a group of insiders and rejecting the culture of its time, these Gothic and "undead" literatures, music, and films, like the Johannine corpus, provide solace and a community for their readers and viewers, reinterpreting apocalyptic metaphor, and informing social identity.

With the final essay in this volume, Andrea Subissati draws upon Clive Barker's cenobites. In Barker's 1986 novella *The Hellbound Heart*, Frank Cotton's search for the ultimate carnal experience leads him to discover and open a gateway into hell. Far from the orgiastic pleasures he had hoped for, hell is a site where sensation of all kind is experienced and the line between pleasure and pain is blurred. He is greeted by undead creatures known as "cenobites," who conduct experimentation on the further reaches of experience. Having summoned the cenobites by opening the portal, Frank is dragged into hell where he becomes their prisoner for an eternity of torture until his lover Julia tries to reincarnate him to his physical form. Barker's novella and the film franchise that came of it are laden with theological concepts, particularly through Barker's modernized conceptions of sin and culpability. His cenobites can be conceived of as contemporary demons, a new and novel take on classic conceptions of "the devil." In this chapter Subissati analyzes Barker's unique mythos of the cenobites and their version of hell with a focus on how they inform/engage with Christian conceptions of heaven and hell, sin and temptation, and the body/soul dichotomy.

We believe you will find the pages that follow interesting and challenging, both in terms of an understanding of various undead creatures in popular culture, and what they may have to tell us by way of theological reflection. In the classic horror film *The Bride of Frankenstein*, Dr. Pretorius offered a toast to his new collaborative venture with the words, "To a new world of gods and monsters." We offer the same sentiments in our collaborative exploration of the undead and theology.

Contributors

ARNOLD T. BLUMBERG is an author, book designer, educator, former museum curator, and internationally recognized zombie expert. He has written numerous books and articles on genre entertainment and pop culture history, and served for many years as Editor of *The Overstreet Comic Book Price Guide*. He co-authored *Zombiemania: 80 Movies to Die For*, contributed to *Triumph of the Walking Dead* and *Braaaiiinnnsss!: From Academics to Zombies* as well as the *Doctor Who: Short Trips* series, and writes for IGN.com and AssignmentX.com. He teaches a course on zombies in popular media at the University of Baltimore that garnered worldwide press coverage, as well as a course in comic book literature at the University of Maryland. He sometimes checks to see how fast he can unlock his door in case of a sudden zombie apocalypse. His website is located at atbpublishing.com.

JESSICA DECOU earned a PhD in theology from the University of Chicago Divinity School in 2012. She has served as a Louisville Institute Dissertation Fellow, a Junior Fellow at the Martin Marty Center for the Advanced Study of Religion, and has taught courses on theology and popular culture at McCormick Theological Seminary. She has written on a range of topics and figures, from Karl Barth's theology of humor to the life and death of Hank Williams to the work of Louis C.K. Her publications include articles in the *International Journal of Systematic Theology*, *Word and World*, *Encyclopedia of the Bible and its Reception*, and *Christianity Today*.

VICKY GILPIN has an EdD in Educational Leadership and is a teacher at Cerro Gordo High School, Richland Community College, and Millikin University in Illinois. She is also a long-time lover of vampires, horror, and fantasy; she credits the Popular Culture Association/American Culture Association (PCA/ACA) with providing her with the courage to explore those realms. Recent publications are "A Female Protagonist,

Sex with Monsters, and Questionable Femmes Fatale: The Continuing Tension of Noir Elements in Laurell K. Hamilton's *Anita Blake, Vampire Hunter* series," in *Women Without Borders* and "Hungering for Appropriate Instruction: Desperately Seeking the Meddling-in-the-Middle Model in Rice's *Interview with the Vampire* and Holland's *Lord of the Dead*," in *Research and Criticism*, and a recent presentation is "If It Weren't Written with Vampires In Mind, It Should Have Been: A Vampiric Analysis of Wallace Stevens' 'Tea at the Palaz of Hoon'" for the PCA/ACA in 2012. Currently, she is pondering thesis topics to complete her Master's degree from Harvard University Extension School.

JOSEPH LAYCOCK is a graduate of Harvard Divinity School's Program in Religion and Secondary Education and worked as a high school teacher for several years. While teaching in Atlanta, he began doing ethnography of the Atlanta Vampire Alliance that resulted in his book *Vampires Today: The Truth About Modern Vampirism* (Praeger, 2009). Laycock briefly rode the *Twilight*-media-train appearing on *Geraldo*, NPR, MSNBC, the History Channel (Canada), and numerous late night radio programs. He now holds a PhD from Boston University and continues to publish on issues of religion as it relates to society, education, and popular culture. Laycock currently teaches at a local college and is a blogger for Religion Dispatches.

JARROD LONGBONS is a doctoral candidate in the Department of Theology and Religious Studies at the University of Nottingham. His thesis focuses on a genealogy of nature-culture dualism in order to understand the ideologies that create our current ecological crisis. In addition to his work as a theologian, he is also the associate minister at Northside Church of Christ in Bloomington, Illinois. There his research is applied through education and communal agriculture. Jarrod keeps a theological blog called www.theartofthegoodlife.blogspot.com where he writes on theology, philosophy, pop-culture, and agriculture. Although his main academic interest is in the theological doctrine of creation, the character of the vampire plays an important role in his understanding of human nature.

JOHN W. MOREHEAD has an MA in intercultural studies from Salt Lake Theological Seminary. He applies his academic background in religious and cultural studies to his work in religion and popular culture. In this area he has taught courses on theology and film, and contributed to *Halos & Avatars: Playing Games with God* (Westminster John Knox, 2010), *Butcher Knives & Body Counts: Essays on the Formula, Frights, and Fun of the Slasher Film* (Dark Scribe Press, 2011), *Horror Films of the 1990s* (McFarland, 2011), and an essay on Matrixism for the *Handbook of Hyper-Real Religion* (Brill, May 2012). He sits on the Editorial Board for *GOLEM: The Journal of Religion and Monsters*, and he regularly explores popular culture, the horrific and fantastic at his blog TheoFantastique.com, and as a contributor to Cinefantastique Online.

ASHLEY JOHN MOYSE is a PhD candidate in religious studies at the University of Newcastle, Australia. He also holds a master of science (N. Colorado) and a master of theological studies (Trinity Western) with specialization in applied physiology and ethics, respectively. He was also conferred the certificate of advanced studies in bioethics and health policy (Loyola-Chicago). His research interests focus on the intersection of theological ethics and/or theological anthropology in relation to the theory and practice of biomedical ethics. Zombie horror and classic western television and film serve as guilty pleasures. Ashley and his wife, Aime, call the Vancouver (Canada) region home but currently reside in the sleepy beach town of Newcastle, NSW, steps from the surf—a great distraction from research and writing.

KIM PAFFENROTH is Professor of Religious Studies at Iona College. He wrote several books on the Bible and theology, before turning his analytical gaze upon religious themes in horror. His examination of the Romero films, *Gospel of the Living Dead: George Romero's Visions of Hell on Earth* (Baylor, 2006), won the Bram Stoker Award. Since then he has written several zombie novels, including the *Dying to Live* series (Permuted Press, 2007–11) and *Valley of the Dead: The Truth Behind Dante's Inferno* (Permuted Press, 2010). He is the Senior Editor of *GOLEM: The Journal of Religion and Monsters*.

J. RYAN PARKER completed his PhD in Religion and the Arts at the Graduate Theological Union in Berkeley, California, with a focus on film and religion, particularly the history of religious cinema and contemporary independent religious films. His dissertation is being published by McFarland & Co. Publishers as *Cinema as Pulpit: Sherwood Pictures and the New Church Film Movement*. Along with his contribution to this collection, he has also contributed an essay to a collection on theology and film entitled *Light Shining in a Dark Place* (Pickwick, 2012). He holds a

Contributors

BA in English from Mississippi College and an MDiv from Wake Forest University Divinity School. He is also the creator and editor of and main contributor to Pop Theology (www.poptheology.com), a website that explores the intersections of religion/theology and popular culture.

W. SCOTT POOLE is the author of *Monsters in America: Our Historical Obsession with the Hideous and the Haunting* (Baylor University Press, 2011), and *Satan in America: The Devil We Know* (Rowman & Littlefield, 2009). A professor of American history at the College of Charleston, he teaches a number of courses related to the history of the supernatural and the fantastic in American society and culture. He is a regular contributor to Popmatters.com and blogs at www.monstersinamerica.com.

BETH M. STOVELL received her Masters degree in Interdisciplinary Studies from Regent College and her Doctorate in Christian Theology with a concentration in Biblical Studies from McMaster Divinity College. Beth is Assistant Professor of Biblical Studies at St. Thomas University in Miami Gardens, Florida. She has authored *Mapping Metaphorical Discourse in the Fourth Gospel: John's Eternal King* (Brill, 2012) and co-edited *Biblical Hermeneutics: Five Views* (InterVarsity, 2012) with Stanley E. Porter. Beth has contributed to several edited volumes including *Global Perspectives on the Bible* (Pearson Prentice Hall, 2012), *Dictionary of the Bible and Western Culture* (Sheffield Phoenix, forthcoming), *The New Testament in its Hellenistic Context* (Brill, forthcoming), and *The Language of the New Testament* (Brill, forthcoming). She is contracted to write a commentary on the Minor Prophets in the forthcoming Zondervan *Regula Fidei* series.

ANDREA SUBISSATI is a sociologist and writer on cultural studies and the horror film genre. In 2010, her first book on the social impact of zombie cinema was published under the title *When There's No More Room In Hell: The Sociology of the Living Dead* (Lambert, 2010). The book has been reviewed in *Rue Morgue* and *Fangoria* magazines, and she has made numerous appearances as a guest on the *Rue Morgue* podcast. Her current projects include chapter contributions for *Terror of the Soul: Essays on the Canadian Horror Film* (slated for release in 2013). Andrea lives and works out of Toronto, Ontario. She continues to indulge in her passion for all things dark and when she is not hunched over her laptop working on her blog (www.LadyHellbat.com), she can be found playing roller derby with The Gore-Gore Rollergirls.

PART ONE

Vampires

1

Vampires and Female Spiritual Transformation

Laurell K. Hamilton's *Anita Blake, Vampire Hunter*

VICKY GILPIN

"I believed in love, but I believed in evil, too. Neither love nor evil conquers all, but evil cheats more."[1]

IN HER SEMINAL WORK *Our Vampires, Ourselves*, Nina Auerbach not only analyzed how vampires signified multiple metaphors within two centuries, but also how they created a specific lens through which audiences and readers could perceive or interpret societal issues of their times. She explored how twentieth-century vampires altered the vampire paradigm, and she predicted that after a "long, restorative sleep," vampires would awaken to begin a new cycle of meaning.[2] The first decade of the twenty-first century has proven Auerbach correct: vampires have re-awakened and transformed. By not merely representing "the other" of one's choice, whether xenophobia, capitalism, or contagion and disease, these vampires continue to force mirrors upon the reader and society.

One interpretation of the vampire is as a symbol of entropy "because it is subversive, perverse, alienated, even evil, turning holy rite by

Part One: Vampires

parody to blasphemy."[3] As vampires have become more complex, developing particularly from the emotional and spiritual concepts explored by Anne Rice, they have become protagonists, lovers, and self-reflective, and in so doing, they directly challenge traditional interpretations, both of vampires and of world issues. Carter notes, "contemporary readers—and writers—more often see the vampire's otherness and sexual ambiguity as alluring. Hence the more or less traditionally supernatural vampire, as transformed in the novels of such authors as Anne Rice and Chelsea Quinn Yarbro, becomes attractive rather than horrible."[4] In *From Demons to Dracula: The Creation of the Modern Vampire Myth*, Matthew Beresford posits that as fascination and desire supersede fear of vampires, the vampires themselves must change.[5] The perception of religion or spirituality represents a provocative aspect of vampiric literary transformation: vampires have so often been depicted as antithetical to positive aspects of religion, like the purity of friendship, that interpreting vampires as anything but soulless and demonic when confronted by the purity of religious conviction, per *Dracula*, may seem contradictory to the commonly held belief of vampires as agents of entropy. However, analyzing vampires in conjunction with religious or spiritual tropes is plausible because of the anthropomorphization of religious as well as literary beings.[6] People attribute a mélange of human and superhuman properties or characteristics to religious and literary supernatural figures; in vampire literature, these characteristics evolve throughout a time period or a series depending on the needs of the readers, author, or literary situation. With vampires, the concern is to make the characters fit or comment on some recognizable vampire mythos while reflecting something fresh or original. For example, in *Vampire God: The Allure of the Undead in Western Culture*, Mary Y. Hallab notes how twentieth-century vampires began to rail against the confines of religious dualism; as perceptions about religious practice and belief altered, so did the vampires usually set in opposition to those perceptions. In addition, one cannot discuss theology and the undead without emphasizing Beth McDonald's *The Vampire as Numinous Experience*. Using Rudolf Otto's concepts of the numinous, particularly the fear and fascination perceived when confronting something powerful and other, McDonald argued that

> a textual experience of the numinous in the form of the vampire propels the subject of the experience on a spiritual journey involving both psychological and religious qualities, and that through that journey the reader, and possibly the main

character, begins to understand the value of his or her existence in the world and to negotiate a new relationship with the divine.[7]

RELIGIOUS ELEMENTS OF
ANITA BLAKE, VAMPIRE HUNTER

Laurell K. Hamilton's *Anita Blake, Vampire Hunter* series represents a transformative journey on many levels, but one lens through which the series can be viewed is that of a spiritual transformation, not only of the interiority of the protagonist and how that affects her personal world, but of how spirituality or religion is depicted within the vampiric world: how does the existence of vampires alter religious beliefs or practices? The works' protagonist and narrator is Anita Blake, a Christian, human, Noir-style civilian advisor to the police's Regional Paranormal Investigation Team who also raises zombies from their graves as part of Animators, Inc., and who is licensed to kill vampires. At first, her opinions echo many religious views about "the other" of all types: They are unknowable and unlovable, thus they are to be held at a distance, regulated, or destroyed. Initially, the soon-to-be Master of St. Louis, Jean-Claude, resonates with stereotypical vampire tropes: a powerful gaze, walking in dreams, simultaneous repulsion/attraction, and soullessness, in Anita's opinion. However, "Hamilton's vampires are not all bad guys, not the Old Enemy of God nor agents of Satan. They are natural beings in the universal order, some good, some bad, who, like most humans, just want to live (although sometimes a bit disreputably)."[8]

Early in the series, Christian symbolism is predominant, but even then, not all depictions are clear-cut in their duality: Jean-Claude bears a cross-shaped scar—as crosses figure heavily in the series as painful to vampires—but so does Anita from when she was tortured. Traditional Christian anti-vampire weapons such as holy water and crosses get mentioned often at the start of the series, but as the series progresses, non-Christian religious beliefs appear. In *Burnt Offerings*, Anita asks an evil vampire how much bad karma he has accumulated and if he is still a good Hindu; her religiously-focused pressure allows her to gain his permission to kill his son who had terrorized the paranormal people of St. Louis under Anita's protection. Several discussions occur about protection through metaphysical weaponry or defenses: in the series, some items such as charms and medicine bags may work whether one believes in

Part One: Vampires

them or not, and others depend on the strength of one's faith, though that faith need not be Christian, as evidenced by a character who carries a small Buddha figure. When Malcolm, the leader of the vampire church, mentions that he would like a priest to hear his sins, but he cannot because their crosses would glow in his presence, Anita answers, "The holy items only go off if the true believer panics, or if you try vampire powers on them." Anita has acquired this information through her journey described in many books because of her constant social contact with vampires, but which many vampires and believers did not know.[9] Religious self-proclamation versus true belief is debated often in the series as Anita ponders her own moral standing.

Through the series, religious methods occasionally meld, supporting the theme that faith, not the flavor of belief, is most important in fighting evil, and evil is usually not neatly divided between humans and vampires. In *Blue Moon*, during a werewolf ritual, Anita likens her psychic impressions and experiences at the lupanar, the werewolf traditional meeting place, to a form of worship. At the end of *Blue Moon*, prayers of multiple faiths mingle, followed by sex as ritual, both equally healing and powerful within that moment. In addition, a Christian witch, a Follower of the Way, is the wife of a coworker. In *Skin Trade*, Anita, a Wiccan warrior, and several assassins of different beliefs combine their preventative measures to defeat the first vampire, Marmee Noir, and her abduction or infestation of Anita. Anita's instruction and support from a Wiccan counselor also assists in her personal spiritual transformation. She continues to see herself as Christian, but she also gains from her interactions with Marianne, her advisor in managing the many spiritual and paranormal challenges with which she deals. In *Incubus Dreams*, Anita prays about sex and her intricate entanglements, and she gets an answer from Marianne via a phone call; this chain of events simultaneously distresses and inspires awe in Anita at a much higher level than Marianne, who demonstrates a blasé attitude for someone giving a deific message to its recipient.[10] As with everything in her life, Anita fights the self-reflection necessary to be comfortable in how her spirituality, while still strong, adapts to changing circumstances.

MONSTROUS INTIMACY AND TRANSFORMATION

Her humanization of "the other" of vampires (and Fey, werewolves, psychics, etc.) also alters her perception of religion through the series. At first, her thoughts about the vampire church, The Church of Eternal Life, are condescendingly derogatory. She and Malcolm, the head of the church, have an antagonistic relationship, particularly as she becomes closer emotionally and magically to Jean-Claude and wants Malcolm to behave more like a vampire who instills the respect, fear, and obedience of his congregation through a blood oath, and less like a benign and charismatic religious leader who expects his congregants to want to be good. Initially, she viewed vampires as soulless corpses. However, in *The Killing Dance*, because of a surplus of her power, she treated some vampires like the bodies of the zombies she animates and accidentally raises several vampires from their coffins. They were moving under her command, but their consciousness and senses of self were absent; a situation that horrified Anita because she knew these vampires as individuals with distinct personalities. While performing a ritual to return the vampires to their regular state of daytime torpor, so they would no longer be under her control, one of the vampire's presence returning at sunset displaces Anita's control from his body. Thus, another layer of the numinous developed in the series: vampires are viewed as more than walking corpses; they are still awe-inspiring, but an automatic definition of vampires as "soulless" became questionable. This realization, as well as her burgeoning powers, makes Anita view the so-called "monsters" differently, enough so that she supports legislation defending vampires who do illegal acts while under the control of stronger vampires, a far cry from when she was unsure if vampires should even be considered legal citizens in the first work, *Guilty Pleasures*.

Initially, even as Anita gains power, she gains it for Jean-Claude, encouraging a traditional masculine approach to the vampire as numinous, with Jean-Claude clearly in the dominant position as the all-powerful paranormal being. He supports this customary view in the eyes of other vampires who often equate his sentimentality toward Anita with weakness: "My human servant and my wolf are merely extensions of my power. Their hands are my hands; their deeds, my deeds. That is council law. So what does it matter where my power comes from?"[11] However, Jean-Claude notes that even with her as his human servant, he fears who might become the actual master, referencing Anita's strength of will and questioning the stability of the normal numinous relationship in their situation. In *Cerulean Sins*, Anita says, "I don't have a Master. I'm not even sure I have an equal,"[12] and Jean-Claude warns the other third of their power base, "Don't you realize by now, Richard, that *ma petite* is either your equal or your master? She knows no other way to be."[13] His fears are reasonable, as Jean-Claude, Richard, and Anita form a powerful triumvirate that allows them to share abilities and increase all of their powers, but then Anita gains another triumvirate that includes her own vampire servant; as she begins gaining powers, often through sex very similar to ritual or attacks from other paranormal creatures, they do not only augment Jean-Claude's power base but also increase her own abilities, and she becomes a numinous force in her own right. However, her increased power and increasingly-intricate relationships cause Anita to question her behavior in regard to standard or socially acceptable religious mores, emphasized when Malcolm, head of the vampire church, indicates that although her influence may at times civilize Jean-Claude's naturally aggressive reactions to transgressors and challengers, he says, "I saw you once as his victim, Anita. Now I am no longer certain who is the victim, and who the victimizer."[14]

PERCEPTIONS OF NORMALCY AND MORALITY IN THE PARANORMAL WORLD

Many characters, including Anita herself, fetishized standard perceptions of normalcy, particularly heteronormative behavior, in a way that echoes adherence to socially acceptable religious guidelines. The series is rife with moments of soul-searching, particularly as Anita grows ever-closer to the monsters. She posits, "I was beginning to wonder if I was still a good Christian. I didn't doubt God. I doubted me. Having premarital sex with a vampire had shaken my faith in a lot of things."[15] However, the closer Anita got to the monsters, the more stereotypically monstrous qualities she embodied, the more she strayed from heteronormative behavior, the richer her interiority and theological depth. She defends her sexual, professional, and spiritual lifestyle, saying, "We're all creatures of light and darkness. Embracing your darkness won't kill the light. Goodness is stronger than that."[16] This theme appears in most of the books, underscoring Anita's spiritual transformation as she learns more about herself and others as individuals rather than representatives of specific ethnicities, religions, or species. In addition, the idea that darkness and light can coexist supports themes within the transforming dialogue of modern vampire literature. In *Narcissus in Chains*, Anita becomes a type of vampire, one who must feed the ardeur with sexual activity, which allows Jean-Claude to share some of his darker numinous aspects with Anita. McDonald notes, "It is through Otto's numinous, with all its attributes of mystery, dread, and fascination, that one finds the transcendence that makes life, as opposed to mere existence, possible."[17] Anita's spiritual journey through the series forces her to discover the difference between life and mere existence, particularly in regard to her sexuality, the meaning of love, and how self-reflection can benefit herself and others.

Keeping up with the needs of the ardeur require Anita to review her own self-image, particularly that of being a moral person.[18] Even when attempting to date only Jean-Claude and Richard, the leader of the werewolves, to maintain their power base causes her opinions based in her Midwestern roots some squeamishness. Gaining a type of vampirism that forces her to feed sexually or she will drain Damien and Nathaniel, her other triumvirate, and then die herself, is both a curse and a blessing. It horrifies the vague part of her that still believes only a single monogamous relationship is morally appropriate and taxes her relationships with those she loves when circumstances require her to have sex with people she does not love. However, the ardeur also forces her to reflect upon her true sexual desires rather than remaining oppressed and miserable because of guilt encouraged by the religious mores of her youth. Anita comments to Richard, the monogamy-minded, self-hating dominant werewolf, "The only true happiness, Richard, lies in knowing who you are—what you are—and making peace with it."[19] This is a hard realization for Anita to maintain because her default modes include anger, self-recrimination, and guilt, but through the series, she learns that she has to love or accept herself, even the parts society would deem monstrous, before she can provide stability or love to anyone else. Self-reflection and acceptance are integral to Anita's transformative journey, as they have been in the life of the author. In her Afterword to *The Laughing Corpse*, Laurell K. Hamilton states,

> In many ways Jean-Claude's seduction of Anita is my own seduction, not by another man, but by who I am. Who I truly am. Not some sanitized version of what other people wanted me to be, but who I truly was meant to be. No, not meant to be, who I was. This was the beginning of me understanding my

own sexuality, my own religious path, and what it meant to truly harm none, not even yourself.[20]

SEX, LOVE, AND FRIENDSHIP AS SPIRITUALLY TRANSFORMATIVE

Sexuality, personal understanding, and spirituality twine together with a common thread in the *Anita Blake, Vampire Hunter* series: love. Despite, or because of, the increase of what some religious practitioners might view as extreme or immoral sexual practices, such as group sex, BDSM, and homoeroticism, when Anita became a succubus through the ardeur, the importance of love became repeatedly emphasized. Love is difficult for Anita: modeled after Noir anti-heroes, she has difficulty with emotional acknowledgement or expression; an example of this is when she notes, "I'd been willing to kill for the people I loved for a very long time; now I had to start living for them."[21] Not only perceived as a certain way because of her petite size and gender, but also betrayed by a fiancé when his family learned of her Mexican heritage, and constantly betrayed by Richard, who hates her comfort with the monsters, her job, and her sexuality, Anita is suspicious that those who declare love want to change her, so self-reflection is a painful and important part of her spiritual transformation.

Her emotional growth is demonstrated in *Incubus Dreams* when Anita mentions,

> There comes a point where you just love someone. Not because they're good, or bad, or anything really. You just love them. It doesn't mean you'll be together forever. It doesn't mean you won't hurt each other. It just means you love them. Sometimes in spite of who they are, and sometimes because of who they are. And you know they love you, sometimes because of who you are, and sometimes in spite of it.[22]

Anita may wish for tolerance from her family and society—as her grandmother prays for her soul because of her necromancy and she could lose her jobs as a grandfathered-in Marshall and part of the Paranormal Investigative Team if she shifts due to the multiple strains of lycanthropy in her veins, or if someone official discovers her psychic vampirism and the true depth of her connections to so many of the monsters—but she wants acceptance from her friends and lovers. In an interview, Laurell K.

Hamilton comments, "Once you look at these creatures and realize that they aren't monsters, they become people to you. That means if you love someone who is a lycanthrope, do you truly love them, or do you only love half of them?"[23]

What is seen as an increased humanization of late twentieth-century American religion can be perceived in correlation to an increased awareness of the power of gender in religion, thus increasing religion's flexibility and ability to meet the needs of more people.[24] This humanization and flexibility emphasized an awareness of the power of the emotional aspects of religiosity and spirituality. Despite her hard-boiled exterior, Anita Blake's emotional self-reflection strengthens her power base as a numinous figure by simultaneously expanding her definitions of love and increasing her ruthlessness for those she loves. One of Anita's prime motivations is to keep safe those under her protection, a type of maternal love; when confronted with yet another challenge to her friends' happiness, she notes, "I thought failure meant them dying, or getting hurt. What I realized suddenly was that the true failure would have been if I hadn't given a damn. You can bandage a wound, set a broken bone, but not caring . . . you can't cure that, and you can't recover from it."[25] Friendship as a form of love and a form of power strengthens Anita and flummoxes older vampires who do not understand friendship or love. Her spiritual transformation in which love is a primary catalyst not only affects Anita. In *Burnt Offerings*, her offer of friendship allows her to gain a strategic advantage with scary council vampire, The Traveller, which allows her to save many of her friends. In *Narcissus in Chains*, her friendship and prior salvation of many shifters allows her to defeat challenges to her authority and set in motion the seeds for a Coalition to encourage more communication among shifters.

Before performing a magical sexual ritual to keep their territory safe, Jean-Claude says, of the potential outcomes, "The worst is that we are dead, and our people will be at the mercy of others that do not love them."[26] The wording is integral in relation to religion as well as traditions of vampire literature. Jean-Claude could have as easily said "protect" or even "care about," but the word "love" is telling: Jean-Claude, Richard, and Anita must protect their territory, but the emotional connection to their people demonstrates love as an integral aspect of the numinous in Hamilton's series; purity of love may be argued as yet another supernatural quality that inspires fear and awe. Though Jean-Claude is no different from most literary vampires in that he craves power and manipulation,[27] his relationships appear to be multi-faceted in contrast with early depictions of vampires who only attempt to befriend for sanguinary advantage. Early vampiric works like *Dracula* and "The Vampyre" promised the intimacy of masculine love and friendship, while "Carmilla" allowed the female characters to achieve a certain intimacy denied to the male vampires.[28] The layers of love and friendship expressed in a variety of ways with concern to sexual, platonic, and emotional needs in the *Anita Blake, Vampire Hunter* series transform vampiric intimacy from the centuries-old promise to a modern reality.

Anita's regular lovers, including several who also love each other, are certainly not the "re-costuming of the heterosexual male lead" that makes Young Adult Paranormal Romance in literature so popular[29] because the series' issues of morality, sexuality, and love exhibit adult complexity as well as spiritual challenges. The difference between love and lust is mentioned often in the series, as understanding love is a key transformative element; the truly evil characters in the series do not see a difference between love and lust, and that is often their downfall when they face Anita and her companions. Interestingly, the original power that started Belle Morte's line, the line responsible for the ardeur, was powered by love,[30] but several times Belle Morte equates love and lust. When Asher, Jean-Claude's vengeful former and future lover enters the series, he threatens Anita because of the difference between love and lust: "You've finally given me what I need to hurt you, Jean-Claude. You love someone else at last. Love is never free, Jean-Claude. It is the most expensive emotion we have, and I am going to see that you pay in full."[31] However, by loving the emotionally and physically scarred Asher for himself, Anita sets him free from some of his anguish, which allows him to pursue a slightly less cruelty-laden relationship with Jean-Claude.

Laurell K. Hamilton emphasizes, "Sex between consenting adults who care for each other is never a bad thing."[32] In this case, the phrase "who care for each other" is integral as an aspect of love. Nathaniel and Asher represent dual sides of love: both have been betrayed in their lives, but Anita's love for them, spiritually healing for Anita as well as for them, may be even more powerful and provocative than her more traditional vampire-lover relationship with Jean-Claude.[33] Several times, Anita has had to come to the rescue of Nathaniel, a submissive leopard shifter with no stopping point; however, Anita's love allows him to not only have faith and hope in her, but also faith in his own strength. At the end of *Narcissus in Chains*, he shoots someone to protect her, and he comes to her rescue at the end of *Flirt*. Her relationships with Asher and Nathaniel "represent active transgression of her own sexual boundaries for the sake of love."[34] Not only does she explore her own sexual boundaries, Anita must plumb her emotional boundaries through reluctant self-reflection.

Anita fights not to love Nathaniel physically or emotionally because she sees him as someone to protect rather than to love; part of her transformation stems from the understanding that people who love each other can protect each other. In *Incubus Dreams*, she startles herself by admitting that she loves him, and in *Danse Macabre*, Nathaniel notes that he had to learn how to love her, a comment that causes chuckles among her friends and other lovers when she attempts to argue that she is not so difficult to love. Anita is told, "You truly want us all to be happy, Anita. You have no idea how rare it is for two people in a relationship to truly want the happiness of the other, but you juggle many hearts and seek happiness for all. It is a rare gift, this desire."[35] In addition, Anita's power of will and self-reflection alters the way she views the ardeur. At first, like with everything else self-reflective, sexual, or spiritual, she fought it as well as what it could teach her, denying the emotional lessons life provides. By working with the ardeur instead of against it, Anita learns that she can transform her perception of the ardeur: "I'd learned that the ardeur could be about friendship and not just romance. In that moment, it was even more than that. It was about that feeling of belonging, of being home."[36] The transformation of her perception of the ardeur represents a major triumph in Anita's spiritual journey because hating the ardeur was, in effect, hating a part of herself, and she could not love those she protects without self-love.

CONFRONTING PERCEPTIONS OF MORALITY

One of the most important works in the series in regard to theology and the undead would be *The Harlequin*, a book that begins with Anita's appointment with Malcolm, the leader of the vampire church, the Church of Eternal Life. He indicates his own sin is pride and is goaded into calling Anita a whore, as he has done before. When he asks if she worries about getting into heaven, she answers, "I did, for a while, but my faith still makes my cross glow. My prayers still have the power to chase the evil things away. God hasn't forsaken me; it's just that all the right-wing fundamentalist Christians want to believe that he has."[37] Richard and

Malcolm both equate lust to evil and non-heteronormative experiences as evil. In this way, they symbolize the dangers of partiality Anton Wilhelm Bohm wrote about in his letter "Universal Love: The surest way to advance the interest of religion, and unite the several contending parties about it" in 1709. Although certainly not discussing paranormal ménage and the intricacies between lust and love as paths to power and safety in a vampire-led city, Bohm asserted that divisions of belief and a reduced emphasis on love lessened religion because such prejudice shaded the eyes to the spiritual potential of oneself and others. He emphasized the importance of love of others as echoes of and encouragement toward love of the Divine.

At the climax of *The Harlequin*, Malcolm blood oaths to Anita, giving her power over him and his congregation; his selflessness toward his congregants transforms the ardeur from sex to love; as their enemies slam the congregants with fear, she promises them love: "love isn't the absence of pain. It's the hand to hold while you're going through it."[38] Her abilities kept the congregation and her friends safe for a moment, but they got buffeted again by more power; Nathaniel's surety and Damien's pain-forged calm kept them safe enough to reach Jean-Claude. However, Richard's self-hate, homophobia, and conviction that lust as an expression of love is bad, weaken them as their opponents pour self-doubt, depression, and horrific memories into them. Even Malcolm defends Anita's choices to Richard by saying, "I felt what Anita and her triumvirate raised earlier. It was friendship, love as pure as any I've known. I begin to believe the ardeur is a jewel with many facets, but it needs light to shine."[39] Malcolm and Richard have felt safely hidden behind their walls of self-righteousness because so many of Anita and Jean-Claude's powers are sexual; however, Malcolm admits that he has been too judgmental in his condemnation. Anita defends herself to Richard, saying, "My cross still works for me, Richard. It still burns with holy light. God hasn't forsaken me." Richard responds by saying, "But he should have. He should have, don't you see? If what I believe is right, if what you say you believe is right, then your cross should not burn. You have broken so many commandments. You've murdered, tortured, fucked, but your cross still works. I don't understand that."[40] At this declaration, Anita realizes that Richard does not just hate her for her closeness to the monsters, but that he thinks she is truly evil. Her response indicates just how much Anita has developed on her spiritual journey since the first book:

> Maybe God isn't the sex police, Richard. Sometimes I think Christians get all hung up on the sex thing because it's easier to worry about sex than to ask yourself, *Am I a good person*? If as long as you don't have sex with a lot of people you're a good person, that's easy. It's easy to avoid that. It's easy to think, *I'm not fucking anyone, so I'm good*. It makes it easy to be cruel because as long as you're not fucking around, nothing you do can be that bad. Is that really all you think of God? Is he just the sex police for you and Malcolm? Or is it that sex is easy to worry about, easy to avoid, and the whole love-your-neighbor-as-you-love-yourself thing that's hard?[41]

At that, she and Jean-Claude release Richard from the embrace of their people, the only safeguard keeping all of their enemies' magic from destroying him with doubt, pain, and loss.

While Jean-Claude peruses the powers of his people for the right strategy to compete with the increased pressure of the painful magic, Anita thinks "He was vampire, which meant he was a cold power, a thing of logic, because emotions do not trouble the dead," but then she realizes he is merely quashing his emotions to give their enemies fewer weapons against them, as Richard's doubt was a weapon against them. That Jean-Claude feels the worst thing that could happen would be that they would all be dead, and their people would go to those who "did not love them," as he noted in *Incubus Dreams*, refutes the concept of vampiric emotionlessness and detachment, reinforcing the multiple layers of the numinous as demonstrated in the *Anita Blake, Vampire Hunter* series. As their enemies make them relive their worst memories of loss, it is Nathaniel's confidence who gives them the strength to defy the dark magic: his certainty born of Anita's love allows the ardeur to wash through them and the congregation, not with the lust Richard had feared, but with the strength of love and friendship.

Anita and Jean-Claude, as numinous figures, not only gain from the power of love, for and from each other as well as for and from those people they are trying to save, the transformation of the ardeur as a conduit for love reinforces the idea that only those people (vampires, shifters, necromancers, etc.) with the capacity to see the positive edge of lust without condemnation and understand the difference between lust and love have the capacity for spiritual growth. Jean-Claude demonstrates his ability to grow spiritually in *Bullet*, when he changes the direction of the ardeur to save their people once again: "My last solid thought was that we

Part One: Vampires

would not feed on death; we fed on life, on love, and I would not have my people serve the dark. We would serve the light."[42] Learning to accept the benefits of her powers and her intimacy with the monsters allowed Anita to recognize the multifaceted aspects of religion and accept herself when again fighting the embodiment of darkness, Marmee Noir, in *Hit List*:

> The power felt so good, and yet I knew I was draining the life out of two people, evil vampires, but still people. I prayed, not for help to do it, but that the power wouldn't corrupt me. That drinking in her darkness wouldn't make me evil, too. Using the most evil power I had, I prayed, and I didn't burst into flames, and no one's holy object glowed. I ate the darkness that existed before God thought light was a good idea, and he was okay with that; he created the darkness, too. He actually liked both just fine.[43]

CONCLUSION

As Anita became more accepting of the monsters and more open to love without the constraints of societal opinion as influenced by religion, she became more open to self-reflection and to religious tolerance. Anita Blake's spiritual journey is a sexual journey as well, but her awareness of the softer aspects of her personality affects everyone she wishes to protect, as Anita is no less ruthless in regard to love as she is when being challenged. However, much of the series focuses on Anita's challenges to herself and her questions of whether she would still be considered a moral person while doing certain activities, whether sexual or as part of her job. Through her continued association with the monsters, her own qualities others would view as monstrous, and reluctant self-reflection, she realizes that the question is not whether she would still be considered a moral person by the guidelines of others but whether she would consider herself a moral person by her own beliefs; beliefs that have expanded through the series. Anita Blake demonstrates the personal transformation created by acceptance—love—of the darker sides of oneself.

END NOTES

1. Hamilton, *Cerulean Sins*, 425.
2. Auerbach, *Our Vampires*, 192.
3. Dennison, *Vampirism: Literary Tropes*.
4. Carter, "Lust, Love, and the Literary Vampire," lines 27–30.
5. Beresford, *From Demons to Dracula*, 167.
6. Shtulman, "Variation in the Anthropomorphization," 1123–38.
7. McDonald, *The Vampire*, 2.
8. Hallab, *Vampire God*, 110.
9. Hamilton, *The Harlequin*, 10.
10. Hamilton, *Incubus Dreams*, 62–67.
11. Hamilton, *Burnt Offerings*, 72.
12. Hamilton, *Cerulean Sins*, 160.
13. Hamilton, *The Killing Dance*, 261.
14. Hamilton, *The Harlequin*, 4.
15. Hamilton, *Burnt Offerings*, 298.
16. Ibid., 208–9.
17. McDonald, *The Vampire*, 141.
18. Benefiel, *Reading Laurell K. Hamilton*, 47.
19. Hamilton, *Narcissus in Chains*, 434.
20. Hamilton, *The Laughing Corpse*, 328.
21. Hamilton, *Danse Macabre*, 302.
22. Hamilton, *Incubus Dreams*, 421.
23. Schindler, "Underworld Seductress," lines 36–39.
24. Porterfield. *The Transformation*.
25. Hamilton, *Narcissus in Chains*, 316.
26. Hamilton, *Incubus Dreams*, 538.
27. Auerbach, *Our Vampires*, 110.
28. Auerbach, "My Vampire, My Friend," 11–16.
29. Murphy, "Someday My Vampire Will Come?," 57.
30. Hamilton, *Skin Trade*, 517.
31. Hamilton, *Burnt Offerings*, 67.
32. Hamilton, *Ardeur*, 58.
33. Ibid. Devon Ellington's "Ardeur's Purpose," and Natasha Fondren's "The Domestication of a Vampire Executioner," examine the roles Asher and Nathaniel play in Anita's life in depth.
34. Clifton, "Showing the Scars," 193.

Part One: Vampires

35. Hamilton, *Danse Macabre*, 301.
36. Hamilton, *Skin Trade*, 236.
37. Hamilton, *The Harlequin*, 10.
38. Ibid., 369.
39. Ibid., 376.
40. Ibid.
41. Ibid., 377–78. Emphasis in the original.
42. Hamilton, *Bullet*, 174.
43. Hamilton, *Hit List*, 317.

2

Crossing the Spiritual Wasteland in *Priest*

JOSEPH LAYCOCK

PRIEST (2011) IS A vampire film that combines elements of the science fiction, Western, and martial arts genres. While theater audiences found this mix difficult to digest, *Priest* does succeed in manipulating audience expectations about vampires and their relationship to the sacred order. A century of vampire films has presented a dualistic worldview in which warriors bearing crosses fight against demonic vampires in the name of God and the Church. This formula is as old as George Melies's *Le Manoir du Diable* (1896—arguably the first vampire film ever made) in which a vampire-like character identified as Mephistopheles is turned to dust by a cavalier brandishing a cross.[1] Contemporary vampire films have offered variations on this formula. *John Carpenter's Vampires* (1998) featured priests more concerned with power than slaying vampires, while television and movies from *Dark Shadows* (1966–71) to *Buffy: The Vampire Slayer* (1997–2003), to *Twilight* (2008) have presented vampires who are more scrupulous and "human" than many of the living. But while these films offer variations on a dualistic framework, *Priest* unmakes the vampire formula almost completely. The Church does have the power to protect us from vampires, but it is also a totalitarian, monster state. The vampires are utterly devoid of humanity and yet they possess a sort of alien divinity. Several characters suggest that the vampires are more righteous than the hypocrisy of the Church. The horror of *Priest* is not the vampires as a manifestation of demonic evil, but the threat of a world where good and evil are no longer meaningful categories. With the protagonist, the audience is left in a wasteland of moral emptiness, where the sacred order appears to lie in ruins.

Priest is set in an alternate timeline in which humanity and vampires have fought an endless war, reducing much of the planet to wasteland. Humanity has gained the upper hand by creating "priests," super-powered humans who have been trained by the Church in vampire slaying. After the war, most of humanity lives in giant walled cities ruled by a theocratic police state. The last vampires are kept on "reservations" and the remaining priests are in retirement. The protagonist is simply named The Priest (Paul Brettany), suggesting that priests sacrifice their identities when they take their vows. Priests also bare large cross tattoos on their foreheads, marking them as living weapons of the Church. When the vampire threat resurfaces, The Priest finds that the Church is more interested in maintaining its power then in protecting humanity from evil. Worse, he learns that his fellow priest and former comrade has risen as one of the undead and is now leading the vampires in an attack against the cities. This vampire anti-priest also has no name. The credits name him as "Black Hat" (Karl Urban). Black Hat argues that the noble savagery of the vampires is preferable to the hypocrisy of the Church. He invites The Priest to join him in a war he claims will purify a sickened planet. The Priest rejects both the Church and the heretical teachings of the vampires, choosing neither the shelter of the city nor the hives of the undead. At the end of the film, we see The Priest heading into the radioactive wasteland alone, disillusioned, and angry. He seems to have overcome his crisis of faith, but it is not clear to the audience where he is going or what he has decided to do.

Priest is the second horror movie directed by Scott Stewart. The first was *Legion* (2009), which also stars Paul Brettany and deals with many of the same themes. In *Legion*, God has grown tired of humanity's wickedness and sends an army of angels to exterminate mankind. Brettany plays the archangel Michael, who chooses to rebel against God in order to defend humanity. Like *Priest*, *Legion* plays on the audience's expectations by presenting the traditional forces of God—angels and the Church—as antagonists. In each case, Brettany's character represents a "faithful remnant" of the sacred order.

What fascinates and horrifies about these films is not the bloodthirsty vampires or angels, but the fear that the world does not work the way we imagined it and that our faith in the sacred order could be misplaced. In *Sacred Terror: Religion and Horror on the Silver Screen*, Douglas Cowan argues that horror movies reveal "sociophobics"—fears that are socially constructed and culturally specific. Cowan suggests that the most frightening horror movies often have religious themes—a claim with which Stewart would certainly agree. Furthermore, by reading horror films as "sociophobic windows" we can learn much about the place of religion in society.

Legion and *Priest* both conform closely to a sociophobic that Cowan calls "the metataxis of horror" or "a shift in dominant or accepted taxonomies of the sacred."[2] In making this claim, Cowan draws heavily on the work of sociologist Peter Berger and his notion of "the sacred canopy." Berger argued that society and indeed our experience of reality have no inherent order and that any meaning must be socially constructed. This socially constructed order, which Berger calls the sacred canopy or "nomos" (a Greek term indicating "law" or "norms"), is necessary for human beings to live and function. When it is compromised, our world descends into primal chaos or *anomie*. *Anomie*, Berger explains is "the nightmare par excellence." Without the support of the sacred canopy:

> the individual is submerged in a world of disorder, senselessness and madness. Reality and identity are malignantly transformed into meaningless figures of horror. To be in society is to be "sane" precisely in the sense of being shielded from the ultimate "insanity" of such anomic terror. Anomy is unbearable to the point where the individual may seek death in preference to it. Conversely existence within a nomic world may be sought at the cost of all sorts of sacrifice and suffering—and even at the cost of life itself, if the individual believes that this ultimate sacrifice has nomic significance.[3]

Priest demonstrates the lengths to which human beings will go to avoid the terror of *anomie*. The humans who huddle in dark polluted cities monitored by the armed guards of the Church prefer this existence to the chaos and uncertainty of living in the wastelands. Early in the film, The Priest sees the corruption of his Church and asks a colleague, "Is this the world I fought for?" His friend responds, "No, but it's the only world we have left." The Church's propaganda, "God protects you. The Church protects you. The City protects you," describes perfectly the

Part One: Vampires

sacred canopy. These institutions protect humanity not from vampires, but from chaos and meaninglessness. Only a small percentage of enterprising humans attempt to form frontier communities in the wastelands. Eventually, we learn that those cast out of human society choose to become "familiars" or servants of the vampires. As Hicks, the wasteland sheriff explains, "Becoming a vampire slave ain't my idea of belonging, but people get all sorts of strange ideas." Even life among the vampires is preferable to one without order.

As an apostate priest, the protagonist is denied even the sense of community experienced by the vampire slaves. After breaking his vows, beating up the Church's soldiers, and leaving the city, The Priest speeds into the desert on a futuristic motorcycle. The motorcycle's monitor flashes the message "Entering Wastelands," signifying that the Priest is now beyond the protection of Church and city. Here, he has no name, no place in society, and is hunted by the Church and vampires alike. The Priest's dilemma demonstrates the true horror of life outside the sacred canopy. It is obvious that no one survives alone in the wasteland for long.

Cowan outlines three narratives commonly used to set up the metataxis of horror in which the sacred canopy is compromised: inversion, invasion, and insignificance. Horror films that feature an inversion of the sacred order reveal that the traditional allies and protectors of humanity are actually plotting against us. In invasion horror movies, an alternate sacred order enters our world represented either by an alien religion or alien gods. Finally, in films such as the *Hellraiser* series (1987–2005), the sacred order is revealed to be insignificant and unable to protect us from spiritual evil. In some ways, *Legion* and *Priest* simply revive plots from earlier horror films that feature the inversion of the sacred order. As Cowan notes, we have already seen deceptive and menacing angels in *The Prophecy* (1995), and *Constantine* (2005). Similarly, the theme of treachery within the Catholic Church appears in films such as *Stigmata* (1999), and *John Carpenter's Vampires* (1998).[4] *Priest* is original in that it uses the rival theologies of the Church and the vampires to present both an inversion and an invasion of the sacred order simultaneously. The world of the Church has become a corrupt police state, even as the heretical Black Hat presents a vision of an alternative world run by vampires. Black Hat invites The Priest to adopt his sacred order, one where human notions of good and evil have no place. In *Priest*, the horror of the vampires is not their slimy fangs or the preternatural speed with which they rend human flesh, it is the sickening possibility that they could actually be more righteous than the Church—that the world truly would be better off if the vampires won. The audience follows The Priest and his allies as they are caught between the inverted sacred order of the Church and the invading sacred order of the vampires.

THE WORLD OF *PRIEST*

Priest is loosely based on a Korean comic of the same name by Hyung Min-woo. The comic has a sprawling plot involving a battle between the forces of God and fallen angels that spreads chronologically across the crusades, the Wild West, and the modern era. Stewart's adaptation has an entirely new plot, but retains from the comic the themes of Manichaean dualism, apostasy, and heresy. In the comic, the protagonist is a fallen priest named Ivan Isaacs who stalks the desert on a quest for vengeance. Isaacs has a cross tattoo on his forehead and hides his face under a tattered Stetson, suggesting he is the basis for both The Priest and Black Hat in the film adaptation.[5] Min-woo himself drew from a milieu of fantasy films, comics, and video games that combined gothic themes with science fiction and the Old West. The PC game *Blood* (1997) featured a gunslinger who had risen from the dead to battle cultists. Black Hat and Ivan Isaacs also seem indebted to the film *Vampire Hunter D* (1985) where a half-vampire in a wide-brimmed hat hunts the undead in a post-apocalyptic wasteland.[6] To a certain extent, modern vampire fiction has always relied on the collision of genres and time periods. In Bram Stoker's novel *Dracula*, the heroes use nineteenth-century technology to battle a pre-modern supernatural evil. Steam trains, Stetson hats, and bowie knives have been *de rigeur* for vampire hunters ever since.

Priest begins with an animated sequence depicting an alternate history in which humans and vampires have warred for eternity. We see medieval knights fighting hordes of vampires followed by World War I-era soldiers armed with gas masks and flamethrowers. No human technology can match the physical prowess of the vampires until the creation of the priests, holy warriors with superhuman strength and speed. With the help of the priests, humanity is victorious and the few remaining vampires are confined to reservations. However, the war has clearly taken an enormous toll. Most of the world appears to be a radioactive wasteland. Ruined cities lie in the desert suggesting that nuclear weapons were used against the vampires. Humans are encouraged to live in dark,

Part One: Vampires

polluted, walled cities that are the seat of the Church's power. However, a few colonists have chosen to dwell in the wastelands and attempt agriculture in the radioactive soil. Monsignor Orelas, the leader of Cathedral City, states, "The wastelands are a haven for the lawless and the immoral."

The film's premise and setting bears a family resemblance to the world of the British comic character Judge Dredd, who first appeared in 1977. Dredd is a "street judge," a sort of futuristic lawman, who patrols "Mega-City One," a fascist urban society surrounded by radioactive wasteland. Judge Dredd upsets the cosmology of the superhero genre in much the same way that *Priest* upsets the cosmology of the vampire genre. Much like The Priest, Dredd has sacrificed his identity and embraced ruthless violence because he believes a totalitarian state is better than criminal lawlessness. Both characters reflect a world where the sacred order has been severely compromised. Danny Fingeroth argues that, "In *Judge Dredd*, the *world* is the monster."[7]

In the alternate history of *Priest* the threat of vampires has apparently always been too dire for other religions or secular governments to arise. All of humanity is ruled by a theocracy called simply "The Church." Although the Church is never explicitly stated to be Catholic, it is clearly inspired by the pre-Reformation Catholic Church. Historically, the vampire legend had little to do with the Catholic Church, as folk traditions surrounding vampires and vampire-like creatures come primarily from Orthodox Christian countries. Catholic theologians did not begin to debate the existence of vampires until the eighteenth century, with the majority dismissing them as superstition. In a letter to the archbishop of Leopolis in Poland, Pope Benedict XIV condemned belief in vampires claiming that these stories were promoted by unscrupulous priests seeking money for exorcisms.[8] However, contemporary fiction has firmly established the Catholic Church as the archenemy of vampires. In *Dracula*, Dr. Van Helsing uses Catholic implements such as holy wafers and crucifixes that disturb his English Protestant allies. The connection between vampires and Catholicism has now been firmly cemented by recent films such as *John Carpenter's Vampires* (1998), *Dracula 2000* (2000), *The Forsaken* (2001), and *Van Helsing* (2004).[9]

It is unclear whether the powers of the vampires and the priests are supernatural or merely superhuman. It is implied that the priests receive their abilities through a combination of natural aptitude, training, and alteration by some technological means. The Priest and his female counter-part, The Priestess, make cryptic comments that priests are usually chosen as children and that becoming a priest requires great sacrifice. The cross that is tattooed onto the priests recalls Revelation 7:3 where those who are to be spared the tribulation receive a seal upon their foreheads.

In addition to seeing the various knives, throwing blades, and other weaponry of the priests, we are also given some insight into their training. *Priest* is in many ways a thought experiment about Catholic history, and the fighting style of the priests may be the most interesting result of this experiment. Much of the priest's skill lies in understanding the nature of vampires, being able to calculate the trajectory of their lightning-fast movements, and intercepting them. The Priest explains to Hicks, "There are always two points: A and B. Know them both, and you'll kill a vampire." During several of the action sequences, The Priest and The Priestess appear to pause and calculate how to hit moving targets. These pauses distinguish *Priest* from similar action films such as *The Matrix*, which slow down action sequences only to further emphasize the speed of the martial artists. The Priest's thoughtful and systematic approach to vampire slaying is reminiscent of Thomism, the philosophical school founded by the Dominican theologian Thomas Aquinas. Thomism draws on Aristotle and emphasizes empirical epistemology, systematic ontology, and practicality. Had the Church been fighting vampires in the thirteenth century, it is possible that Aquinas might have given some thought to more efficient vampire slaying, resulting in a fighting style that relies more on geometry and ontology more than on militaristic fury.

A more obvious historical inspiration for the priests is the Knights Templar. The priests are not actually religious leaders but holy warriors. In the film, the term "clergy" is used to describe ecclesiastical authorities. Priests are subservient to clergy and, much like medieval knights, they genuflect when addressing them. (Notably, while we see a priestess, there are no female clergy, suggesting that women are still barred from ordination). The Knights Templar was an order of warrior monks created in the eleventh century to protect Christian pilgrims traveling to Jerusalem. Like the priests, the Templars were required to take a vow of chastity and were marked by large crosses on their uniforms. The Templars grew increasingly wealthy and powerful to the dismay of European monarchs. In 1314, King Philip IV of France accused the Templars of heresy, arrested as many as he could, confiscated their property, and executed their grand master, Jacque de Molay. Other European powers, including the pope, condoned Philip's suppression of the Templars.[10] This trope repeats itself in *Priest*, where the Church has come to fear the power of an order of holy warriors it has created. At the end of the film, The Priest appears to be organizing the remaining priests into some sort of secret order, much as the Templars are believed to have done.

THE INVERTED SACRED ORDER OF THE CHURCH

The Priest comes from "Cathedral City," one of several walled cities inhabited by the remaining humans. Cathedral City is an Orwellian dystopia run by The Church and united by fear. Audible and visual propaganda is everywhere, displaying messages such as "Faith. Work. Security." Whatever work is done in Cathedral City is clearly industrial as demonstrated by the harsh metal sets and a constant cloud of smog. We learn that since the war ended, the smog has placed Cathedral City in a state of perpetual darkness, making it ripe for vampire invasion.

Throughout the film, clergy repeat that, "To go against the Church, is to go against God." The rather ham-fisted message is clear: This is not a holy city, but a fascist city that uses religion as a tool of control. Cathedral City represents a mockery of Augustine's notion of "the city of God." (The town protected by Sheriff Hicks is named "Augustine," another reference to this theologian.) Appropriately, Augustine's work, *De Civitate Dei*, is, in a sense, a post-apocalyptic text. It was composed shortly after Rome was sacked by the Visigoths in 410 CE, an event that ushered in the so-called Dark Ages. Augustine framed human history as a struggle between two rival cities—the city of Man, which he associated with paganism and the Roman empire; and the city of God, a New Jerusalem governed by heavenly, rather than worldly, politics. The city of God, according to Augustine, will ultimately be triumphant. Superficially, Cathedral City resembles the city of God. It exists in the far future and is ruled by the Church rather than secular authorities. Its citizens are pious and austere, apparently taking no interest in worldly pleasures. But in reality, Cathedral City is a city of Man, and its leaders are preoccupied with worldly power rather than transcendent truth. Augustine writes that the city of Man is ruled by small gods who are "reduced to a kind of poverty-stricken power and eagerly grasp at their own private privileges and seek honor from their deluded subjects."[11] This is an apt description of the clergy of Cathedral City. However, Augustine argued that the City of man, while imperfect, still retained some virtues; life in Cathedral City resembles a kind of underworld, a true inversion of the City of God.

There are also two scenes depicting religious life in Cathedral City. We see the sacrament of confession at the beginning of the film and the sacrament of communion at the end. Both rituals are parodies of the proper Catholic sacraments. In the beginning of the film, The Priest is shown standing in a line waiting to enter a futuristic confessional. Heavily armed soldiers regulate the line, suggesting that confession is mandatory. While Catholic confessionals are designed to protect the identity of the penitent, in Cathedral City they are designed to expose their identity. The Priest enters the booth and states, "Bless me, father, for I have sinned," at which point a biometric computer program identifies his voice pattern and Monsignor Orelas appears on a videoscreen to take his confession. The sacrament of confession has been seamlessly fused with Orwellian surveillance technology. Adding insult to injury, the image of Orelas appears to be a recording. Rather than listening to the Priest's doubts, the image on the videoscreen offers an empty platitude, assigns an arbitrary penance, and sends him back onto the street.

At the end of the film, The Priest barges in on Monsignor Orelas as he is giving communion. Holding a cup of wine, Orelas intones Leviticus 17:11, "For the life of the flesh is in the blood, and I have given it for you on the altar to make atonement for your souls." Needless to say, this is not the normal liturgy for the sacrament of communion. Instead it is an Old Testament law describing proper procedure for animal sacrifice. This discussion of blood may also hint that the clergy are simply another form of vampire, feeding on humanity's blood. Voltaire first made this connection during the Enlightenment, when he equated the economic exploitation of clergy with vampirism.[12]

These distortions of Catholic tradition set up the metataxis of horror by inversion: The Church is supposed to protect humanity from vampires and instead it has become itself dangerous and predatory. However, *Priest* also draws on five hundred years of Protestant criticism of Catholicism. After renouncing the Church, the Priestess explains to The Priest, "Our power doesn't come from the Church, it comes from God. With or without the clergy, we're still priests." This is essentially Martin Luther's claim that every man is a priest from the moment of baptism.[13] The image of the wicked Catholic authority actually preceded the vampire as a Gothic villain in novels such as *The Monk* (1796) and *The Italian* (1797). In the nineteenth century, Catholic immigration to the United States inspired a Nativist backlash against "Popery." A slew of Victorian novels portrayed Catholicism as an idolatrous and authoritarian religion

Part One: Vampires

in which nuns were kept in captivity as "holy harems" for priests. The sacrament of confession in particular was seen as a ceding of autonomy to Church authorities.[14] In *A Culture of Conspiracy*, Michael Barkun demonstrates how fears of corrupt Catholic priests have elided into fears of corrupt government. He argues that in the modern era, anti-Catholic conspiracy theorists no longer have theological objections to the Church, but still fear its hierarchical structure, its global reach, and its capacity for secrecy.[15] This development is apparent in *Priest*, where the Catholic Church has fused with a modern police state.

THE INVADING SACRED ORDER OF THE VAMPIRES

The vampires of *Priest* are perhaps the most hideous ever presented in modern cinema. Clearly inspired by the work of artist H. R. Giger for the *Alien* series, the vampires have no eyes and prefer to live in "hives"—earthen structures resembling giant insect mounds and ruled over by a queen. Hives are apparently constructed with slime that the vampires secrete from their bodies. The vampires also invoke one of Giger's influences, pulp horror-writer H. P. Lovecraft. Cowan argues that Lovecraft's themes of alien beings utterly indifferent to humanity represent a classic example of an invading sacred order.[16] Much like the flesh-eating antagonists of the *Aliens* movies or some of Lovecraft's nameless horrors, the vampires display an intelligence that is totally other. They are incapable of speech and run on all fours like animals. Yet they display an ability to wage organized warfare. They are only able to communicate through familiars, humans who have been partially turned into vampires, who speak on their behalf.

The monstrousness of Stewart's vampires is part of a cycle in popular culture wherein alluring, Romantic representations of the vampire are met by a backlash of vile vampires. In the 1990s, a backlash occurred after the film *Interview with the Vampire* (1994), featuring beautiful, sensitive vampires played by Tom Cruise and Brad Pitt. That year, horror writer F. Paul Wilson described his concern that the vampire has become "trivialized" instead of frightening.[17] In 1996, the film *Dusk till Dawn* presented soulless, animal-like vampires in deliberate contrast to Anne Rice's tragic and beautiful immortals. *Priest* was produced in the midst of another vampire boom characterized by the *Twilight* series and

True Blood. Eyeless vampires are a resounding counter-point to romantic characters like Edward Cullen and Bill Compton. Perhaps to emphasize this point, Stephen Moyer, the actor who plays Bill Compton, plays The Priest's brother who is savagely maimed by the undead. The total otherness of the vampires in *Priest* is necessary to set up the metataxis of terror. The fact that the vampires are not remotely human makes it that much more unsettling when Black Hat argues that they are more virtuous than the Church.

The way vampires are dealt with in *Priest* references both the treatment of Native Americans by Catholic conquistadors and European settlers and the dehumanizing conditions faced by imprisoned populations in our own society. The vampires are forced to live on "reservations," a label that references displaced Native Americans. However, the reservations are actually guarded facilities surrounded by concrete and barbed wire. They resemble modern prisons more than reservations of Native Americans.

Native peoples were also the subject of theological debate. In 1550, Charles V of Spain called an assembly of Catholic theologians to debate the nature of Indians and whether a just war could be waged against them in the name of spreading Christianity. Some argued that Indians are rational beings and that invading them to stamp out their religion would not meet Catholic standards of a just war. Others claimed that Indians are inherently inferior and that slavery is their natural position in life.[18] In *Priest*, the Church has apparently held a similar debate. Black Hat explains the Church's teaching that the eyes are windows to the soul and as the vampire evolved without eyes, "It is a soulless creature to be eradicated."

But while the Church condemns vampires, Black Hat and the familiars offer a different perspective. A familiar tells The Priest, "Look what you've done to them! They once ruled this land! They were warriors! They were gods!"[19] Black Hat describes the vampire queen as his "angel of mercy," and declares, "I have seen the soul of a vampire and let me tell you it is far more pure than that of any man." These statements represent another European reading of Native Americans: The fantasy of the noble savage. For humans who have sided with the vampires, vampirism represents everything the Church is not. Vampires have no delusions or hypocrisy and no notion of sin: they simply kill in accordance with their nature.

Part One: Vampires

Black Hat becomes a prophetic figure, promising an apocalyptic battle in which the righteous order of the vampires will defeat the hypocritical order of the Church. At the beginning of the film, we see that Black Hat was captured while raiding a vampire hive with The Priest and left for dead. Only at the film's denouement do we learn what happened to him afterwards: On the brink of death, he was given the blood of the vampire queen and resurrected as a "human vampire." Black Hat becomes a liminal being stronger than either the priests or the vampires and able to walk in the daylight. In a scene showing his capture by vampires, he enters the hive and remarks, "Feels like our grave." When he meets The Priest again as Black Hat, he explains, "In the depths of that hive, I crossed the threshold between life and death." The character's back-story parallels the resurrection of Christ, with the vampire hive acting as a substitute for the tomb. Black Hat becomes a kind of inverted vampire messiah, promising, "I am the bringer of the tide, I am the wave that will wash clean this unclean world." He attempts to convert The Priest inviting him to "accept the blood of the queen." Like the Church, Black Hat also offers a form of communion and belonging. When Black Hat is finally defeated, he is incinerated by an explosion that knocks him off his feet. We last see him in mid-air with his arms out, in a cruciform pose, as if to emphasize his messiah-like qualities.[20]

Giving vampires spiritual significance only makes them more horrific. In *Religion and Its Monsters*, Timothy Beale makes a distinction between "demonized" and "deified" monsters. Demonized monsters exist in total opposition to the sacred and by opposing them we draw closer to God. Deified monsters, however, are so frightening and so other that they inspire a sense of the sacred—what Rudolph Otto called the *mysterium tremendum*. Beale explains:

> Here the monster is an envoy of the divine or the sacred as radically other than "our" established order of things. It is an invasion of what we might call *sacred chaos* and disorientation within self, society and world....
>
> If demonizing a monster keeps God on our side, then deifying it often puts us in a world of religious disorientation and horror.[21]

This "sacred chaos" is Cowan's metaxis of horror and Berger's *anomie*. The vampire apologists—Black Hat and the familiars—transform the vampire from a demonized monster to a deified one. By giving vampires qualities of the sacred, *Priest* sets up an invasion of the sacred order.

THE VIEW FROM THE WASTELAND

The parallels between the Church and the vampires become increasingly stark by the end of the film. Humans huddle in their cities ruled over by the clergy and vampires lurk in hives ruled over by a queen. Both communities are surrounded by wasteland and draw in humans who fear being alone. Neither community has the luxury of sunlight. There are also strong parallels between The Priest and Black Hat. One loses his humanity in the city by becoming a human weapon, the other loses it in the hive by becoming a human vampire. Both men operate in the wasteland between city and hive. Both are heretics and enemies of the Church. After a battle with vampires in a reservation, The Priest is forced to confront the fact that he is as much of a living weapon as the vampires he fights. A familiar tells him, "They [vampires] were what nature made them to be, just like you." On seeing The Priest fight, Hicks remarks that killing comes easy to him. The Priest responds, "It just comes. Easy's got nothing to do with it."

This blurred line between the flawed hero and the tragic villain is indebted to Gothic literature. The Gothic villain is often a failed hero whose potential has been somehow corrupted. Similarly, Gothic literature gave rise to the "Byronic hero," a tragic figure that is idealized but flawed. However, this connection also has precedent in the original folklore of Eastern Europe where the vampire and the slayer were often connected. In *Slayers and their Vampires*, Bruce McClelland explains that only certain people were believed to be born with the power to detect and slay vampires. Furthermore, the same conditions that would produce a vampire were also likely to produce a slayer. In Bulgarian culture, the twelve days between Christmas Eve and January 6 were "unclean days." It was believed that children born during this time were likely to become vampires in death and a number of ritual taboos were enforced to prevent this from happening. But children born during the unclean days were also likely to have the powers of a vampire slayer. McClelland writes, "The vampire slayer is cut from the same cloth, is the product of the same social or religious violations as the vampire."[22] He notes that reciprocal relationship between vampire and slayer is perpetuated in popular culture through shows such as *Buffy: The Vampire Slayer*. It is also apparent in *Priest*.

With regards to the metataxis of horror, these parallels serve to reinforce the idea that the order represented by the Church and the vampires are arbitrary and therefore factitious. The Church has invented one horrific regime and the vampires have invented another. Transcendent truth is nowhere to be found. This is the view from the wasteland where both the city and the hive can be examined side by side. At the end of the film, humanity is spared from the vampires but The Priest is still exiled in the wasteland. Monsignor Osilas tells him, "The war is over!" He responds, "No. It's just beginning." It is unclear whether The Priest is referring to the old war between vampires and humans or a new war between priests and the Church.

The reason that audiences may admire or sympathize with The Priest is that his disillusionment and alienation reflect our own experience of modernity. Berger argued that modern people are assailed by a plurality of competing religious and social realities that weakens the sacred canopy and creates a "crisis of credibility" in which claims about reality that were once taken for granted are called into question.[23] Berger predicted that religious pluralism would lead to secularization as the crisis of credibility caused people to lose faith in all religious claims. He has since recanted the secularization hypothesis; however, the crisis of credibility remains. Radical doubt is now an inherent condition of living in the modern world.[24] Unlike pre-modern cultures, we no longer inherit a shared sacred canopy. Instead, modern people are burdened with navigating competing views of reality. As Jean-Paul Sartre said, "Every man is condemned to freedom." Like The Priest, we can take nothing for granted and must discover the truth for ourselves. Tellingly, Berger dubbed this condition of modernity "the heretical imperative" after the Greek "hairesis"—to choose.[25] Like the Priest who sees both the corruption of the Church and the alien order of the vampires, we are all heretics standing in the wasteland with an uncertain future. It is a frightening place to be.

END NOTES

1. Abbot, *Celluloid Vampires*, 1.
2. Cowan, *Sacred Terror*, 67.
3. Berger, *The Sacred Canopy*, 22. Berger's use of the word "anomy" is an Anglicization of the French *anomie*. This term has its origins in sociology with the French theorist Emile Durkheim.
4. Berger, *The Sacred Canopy*, 67–71.
5. Min-woo, *Priest*.
6. For a detailed analysis of "Vampire Hunter D," and the significance of genre blending in Asian popular culture, see Browning, "The Western Eastern" in Browning and Picart, *Draculas, Vampires*, 279–94.
7. Fingeroth, *Superman on the Couch*, 130.
8. Introvigne, "Satanism Scares."
9. PiPaoulo, "Vampires," 447.
10. Melton, *The Encyclopedia of Religious Phenomena*, 326–27.
11. Augustine and Dods, *The City of God*, 310.
12. Heldreth and Pharr, *The Blood Is the Life*, 211.
13. Luther, "Address to the Christian Nobility."
14. Griffin, *Anti-Catholicism and Nineteenth-Century Fiction*, 153–54.
15. Barkun, *A Culture of Conspiracy*, 131.
16. Cowan, *Sacred Terror*, 65.
17. Guiley and Macabre, *The Complete Vampire*, 98.
18. Carrasco, *Religions of Mesoamerica*, 7–8.
19. The term "familiar" now appears in a number of modern vampire films. However, the original familiar is Renfield, Dracula's human servant in Bram Stoker's novel. Interestingly, Renfield also regards his undead master as God. He compares himself to the biblical Enoch who walked with God. See Stoker, *Dracula*, 436.
20. Several critics have noted that the cruciform pose is used heavily in the *Alien* quadrilogy directed by James Cameron. These films were an obvious influence on *Priest's* eyeless vampires and Black Hat's cruciform death may be another element borrowed from Cameron. See Lynda K. Bundtzen, "Monstrous Mothers," 103; Kearney, *Strangers, Gods, and Monsters*, 116.
21. Beal, *Religion and Its Monsters*, 6.
22. McClelland, *Slayers and Their Vampires*, 101.
23. Berger, *The Sacred Canopy*, 127.
24. Giddens, *Modernity and Self-Identity*, 181.
25. Berger, *The Heretical Imperative*.

3

Vampires are People, Too
Personalism in the Buffyverse

JARROD LONGBONS

CONTEMPORARY THEOLOGY MUST REFLECT on the vampire.[1] Admittedly, this sounds like medieval superstition, and it is. But while contemporary theologians may not reflect much by way of vampirism, this was not the way it was in the past. The main systematic theological treatment of vampires was written in 1645 by Leo Allatius. By the eighteenth century, belief in vampirism was all but laid to rest.[2] So why reflect on the vampire today? Because the image of the vampire persists in the popular consciousness as a metaphor for the *zeitgeist* of the times in which these stories are penned. They, like all literary monsters, reveal the basic concerns of the culture that creates them, and as Gregory Erickson writes, "a cultural phenomenon like vampires is both produced by and part of a society inextricably tied up in its religion."[3] So what can a reading of our current vampire myths tell us about our contemporary concerns and religious assumptions?

Among millennial vampire stories, none are more compelling than *Buffy the Vampire Slayer*, created by Joss Whedon, an absurdist atheist television auteur.[4] The show follows a young girl, the chosen one of her generation, who is gifted with the supernatural ability to fight vampires. She is the slayer. *BtVS* is compelling for many reasons: it is a self-referential story about growing up, it interacts with pop-culture, it engages relevant social issues, and reflects on life, death, and philosophy. And it does all of this, of course, without taking itself too seriously. Of note, Buffy represents an inversion of typical American horror—she does the saving, and does not need a man to save her.[5] *BtVS* is indeed an ingenious piece of television.

Of particular relevance to the subject of the "undead" is one of *BtVS*'s most rich and fully developed characters—Spike.[6] Spike journeys from being a vampire—a person *diabolique*—to a vampire with a soul—a person for others—which leads to his ultimate redemption. Interestingly, the soul in *BtVS*, a distinguishing factor for the living, is not a transcendent element of selfhood that orientates one toward the divine; rather, it functions as the personalizing part of the self, which activates a propensity to action on behalf of and for others. Therefore, theology can engage *BtVS* through a reading of the show along with a comparison to Christian personalism. Specifically, I will show that the soul in *BtVS* is a secular parody of a more robust Christian personalism put forward by Pope John Paul II and Pope Benedict XVI. And since the show is immanent in scope, I will show that its personalistic soul ultimately fails to satisfy the current anxieties of our time, though they are demonstrated so well by the show itself.

THE BIRTH OF THE MODERN SECULAR VAMPIRE

Though vampire stories can be found throughout history, most of them are positioned within a Judeo-Christian *Weltanschauung*. Let's begin with the archetype for all modern vampire mythologizing, Bram Stoker's *Dracula*. Stoker's vampire is, classically, a Roman Catholic vampire tale,[7] as evidenced by *Dracula*'s repellants: the consecrated wafer of the Eucharist and the crucifix.[8] The rationale for this motif is inherently Catholic, because the sacraments represent the real presence of Christ, and are therefore efficacious in repelling the unholy.[9] The story of *Dracula* puts forward the clear message that vampires are in league with Satan and are opposed by those who stand on the side of God. And while the story has many metaphors to be examined, the basic reflection of its time is clear: it is a story of conservative Victorian perspective, a basic tale of good versus evil.

Part One: Vampires

A gestalt shift took place in popular vampire literature with Anne Rice's *Vampire Chronicles*. Unlike Stoker's Victorian tale, Rice's represents a change in theology and popular concerns. Her vampires are much more Protestant[10] than the ones fashioned from Stoker's archetype. Rice's vampires do not coil in fear in the presence of the cross, the Eucharistic wafer, or the church building. In fact, as Lloyd Worley shows, Rice's vampire regularly "approaches and handles" these icons.[11] Worley argues that since the vampires do not have faith in the elements they touch, the elements have no inherent authority and pose no threat to the "undead." This is a decisive break from a Catholic sensibility for which the elements are imbued with the real presence of Christ. Rice's world reflects a Protestant faith wherein the elements are efficacious only when the believer believes in them. Protestantism does not hold a doctrine of presence within the sacrament, but at its nearest to Catholicism, presence is only *with* the sacrament when the participant has faith in it. Rice's vampires reflect a faithless existential angst related to the Reformation,[12] but did not appear in full until the existentialism of the twentieth century. Their angst runs parallel to the angst of our hyper-consumerist, and postmodern times. Rice's vampire Louis might even ask, "What is all our consumption really for?"

If Stoker's vampire is a Catholic one, and Rice's is a secular one (with elements of Protestantism),[13] then *BtVS* represents a thoroughly postmodern (and secular) vampire world. Being postmodern, the Buffyverse (a term to describe *BtVS* and its spinoff *Angel*) is able to draw on various mythologies, theologies, and religions to develop its unique story without being faithful to any particular one. Vampires in *BtVS* are harmed by the cross, but the show is iconoclastic toward Christianity and other traditional religions. In a humorous scene echoing Rice's vampire *Louis*,[14] some vampires enter a church. They do not find God there; instead, they reflect on why they were once so afraid of that old beautiful building.[15] Like the cross, holy water can cause harm to the vampire in *BtVS*, but ironically, Christianity and the church have nothing to say in the Buffyverse; they are dubious at best and mocked at worst. A fairytale form of Wicca, with a blending of pagan reconstruction, is the only religion taken seriously in the Buffyverse. Zoe-Jane Playdon suggests the reason for the use of Christian icons in *BtVS* is only because they "belong more forcefully to the world of vampires and demons"[16] and ultimately, they are hold-overs from tradition. Playdon further suggests their power has no sway over Buffy's evil-fighting crew, the "Scoobies." For them, these icons are merely instrumental without essential significance.[17] *BtVS*' mythologizing is inherently American, for it starts from the old world but develops with its own unique, iconoclastic take.

As far as the metaphysical goes, *Buffy's* world is thoroughly immanent.[18] Wiccan magic is a powerful force, used for good or evil, but its power is drawn from completely immanent relations. By immanent relations, I mean that there is no deity outside the universe who bestows power. Rather, magic happens through appeal to artifacts within the Buffyverse or petition to deities of alternate dimensions. There are gods in *BtVS*, but they are not totally transcendent. They are found in alternate and parallel dimensions; they are connected to Buffy's world in a wholly immanent way. When dealing with such a deity (Glorificus for example, in season 5), the Scoobies encounter not a truly transcendent God, but a being that resembles a human but with much more power. *BtVS*' deities are ill-tempered, contingent, and even immoral, much like the ancient Greek pantheon.

The Buffyverse is an anxious place void of transcendent or revealed knowledge that defines the good life. Truth is mediated through friendships and power, tradition is mocked while esoteric practices are praised, and the Scoobies often sense that they are all alone in a dark and lonely world. Their community is their only respite for loneliness, and the mysterious (albeit immanent) gifts of the slayer represent their only hope for goodness to prevail over evil. The Buffyverse reflects our current postmodern condition of anxiety, wherein participants must create both truth and ethics, since appeal to an external force is seen as desperate, blind faith.

So enters the vampire. The vampire and other demons serve as helpful plot pieces to deal with community, truth, and ethics. When right and wrong are difficult to discern, the Scoobies know, at least, that vampires are evil. This much is clear. All demons, but vampires in particular as demons *par excellence*, demonstrate radical evil because they parasite the life of humans. The dignity of the human person is the result of his or her soul, and vampires are diabolical because they lack a soul. This soul, however, is ambiguous, and will be parsed out below in the character arc of the vampire Spike.

To preface the conversation about the soul in Spike, I would like to highlight how the conception of the soul in *BtVS* is a secular immanent one. For Christian thinkers, the soul is the rational part of the self that is inseparable from the body, except in death.[19] It is the transcendent part of the body that orientates the self toward God. The soul's greatest ethical achievement is to bring the person to prayerful submission before God. In the Buffyverse, however, the soul has nothing to do with relating to the divine. Rather, it seems the real difference between the human and the vampire is not only their diet, but their ability to have a conscience, feel guilt, and act through self-sacrifice.[20] Interest in the soul in *BtVS* follows the modern interest in the ambiguous inner-life of a self, as Kenneth L. Schmitz writes,

> For there has been a deep fascination with and cultivation of the inner character of human consciousness in modern times, quite unlike the religious journey within the soul. The inner-directedness of much of modern thought is not to be confused with the interior movement of transcendence that has always animated and still animates the religious thought and prayer of Christians. Perhaps it is not too much to call the modern movement inward the "secularization of interiority." The religious journey within seeks to lay the prayerful soul before God, whereas the modern journey within seeks to find and test the self as the human foundation for certitude and the basis for evaluation.[21]

Spike's reacquired soul reveals more of this modern "secularization of interiority" in *BtVS* as it leads him to consider others ethically, but in no way leads him to transcendence.[22] Again, the soul in the Buffyverse can be nothing more than a secular caricature of Christian personalism. As will be shown, the soul allows humans to be persons in relation to one another and ultimately to God; it allows for persons to be persons for others, which is beyond the parasitic nature of the vampire. Spike, however, though he finds redemption, is never able to truly enter into a relationship with the divine; at best, he becomes a person in relation to other immanent persons, thus revealing a distortion of Christian doctrine. Before we approach Christian personalism, let's examine character arc of Spike to get a better understanding of the "undead" and its relationship to soul in the *BtVS*.

SPIKE: ON THE WAY TO PERSONHOOD

Gleaning the function of soul in *BtVS* best arises with a reading of the character arc of Spike, one of the Buffy's most complicated characters. When Buffy's boyfriend is interested in the immortality of the vampire, she explains its true nature, "You die. And a demon sets up shop in your old house. It walks and talks and remembers your life, but it's not you."[23] Chiefly, vampires function like the id of the bodies they possess; they express the dark side of the former person's desires.[24] Simple as this may sound, it assists in understanding much of the motivation of Spike.

Though Spike first appears in season 2 as a self-assured Billy Idol look-alike villain, flashbacks from season 5 reveal that he was once someone far more passive. These flashbacks illustrate that Spike, or William, his human name, was a very different person from the one who becomes the nemesis of the slayer.

WILLIAM

Unlike his dark counterpart, Spike, William is three piece-suited poetic dilettante. He ignores an outbreak of missing persons because he is preoccupied with romantic poetic naiveté. The muse for his poetry is Cecily; she is the subject of his poetry and unrequited love. He is single-mindedly focused on possessing her; William's poetry is scarcely devoted to anything else. Unbeknownst to William, his poetry is the topic of ridicule for his contemporaries. They call it "bloody awful" and claim that they'd rather have a "railroad spike driven through their head" than be forced to listen to it.[25]

In a London salon, William finally reveals his love to Cecily. Embarrassed by William's obsession, Cecily rejects him because he is beneath her. Devastated, William flees into the city streets. He wanders into a dark alley where he meets Drusilla (once a postulant in a nunnery). William finds himself in her dark vampiric embrace. She sires him, William becomes a dark vision of himself, and he becomes Spike the vampire. The two are a diabolical pair of lovers who eventually show up in Sunnydale looking like a vampiric Sid and Nancy. It is during the earliest days of Buffy's tenure as slayer when they enter the seedy underbelly of Sunnydale's "Hell mouth" community.[26] Spike is everything that William is not. He is not pathetic in body nor a "fool for love;" he is a ruthless killer who can possess and consume anyone woman that he desires.

SPIKE THE VAMPIRE

Whereas William inspired the nickname "William the Bloody" from his awful poetry, Spike lived out the moniker in literalistic fashion. He

Part One: Vampires

became "Spike" not because of what his poetry inspired in people but the nature of his violence. Spike became the definition of a diabolical person, someone who treats others as only a means for pleasure. He delights in dominating; this is his single greatest *raison d'etre*. His fascination with the slayer is the best evidence of this. Spike has already drained the blood of two slayers, and his initial desire to live in Sunnydale is to consume the blood of Buffy. No woman, not even the slayer, is beyond him.

Spike's other romantic passion is Drusilla. For most of Spike's vampire life, Drusilla was his partner in the bedroom and in bedlam. Through seasons 2 and 3, Spike perversely loves Drusilla. His love for her is not one of self-giving but of possession. His love was based on what she added to his life—a perverse and dark fulfillment of William's desire for Cecily. As for Drusilla, her love for Spike continued only when he accomplished evil; if he failed or wavered, her love waned.

When the diabolical duo leaves Sunnydale, Drusilla cheats on Spike with a chaos demon. Distraught, Spike confronts her. She tells him that she is sickened by his obsession with and inability to destroy Buffy. So, Spike leaves Drusilla and journeys back to Sunnydale to destroy Buffy. His subsequent encounters with Buffy and the Scoobies are mixed: he comically mourns Drusilla while sharing a cup of cocoa with Buffy's mother, Joyce, and at other times he resents Buffy, plotting her demise. Finally getting over his sadness, Spike exits the narrative with renewed vigor for evil.

SPIKE WITH A CHIP

Season 4 is a turning point for Spike. It is freshman year in college for the Scoobies, and the gang learns of a covert government agency, ominously labeled "The Initiative." Its aim is to study, understand and fight demons. Spike resurfaces in Sunnydale with a new found sense of self. But before he can enact mayhem, he is captured by The Initiative. While in captivity, staff at The Initiative inserts a neurobiological chip that causes severe pain whenever Spike thinks of harming human life. This chip effectively "de-fangs" Spike, leaving him helpless against the Slayer and The Initiative.

The turning point comes as Spike tries to ally the Slayer. He does so, at first, to find protection from The Initiative, and secondly because he discovers that he can still hurt other demons. Violence, even toward demons, is just enough for Spike to quell his appetite for hostility. Slowly,

Spike becomes a liminal character in the Scooby gang. It would appear that with the chip, Spike enters the realm of the ethical, as he finds renewed identity fighting on the side of good. However, his actions are cursory, because it is a result of a mechanical chip and not of free will. What the chip does for Spike's journey to redemption, however, is to create room for him to see the good and live in proximity to it. Through this proximity (alignment with the Scoobies), Spike develops a sexual obsession for Buffy. Unable to defeat her, sexual fulfillment is the only way to possess her.

This obsession with Buffy takes many dark and humorous turns through seasons 4 to 6. Of the Scoobies, Spike relates more naturally with Buffy, perhaps because she is the one who sees his potential for good. Eventually, Buffy will identify more with Spike than her living friends. Until then, however, Buffy's friends, including her watcher Giles, are steadfastly suspicious of Spike's intentions.

A major climax in the narrative is Buffy's self-sacrificial death. Buffy and the scoobies are faced with, yet again, apocalypse. A hell dimension is opened, threatening to engulf the world, and the only way to close the door is for someone in Buffy's family to fill it with her life. The key to this dimension is Dawn, Buffy's sister, but Buffy will not allow her younger sister to be the sacrifice. The only one left is Buffy, and it can only be Buffy. The tragic scene is an immanently analogous to Christ's *Via Dolorosa*; Rhonda Wilcox describes the scene as follows, "Buffy had sacrificed her life to save the world, and above all, her sister. In spite of the efforts of her friends and the Scooby Gang (including Spike), a wound has been opened in the world, which Buffy has healed with her own body."[27] The season ends in tragedy with Buffy's friends around her sacrificial body. Chief among the mourners is the inconsolable Spike. The sting of loss and the grief of failure to protect Buffy's sister as he had promised are evidenced by his uncontrollable mourning.

The next season begins somberly. Buffy is dead, and the Scoobies are doing everything they can to keep it together. Spike is among them in solidarity; he spends his nights slaying demons and watching out for Dawn. He is grief stricken, and though he still has the chip, it appears that he is living the good life out of his own free will.

Then, the narrative takes a dramatic turn: Buffy is resurrected through the magic enacted by several of the Scoobies. This act again exposes its secular parody of the Christian story, because Buffy dies for the life of the world and is resurrected not by the power of a transcendent

God, but by a group of friends. Simply put, Buffy *needs* them to be resurrected. From the Scoobies' perspective, Buffy is resurrected and justice has prevailed, but the truth is much graver; Buffy has been wrested from a heaven dimension, and then she dug herself out of her own grave. Buffy's resurrected life is arduous, she's numb and relates to no one. The season is about Buffy's attempt to cope with the realities of life again.

This experience allows Spike and Buffy to relate to one another in a new way, through mutual understanding, Spike's obsession with Buffy grows, and through a majority of the season, he and Buffy participate in a licentious sexual relationship. Buffy, ashamed, hides the relationship from her friends and family. She uses Spike as a tool to feel anything at all. Eventually Buffy ends the relationship. Spike panics; he attempts to get Buffy to sleep with him one more time. He is convinced one more night of passion will convince Buffy of her love for Spike. Buffy refuses, and Spike attempts to rape Buffy. She fends him off, terrified by his obsession. Spike understands his depravity through Buffy's terror, and he flees in shame. By the end of the season, the audience does not know where Spike is going, but he promises to give the Slayer what she wants, or rather what she truly deserves.

SPIKE WITH A SOUL

Fleeing in rejection like William did after Cecily's rejection; Spike travels to a distant land to win back his soul. Through various grueling challenges, Spike prevails. By season 7 he is back in Sunnydale, soul intact. Winning Buffy's trust again, Spike begins to fight with the Scoobies against the "big bad" of the season which is the biggest and badest evil of the whole mythology: The First Evil, or simply The First.[28]

This season is one of becoming for Spike, for if the chip got him close to the ethical sphere of life, his soul will enable him to come close to something of a religious sphere.[29] Spike is filled with insecurity and grief; even with a soul, can he ever overcome his past? Spike's soul does not exactly reinstate William the dilettante poet. Spike still has the make-up of a vampire, but with a soul he has a conscience, free will and the ability to empathize with others like when he was William the human.

The final season of *BtVS* is harrowing. "The First" appears to be an indomitable enemy. And Buffy's friends doubt her leadership on many occasions, but Spike is always there to defend her and follow her lead. He is faithful to her because he loves her and senses his debt to her, trusting her when everyone else does not. Throughout the season, The First attacks Spike physically and emotionally and even tries to tempt his desire for blood lust. The newly "ensouled" Spike, however, remains mostly steadfast. Even under pain and torture he will not betray Buffy.

By the end of the season, Angel arrives with an enchanted medallion, *deus ex machina*. It is to be worn by someone with a soul but who is stronger than a human. It is to be worn by a champion. The medallion's power will aid the champion in defeating The First, and Angel believes he should be this champion. Buffy will not permit Angel this role, however, because she needs him to be ready in L.A. as a second front in case she cannot contain The First. It is clear that the champion must be Spike.

Returning home with the medallion, Buffy relates the story to Spike. Spike withdraws in shame, believing he could never be the champion to wear the powerful emblem, since he's mostly been a monster. The following moment is profound. Buffy proclaims that Spike *is* the champion worthy to wear the medallion; her faith in him "en-courages" Spike to be the man he needs to be. Buffy's faith in Spike is constructive for his own self-understanding. After this gift of faith, the two spend the night sweetly in each other's arms. They do not use each other as they did before; instead they give themselves to each other in love.

Spike dons the medallion for *BtVS'* Armageddon. At the climax of the battle, the medallion begins to glow with a brilliant light. Directly before Buffy and the gang escape the collapsing Hell Mouth, Spike holds the threshold, allowing the others to pass in safety. The light from the medallion shoots upward and Spike, the once creature of darkness, bathes in the effulgent[30] light of the sun. Buffy pleads with Spike to escape with her. Denying her, Spike realizes his destiny of redemption and replies, "I want to see how it ends." Before Buffy escapes the threshold of hell, she grabs Spike's hand; as they take a last look at one another, their hands combust into flame. Buffy looks at her hand, then turns to Spike with tear-filled eyes and breathes, "I love you," speaking that for which he has desired to hear for so long. The light from above shoots through Spike and kills the vampire horde in the Hell Mouth. The ridge collapses, and Spike perishes along with the army of The First. Buffy's love and faith in Spike gave him the strength to give his life for the world. Spike became the man for others that he never was as a soulless vampire. Through self-giving, Spike found his redemption.

Part One: Vampires

THE MEANING OF THE SOUL IN BUFFY THE VAMPIRE SLAYER

What can this story tell us about the nature of the undead in the Buffy-verse? Vampires in the mythology are not living persons due to absence of the soul.[31] They are like animals with superhuman strength used for parasitism, which emanates from absolute egoism and disregard for the dignity of others. This contempt for human life is the very nature of evil in *BtVS*, and for this reason, vampires are to be killed without question. But ambiguity about vampiric dignity arises when the vampire acquires a soul; though the soul does not make a vampire a human, it does make them a person. So just what is it about the soul that makes a self a person?

As noted, there are many ambiguities within the mythology of *Buffy*. For example, two vampires in the story attain their souls: Angel and Spike. Angel is introduced to the show having already received a soul, which makes him a brooding ally of Buffy and the Scoobies. But the first and primary vision of Spike is of a soulless vampire, and only through time and circumstance does he become a liminal character in the Scooby gang. Spike does not receive his soul until later, and that is not his moment of redemption. For both of these characters, the presence of the soul allows the self to be fully ethical, but Angel's soul represents an essentialist idea of the person, while Spike's personhood bears an existentialist notion.[32] The difference is probably due to audience perception of Angel as an inherent good guy character, while Spike is presented as a villain. In the end, however, Spike represents the most fully developed character in *BtVS*, so his character can reveal more about what the mythology has to say for the soul and the undead.

The soul, here, is not an essentialist entity of transcendence that orientates one toward others and God; rather, as Spike shows, the soul existentially allows him to act ethically toward others. There are similarities, to be sure, with traditional views of the soul. First, the soul allows Spike to be a man for others, complete with empathy, conscience, free will, and the ability to self-sacrifice. But as an ontologically transcendent part of the human, this presentation of the soul is ambiguous at best. The soul cannot orientate toward the divine because there is no divine in the show. As with the Christian notion, the soul enables a self to be a person in relation, even a self-giving person, but without the ultimate *telos* of giving oneself to Christ.

Sure, monomythically,[33] Spike gives his life for a Christ-figure by dying for Buffy.[34] She is his muse for living the good life. But Buffy is an inverted Christ-figure at best, as she is finite and reliant upon her friends for her strength and even for her resurrection. In an immanent universe, like the Buffyverse, there can never be a true Christ-figure; all attempts at constructing one are nothing more than secular caricatures.

And because of this immanent imagination, the eschatological sense of *BtVS* never overcomes the anxiety of nihilism. Sure, we the viewers are given hope because the spirit of the Slayer is made "transpiritual." The confident, powerful essence has been magically spread to countless would-be Slayers around the world. Democratically, the spirit of the slayer has been seized away from the old patriarchal architects of the slayer's power, which is good for the world. What cannot be escaped, however, is the eternal struggle built in to the fabric of the world: a balance between good and evil. Radical evil is still possible, and there is no one standing completely "other" to Buffyverse, beyond good and evil, who can eradicate evil from it *in toto*. Ultimately, all that the citizens of the Buffyverse have is each other; their only hope is immanent and corruptible love between finite persons. Secular personalism can never overcome this impasse. We must move to Christian personalism to glimpse a mythology that is more complete, one that completely defeats the anxiety of our modern world which is the same as the one found in the Buffyverse.

CHRISTIAN PERSONALISM

Pope Benedict XVI writes, "the concept of person, as well as the idea that stands behind this concept, is a product of Christian theology."[35] This contribution to Western human thought was developed as a result of the Christian quest to understand the Triune God. Essentially, the term "person" has two Western antecedents: the Greek *prosopon* and Latin *persona*. Both words were used in antiquity to describe the "face" or masks actors wore in the theatre. A mask worn by an actor defined the character's role by a certain set of relations with other characters. In this way, early Christian thinkers used the term "person" to describe God. Benedict writes that Tertullian gave the full expression of personhood to God with his formula, "God is the '*una substantia-tres personae*,' one being in three persons. It was here that the word 'person' entered intellectual history for the first time with its full weight."[36] For Benedict, the idea of person as it relates to God comes through reading the Bible and seeing "intra-divine" dialogue between the Father, Son, and Holy Spirit; thus in Scripture we find the "idea of God as the dialogical being. It refers to God as the being that lives in the word and consists of the word as 'I' and 'you' and 'we.'"[37] So "God is a being in three persons"[38] and therefore God is rightly "understood as a relation."[39] This is important, because the persons of the Trinity are not separate substances that merely adhere to one another; rather, the relation of persons determines each person. Benedict continues, "in God, person means relation. Relation, being related, is not something superadded to the person, but it *is* the person itself. In its nature, the person exists only *as* relation."[40] Therefore, the substance of God is determined by relations, and it is a mistake to think that the relations are a product of some base substance. Benedict defines the first person "as self-donation in fruitful knowledge and love; it is not the one who gives himself, in whom the act of self-donation is found, but it is this self-donation, pure reality of act."[41] Again, we can conclude that the substance of God is determined from the divine donation of persons: The Father is *for* the Son, the Son is *for* the Spirit, the Spirit is *for* the Father and every other which way in between.

Benedict's trinitarian personalism aids in understanding both God and human persons. He writes, "the decisive illumination of what person must mean in terms of scripture: *not* a substance that closes itself in itself, but the phenomenon of complete relativity, which is, of course, realized in its entirety only in the one who is God, but which indicates the direction of all personal being."[42] And for Benedict, this model of personhood informs anthropology. For Benedict, "the human person is the event or being of relativity"[43] as well. This relativity has everything to do with humans relating to other humans, but unlike Spike, it does not end there, because "the more the person's relativity aims totally and directly at its final goal, at transcendence, the more the person is itself."[44] For Christian personalism, the human finds its greatest self in relating to the transcendent God. This is why Augustine confesses to God, "our heart is restless until it finds rest in you."[45]

Finally, Christian reflection on the Trinity reveals that God is not a simple "I" but a self-giving "we." In like manner, human beings are not defined by strict "I" and "you" Cartesianism, because like God, human persons are defined, first, by their relations. Like the persons of the Trinity, humans are most fully human when they live lives of self-donation. Just what does this relativity look like for humans? To answer this we will turn our attention to the "personalistic norm" of Benedict's predecessor, Pope John Paul II.

PERSONALISTIC NORM

"Love is the sincere gift of self. In this sense *the person is realized through love.*"[46]

The personalistic norm begins with the New Testament command to love neighbors. For John Paul II, this really implies love for persons. He writes, "for God, whom the commandment to love names first, is the most perfect personal being. The whole world of created persons derives its distinctness from and its natural superiority over the world of things (non-persons) from a very particular resemblance to God."[47] Excluding the reference to God, this is the case for the Buffyverse. Humans are valued because they are persons (with soul) and vampires are not valued because they are non-persons (lacking soul). So what is a person according to John Paul II? He writes, "a person is an objective entity, which as a definite subject has the closest contacts with the whole (external) world and is most intimately involved with it precisely because of its inwardness, its interior life."[48] For him, a person is an object, the person is an entity, but is also a subject, and is to be treated as such. Persons too, have an inner life, which for the Pope means the spiritual life. This spiritual life is possible for the human person because of its rational nature, which is the same reason why human persons can exhibit free will. He writes, "man's nature differs fundamentally from that of the animals. It includes the power of self-determination, based on reflection, and manifested in the fact that man acts from choice. This power is called free will."[49] The human person then, is *sui juris*—master of self—which certainly parallels the differences in the life of persons and vampires in *BtVS*. Vampires act like animals, controlled by instinct, slaves to desire, while humans can self-transcend ecstatically.

The personalistic norm is identified with love. Or rather, as John Paul II has it, "the commandment to love *is* the personalistic norm."[50] Under this norm, persons are not to be used as means to an end in some utilitarian notion of pleasure; rather persons are to be treated with dignity, fairness, and justice. These virtues mean that a person is to be treated as an "object of love, not as an object for use."[51] But when abstracted from love, these virtues only concern themselves with the material world;

rather they must be seen under the jurisdiction of love. Only then do these virtues reflect an "affirmation of the value of the person as such is of its essence."[52] Seeing others as an object of love deeply affects the way persons are in action. Of love and the person John Paul II writes, "but love forcibly detaches the person, so to speak, from this natural inviolability and inalienability. It makes a person want to do just that—surrender itself to another, to the one it loves."[53]

Consider sexual unions. In these relationships, two persons give themselves as gifts to one another. But this cannot be, because as an objective entity, the person is "untransferable, *alteri incommunicabilis*";[54] because of the person's inner life, the person is his or her own master, and therefore cannot be the property of another in a physical sense. But the Pontiff writes that one can give oneself "in a moral sense. In this sense, one person can give himself or herself, can surrender entirely to another, whether to human person or to God, and such a giving of the self creates a special form of love which we define as betrothed love."[55] The deepest love between humans is this self-giving, morally, to another, handing over the ownership of one's own life. He continues, "this is doubly paradoxical: firstly in that it is possible to step outside one's own 'I' in this way, and secondly in that 'I' far from being destroyed or impaired as a result is enlarged and enriched—of course in a super physical, a moral sense."[56] When a person's aim is not to possess but to self-give and be possessed instead, he receives the life back in full. Luke's gospel teaches, "For whoever wants to save his life will lose it, but whoever loses his life for me will save it" (Luke 9:24 NIV). Christian personalism, ontologically, means that a person is first defined by their relations; ethically, it means that a person is in full when they become a person for others. There is no separation from ontology and ethics here. The highest moral act is the one of self-giving, which Pope John Paul II summarizes, "The person no longer wishes to be its own exclusive property, but instead to become the property of that other."[57]

It is only when Spike has a soul that he and Buffy can establish a healthy intimate relationship. No longer is the relationship based on utilitarian pleasure, but on self-giving and thus self-receiving. Indeed, Buffy and Spike can utilize each other for self-interested pleasure more easily when Spike is not fully a person. The soul makes the person, and hence the love, possible.

CONCLUSION

In *BtVS*, the "undead" vampire is a demon-possessed body, soul *in absentia*. But as we have seen, the vampire can reacquire its soul; though still not a human, vampires can be people with dignity. As I have argued, the soul in *BtVS* is not a transcendent essentialist entity, but an existential tool enabling the undead vampire to become a person in relation. This in part echoes Christian personalism, but it fails to compare because in the end, a character like Spike can only give himself for finite, immanent beings. There is nothing external for which he or anyone else can give themselves; there is nothing that grants their self-giving lasting significance. At its deepest meaning, the fight against evil can continue, and they can live to fight another day.

Christian personalism, on the other hand, goes an important step further. It understands that a person's greatest happiness is discovered in offering oneself to God. John Paul II reminds us that humans are the only animals in which God creates for himself, therefore as persons, as souls even, we find our highest meaning and happiness when humans participate in the life of God.[58]

Our age is anxious, as our vampire myths witness to us. Is there meaning? Do we matter? Who am I? What is living, and what is dead? These are important questions when much of our life reflects the vampire's: negligent consumerism. *BtVS* is a helpful mythology for asking those questions, but it cannot escape the anxiety of our times; in fact, its answer is nihilistic. It says that we are all alone, save our friends who are in the same predicament, and the only thing we can do is find our meaning in our community. Evil will always be there, and it is enough if we have friends to cope with us in our struggle. For Christianity and its personalism, on the other hand, we are not alone. In fact we can't be alone, because we are defined by our relations; the most basic and profound relation we have, in fact, is with the Triune God in whom we have our ultimate meaning and destiny. God is the person who grants meaning, goodness, and beauty; it is in our relation to God that we find Sabbath, true redemption. Even the Church—God's community of celebration—acknowledges this personalistic norm on a regular basis. Regularly, the Church gathers to participate in the Eucharist, and no matter one's view of "presence," all traditions affirm that it is the meal that identifies us with a self-giving God. When consuming it, the participants, themselves, are consumed into the body of Christ. Simply put, it reminds the Christian

Part One: Vampires

person that their fate is bound up with others. This is not incidental to one's local situation; rather it is a radical commitment to relation, both to God and God's people.[59] The closest the Scoobies come to Eucharistic life of relation happens when they gather to celebrate and to rest from their timely and quotidian victories, knowing that another day means another chance for evil to prevail.

END NOTES

1. This essay is dedicated to my mother, Junie Longbons, and to Ryan "Gimpy" Stewart. Thank you, Mom, for instilling in me what Lint Hatcher calls the "spooky gene." And thank you, Ryan, for countless hours of waxing theological about Buffy and the horror genre.
2. Melton, *The Vampire Book*, 118–19.
3. Erickson, "Sometimes You Need A Story," 109–10.
4. For Whedon's personal philosophy see "Joss Whedon Atheist and Absurdist" video, online at http://www.youtube.com/watch?v=EReyF2ZzXGA.
5. For Whedon's feminism see the interview at ign.com, online at http://movies.ign.com/articles/425/425492p2.html.
6. See http://www.scifitv.com.au/Blog/2010/08/joss-whedon-says-serenity-was-firefly-season-2/.
7. It must be pointed out that Stoker was an Irish Anglican. The character Jonathan Harker, a primary protagonist in *Dracula*, was also an Anglican. However, Dr. Van Helsing uses Roman Catholic sacramental elements as weapons to combat Dracula, such as the crucifix and the consecrated wafer of the Eucharist. I am in no way arguing that Stoker intended to write a Catholic vampire story, rather the argument is simply that the world he creates is metaphysically (albeit implicitly) Catholic in its engagement with religion precisely because of the divine presence within the sacramental elements used for defeating vampires.
8. Worley, "Anne Rice's Protestant Vampires," 79.
9. See http://www.newadvent.org/cathen/05573a.htm and Graham, *Cities of God*. Ward argues that when Jesus says "this *is* my body," the word "is" is an ontological scandal that we must deal with.
10. Admittedly, like Stoker, Anne Rice is not attempting to write a specifically Protestant or Catholic vampire story. At the time of publication, Rice had rejected her Catholic upbringing and accepted a secular life-view. While her stories contain elements of secularism and paganism, the point I am making, in relation to the Christian religion and sacramentality, is that her stories take on a more Protestant metaphysic. No longer, in Rice's vampire world, are sacraments imbued with the presence of Christ. Faith is now needed in order for them to have any power. Noting Rice's vampire stories for this essay is meant to

give an example of shifting religious attitudes in which vampire stories are told. Stoker presents a more Christian worldview while Rice is closer to Whedon's secular one.

11. Worley, "Anne Rice's Protestant Vampires," 80.
12. This point is certainly complex and filled with a long history. For our purposes we must note that there was a monumental theological shift around the sixteenth century with the rise of nominalism and voluntarism. Put simply, theologians began conceiving of God as supremely distant from creation. The theological landscape was dominated by total transcendence. The Reformation, along with its shifting understanding of religious mediation, was born during this era and helped to solidify an abstracted view of God. Through these theological developments, Nietzsche could argue that society had "killed God"; society has no more need of a transcendent meaning for the world. This provided a firm foundation for existential philosophy, especially after the calamities of the twentieth century. See Szerszynski, *Nature, Technology*. This point is not to say that the Reformation is responsible for existentialism, rather its attitudes about where to "locate" God are genealogically related to later secular ideologies.
13. After all, Rice wrote her stories in the context of America, which is shaped more so by Protestant sensibilities than Catholic ones.
14. Worley cites *Interview with the Vampire*, when Louis discovers that he has nothing to fear from a New Orleans cathedral.
15. *Buffy the Vampire Slayer*. Episode no. 4.16 "Who Are You," first broadcast 29 February 2000 by WB Television Network. Directed and Written by Joss Whedon.
16. Playdon, "What You Are, What's to Come," 171.
17. Ibid.
18. Ibid.
19. See Maximus the Confessor, *Ambiguum 7*, 71.
20. It is important to note that in *BtVS* humans can act less than human. This usually happens when they act selfishly without regard to the well-being of other persons. Demons, too, can act more humanly than humans, when they exchange parasitism for *kenosis*.
21. Schmitz, *At the Center of Human Drama*, 37–38.
22. The criticism that Spike is never directed toward transcendence does not aim to negate immanence. For Christian theology, a God who is totally transcendent is also more immanent than creatures are. I am not implying any dualism here; the real criticism lies in the fact that Spike's meaning is found completely within immanent relations without a proper transcendent one. He never gives himself (or is able to give himself) for the transcendent source of all being, because in the Buffyverse the existence of such a being is *aporetic* at best.

Part One: Vampires

23. *Buffy the Vampire Slayer*. Episode no. 2.7 "Lie to Me," first broadcast 3 November 1997 by WB Television Network. Directed and Written by Joss Whedon.
24. Busse, "Crossing the Final Taboo," 212.
25. *Buffy the Vampire Slayer*. Episode no. 5.7 "Fool for Love," first broadcast 14 November 2000 by WB Television Network. Directed by Nick Marck and Written by Joss Whedon and Douglas Petrie.
26. Sunnydale, California, the setting for the show, lies on top of a "Hell Mouth." A Hell Mouth is a gateway to hell and for *BtVS* it functions as the source of dark energy that allows for a demon subculture.
27. Wilcox, *Why Buffy Matters*, 84.
28. Interestingly, *BtVS* seems to have a more fully developed notion of a transcendent source in relation to evil as opposed to good. To be sure, this is still an immanent concept, but there is more represented on the side of evil in *BtVS* than good.
29. I am indebted to an unpublished paper by Ryan Stewart called "Cultural Artifacts: *Buffy the Vampire Slayer*," written for Christopher Ben Simpson's Kierkegaard class at Lincoln Christian University, Lincoln, Illinois, 2008. In the paper, Stewart argues that Spike's character arc follows the three main life-views in the philosophy of Kierkegaard: the aesthetic (life-view of pleasure), the ethical (life-view of others), and the religious (a life-view encompassing the other two, lived for God, where the aesthetic and ethical are properly contextualized).
30. William's poetry for Cecily made use of this term, he writes, "My heart expands, 'tis grown a bulge in it, inspired by your beauty effulgent," in "Fool for Love."
31. Giles explains this in episode 1.7 "Angel," first broadcast 14 April 1997 by WB Television Network. Directed by Scott Brazil and Written by David Greenwalt.
32. Wilcox, *Why Buffy Matters*, 87.
33. See Campbell, *The Hero with a Thousand Faces*. In it, Campbell claims that all myths are variations of the same myth, just told in different cultures to different audiences.
34. Read through the lens of Christianity, Spike can also be seen as a "Christ-figure" in the show.
35. Ratzinger, "Receiving the Tradition."
36. Ibid., 440.
37. Ibid., 443.
38. Ibid., 444.
39. Ibid., 445.
40. Ibid.
41. Ibid.
42. Ibid.
43. Ibid., 452.
44. Ibid.

45. Augustine, *The Confessions*, 43.
46. John Paul II, *Crossing the Threshold of Hope*, 202.
47. John Paul II, *Love and Responsibility*, 40.
48. Ibid., 23.
49. Ibid., 23–24.
50. Ibid., 41.
51. Ibid., 42.
52. Ibid.
53. Ibid., 125.
54. Ibid., 96.
55. Ibid., 96–97.
56. Ibid., 97.
57. Ibid., 125.
58. John Paul II, *Crossing the Threshold of Hope*, 201.
59. I am indebted to Cavanaugh's *Being Consumed*, for this personalistic understanding of the Eucharist.

4

The Vampire that Haunts Highgate
Theological Evil, Hammer Horror,
and the Highgate Vampire Panic in Britain, 1963–1974

W. Scott Poole

"Does a Wampyr haunt Highgate?"[1]

On February 6, 1970, the *Hampstead and Highgate Express* luridly raised this question by using it to headline a letter from paranormal investigator Sean Manchester. Manchester insisted that a dark Vampire Lord from eastern Europe came London with the help of his occult supporters in the eighteenth century. This monarch of the undead, who Manchester described in terms remarkably reminiscent of Christopher Lee's portrayal of Count Dracula in the immensely popular Hammer horror series, still haunted the overgrown and brambled paths of the Victorian cemetery. He had been quiescent for almost two centuries until a circle of Satanists raised him from the dead.[2]

Manchester had come late to the undead, satanic, party. For more than a decade, various strains of theology and popular culture in British society intermingled themes of desecrated graveyards, satanic rites, demons hunting the innocent, and tall, dark vampires craving blood and its dark ecstasies. Speculation, theological writing, pop culture mania, and outbreaks of moral panic occurred against the backdrop of growing chaos in Great Britain. In fact, the panic inspired by the historical context has led historian and cultural critic Francis Wheen to call the 1970s "the golden age of paranoia."[3]

Vampire panics had not been uncommon in early modern Europe, at least in Eastern Europe, where the folklore about blood-sucking revenants and vampire-hunting flourished in the early modern period. Historian Paul Barber uncovered a whole world of legendary vampire material in this region, much of it centered on anxiety about improper burial and the after-life of murderers and suicides. In fact, as late as the nineteenth century, he found cases in Bulgaria of iron stakes being driven through the hearts of the recent dead and the corpses being set on fire. In the same era, panicky Serbians removed the hearts of alleged vampires and boiled them in wine.[4]

The vampire panic has been uncommon, indeed almost unknown, in the modern West. This has remained the case since the end of the Second World War, a period future historians and folklorists will likely view as a bubbling cauldron of rumor and legend based on beliefs in the supernatural and the paranormal. During this period, alien abduction panics, cult panics, cattle mutilation panics, possession panics, and satanic ritual abuse panics have resounded through Britain and America's cultural echo chamber. Strangely, given their pop culture notoriety, vampires have played little role in this monster mash of social legend and rumor panic.[5]

This is true with the exception of the vampire panic Britain experienced in the late 1960s and early 70s. The bizarre affair centered on Highgate Cemetery, a large burial ground north of London between Lower Holloway and East Finchley. Built as a "overflow plots" for Victorian Londoners who could not be buried in a parish church, more than a hundred thousand tombs are found there. These range from small plots to large crypts sculpted in the faux Egyptian and faux classical styles so beloved of the cemetery's first decades of existence. Other than its alleged vampires, the most famous residents of Highgate are Christina Rossetti, George Eliot, and Karl Marx. Douglas Adams, author of *Hitchhiker's Guide to the Galaxy*, also molders here.[6]

The cemetery also became famous in the twentieth century for becoming a ruinous pile. All plots had been filled by the time of the First World War and local authorities ceased to maintain it. Many of the ornate vaults incurred significant damage during German bombing raids during World War II. By the 1960s, graves had been left open, wild shrub, weeds, and second growth foliage had taken over the once well-maintained

Part One: Vampires

garden-like paths. A visitor in the mid-60s described underbrush as "hip high" and advised adventurers in the cemetery to bring a machete.[7]

Future Highgate visitors instead came with wooden stakes and holy water . . . and the desire to kill vampires, see vampires, see someone trying to kill vampires, to see something supernatural or maybe just to see something. Between 1969 and 1973—with bizarre flare-ups occurring as late as the 80s—local media issued a steady stream of stories that a vampire walked Highgate. Meanwhile, two "occult experts"—David Farrant and Sean Manchester—became the Van Helsings that would destroy the monster. In certain respects, the bizarre chain of events climaxed with a mob descending on the cemetery on March 13, 1970 (a Friday the 13th), while police frantically tried to hold back perhaps hundreds of people who rampaged through the Highgate underbrush.

This essay seeks to place this vampire hunt, *sui generis* in the history of late twentieth-century moral panics, in the midst of a particular set of social conditions, pop culture phenomenon, and theological discourse about the nature of evil. A vampire walked the ruined paths of Highgate at a moment when British society descended into a maelstrom of economic chaos and free-floating cultural anxiety. Moreover, he appeared in the midst of a discourse about the work of the devil that emerged out of the small but vibrant British evangelical and charismatic movements in the 60s and 70s. This discourse provided a legitimizing theological language of evil. Finally, the Highgate panic shows us much about the complex relationship between religion and popular culture in modern society, the strange alliances they sometimes forge in relation to supernatural discourses. Religious conservatives, horror films, and the disastrous state of British life in the early 70s ensured that, in the midst of an increasingly secular society, the devil got his due.

A number of previous studies have examined the issue of moral panics in relation to supernatural beliefs. Folklorist Bill Ellis and sociologist Jeffrey Victor created the most comprehensive of these studies. Ellis has fashioned a significant body of work detailing how supernatural beliefs become the basis of "rumor panic," which he defines as "brief but intense events in which rumors about a menacing person or group circulate in the community. . . . [T]he only defense is a strong offense by concerned citizens." The monster is loose, the monster is after us, and it's the responsibility of angry villagers to grab their torch and join the mob.[8]

The work of Ellis and Victor has focused on the panics largely from a folkloric and sociological perspective. They have carefully explored and explained the basic mechanics of rumor panic and how these panics have frequently found expression in public life. Victor's *Satanic Panic* is astoundingly rich in detail and the perfect complement to Ellis' more theoretical discussions of how folklorists should read moral panic.[9]

Ellis in particular has given a detailed guide to the events surrounding Highgate in his important book *Raising the Devil: Satanism, New Religions and the Media*. Ellis, as he has done throughout his extraordinary body of work, mapped the cultural topography of the Highgate panic, showing the role of earlier conceptions of "black magic circles" in Britain, the variables related to the transatlantic conceptions of "Satanism," and the role played by radio, television, and newspapers in shaping social rumor into a major media event. Ellis also argues that the Hammer Studios horror films of the early 70s drew on "the popular interest in black magic" by borrowing folk beliefs about black magic, Satanism and vampires in films such as *The Satanic Rites of Dracula*.[10]

The current study builds on rather than contradicts these insights. Instead of looking for specific social triggers for the weird goings-on at Highgate, it situates the panic into a total environment of popular belief, a free, easy, and largely unconscious exchange between pop culture and religious belief, popular entertainment and the Christian theology of the supernatural. In twentieth-century North America, religion and popular culture had an uneasy alliance in representations of the demonic. The story in Britain is far more complicated and, in some respects, more interesting. So interesting, that we need a broader understanding of historical context to make sense of these events rather than relying on the theoretical construction of moral panic.

A look at the Highgate Vampire Panic in historical context shows that cultural discourses are produced by, and also further incite, historical experience. The British historical context of the late 60s and early 70s provides some explanation for Ellis' contention that "Satanism was a growth industry in Great Britain" during this period. British evangelical theology and its conceptions of spiritual warfare provide further context. In the first section of this essay, I'd like to explore how demonic discourses among both British evangelicals and the newly emerging charismatic movement helped shape the experience and meaning of Highgate.[11]

Part One: Vampires

A BRITISH THEOLOGY OF THE DEVIL

The modern phase of the British evangelical movement had its origins in the 1920s and 30s and received transatlantic influences from the rise of American Fundamentalism of the same period. The work of C. S. Lewis during and after World War II particularly affected the shape of British evangelical life, though Lewis himself was not an evangelical. Lewis' influence tended to make British evangelicalism both more sophisticated theologically and far more invested in its identity as part of a historic Christian tradition than has been the case in American evangelicalism. Perhaps for this reason, British evangelicalism tended to become less entangled in political controversies over topics such as changing sexual mores and the widespread acceptance of evolution. Given the unique nature of the Church of England, evangelical involvement in British politics, to the degree it occurred, centered on efforts to involve parliament in struggles over various revisions of the *Book of Common Prayer*, the liturgical and devotional manual of the Anglican tradition.[12]

As the Church of England liberalized its views of the authority of the Bible and renegotiated its relationship with modernity, evangelicals (in and outside the established church) increasingly came together in small networks. Much like their American cousins, they tended to identify around the issue of biblical inerrancy and a resistance to what they denominated as "liberalism" or "modernism." Although "nonconformist" or "free churches" certainly provided much of the backbone of British evangelicalism, its important to note that many evangelicals remained within the Anglican tradition, often creating infra-church networks for support such as the Fellowship of Evangelical Churchmen.[13]

1966 represents a major turning point in the life of the movement. In that year, D. Martyn Lloyd-Jones, the leading spokesman for the Free Church evangelicals, used a meeting of the British Evangelical Alliance to call on his co-religionists within the Church of England to abandon the established church as a sinking theological ship. He asked his fellow conservatives to take the classic separatist position of "coming out from among them" and join one of the Free Church traditions or simply create independent congregations. John Stott, another significant leader figure among British evangelicals, took the podium to rebuke Jones and urge caution on the part of his fellow Anglicans.[14]

This religious conflict, triggered by evangelicalism's troubled relationship with modernity and its continued debt to the Puritan impulse, pushed Lloyd-Jones in an increasingly conservative direction even as his popularity as a preacher and biblical interpreter grew. In fact, he (along with his sometime nemesis Stott) became celebrity preachers in the midst of an increasingly secular England.

Lloyd-Jones had served as the highly popular preacher of Westminster Chapel since 1943. Indeed, at a time when religious practice in Great Britain had entered a slump from which it has never recovered, Lloyd-Jones attracted gigantic London crowds with his courtly manner and warm scholarly style of expository preaching. Giving sermons that ran close to an hour in length, he marched his listeners through entire books of the Bible over many months of exposition. Lloyd-Jones most famously expounded the books of Romans and Ephesians, exegetical material later published in many volumes. His sermons reached a wide audience in the 1960s being printed, usually verbatim, in the weekly *Westminster Record*.[15]

Throughout the 1960s, Lloyd-Jones preaching focused on the reality of the devil and his influence over contemporary Britain. In sermons such as "The Devil and the Nations" (1960), "Attacked by the Devil" (1963), and "Questions and Answers on Healing and Demon Possession" (1971), he asserted the reality of Satan as well as an entire world of malevolent forces that threatened unbelievers, the Christian church, and all of human society. Outright demon possession represented at least part of the devil's efforts in the world. Moreover, and in contradistinction to many evangelical ideas on the subject, Lloyd-Jones believed that Christians, and not just unbelievers, could become possessed by diabolical spirits.[16]

Society could also become the focus of demonic attack. Indeed, while he never numbered vampires among the evils hordes assembled by the devil, Lloyd-Jones did claim that there are "thousands, perhaps millions, of evil spirits "active in modern society. Indeed, he believed them to be especially active in the UK during the 1960s and 1970s. This idea grew out of his belief that the devil concentrated on certain nations at certain times and Britain faced just such a period at the end of the twentieth century. Noting an "increase" in demonic activity during the 1960s, Lloyd-Jones blamed these new manifestations of evil on "the lowered spirituality and the godlessness of the whole country."[17]

These ideas found fullest expression in his expository sermons on the Book of Ephesians that became available in book form (apparently with very little redaction) in 1976. One of these books entitled *The Christian Warfare*, focused close to four hundred pages on Ephesians

6:10–13. Modeled on a Puritan classic, William Gurnell's *The Christian in Compleat Armor*, Lloyd-Jones imagined Christians in constant spiritual warfare with Ephesians' "powers and principalities" in a Britain that had fallen, according to him, into a state of "lawlessness." He connected this growing anarchy in the UK to the devil's ability to convince the young to revolt against established authority.[18]

Given the sheer amount of time of time Lloyd-Jones spent on these several verses in Ephesians, his exegesis warrants a closer reading. In general, his exposition moves in two different but complementary directions. On the one hand, he recounts the Miltonic reading of Lucifer's fall and insists on a literal understanding of this element in the Christian tradition. On the other, he launches a series of broadsides against "rationalists" and the "scientific-minded" that have allegedly banished the idea of satanic evil from public discourse.[19]

Lloyd-Jones also concentrates on what he sees as the devil's almost constant work in the world. The popular preacher created a universe filled with powerful, pernicious creatures, with the devil as their high king. Satan worked tirelessly against the Church and the fight against him involved much more than resisting temptation, doing good deeds or trying to improve one's moral life. Lloyd-Jones and other British evangelicals imagined a literal struggle against very literal forces of darkness. At a time when some called for a demythologizing of Christianity, Lloyd-Jones became a leading voice arguing for what could be called its remythologization.[20]

Indeed, reading Lloyd-Jones' Ephesians sermons at times feels like a trip to Tolkien's Middle Earth during time of war. Satan becomes, not the tempter or even simply the enemy of God causing chaos, but rather a Lord of Evil, Sauron in his might, leading what Lloyd-Jones calls "Cohorts, battalions, legions" of evil spirits running rampant on the earth. "The devil is not a solitary power," Lloyd-Jones claimed; "he has his agents and agencies."[21]

In order to underscore this point, Lloyd-Jones insisted on a retranslation of the King James' version of Ephesians 6:12. The description of "wickedness in high places," he argues, must be translated as "wicked spirits" or even "spiritual cohorts of evil." Lloyd-Jones argued that such a translation fit better with the writer's general insistence on the reality of "myriads of spirits of evil . . . their nature is evil, their commission is evil and their work is evil."[22]

This much-beloved leader among British Free Church evangelicals represented anything but a marginal theological position. Notably, while Lloyd-Jones and John Stott disagreed over issues of church polity, they came together in a common belief in the active work of Satan in the world. Indeed, in the midst of the Highgate panic, Stott delivered at least one sermon on the idea of "satanic oppression" and "a devil bent on taking men alive."[23]

The influence of these leading evangelicals, though significant, does not explain the level of satanic discourse that became current in a society that had frankly, stopped going to church. A new and vital religious movement had appeared, very different in many respects from the evangelicals but just as insistent on the work of Satan on earth and the need for Christians to engage in spiritual warfare. Largely an American import, the British charismatic movement borrowed their transatlantic cousins' ideas about healing, glossolalia, and the need to do battle with the Prince of Darkness.

Most accounts link the beginning of charismatic renewal movement in England to a town in Greater London called Beckenham in 1963. Influenced by the traditional teachings of Pentecostalism regarding the "gifts of the spirit," the British charismatic movement thrived both in "house churches" and in certain corners of the Anglican establishment. The latter can be explained in part by the contemporary influence of the charismatic movement in the American Episcopal Church.[24]

Charismatic influences changed worship styles in a few Anglican parishes and among some of its leaders. Indeed, at least one report exists of some Anglican bishops at charismatic renewal conference dancing joyfully around a communion table in 1978. However, the idea of spiritual warfare and the ability to exorcise demons also played a substantial role, with some C of E parishes focusing their attention almost exclusively on doing battle with demons and other monstrous satanic creatures. [25]

The idea of Stott and Lloyd-Jones out on a vampire hunt seems more than a little ridiculous. Nor do we find references to vampires in the writings and sermons of the British charismatic movement. However, Bill Ellis certainly uncovered evidence that ideas about Satan's malevolent influence seeped down into the ranks of local clergy, even among the ranks of evangelicals in the Church of England. In 1963, the Reverend Leslie Barker, the rector responsible for the crumbling tenth-century parish of St. Mary's in Luton suggested that what he simply referred to as "Satan worshippers" had been responsible for a recent wave of "grave

Part One: Vampires

desecrations." Barker made this seemingly outrageous claim after some teenage boys insisted that they seen a skull skewered on top of a pike in the crumbling remains of the Chapel.[26]

Ellis notes that a discourse of about "grave desecration" and churches became very common in 1960s Britain, a discourse that made frequent reference to the work of Satanists. By the mid-1960s, the British police got in on the act, claiming they had uncovered "more than two hundred" incidents of ritual grave desecration.[27]

Anxieties over grave desecration created a popular mentality about evil goings-on in burial grounds. Religious leaders often played a key role in these panics. During the Highgate panic itself, an Anglican priest named Christopher Neil-Smith became involved, even though he seems to have regarded some of the talk of vampires as a "novelistic embellishment." Nevertheless, he took the power of Satan seriously and believed that the devil had been doing his work at Highgate.[28]

In fact, Neil-Smith had been performing exorcisms since the late 1940s and at the time of his death in 1995, he had allegedly performed "many thousands of exorcisms." In one especially sensationalized incident, he allegedly exorcised what he described as "the high priestess of a witches coven." Certainly no skeptic, he was given to novelistic embellishment himself, claiming that expelling demons tended to cause church altars to "vibrate" and that he had been "thrown across the floor" during exorcisms.[29]

How did conservative, charismatic, and evangelical religious leaders come to know so much about the devil in the 1960s and 1970s? Certainly we have to pay attention to the wide influence of Lloyd-Jones preaching and his insistence on the reality of spiritual warfare. Moreover, the Charismatic movement, both in Britain and in the United States, certainly placed a heavy emphasis on the role of demonic possession and the spiritual necessity of exorcism, ideas that became increasingly important to them in the post-World War II era.[30]

It's also very likely, that many of them rediscovered the devil at the movies.

THE SATANIC RITES OF HAMMER

Hammer Studios created one of the most successful brand names in film history. The production company had existed in various forms since the

1930s and dabbled in Gothic thrillers from its inception. Bolstered by the British government's heavy taxation of American films in 1947, Hammer explored a variety of genres, particularly focusing on films based on radio shows dealing with mystery and suspense. By the mid-1950s, and under the leadership of James Carreras, Hammer began experimenting with the popular sci-fi genre, producing interesting hybrid material that tended to have more complexity than the standard American alien invasion narrative.[31]

Hammer entered an era of wild popularity with the 1957 production *The Curse of Frankenstein*. Rather than worrying over the copyright issues that might emerge if they attempted a remake of James Whale's 1932 *Frankenstein* for Universal Studios, Hammer created an entirely new mad scientist and an entirely new monster. A medical student, (he's no Baron) Frankenstein became a rebel without a cause, an anti-hero for the late 1950s. The Monster became zombie-like in its look, with gruesome, bloody, peeling skin. Hammer's Monster truly looked like a thing made from corpses rather than the art deco masterpiece that James Whale and Boris Karloff had created. Hammer cast the whole affair in a Gothic/Victorian/medieval never-never land that still, sometimes, seemed suspiciously like the modish Britain of the 60s.[32]

Critics warmly despised most Hammer productions, viewing them as exploitative in their tendency to mix gallons of Technicolor blood with heaving bosoms eager to burst out of corsets. The British public, and eventually American fans, loved the films. A Hammer horror marquee always insured long lines at theatres and became part of the pop iconography of the 1960s.

Success beyond their wildest dreams came to Hammer with *Curse* and so the studio set about to rehabilitate and reimagine all the classic monster paradigms, creating their version of the Mummy, the Wolf Man and, of course, Count Dracula, played as a disturbing combination of regal and bloodthirsty, aristocrat and savage animal, by Christopher Lee. Lee created a Dracula as sinister as Lugosi's. But he also heightened the erotic aspects of the character, transforming his appeal, as Denis Meikle has said "from chill charm ... [to] the warm embrace of a demon lover."[33]

Dracula (1958; *Horror of Dracula* in the U.S.) came first and drove England into vampire hysteria. The reimagining of the lord of the vampires topped *Curse* at the box office and Lee's Dracula, usually surrounded by female victims more or less falling out their clothes, became the iconic symbol of the Hammer horror tradition. The films that followed the Lee

Part One: Vampires

(and Peter Cushing) masterpiece, while generally viewed as inferior by fans today, fed from, and fed into, Britain's growing fascination with the occult.

This fascination both filtered up through the growing unease over "grave desecrations" and their possible satanic implications and filtered down through a growing movement of what might be called satanic chic in British celebrity culture. Filmmaker, alleged magus and startlingly successful self-promoter Kenneth Anger became a confidante of the Rolling Stones during this era and, according to an unconfirmed rumor, came close to convincing Richards and Jagger to put together a concept album based on the works of William Blake. He certainly had them reading De Sade and Aleister Crowley and provided some inspiration for the controversial *Their Satanic Majesties Request* album and the infamous "Sympathy for the Devil" cut on *Beggars Banquet*.[34]

Hammer Horror helped shape this black magic zeitgeist in the years leading up to the Highgate Panic. Two films in particular, *Dracula Has Risen from the Grave* (1968) and *Taste the Blood of Dracula* (1970) are worth close examination given their appearance immediately before and during the Highgate Panic. They also suggest ways in which popular culture may have been borrowing heavily from themes in British religious life and how British religious life borrowed those themes right back.[35]

Famous horror film host, critic, and aficionado John Stanley described *Dracula Has Risen from the Grave* as filled with the "heavy handed use of religious symbolism." In fact, it does swerve unevenly back and forth between religious parable and critique of the religion. Leitmotifs in the film include angst over the corruption of innocence and the sexuality in relation to religious structures while the struggle over the nature of religious belief remains paramount throughout. Indeed, the film's confused mish-mash of a message poses a question, perhaps unwittingly, about the struggle between belief and unbelief in a world where evil, everybody at least agrees, exists in abundance.[36]

Notably, given the cultural context, the narrative opens with a "vilely desecrated church." No one in the faux medieval/Victorian mash-up of a village ever attends "the empty church" because of "the Shadow" that has fallen across it. Monsignor Ernst, a "spiritual warrior" of the Christopher Neil-Smith sort, demands that the local village priest go with him to the source of the "Shadow" and exorcise it. While the Monsignor places the most gigantic crucifix you have ever seen on the door of Castle

Dracula, his hapless helper manages to resurrect the Count through a freak accident.[37]

Lee's Dracula remains as menacing in this film as in most of the other Hammer vampire fests, even as the plot crumbles around him. Dracula decides to take revenge on the Monsignor for, apparently, denying him access to his castle. Despite the silliness of the plot, Lee does become here, as Mary Y. Hallab argues, "a powerful, chthonic godlike authority . . . effectively satanic in his contempt for puny mortals." Indeed, his revenge on "puny mortals" involves the seduction and victimization of the Monsignor's niece who is, of course, named Mary. Her human paramour Paul happens to be an atheist at odds with the Monsignor.[38]

The film's narrative logic insists that Paul the atheist must come to believe in vampires, and in God, in order to save his beloved from her demon lover. Indeed, the Monsignor (who Dracula completely puts out of commission by hurling across a roof) gives to Paul a mystical text of exorcism ("in Latin"). Religious faith triumphs over both Paul's atheism and the King of the Vampires. The young unbeliever defeats Dracula through spiritual warfare. In the last shot, we see Paul holding Mary and crossing himself. Yet another gigantic cross skewers the now empty cape of Dracula as the credits roll. Religion 1, demonic vampires 0.

Many of the elements that British evangelicals and charismatics made central to their religious experience appear in this film. Sublimated somewhat by placing the story within a faux medieval Catholic England (that, again, also seems Victorian), a clear emphasis remains on spiritual warfare and the efficacy of exorcism. Moreover, Hammer added an interesting tidbit to the Vampire mythos in this production. Paul manages to stake Dracula at the midpoint in the film but, according to a priest, Dracula will only die if Paul also agrees to pray over the corpse. In almost every respect, the battle against the demon prince as played by Lee resembles the concepts of spiritual warfare. *Dracula has Risen from the Grave* also played with the notion of desecrated churches which, as we have seen, had become a central symbol of 1960s Britain's discourse about the growing power of the devil. It's also worth noting that this became the highest grossing film in Hammer history.[39]

In a film that hit screens in the middle of the Highgate panic, Hammer extrapolated further from these themes. In *Taste the Blood of Dracula* (1970), we see almost a complete identification of Satan, black magic and the Vampire Lord.

Part One: Vampires

Taste centers on the story of a group of debauched sexual adventurers who, except for the last Sunday of the month, masquerade as proper, church-going Victorian gentlemen. During one of their orgies (taking place while their families think they are "doing charity work in the East End"), they come in contact with young Lord Courtly who, rumor has it, has been "possessed by the devil" and repudiated by his family after "performing a black mass in the family chapel." Courtly interests the group, a bit bored with their brothel-visiting, in the black arts. In fact, he invites them to help him purchase an amulet and a cloak that belonged to (guess who) Dracula himself.[40]

Conforming almost completely to the scripts of grave desecration/church desecration panics of the 1960s, the group holds black mass in a crumbling parish. The ritual, at first, seems to only end in the death of the young wastrel Courtly. Dracula does however, come back from the dead and targets the virginal young daughter of the leader of the debauchee's as his latest target. "Alice" is, in true Hammer style, portrayed as a blonde innocent at the very height of pulchritude and fairly exploding out of various dresses and nightgowns.[41]

Count Dracula himself seems more than little incidental to the narrative and a look at early treatments for the film confirm that this is the case. This odd shift in Dracula films away from their central character had something to do, of course, with the growing expense of keeping Christopher Lee in the lead role (and convincing him to don the cape for these increasingly cartoonish sequels).[42]

Contract negotiations aside, Hammer also sought to tap the zeitgeist that had become increasingly fascinated with black magic, witch covens, and unholy sacrifices taking place in desecrated churches. In *Taste the Blood of Dracula,* the Count himself does not show up until almost an hour into the proceedings. The worship of Satan and evil rites are present almost from the start. In fact, the very title, meant to shock with schlock, referenced a satanic rite in which the young, handsome, and satanic Lord Courtly (Crowley meets Anger meets Jagger?) drinks the Count's blood on the altar of a desecrated church.

Hammer produced these films in the same historical context that gave Britain its grave desecration anxieties. It traded in the previous decade's fascination with what the period's popular writer about the occult, Eric Maple, described as the recurring belief that "some village church had been profaned by homespun Satanists" and the general "revival of interest in witchcraft." Such beliefs received enormous legitimacy from the fact that one of London's most popular preachers insisted on the reality of the devil and the dark prince's interest in destroying Great Britain.[43]

The influence of these films becomes apparent when reading them against the rhetoric of the Highgate Vampire hunts. Much of the rhetoric about the strange happenings at Highgate could have been borrowed directly from the script of *Dracula has Risen from the Grave* and *Taste the Blood of Dracula*. Or extrapolated from a solid decade of satanic discourses coming from Britain's conservative religious community. Or, as this essay argues, intertwining them into a public spectacle that the media and public would love, the lurid sensationalism of what became the tale of the Highgate Vampire. A vampire called from its grave both by social discourse and social chaos.

VAMPING IT UP AT HIGHGATE

The details of the Highgate vampire panic have been fully explored by Ellis in several different works. Another good brief description appears in Joseph Laycock's *Vampires Today*. Only a brief review seems necessary in order to place this event in a much larger cultural matrix of theological discourse, popular culture and contemporaneous British history.[44]

Occult investigators and alleged psychics David Farrant and Sean Manchester may have been the immediate triggers for the event. In early 1969, both made repeated visits to Highgate cemetery, claiming that vandalism and graffiti found there pointed to satanic rites. Farrant spent the night in Highgate Christmas Eve, 1969 and reported to *The Hampstead and Highgate Express* that saw a "grey figure" walking down one of the overgrown lanes.[45]

Farrant's claims seized the public imagination and soon the local newspapers filled with reports of various kinds of specters haunting Highgate, some of them seeming like vampires and some of them not (one report told of "ghost bicyclist" who chased a woman through one of the cemeteries lonely lanes). These various, conflicting versions of supernatural visitations only coagulated (sorry, couldn't help it) into a vampire tale with Sean Manchester's public claims about "a King Vampire from Wallachia" at the cemetery. He claimed that the creature must be destroyed "by the traditional and approved method—drive a stake through his heart with one blow just before dawn between Friday and Saturday, chop off his head with a gravediggers shovel and burn what remains."[46]

Local television specials encouraged the vampire speculation. One of these "special reports" included a young child's claim that he "actually saw its face and it looked like it had been dead for a long time." The broadcast, held on Friday March 13, led to an enormous gathering at Swain's Lane, the major road through Highgate. Police feared that the crowd, which may have numbered in the hundreds, might scale the wall and start a bizarre cemetery riot. Local teenagers and twenty-somethings filled the cemetery through much of the weekend, searching for vampires, satanic rituals, and probably drawing plenty of pentagrams themselves in the process.

All of this activity served to further increase the rumor legend of vampires and black magic at Highgate and beyond. In February of 1971, St. Michael's Parish, an Anglican congregation in Islington, allowed Manchester to come and perform an "exorcism." The Reverend Denis Pauley, an assistant to the actual rector but serving as "priest in charge" at the time of the incident, alleged that the reserve sacrament had been taken from the altar and publicly commented that he believed "those concerned took the Blessed Sacrament to use in their devil-worship." In the exorcism that followed, Pauley reportedly read from the Bible while Manchester threw some unidentified powder over the altar and its implements. The incident further advanced Manchester's reputation as a fearless vampire hunter and kept the Highgate story alive.[47]

In fact, the vampire of Highgate continued to walk through the 1970s and into the 1980s. In 1972 and 1973, the police captured a number of "legend-tripping" teenagers and at one point David Farrant found himself on trial for various minor offenses (including, according to Ellis, "threatening detectives with voodoo dolls."). As late as the 1990s, Manchester remained a media darling, regularly called upon during periods of rumor panic.[48]

Notably, the panic over vampires and black magic occurred in the middle of an almost unprecedented period of social, political, and economic upheaval in British society. A severe economic downturn in the 1960s had created a large, marginalized population of young people, bored, angry and sometimes wandering through literal ruins of former industrial boomtowns. In 1972, Britain had a million unemployed people and an inflation rate of 14 percent.[49]

Politically, the UK seemed on the point of complete collapse. Under the faltering hand of Prime Minister Edward Heath, the years of the Highgate Vampire panic included no less than five declarations of national emergencies. Meanwhile, Heath's draconian policies in Northern Ireland included internment without trial and likely acted as an accelerant to domestic terrorism. Indeed, many historians understand his policies as part of a larger sequence of events that led to 30 January, 1972 ... Bloody Sunday.[50]

Northern Ireland, for good reason, received world attention for its "troubles." In truth, trouble appeared everywhere in British life. Along with it came open discussion of social revolution and the possibility of an apocalyptic collapse of British society. Conservative, traditionalist historian A. J. P. Taylor announced, "there's no future for this country ... Revolution is knocking at the door." Books with titles like the 1971 *The Coming British Revolution* suggested that miner's strikes, the country's economic doldrums, and the Heath government's wavering political leadership created conditions for a new 1917, a complete reordering of life in the UK.[51]

These social conditions certainly strained the much-vaunted national mythology of "stiff-upper lips." In fact, even the highest reaches of the Heath's government fell prey to a growing sense of paranoia. William Armstrong, head of the British Civil service under Heath and sometimes referred to as the "assistant Prime Minister," became the symbolic incarnation of this public anxiety. In January of 1974, Armstrong attended a seminar held in Oxfordshire that's guests included most of the major leaders in British government and business. Armstrong spoke to informally to many of the attendees about how communism had infiltrated every sector of British society; talk not so strange for that period. However, he spoke more formally about the need of all the delegates to "go home and prepare for Armageddon" and worried aloud that the premises had been "bugged." At one point, the President of the Bank of England found Armstrong laying on the floor of a parlor in front of a roaring fire at the Ditchley Park estate, stripped almost completely naked, and mumbling about the end of the world, the Soviets and "moving the Red Army from here and the Blue Army from there." The following day, Heath received the news that the country's chief civil servant had been admitted to a mental institution.[52]

This period of intense paranoia drew from an underground cistern of anxiety, feeding directly the fountains of supernatural panic that appeared in such flumes throughout the 1960s and exploded like a geyser in 1969. The decade became a time when worries over the state of society blended into rumors of supernatural malfeasance.

Part One: Vampires

Ironically, the "grave desecrations" that formed the general background of the public discourse about Satanism are likely themselves the product of Britain's economic crisis. Bill Ellis' thorough investigation of the background of Highgate attributes a significant portion of the cemetery hijinks to young people out for pranking and fun. It's important to note that many of these disaffected and marginalized young people are of that demographic represented disproportionately in British unemployment statistics of this era.[53]

Economic doldrums, disaffected youth, and a society gripped with a growing sense of paranoia are not enough to explain vampire panics. In fact, this look at the total environment that created and shaped what happened at Highgate forces us beyond the idea of moral panic and to think in new ways about how societies interact with beliefs about the supernatural. The story is both cultural and theological. It has to do with the church and the movies and the places where they meet. It's a story firmly rooted in the historical moment, so much so that "historical panic" maybe offers a better language of interpretation than the frequently used concept of "moral panic."

CONCLUSION: HISTORY AND ITS WORLDS OF ENCHANTMENT

A number of folklorists, sociologists, cultural anthropologists, and psychologists have tried to make sense of how fantastic beliefs interact with the quotidian world, how people use their belief in religion and in the supernatural to conceptualize their worldviews and to understand their social location and cultural context.

The idea of moral panic has, as we have seen, proven useful in explaining the mechanics of these processes. Tensions within communities often do lead directly to the creation of a supernatural scapegoat, or even a natural one, that can be easily identified and destroyed, restoring social unity and reaffirming the significance of widely-held values and the authorities that support them.[54]

But not all beliefs in the supernatural lead to moral panic. They also create wonder, curiosity, and a desire for further investigation and knowledge. Christopher D. Bader, F. Carson Menken, and Joseph D. Baker explore this aspect of what they define as "the paranormal" in their book *Paranormal America*. They examine belief patterns about Bigfoot, ghosts, and alien abductions existing across a rather large spectrum of the American public. Interestingly, in relation to the discussion here, they argue that, "conservative religion has a dampening effect upon paranormal belief." This ignores the fact that conservative religious movements insist on a strong belief in the supernatural. Bader, Menken, and Baker exclude from their investigation beliefs in demons, angels, the efficacy of exorcism, and, in fact, vampires. A category we could simply call "religious monsters" does not play a role in their analysis.[55]

Scholars must remember that believers in the supernatural often reject one set of "paranormal" beliefs in favor of another. In this sense, conservative religious faith enlivens and complicates, rather than dampens, supernatural belief. Billy Graham, for example, entertains the idea that UFOs are examples of "angels" acting as God's secret agents rather than extraterrestrial visitations. He also rejects "new age" spirituality as the work of Satan and demonic forces. He may or not believe in Bigfoot, or in vampires, but he and millions of other evangelicals certainly believe in the reality of religious monsters and monsters of religion.[56]

Certainly the climate of British society in the 1960s and 1970s had been significantly influenced by the power of monsters of religion, creatures born on the dark side of the sacred. What makes these beliefs survive together in the modern world? In particular, how did they survive in a fairly secular Britain?

One fascinating possibility comes from Christopher Partridge's argument in his two-volume work *Re-Enchanting the West*, a set of ideas adapted usefully by Joseph Laycock for his study *Vampires Today*. Partridge takes the long view of these beliefs in the Western world, arguing that beliefs in the fantastic constitute something on the order of imaginative revolts against Enlightenment rationalism. These beliefs often include an intertwining of pop culture fascinations with folk belief.[57]

The idea of an enchanted world seems a useful one and Partridge's narrative has the appeal of placing such ideas in the context of a larger reading of the history of Western Europe. The idea becomes problematic, however, when considering ways in which the Enlightenment itself had its own fascination with the irrational. Even Carl Linnaeus, whose *Systema Naturae* promised to create what Stephen Asma calls "a conceptual filing cabinet of the world," held out for the possibility of dragons. Voltaire wondered if Satyrs existed in the forgotten or unknown places of the earth. Far too many historians study the massive trans-Atlantic revivals in Britain and America and the Enlightenment as if they existed in vacuum-sealed compartments, rather than contemporaneous events.[58]

D. Martin-Lloyd-Jones fought the devil in mid-century Britain as an heir of those revivals. The continued existence of a vibrant subculture of charismatics and evangelicals in Britain reminds us of the complexities of the post-Enlightenment world, how enchanted worlds exist and even thrive in the interstices of modernity. Hammer Horror fed off and fed into these worlds of enchantment and helped create new ones in the vampire panics at Highgate. Individuals and communities do not always need to re-enchant their worlds as they live out of mentalities and in historical structures that have enchantment to spare.

Today, St. Mary's of Luton, a desolate tenth-century ruin in 1963 when the Reverend Leslie Parker claimed it had been a haunt of "Satan worshippers," has become a living, restored congregation that describes itself as "part of the worldwide Anglican communion and the evangelical and charismatic traditions that shape us." This parish and its role in both the vampire panic and the emergence of the charismatic movement in England testifies to how a supernatural world of enchantment survives and thrives in the middle of a society that must be described as highly secular.[59]

Perhaps the resurgence of a faith that makes the supernatural a central premise should not surprise us at all. St. Mary's Luton, like Highgate Cemetery, has found itself at the interstices of a religious faith that asserts itself aggressively against modernity, while borrowing and swapping its themes with popular culture. The peculiar alliances of rumor panics and movies, demons and vampires, evangelical warriors and amateur Van Helsings, all point us back to the surprising ways historical context can work its dark magic.

Indeed, history not only includes what Slavoj Zizek calls "fantasy scenarios that obscure the true horror of the situation." It includes fantasy scenarios that fully illuminate the true horror of the situation, making the fantastic itself into a historical variable and allowing participants to live out their enchanted worldviews. The fantastic in theology, in popular culture and as an expression of the angst of history can, and did, create a historical moment that allowed a vampire to haunt Highgate.[60]

END NOTES

1. The German word for "Vampire" seems very peculiar here. The term "vampire" certainly was in general currency in British society. Bram Stoker made use of Wampyr and originally referred to his villain in Dracula as "Count Wampyr." *The H&H Express* writer may have been aware of this usage. See Wolf, *Dracula*.
2. "Does a Wampyr Haunt Highgate?" 3.
3. The subtitle to Wheen's excellent, and frightening, *Strange Days Indeed*.
4. Barber, *Vampires, Burial and Death*, 37–38, 63. One useful line of inquiry regarding Highgate, a much more anthropological one might be to examine it in relation to folklore and anxiety about the restless dead. Hallab points out in *Vampire God* that the "vampire's real crime is his excessive love of love." Or, perhaps more to the point, the vampire's refusal to stay dead. See Hallab, *Vampire God*, 135–36.
5. In his outstanding study of modern vampire communities, Joseph Laycock discusses two such panics since the 1960s, one of them being Highgate. The other involved the 1996 disappearance of Susan Walsh who had done a story on "modern day vampires" for the *Village Voice*. Laycock found evidence that the NYPD briefly investigated this case as some sort of occult crime but his own informant described that investigation as "half-hearted." Walsh struggled with alcoholism, prescription drug addiction and may have been the victim of organized crime because of a story she had written on the Russian mob. It's difficult to describe the response to the story, which garnered some public attention for obvious reasons, as a true "panic." See Laycock, *Vampires Today*, 140–41.
6. "A Short History of Highgate," http://www.highgate-cemetery.org/index.php/history.
7. Altick, *To Be In England*, 194–95.
8. Ellis has written at length about the nature of legends, rumors, and moral panics. This quote comes from his classic *Raising the Devil*, 203. See also his extraordinary collection exploring folk belief, rumor panic, and "ostensive" action, *Aliens, Ghosts and Cults*.
9. See Victor, *Satanic Panic*, especially 40–42, 73, 201–5, 304–5, for a bit of an introduction to significant terms and arguments of this incredibly thorough study.
10. See especially *Raising the Devil*, 208–15.
11. Ibid., 202.
12. Bebbington, *Evangelicalism in Modern Britain*, 205.
13. Ibid., 251.
14. Bebbington, "British and American Evangelicalism Since 1940," in *Evangelicalism: Comparative Studies*, 30.
15. Murray, *D. Martin Lloyd-Jones*. A definitive, critical biography of Lloyd-Jones does not exist.

Part One: Vampires

16. Sargent (ed.), *Gems from Martin-Lloyd Jones*, 90.
17. Ibid
18. Lloyd-Jones, *The Christian's Warfare*, 14.
19. Lloyd-Jones attack on secularism as a force that disenchants the world joins with numerous critiques of the post-enlightenment west that have raised questions about the legacy of rationalism. The Enlightenment itself, as I suggest in the conclusion of this essay, represents an incredibly complex phenomenon in relation to attitudes about the supernatural.
20. Historian George M. Marsden describes the rise of religious fundamentalism as both a response to Darwinism and to literary/historical/critical readings of the Bible. See Marsden, *Fundamentalism and American Culture*, 17–19.
21. Lloyd-Jones, *The Christian's Warfare*, 63.
22. Ibid.
23. Stott, "The Message of Second Timothy," 126.
24. Bebbington, *Evangelicalism in Modern Britain*, 229; See also Tweed, *Re-telling U.S. Religious History*, 221; California Episcopal priest Dennis J. Bennett played a key role in the charismatic movement in America during the 1960s, experiences recounted in his 1970 *Nine O'clock in the Morning*, now a classic among Anglican charismatics.
25. Bebbington, *Evangelicalism in Modern Britain*, 241–42.
26. Quoted in Ellis, *Raising the Devil*, 212.
27. Ibid., 215.
28. Ibid., 222.
29. Beeson, *Priests and Prelates*, 128.
30. See Cuneo, *American Exorcism*, 111–14.
31. Much of my description of the history of Hammer comes from Meikle, *A History of Horrors*, 19, 22–26.
32. Ibid., 39–43.
33. Ibid., 58
34. Baddeley, *Lucifer Rising*, 45–48. For the record, Baddely is a gonzo journalist heartily in favor of all three of the ideals in his sub-title. His ironist style forces you to take some of his claims with a grain of salt, however the case for Anger's influence over the Stones and a small group of "black magic" dilettantes seems airtight. A closer examination of this phenomenon seems warranted given its similarity to another period of "satanic chic" that developed among the aristocratic classes of eighteenth century France.
35. See Leggett, *Terence Fisher*. Leggett argues that Fisher came close to creating Christian allegory in many Hammer films. Freddie Francis, however, directed the two films we are considering, probably the Hammer "Dracula" productions with the most obvious religious references.
36. Stanley, *Creature Features*, 152.

37. *Dracula Has Risen from the Grave,* Directed by Freddie Francis, Hammer Productions (1968).
38. Hallab, *Vampire God,* 119.
39. Meikle, *A History,* 217.
40. *Taste the Blood of Dracula,* Directed by Freddie Francis, Hammer Productions (1970).
41. This became a theme in both the films and the painted posters that have become cult classics. See Hearn, *The Art of Hammer,* for numerous examples.
42. The script seems to have originally been written with the idea that Lee would not appear and this resulted in what Hammer historian Denis Meikle describes as a movie "intended to be a Dracula film in name only." See Meikle, *History of Horror,* 228–29.
43. Maple, *The Dark World of Witches,* 199; Ellis, argues in *Raising the Devil* that, "Hammer Studios was . . . quick to pick up on the popular interest in black magic" (229). He is not incorrect but dates this use of popular mythology from Hammer's 1972 *Satanic Rites of Dracula.* This film, despite its title, actually functions as an espionage tale in which a modern-day Count plays a kind of Bond villain seeking to destroy the world. Meikle suggests that Hammer largely borrowed (stole?) the plotline from *Diamonds are Forever* and in this way, ironically, prepared Christopher Lee "for his impending role as a real Bond villain" in *The Man with the Golden Gun.* See Meikle, *A History,* 272–73.
44. Laycock, *Vampires Today,* 141–43.
45. Both Manchester and Farrant wrote full accounts of the events at Highgate. They are not useful for the current study as they are mostly tendentious and center on the conflict of the two men, something I do not explore because Ellis examines the fairly pathetic tale in *Raising the Devil,* esp. 231–39. At one point, Manchester and Farrant even challenged one another to a highly publicized "magical duel."
46. Manchester quoted in Ellis, *Raising the Devil,* 221.
47. "Beat the Devil: Priest Calls in Magicians."
48. Ellis, *Raising the Devil,* 226–27, 237–38
49. It important to note that some of the original worries over strange goings on in graveyards related to more generalized moral panic over "mods" and "rockers" who became, in the words of a 1971 sociological examination of crime in Britain, "stereotypes symbolic of predatory and organized attack on cherished social values." See Downes and Rock, "Social Reaction to Deviance and Its Effect on Crime and Criminal Careers," 351–64. Economic statistics in Wheen, *Strange Days Indeed,* 45; and for a more detailed discussion, see Sinclair, The Economy—A Study in Failure," 94–121.
50. See Arthur's, "The Heath Government and Northern Ireland," 235–58. See Dillon, *The Enemy Within.*
51. Taylor quoted in Cohen, "The Eurozone; Ali, *The Coming British Revolution.*

Part One: Vampires

52. Taken from Wheen, *Strange Days*, 61; Morgan, *Britain Since 1945*, 347, 352, simply describes Armstrong's resignation as coming about due to "a nervous breakdown."
53. Ellis, *Raising the Devil*, 210.
54. See Hunt, "Moral Panic and Moral Language in Media," 629–48.
55. Bader, et al., *Paranormal America*, esp. 12–15, 196–97, and 200.
56. Graham, *Angels*, 8–13.
57. Partridge, *Re-Enchantment of the West*. Cf. Laycock, *Vampires Today*, 32, 34, 122.
58. Asma, *Stuffed Animals and Pickled Heads*, 84; Curran and Graille, "The Faces of Eighteenth-Century Monstrosity," 1–15; Poole, *Monsters in America*, 9–12.
59. Taken from the parish website http://www.stmarysluton.org/home.
60. Zizek, "Fantasy as a Political Category," 91.

PART TWO

Zombies

5

The Living Christ and *The Walking Dead*
Karl Barth and the Theological Zombie

Jessica DeCou

PREFACE

Rather than talking about AMC's *The Walking Dead* (*TWD*),[1] the following will attempt to step *into* the world of *TWD* (addressing the series itself in the preface and footnotes), in order to consider the "theological zombie" through a Barthian lens. Unlike the philosophical zombie, who behaves like the rest of us but lacks conscious experience,[2] the theological zombie is the fetid corpse of popular imagination, rising from its grave to consume the living for the sake of the dead. What are the implications of a zombie outbreak for our understanding of fellow-humanity, eschatological hope, and the doctrine of bodily resurrection? And what does our zombie test-subject reveal about our rights and duties in relation to him? Of course, in deference to the incomparable Daryl Dixon (who exclaimed, in response to all the whining and moping, "What, am I the only one who's Zen around here? Good lord!"), I admit that a Zen approach might be more adequate for surviving a zombie apocalypse because of its insights into the nature, cause, and

Part Two: Zombies

cure of suffering. But lacking sufficient training in Buddhist Studies, the following will consider whether a Christian perspective might also be tenable.

Unlike breeds of the undead that can co-exist with humans, zombies are compelled to devour every living creature *and* the horse they rode in on (literally).[3] As depictions of TEOTWAWKI,[4] therefore, zombie stories typically paint an atmosphere of divine absence. For its part, the increasingly bleak *TWD* tends less to declare, "God does not exist" than to present a growing pile of evidence that, "God has abandoned us." In the series pilot, we see the words, "God Forgive Us," scrawled in blood on the wall above an apparent murder-suicide—a chilling plea from those who took lethal measures to avoid a fate worse than death. In the second season opener, Rick and the others follow the peal of church bells in search of a missing child, but the sense of spiritual abandonment is felt more profoundly than ever before, when they come upon a lifeless church with nothing but a convincing recording that continues to operate on a timer even though those it once beckoned have long since evacuated, been killed, or succumbed to the infection. Inside, the group is met by a small congregation of zombies similarly lured by the bell's tolls (as zombies are attracted by light and sound), endowing the scene with an eerie, eschatological atmosphere. After destroying the pew-zombies, Rick addresses a wooden figure of Jesus on the cross, pleading to someone who himself cried out, "My God, My God, why have you forsaken me," and whose body later rose from the grave:

> I don't know if you're looking at me with what—sadness? Scorn? Pity? Love? Maybe it's just indifference. I guess you already know I'm not much of a believer. . . . The thing is we—I could use a little something to help keep us going. Some kind of acknowledgement, some indication I'm doing the right thing. You don't know how hard that is to know. Well, maybe you do. Hey look, I don't need all the answers. Just a little nod, a sign. Any sign will do.[5]

The sign he gets is the accidental shooting and near death of his young son, which he takes as proof that "God's got a strange sense of humor."[6]

Others, such as Hershel Greene, a veterinarian turned country doctor who enjoys scenic landscapes and Bible study, interpret the boy's survival (and Rick's own) as a sign of divine benevolence. The conflict that drives the action of the mid-season finale centers around another fundamental disagreement between Rick's group and Hershel's, this one concerning the nature of the outbreak and its impact on the humanity of the afflicted, their respective positions summed up in the following exchange.

> Dale: We put down a walker.
>
> Hershel: You killed a person.

Hershel stands in the "zombies are people too" camp, seeing them as folks "who haven't been in their right minds; people who I believe can be restored" (another statement with potentially significant theological implications). Rather than destroying them, then, he collects them by the barn full, trapping them with snare poles and hiding them away under lock and key. At first, Rick had also been moved by their seeming humanity,[7] but intervening traumas have desensitized him such that now he and the rest of his group can see them only as man-eating savages. Hershel, so focused on preserving the walking dead and respecting their humanity, threatens to send his living companions back out into the tumult, partly because they are relentlessly quarrelsome and reckless (so, honestly, who could blame him?) and partly out of fear that they will discover his zombie sanctuary inside the barn. While Hershel's motivations are vaguely (though inconsistently) religious, his daughter points out that by favoring the dead over the living he is violating the very commandment he had taught her to live by: "A new commandment I give to you, that you love one another, even as I have loved you."[8]

The following attempts to address these and related issues from a more consistent and systematic theological perspective. As a thought experiment concerning a fictional world, I have chosen to present this analysis in form of a fictional treatise, its "author" caught in the same dark and dangerous universe as *TWD*. Though aware of the generic risks (i.e. of veering over the line into cheesy fan-fiction), I have chosen this form because it allows for a more penetrating exploration of the complexities facing such a world than would cold academic prose. However, a few prefatory remarks are necessary. 1) The footnotes are mine rather than the "author's" and will fill in pieces that our fictional author is missing, offering citations and analyses as needed. 2) In an effort to remain as faithful as possible to this universe, and in accordance with the rule that people in zombie movies are never permitted use of the word "zombie," our fictional author will also avoid the z-word,[9] using terms from *TWD* (walkers, geeks) and a few of her own invention in its stead. 3) Finally,

PART TWO: ZOMBIES

when I first sat down to write this contribution to the volume, I did so under the assumption that the task would be fun, and the product funny. Neither turned out to be true. This world is *bleak*—and, therefore, because our make-believe theologian is caught up in TEOTWAWKI, I ask that you forgive her occasional use of profanity as efforts to avoid them rang false (the following is rated TV-MA LV for strong language and violence, viewer discretion advised).

RAZING NECROPOLIS

A Theological Treatise

BY B. B.

THE DEAD OF WINTER

APPARENTLY, I LUCKED OUT (first time for everything). While most people were bugging out, I stayed right where I was, not as part of some ingenious plan, but because I simply did not have the wherewithal to up and leave—and to my good fortune, if the rumor-mill-of-the-post-apocalypse is to be believed. The latter weeks of winter were brutal, even for Chicago, but in their panic to flee the city during the initial SHTF[10] event, people failed to consider what the consequences of lake-enhanced snowstorms and sub-zero wind chills might be for something with no circulatory system and no common sense.[11] One good cold snap and they just lay there, frozen solid, until the sun eventually thaws them out to resume their gruesome pursuits—and in the meantime you can nip that particular problem in the bud. This is why the term "walker," common parlance in parts south and west of here, is only just now catching on. Around here, I've heard them called geeks, drones, slugs, goons, leeches, and so on. The term "Bob" was popular for a while due to the large number carried off into Lake Michigan—geeks can't die but they also can't swim worth a damn, so we could go out to the

The Living Christ and The Walking Dead

Point and aim our binoculars toward Museum Campus to watch them bob and rot amid unmoored bowriders and trawlers until a riptide hurried them off beyond the horizon or a shoreward current washed them up on the rocks, bloated and frostbitten. I was part of a small group of remainders that went around on the coldest days "defusing" the corpsicles with crossbows (de rigueur for the necropolitan fashionista), pick-axes, crowbars, and some guns we borrowed (looted) from the 1-178th Armory a few block north of here, where we first camped after the military/government/utilities threw up their hands in a collective "fuck this" and ran off to their secret bunkers or wherever. We would then cremate the remains in crowded midday funeral pyres, and while we knew we couldn't take care of all of them, we figured they would make enticing carrion for the strays, wildlife, and escaped zoo animals. Between us and them, we thought we were in pretty good shape. We were wrong. Spring having sprung, it is clear that we (both man and beast) missed more than just a few, who have since become unrepentant loiterers as their mobility is gradually restored, leading to renewed panic and a second wave of suicides. If things are quieting down elsewhere (as we've heard), they're just getting started up here—leaving us to face questions we had previously managed to evade.

And so, I will begin this exploration by copying out a rather long quote from Karl Barth's *Church Dogmatics*.

> Man collectively may take on a terrifying and monstrous appearance. But these critical periods usually pass, and they are followed by periods of relative calm in which civilised life is resumed and these dangerous manifestations are again regarded as exceptional. The inhuman element withdraws for the most part into the wings. We are again ashamed of it. We would rather not mention the names which it has assumed and the events which betray its savagery. The face of society is again dominated by more or less sacred causes and the more or less sacred devotion they inspire. And in the light or half-light which they shed the situation again becomes fairly normal and tolerable. It again appears to be an excited and pessimistic and unjustifiable and disruptive exaggeration to point to certain unsettling but isolated phenomena as a reason for maintaining that this inhuman element is always present; that it is at work even in these various forms of philanthropy; that every man is at bottom inhuman; that according to the well-known and much contested formula of the *Heidelberg Catechism* he is inclined by nature to

Part Two: Zombies

> hate God and his neighbour. Those who say this are themselves open to accusation as troublers of Israel, enemies of the human race, and guilty of a genuine inhumanity. The inhuman nature within us laughs at prophets of this kind, lurking, until the next outbreak, where it best loves to lurk, in the concealment of a good and necessary and solemnly exercised activity. In the same way its outbreaks in the life of the individual are only the relatively few interruptions of its normal existence in the concealment in which its words and acts and attitudes are remembered as though it had never been, its whole activity now taking the very human rather than inhuman form of devotion to a cause. Everything now seems to be intact and in order again, so that the charge that everything is really in disorder, and profoundly inhuman, may easily be dismissed as irrelevant.[12]

Of course, Barth is not speaking of an apocalypse of the undead, but his words are both strangely comforting and deeply disturbing when standing before a geek like this one—*especially* a geek like this one, who likely chased a rat into the dumpster and now finds himself unable to escape. No bloated lake-bobber he, nor disfigured by wounds or made grotesque with rot. He's fresh—he still looks like one of us. Observing him from the relatively safe vantage point of my window above, a slew of theological/ethical questions begin to crystallize. What are our moral obligations toward fellow humans? Toward the non-human? Toward the living, the dead, and the undead? How do we even define "human being" now? More basically, should there even be such a thing as a "theological" question in a world so seemingly bereft of divine presence? Is faith more unreasonable now than it often seemed even before this outbreak?

To be perfectly pointed about it, the real question here is whether we should destroy him and, if so, how bad we should feel about it afterwards.

It's a ridiculous question, I know.

What with all hell breaking loose, it's a safe assumption that if you are still among us (un)lucky living then you have already taken down your fair share of the undead, and so the question seems outdated. But, while the question of destroying them may be a "no brainer" (. . . sorry), I have not had to wrestle with it to the degree that many of you have. Nor have I had to decide what to do with infected/reanimated loved ones[13] (I moved here to get *away* from my family).

Of the group I ran with for a time this winter, some could not even cope with disposing of frozen strangers and chose to "call it quits" early rather than confront these kinds of decisions. Others went the opposite direction, reveling in the morbid task and turning civil collapse to their advantage over the living as well (less so during the initial chaos—*spectacularly* so when all the drugs, liquor, and cigarettes ran out), hoarding resources and leaving us weaklings to either hole up alone or submit to every whim and demand of the stronger.

But unlike lord-of-the-flies out there, Dumpster-Geek is not hurting anyone at the moment, so things get more complicated. Is a preemptive strike justified in its case where it would not be in the case of the living (else I would have license to kill anyone I meet in anticipation of what they *might* do someday)? The geek-pops weren't hurting anyone either, but it is very different to act against something that *is* dead (however temporarily) than something that *seems* alive (even if it is not really alive). The former quickly became a matter of routine—but hasn't it always been sin's clever skill to become so run of the mill that we cease to question and correct our behaviors?

In the following pages, I will reflect on these issues in light of the work of Karl Barth and a handful of others (selected, as you might have guessed, based on the limited materials at hand, most everything else having been consigned to the flames during winter). Much of the other information comes largely from accounts told me by a northbound caravan claiming to have heard them from a small group returning from some fool's errand at the CDC and off to pursue another at Fort Benning. In fact, what sparked my decision to write this little treatise was a story they related about a Georgia farmer who, for ostensibly theological reasons, established some sort of geek conservation program in his barn, preserving them in their reanimated state in anticipation of a future cure. This did not end well (the term I heard was "barnageddon"[14]), and the whole thing would be laugh-out-loud stupid if it weren't so tragic. My guess is that he is not the only one who feels this way, and since my skills as a theologian have not often shown their value in this dystopia, I thought this might be my chance to contribute something constructive that could help others avoid disaster. As third-hand information from the Thunderdome Telegraph, I cannot vouch for its accuracy, but with such information scarce—not knowing, I choose to believe.

Part Two: Zombies

"WHAT IS MAN THAT YOU ARE MINDFUL OF HIM . . . ?"

According to a pre-doomsday novel, the U.N. and World Interfaith Council responded to the urgent necessities of a similar pandemic by defining the human in terms of the capacity for social connectedness and emotional recognition of the humanity of others, special allowances being made for those who lack these attributes due to unrelated medical conditions. Death was understood to occur at the onset of the final stage of infection, at which time traditional funerary rites could go forward with or without a body. The practical objective to which these definitions were aimed was to confirm that the infected are *not human*, have no rights, and can be destroyed with impunity.[15] Though I find this definition problematic (and it is quite a leap from "not human" to "destroy with impunity"!), Karl Barth understood humanity in similar terms of relationality and recognition.

Barth held that the *imago dei* is found not in the immortality of the soul but in "being in encounter" with our fellow human. We are not human in and of ourselves but only in relation to the other, reflecting the trinitarian relations of the divine inner life just as the covenant we have with one another reflects the covenant that God has established with us. As a being-with-others, genuine humanity involves four components: mutual seeing, communication, assistance, and gladness.[16] Mutual seeing simply means looking one another in the eye. This intimate personal connection is lacking in the blind encounters of institutional bureaucracies, but once a personal connection is made the mistreatment or neglect of the other becomes more difficult.[17] Mutual communication is a "two-sided openness" in which each conversation partner is willing to address the other candidly and reveal oneself truthfully and also willing to be addressed by the other—otherwise all we have are two monologues talking past each other. We cannot understand the other's self-declaration unless we are open to learning something we did not know before and to letting our preconceived ideas about him/her be proven false.[18] Mutual assistance consists in the willingness not only to offer assistance but to accept help from others (reciprocity vs. pride and condescension). This is where altruism often stumbles, becoming "supremely inhuman" because it originates from an attitude of superiority in which the giver believes herself a savior and cannot fathom needing help from the object of her charity nor his being equipped to provide it. Finally, these three forms of mutual interaction must take place, on both sides, freely and gladly. In genuine human encounter we cannot seek to dominate or manipulate the other, nor can we allow ourselves to be exploited or subjugated by him.[19] This final element of gladness is both the root and the crown of humanity, without which our encounter with the other cannot be fully human.

In describing humanity as a being-*with*-others, Barth is attempting to distinguish our humanity from the humanity of Jesus (through whom alone we are able to understand our own human nature), for only the latter "can be absolutely exhaustively and exclusively described as a being *for* man." In other words, human being as a being-with-others involves reciprocity—one can be and act "for" the other and the other can be and act "for" her—but in Christ, who is both supremely human and truly divine, there is no such reciprocity. In giving himself over to die on behalf of all humanity, thereby winning for them reconciliation and eternal life, it is only he who can claim to exist wholly "for" fellow humanity.[20]

This brings us to the very topical issue of resurrection. Obviously, the recent outbreak had immediate import for a religious tradition with a "re-animated" founder and an accompanying doctrine of bodily resurrection. As the one whose existence was a being-*for*-others, Christ vanquished death on behalf of all humankind, who will rise from their graves when he returns to judge the living and the dead. With the resurrection of Jesus as the model, the general resurrection of the dead has traditionally been understood as a *bodily* resurrection, and for Barth, the relationality that defines genuine human being extends also to the constitution of each individual as a relation of body and soul together—neither a disembodied soul nor an unbesouled body would be genuinely human. "That he 'lives' his life obviously cannot mean that he takes and gives himself life from somewhere," says Barth, but rather a human being lives because he "has spirit," which is the particular interconnection of body and soul made possible by the ongoing activity of the divine Spirit, "and if God were to withdraw what He alone can and does give in this event, not only would his body sink back to the status of a purely material body, to rise and disintegrate even as a material body in the surrounding world of all other bodies, but he himself would necessarily become a shadow and less than a shadow, a departed soul which once was but now has been, an extinct life."[21] Without our bodies we would not be whole, even in eternity, and therefore the content of God's promise of redemption and our source of hope is not our "immortality" in a Platonic dualistic sense of the immortality of the soul separated from its material body, but

Part Two: Zombies

our future redemption in bodily resurrection from the dead.[22] What has been won for humanity is eternal *life*, defeating death so that we "may live and be happy" now—with the knowledge that we are justified and reconciled—and in the eschatological future—having been raised, judged, and redeemed to live in wholeness (as soul and body) forever in the kingdom of God.

In accord with the justice of the eschatological kingdom, the Christian community is called to preserve genuine humanity by defending the rights, freedom, and dignity of all humankind. They must therefore fight against what Barth calls the "lordless powers" (aka "principalities and powers"), which are defined as intrinsically harmless human abilities and achievements that take on a life of their own. They soon "emancipate themselves from him and become his master,"[23] transmuted into *in*human forces of *dis*order and *un*rest. Submission to these lordless powers results in alienation not only from God but from the fellow-human through a "changing of their being with one another, which corresponds to their being with God, into a general being without and against one another." If humanity is a being-with-others, then these powers endanger the species as a whole: "As the powers tear apart the individual, so—because there are so many of them and in such competition—they tear apart society" (. . . never did I expect to read this quote so literally!).

It is the responsibility of the Christian community, Barth declares, to revolt against the disorder wrought by the lordless powers as the community "responsible for . . . the preservation and renewal, the deepening and extending, of the divinely ordained human safeguards of human rights, human freedom, and human peace on earth." This work, though weak and decidedly unequal to the task, takes on a "kingdom-likeness" as a reflection, however dim, of the coming kingdom for which they pray.[24] For Barth, this "revolt against disorder" is *never* a revolt against fellow humans, but always in solidarity with them against the unjust tyranny of the lordless powers.[25]

But what does this revolt against disorder demand from us now, post-WAHBL[26] when we find ourselves battling against what were once fellow human beings but seem no longer to be so?

OF MICE AND MEN AND GEEKS

As the caravanners recounted it, having heard it from those who, in turn, claimed to have heard it directly from a mad but reliable CDC scientist, the infection attacks the brain, promptly causing brain death followed soon thereafter by total clinical death. After a variable interval, the still living virus/bacteria (the epidemiology remains unknown) re-activates the brain stem only, allowing movement without the consciousness or experience or memory that would require significant activity in the cerebrum (hence the need to destroy the brain stem in order to de-animate the corpse).[27] Whatever this undeath is, it is not life, whether we choose to define that term biologically or religiously. What the drones have been granted therefore cannot be the fulfillment of the promise of eternal life. The current contagion is a macabre inversion of the "good news" of redemption—and its issue a perversion of genuine humanity as described above.

In his sluggish but relentless pursuit of living flesh, Dumpster-Geek's inhumanity is undeniable, and, though driven by instinct like any number of other species, his corruption is so complete that his being does not even approach that of an animal. I think about this last point quite often. After the shit's initial hitting of the fan, when some peace was to be found in the dead of winter, the local strays began to emerge from wherever they had hid themselves. Surrounded by so much death, it was startling to encounter life—here in the little form of a cat that I guessed was called Phil. In the weeks since, I often consider the walkers in relation to him, whose eyes disclose such alert engagement and calculating intelligence. Phil has adapted well to this new environment and has learned somewhere along the way to keep quiet lest he attract the walkers (unlike a certain other, now-expired, pet I once knew, who failed this lesson spectacularly). When unsure, he misguidedly looks to me for counsel, meeting my eyes with a piercing scrutiny intended to discern the mental processes behind them, which I typically answer with an indecisive shrug (having hoped to follow his lead on the theory that his is a more refined survival instinct). Phil certainly communicates clearly (even if he is kind of a jerk about it sometimes), and he also offers assistance—bringing me frequent "gifts" of twitching, half-dead birds and bugs to eat—and happily accepts my offerings as well. Moreover, all signs point to his doing these things freely and gladly.

Part Two: Zombies

Now, I should note that Barth would be opposed to ascribing these attributes to non-human animals,[28] and obviously Phil does not quite make up for the lack of human companionship. So, when I first discovered Dumpster-Geek loitering below my window, and recognizing that he posed no immediate danger (though his clattering around threatens to attract every geek in the greater-necropolitan area), I sat on the sill trying to imagine who he might have been in life—whether he voted and for whom, whether he had hobbies, and so on. I felt most sorry for him when it occurred to me that he might have been vegan, or kosher, or a pacifist, or a musical virtuoso, and this brought to mind the indignity of neurodegenerative disorders like Alzheimer's that lead people to do or say things that would have humiliated them before (I've witnessed the anguish in those condemned to a future robbed of freedom and self-control, of memories and self-identity—and obviously we don't kill them, just put them out to pasture). I even considered naming him, in an effort to restore something of his former identity. His appearance still so "lifelike," I wanted to think of him as a companion of sorts. But his uncoordinated slapstick, self-serving brutishness, and inarticulate moaning ultimately made this impossible, and Phil's judicious grumbling upon perceiving the threat below quickly snapped me back to reality.

Dumpster-Geek would be a rotten companion (. . . sorry again). He cannot make eye contact, for he does not recognize the countenance of the other. He cannot engage in mutual communication, for even if he could speak, he could not empathize and therefore would not be driven to offer assistance. Indeed, he cannot even match the empathic abilities of the rodent that likely got him trapped in that dumpster in the first place, for even the lowly lab rat has exhibited a surprising capacity to recognize and end the suffering of his fellow-rat.[29] However many fellow-geeks DG attracts with his clumsy rattling, none of them will pause to reflect on his predicament or give him a hand (in either applicable sense). Moreover, his motivations for interacting with me would be morally questionable to say the least. Mindlessly driven by some aberrant instinct, he can use our encounter only for his own grotesque gain. Incapable of fellowship, he experiences no gladness (though they sometimes roam in packs—some disturbing shadow of their humanity, perhaps?). He cannot recognize life except to consume it—and he is never satiated.

In DG's defense, however, I would cite all the people I knew who fit this description perfectly even before SHTF—not to mention those I have met since. But, while no one ever accused me of being a "people person," I also never went around killing them (even though, in certain specific cases, I could have made a very convincing argument for the social benefits of doing so).

And yet, in his cadaverous features, this malingerer resembles something near akin and awakens a nostalgia for what has been lost. How can destroying him possibly be understood as a reflection, however dim, of the divine order of redemption?

THE EXCEPTIONAL CASE

Of course, many would ask what sense it makes to speak of "killing" what is already dead (recall your many failed attempts in that first terrifying week to stop them with bullets to the heart or blades to the throat), preferring terms like put down, neutralize, or defuse. Even before the current pandemic, scientists in Canada published a study (widely circulated just after our outbreak) that mapped out four mathematical models of the spread of a similar infection and warned that such an outbreak "is likely to be disastrous, unless extremely aggressive tactics are employed against the undead." By disastrous, they meant "the collapse of civilisation, with every human infected, or dead" and therefore the complete extinction of the human species. The fierceness of the infection (which spreads itself with an aggression and efficiency akin to rabies) means that "only sufficiently frequent attacks [against the infected], with increasing force, will result in eradication [of the infection], assuming the available resources can be mustered in time."[30] In theology, there is nothing of *direct* relevance to be found, save for one account from the twelfth century that details a small but similar outbreak in rural England. William of Newburgh, historian and Augustinian canon, admitted that he would not believe it possible for corpses to "sally forth from the grave" if he had not heard several such detailed testimonies recounted by such reliable sources. Alarmed by these events, and recognizing the threat such an outbreak posed, he chose to include some representative accounts in his historical chronicle as a warning to future generations. For example, one account tells of a Berwick man who "sallied forth" from his grave and incited such terror among villagers that they took to sequestering themselves indoors after dark. Though he seems to have caused no real trouble, the town elders determined that a rotting corpse traipsing about town would likely spread disease, so they drafted some strong young men

Part Two: Zombies

to cut him to bits and set him ablaze. We are also told of a local man who schemed to catch his cheating wife by faking a trip out of town, but who proceeded to injure himself in his clumsy effort to ambush the two lovers. During his convalescence, infection set in. So consumed with jealousy as he lay dying, he chose to put off his last confession until the next morning but died overnight (of course). Though he was nonetheless given a Christian burial, he soon rose from his grave, pestilence following in his path. When people had finally had it up to here with the risen dead giving their loved ones plague (which took longer than you would think), they exhumed his grave (finding a swollen, blood-drenched carcass whose burial cloths had been torn to shreds), tore out his heart, and burned the remains, after which time the plague finally ceased.[31]

On the other hand, some now preach against destroying the undead in devotion to the sixth commandment or to hope for some future cure. The rural man mentioned above saw "killing walkers" (the latter term he rejected in defense of their humanity, the former term he would endorse for the same reason and due to his apparent misunderstanding of the nature of the infection) as a transgression of the prohibition against murder and a violation of the command to love and care for one another whether in sickness or in health.[32] But in defending the humanity of the undead, he threatened the safety of the living. According to the necropolitan-grapevine, this man and his group trapped stray geeks with snare poles, herded them into a barn, and then went so far as to "feed" them live animals even though the dead require no such sustenance, thereby depriving the community of life-sustaining resources and inflicting needless suffering on the animals that were maimed before being eaten alive (the drones being too uncoordinated and dim-witted to catch a fully mobile chicken was, I guess, the thinking on that score). Predictably, the discovery of his secret geek stash caused considerable unrest among his guests. Against the man's pleas for mercy (the barn providing sanctuary for his own wife and other family and friends), the others threw open the doors and "executed" the walkers one by one right in front of him.

Now, to formulate a response to this tragic series of events, we could first point to Barth's warning that the danger of humanitarian "causes" lies in their tendency to overshadow actual human beings (just consider all the atrocities committed in the name of this or that "cause"). This is true even in relation to fulfilling the divine command, which "must have the freedom to move within limits" and, therefore, "if we are genuinely ready to obey the command of God, we cannot go so far either to the right or to the left as to maintain such absolute ethical tenets and modes of action in loyalty to Him." Barth is therefore willing to make allowances for the "exceptional case" in which killing (in war, self-defense, tyrannicide, suicide, abortion, euthanasia, hunting food, etc.) is justified. But he also reminds us frequently of the limits of human understanding, such that we cannot know with any certainty whether we are faced, at any particular moment, with such an exceptional case. One must therefore proceed with humility, recognizing "that he may be mistaken, that he may not really have the command of God on his side at all, and that he thus runs the risk of being a rebel."[33] Still, each individual must also follow his/her conscience and, once so convinced, is compelled to act according to these convictions whether driven to contentious objection or mobilization.

When confronted with the exceptional case, this rare instance of justified carnage must be understood as having an "eschatological character. It can be accomplished with a good conscience only as we glance backward to creation and forward to the consummation as the boundaries of the sphere in which alone there can be any question of its necessity."[34] Barth made this statement in reference to the killing of animals for the purpose of prolonging human life, whereas now we kill to avoid getting eaten by the dead. These are not similar, even if similar observations or conclusions apply; nor are we talking about euthanasia or acts of war.[35] Indeed, one reason that Barth has such an aversion to prescribing specific programs of action for Christian response to the command of God is that each situation is unique and must be judged on its own facts.

Unique indeed. Today, determining just what our facts really are is a formidable task unto itself, but we have hopefully made some progress in this regard over the course of these few pages. If genuine humanity consists in recognition of the rights and dignity of the fellow-human, in the openness to mutual understanding and assistance, and in encountering the other gladly, then the afflicted are clearly no longer human. If life is defined as the existence of the individual in the ordered relation of body and soul made possible by the continuous work of the divine without which our bodies would "sink back to the status of a purely material body, to rise and disintegrate," then we are clearly not "killing" in any sense we might have understood that term before. If resurrection is eternal life (continuous in memory and experience with our temporal lives), in which we "may live and be happy" in the order of love and justice that characterize the divine kingdom, then we cannot be witnessing anything but a "lordless" distortion of this promise. (And I should here make explicit my working assumption that in its temporary state of re-animation the geek is an "unbesouled body," but this should be approached as yet another "exceptional case" in which I am obliged to humbly acknowledge the possibility that I am grievously mistaken.[36])

TO HELL AND BACK AGAIN

In light of all the above considerations, I arrive at the very predictable conclusion that destroying the walking dead is not only permitted but commanded. Any other conclusion would be preposterous—you didn't need me to tell you that. Our solemn obligation to the living requires us to commend the dead to Christ, trusting in the promise of reconciliation and redemption. The more sensitive could perhaps be counseled, though only with extraordinary caution, to see it as a form of assistance to those who were once human and who will be again in the eschaton, affirming that "this cry for help always reaches me," and that I hear and understand. With caution, I say, because this could easily be misappropriated to justify euthanizing the living—a question I wouldn't want to touch with a ten foot snare pole—and on down the slippery slope of no-appreciation-for-context. Moreover, this conclusion does not sanction cruelty against those who remain conscientious objectors, lest we forget the nature of "the exceptional case" and forfeit our honest intentions.

But if this grim burden can be understood as an eschatological act that requires us to "glance backward to creation and forward to the consummation as the boundaries of the sphere in which alone there can be any question of its necessity," then rather than losing faith, we should let this tragedy revive our hope in the promise of final future redemption through the resurrection and cleansing of all creation. And, though the future seems remote and inaccessible, Barth counseled that "the future as such is not absent, and therefore we cannot say that what it brings, our own future reality, is absent."[37]

For many, however, the sense of divine abandonment has been so profound that they have lost this hope and turned to suicide, choosing this over a life of grief, a gruesome death, and an undeath that would condemn them to stagger the earth perpetrating these crimes on others. Some have come to see suicide as freedom—a way of seizing life by seizing death—and even Barth acknowledges suicide as another "exceptional case" that must not be judged too harshly, for "who can say that it is absolutely impossible for the gracious God Himself to help a man in affliction by telling him to take this way out? . . . Have we not to take into account the possibility that suicide might not be committed as a crime and therefore as murder, but in faith and therefore in peace with God?"[38] In the interest of full disclosure, I will confide that, of late, I have often been overcome by this darkness and have routinely lulled myself to sleep with the perversely soothing fantasy of eating a bullet to avoid a fate worse than death (and what a vast selection of such fates we now have to choose from). I haven't just *felt* this darkness, I've *wallowed* in it, savored it. (Helpful tip: don't read Ecclesiastes.) My pleas for respite have often taken the form of a plea for death. I have looked with disgust upon my continuing impulse to believe and have questioned my sanity for this and any number of other reasons.

I will further confess that, having witnessed what people are so easily capable of in the name of "survival of the fittest," I have grown to detest the very being-with-others that I endorsed above as the defining characteristic of genuine human being. People have become clannish, impetuous, and paranoid in response to social collapse and the want of bare essentials, prone to melodramatic outbursts of self-justifying bullshit to rival Scarlett O'Hara herself. Earlier, during the dark winter when we roamed the streets defusing and disposing of frozen bodies like some ghoulish road kill removal crew, most had been content to dull themselves to the morbid tasks and frigid winds with generous servings of alcohol. Chicago's wells were deep—very deep—but not bottomless. Once bereft of these mollifying spirits, people had to cotton to their bleak new reality and hew to its severe demands. From this lethal combination of calamity and sobriety came confirmation that "the sons of men are full of evil, and madness is in their heart while they live, and after that they go to the dead" (Eccl 9:3). Pushed beyond their extremity, whatever simmered underneath now surfaced, whether violence, bitterness, despair, narcissism, greed—or in my case a misanthropic predisposition. (My internal soliloquies and tirades now sound like something from the mouth of the "Ancient Booer" of Florin.) I have isolated myself at the expense of my own humanity as we have defined that term here, favoring the company of Phil and even of Dumpster-Geek as one who, at the very least, lacks our unbridled hypocrisy while exceeding our brutality and our stupidity only by a shade.

But I have also been struck by moments of seemingly groundless hope and this (along with an equal portion of cowardice) has kept me

Part Two: Zombies

from turning against myself. One time, after bitter winds suspended our geek-defusing detail for that day, we had to bivouac at the Checkerboard Lounge. The walls were still plastered with posters and photos of jazz greats and local legends, and while looting liquor and other supplies by lantern light, some were inspired to sing—one guy even took to the stage to offer his rendition of "St. James Infirmary." We didn't have to be so quiet then as we do now, and so we soon had an honest-to-goodness party on our hands. There was a lot of mumbling through unknown lyrics (though one talented bloke managed to recite "The Cremation of Sam McGee" in its entirety—*outstanding*), and these were probably the worst performances the Checkerboard (and the world) had ever heard. But it reminded us of the creativity and beauty human civilization can foster at its heights and also of human tenacity in the face of overwhelming adversity.

Though I am not one of those lucky others in whom this crisis has aroused some natural inclination toward fellowship and hope, these moments serve as a reminder that Christian hope is never to be "bound to either the lighter or the darker side," but "is free in face of both possibilities," and will expect indications of the dynamic movement of time toward its ultimate end, "even in relation to aspects which are absolutely black and desperate from the human standpoint."[39] These "intimations of the ultimate in the penultimate" serve as a necessary buttress for sustaining Christian hope, without which our hope devolves into either hopelessness in the face of suffering, or an exclusively other-worldly hope that turns a blind eye to suffering. Genuine hope is always active, and therefore the one who possesses it "will not sit down waiting for something to come and snatch him away, but will manfully go forward hoping for the concrete help needed."[40] Of course, many have suggested that this outbreak is a meting out of divine wrath and that to act against it would be disobedience to the divine will (but how often has that excuse been put to nefarious purpose?), but while we cannot know for sure that it is not a divine reckoning, we must proceed as if not, lest we become callous to the suffering of others and transgress our calling to safeguard freedom, dignity, and peace as we "wait to be snatched away." True Christian hope can never be passive or self-serving or private, but must always act on behalf of the entire world, including those who have succumbed to this "lordless" contagion, recognizing them always as among those who "will also be set free from the bondage of decay into the glorious freedom of

God's children. For we know that the whole creation groans and suffers together until now" (Rom 8:21-22).

Our present sufferings must be seen, as Paul exhorts us, in the light of the eschatological future. We must keep our eyes open for "feeble lights" to sustain our hope and guide our way—and they are out there, even still. Indeed, for Barth, the human conscience (with which we have so struggled recently) is one manifestation of this future in the present—somehow aware of our future perfection, we judge our thoughts and actions according to a future measure that is otherwise unfitting for us as justified sinners.[41] Therefore, the "absolutely black and desperate" burden that we ourselves must now carry need not eat away at our conscience, but can remind us that our hesitations and doubts about the rightness of acts that are clearly right and necessary according to the standards of this imperfect and unjust realm is itself an intimation of the ultimate, pointing beyond the present to the perfection and righteousness of our future selves in the realm of redemption. The revolt against the disorder wrought by the lordless powers, waged *in solidarity with all who have ever lived and died*, is intended to be a dim reflection of this future realm.

Some glad morning we will all rise together.
But now it is time to let the dead rest in peace.

END NOTES

1. Please note that the following concerns only the television series and not the comic book of the same name that is the series' source material. Also, the second season of the series aired in two halves (the first ending in November 2011 and the second premiering in February 2012) and, because the deadline fell in between the two, this essay assumes only that which was revealed from episode 1.1 to episode 2.6. (In other words, readers need not fear spoilers from the comic book or the later episodes).
2. See, for example, Chalmers, *The Conscious Mind*; Kirk, "Zombies v. Materialists," 135–52; Kirk, *Zombies and Consciousness*; Block, "Are Absent Qualia Impossible?," 257–74; Flanagan and Polger, "Zombies and the Function of Consciousness," 313–21.
3. "Days Gone Bye," *The Walking Dead* (*TWD*) 1.1, first broadcast 31 October 2010 by AMC, written and directed by F. Darabont.
4. TEOTWAWKI = The End of the World As We Know It.
5. "What Lies Ahead," *TWD* 2.1, first broadcast 16 October 2011 by AMC, written by F. Darabont and R. Kirkman, directed by G. Horder-Payton.

Part Two: Zombies

6. "Cherokee Rose," *TWD* 2.4, first broadcast 6 November 2011 by AMC, written by E. Reilly, directed by B. Gierhart.
7. As when he knelt before a bisected zombie to say, "I'm sorry this happened to you," before putting her/it down. "Days Gone Bye," *TWD* 1.1.
8. John 13:34. See "Pretty Much Dead Already," *TWD* 2.7, first broadcast 27 November 2011 by AMC, written by S. Gimple, directed by M. MacLaren. Though Hershel wants to respect the zombies' humanity and protect them from harm, he also argues that the outbreak is "nature's way of correcting herself" and thinning out the population; these strike me as inconsistent, especially when his belief in the benevolence of the biblical God is added to the mix.
9. The "z-word" trope gets its name from the following exchange in the zombie comedy *Shaun of the Dead*: Ed: "Any zombies out there?" Shaun: "Don't say that!" Ed: "What?" Shaun: "That! " Ed: "What?!" Shaun: "That! The Zed word! Don't say it!" Ed: "Why not?!" Shaun: "Because it's ridiculous!" Ed: "Alright! Are there any out there though?" S. Pegg and E. Wright, *Shaun of the Dead*, directed by E. Wright, Universal Pictures, 2004.
10. SHTF = Shit Hits the Fan.
11. Though this has not been discussed in *TWD* (since it takes place in the south), see Brooks (whose conception of zombies is very similar to Kirkman's), *The Zombie Survival Guide*.
12. Barth, *Church Dogmatics* (*CD*) IV/2, 441.
13. For *TWD*'s debates on this issue see e.g., "Days Gone Bye," *TWD* 1.1; "Wildfire," *TWD* 1.5, first broadcast on 28 November 2010 by AMC, directed by G. Mazzara, written by E. Dickerson; "Pretty Much Dead Already," *TWD* 2.7.
14. Though I wish I could claim it as my own, this term came from: "Noam Sane" (*pseud.*), comment on Handlen, "Pretty Much Dead Already," *A.V. Club* (blog).
15. Schlozman, *The Zombie Autopsies*, 168f. Those "infected with Stage IV ANSD are NOT HUMAN. . . . The promotion and protection of the rights of persons does not apply to them," and therefore, "all citizens may with impunity destroy Stage IV humanoids." ANSD stands for Ataxic Neurodegenerative Satiety Deficiency Syndrome (a prion infection similar to Mad Cow disease and also related to non-infectious neurodegenerative conditions such as Parkinson's and Alzheimer's), which Schlozman coined in his fictional epidemiology of zombism. See ibid., 147–61.
16. See Barth, *CD* III/2, 250–65.
17. Barth, *CD* III/2, 252.
18. Barth, "Rudolph Bultmann," 126. In Barth's words, "it is impossible to understand any other person unless we are ready to let him tell us something we did not know before, something we could not find in ourselves, something we have hitherto been prejudiced against, perhaps with much justification. We shall never understand him if we are sure we know beforehand the limits of

our understanding. We shall never understand him if we lay down these limits before we have given him a chance to speak for himself."
19. Barth, *CD* III/2, 269f.
20. Barth, *CD* III/2, 214f. "What is accomplished by Him is the destruction of human sin and the death which is its consequence. And it is done effectively and positively. In His resurrection He reveals Himself as the One He is—the genuine, true and righteous man, the real man, who kept the covenant which all others broke. He kept it in His self-offering, in His death for their sin . . . He has only one goal: to maintain the cause of these men in death and the conquest of death; to offer up His life for them that they may live and be happy. He therefore serves them, without prospect of reward or repayment, without expecting to receive anything from them which He cannot have far better and more richly without them."
21. Barth, *CD* III/2, 353.
22. Barth, *CD* III/2, 379.
23. Barth discusses the "lordless powers," in *The Christian Life*, 213–33. Examples of "lordless powers" include political absolutism, Mammon (resources), ideologies/propaganda, etc.
24. Barth discusses the "revolt against disorder," in *The Christian Life*, 233–71.
25. See Demson, "The Advantages and Limits of Irregular and Regular Dogmatics, 95.
26. WAHBL = When All Hell Breaks/Broke Loose.
27. See "TS-19," *TWD* 1.6 first broadcast 5 December 2010 by AMC, written by A. Fierro and F. Darabont, directed by G. Ferland.
28. See Barth, *CD* III/4, 348ff.
29. Bartal et al, "Empathy and Pro-Social Behavior in Rats," 1427–30.
30. Munz et. al., "When Zombies Attack!," 146.
31. These accounts are found in William of Newburgh, *Historia Rerum Anglicarum*, 657–61. The original Latin text is found in *Historia Rerum Anglicarum*, 185–90.
32. Hershel Greene makes this point in "Secrets," *TWD* 2.6, first broadcast 20 November 2011 by AMC, written by A. Kang, directed by D. Boyd, countering the argument for killing zombies because they are dangerous by pointing out that we do not kill schizophrenics even though they may pose an immediate danger to themselves and others.
33. Barth, *CD* III/4, 422, 468f.
34. Barth, *CD* III/4, 355.
35. Caveat: this essay is not *in any way* a veiled tract on hot button issues like euthanasia, suicide, etc., and should simply be taken at face value. The conclusions reached herein are unique to these very fictional circumstances, and it would be *wholly inappropriate* to transfer them out of that world and into ours.

Part Two: Zombies

36. Barth includes a similar caveat regarding the possibility of non-human animals possessing souls. See *CD* III/2, 394ff. and *CD* III/4, 348.
37. Barth, *Ethics*, 465.
38. Barth, *CD* III/4, 404 and 410.
39. Barth, *CD* IV/3, 938f.
40. Barth, *Ethics*, 485f.

6

Zombie Walks, Zombie Jesus, and the Eschatology of Postmodern Flesh

JOHN W. MOREHEAD

"I can't profess to understand God's plan, but when Christ promised a resurrection of the dead, I just thought he had something a little different in mind."

—HERSHEL IN *THE WALKING DEAD*

INTRODUCTION

CULTURES NEED STORIES so that human beings can make sense of the purpose of, and their place in, the cosmos. In the West these are stories of both beginnings and endings—of how things came to be, and how they will ultimately end. The late modern (or postmodern) West is no exception, and given the existential angst that continues to linger in the second decade of the twenty-first century, stories of "the End" are especially prevalent. In our time, examples of these stories of the end of civilization are not only found in sacred written texts such as the Bible of the Judeo-Christian tradition, they are also found in a variety of pop-culture manifestations. One example of this is the Zombie Walk. On the surface these gatherings of those dressed as the living

PART TWO: ZOMBIES

dead may look like little more than fun and identification with the pop-culture monstrous icon of the moment, and many times this is the case. But by probing the Zombie Walk phenomenon more deeply it can be understood as a piece of eschatological theater shaped by the postmodern apocalyptic imagination. As a result it involves significant theological implications. Reflection on the deeper meaning found in some expressions of the Zombie Walk can relay important considerations for theologians interacting with popular culture. In the essay that follows I will explore various aspects, including the phenomenon as a form of postmodern apocalyptic that puts an imaginative twist on the Judeo-Christian apocalypse; attitudes toward death; the body and new concepts of the self; and how this relates to resurrection and a broader Christian eschatology of hope in the face of postmodern nihilism.

ZOMBIE WALKS AND ZOMBIE JESUS

In November 2011 thousands of people gathered in Mexico City to participate in a ghoulish event. The group included men and women, as well as children, who dressed in torn, dirty, and bloody clothing, and wore makeup designed to make them look like rotting corpses. In a country ravaged by violence and murder over the drug trade, Mexico would seem a least likely place for people to want to dress up in ways that identify with death, decay, and the potential for cannibalistic violence. But came they did, and were very vocal about their desire to gather for fun in order to try to set a world record for the most people participating in a Zombie Walk. Nearly 10,000 people were part of this gathering,[1] one of many which pit various cities around the world against one another as they vie for the record for largest Zombie Walk.

The first documented Zombie Walk took place in Sacramento, California in August of 2001.[2] They now take place in many communities as a global phenomenon. Zombie Walks represent a mixture of other performative expressions, including costume play ("cosplay"), and flash mobs. Cosplay is a form of performance art where individuals dress up as their favorite characters and go to public events. This is popular in Japan with participants dressing up as representations of their favorite manga and anime characters, but it is also a phenomenon that is extremely popular in connection with comic book conventions such as Comic-Con as well as science fiction conventions in the United States. Flash mobs involve groups of people who come together in a public place in order to engage in some kind of performance activity on behalf of the surrounding crowds who are taken by surprise by the appearance of the performing group. Elements of cosplay and flash mobs come together as part of participatory culture,[3] with zombie fans organizing events wherein hundreds, many times thousands of people, come together at a prearranged time dressed as zombies in order to shamble about as walking corpses amusing, bewildering, and frightening observers.

At times a religious figure rises from the masses at Zombie Walks, the Zombie Jesus. The Philly Zombie Crawl[4] includes an annual event at Easter and Zombie Jesus is an important part of this gathering. He has also made appearances at a Zombie Crawl in Denver.[5] Zombie Jesus has become a widespread pop-culture phenomenon, as any Google search will confirm, surfacing on t-shirts, mugs, bumper stickers, numerous images found on the Internet, dedicated websites, an *Uncyclopedia* entry,[6] a series of fan-produced comedy-horror films on YouTube and other video venues;[7] is featured in the film *Dead Meat Walking: A Zombie Walk Documentary*,[8] and is even associated with a satirical Church of the Resurrection.[9]

Tracing the origins of Zombie Jesus is difficult, but it seems that the figure arose out of the atheist community online as a form of parody of the Christian message related to Christ and his resurrection. Although the idea is offensive to many conservative Christians,[10] it is understandable how one could read the resurrection of Jesus in zombie-like fashion. The Zombie Jesus Day website argues, "Everything that rises from the dead is a zombie. Easter is touted as the death and resurrection of Jesus Christ. So let's call a spade a spade, eat lots of chocolate, and celebrate Zombie Jesus Day."[11] In addition, the Jesus Was a Zombie! website[12] connects New Testament texts to the concept, arguing that Jesus came back from the dead in keeping with Acts 2:24, and that he "encourages zombie like behavior," referencing John 6:53: "Jesus said to them, 'I tell you the truth, unless you eat the flesh of the Son of Man and drink his blood, you have no life in you.'"

The presence of a satirical religious figure at some of the Zombie Walks provides hints that these events can at times reveal more than an expression of fun or performance art.[13] Scholars and film critics have long noted that zombie films provide commentary on contemporary social life, and their related pop-cultural spinoffs, including Zombie Walks, should be no exception.[14] Some of the commentary comes in the form of

Part Two: Zombies

political critique as evident in certain Occupy Movement protests where several participants dressed up as zombies.[15] But the presence of Zombie Jesus at various gatherings indicates that at times satirical religious commentary related to "the End" is also present. When the Zombie Walk and Zombie Jesus come together it represents a form of postmodern apocalyptic reimagining.

POSTMODERN APOCALYPTIC IMAGINATION AND THE "END-TIMES"

America has a long history of would-be prophets setting dates for the end of the world. Harold Camping of Family Radio, in one recent example, made repeated predictions about the end of the world and the Second Coming of Christ beginning in 1994, but almost two decades later fine-tuned his calculations, and as a result two different sets of dates were presented for May and later October of 2011. The apocalypse did not come on these dates either, and after apologizing, Camping resigned from his ministry. As of the time of this writing yet another would-be apocalyptic scenario is on the horizon as one of the Mayan cyclical calendar systems is set to end in December 2012. A diverse group of individuals across the globe are united in their doomsday panic concerning this event, from New Spirituality adherents to survivalists to entrepreneurs cashing in on items for purchase related to the coming day of doom, whether weapons, food, survival gear, or shelter.

But it is not only people with religious orientations who speak of apocalypse. It is not uncommon to hear commentators refer to any number of events as potential doomsday happenings and label them as apocalyptic, whether global warming, an asteroid strike, the threat of nuclear war, or the potential for worldwide economic collapse. A major secular apocalyptic threat (overlapping with various religious communities) presented itself as the year 2000 approached and with it a great deal of controversy arose, with concerns over the alleged Y2K computer problem. Proponents of this doomsday scenario argued that when the world's computers switched from 1999 to 2000 great problems would arise that would lead to the collapse of international banking computer systems, the failure of power grids, and even aircraft falling from the sky. The world's calendars saw January 1, 2000 arrive without a major Y2K incident, but this was hardly the only apocalyptic panic to grip the public consciousness.

Apocalyptic imagery is often at the forefront of the Western imagination, particularly in the United States. Daniel Wojcik has traced the pervasive influence of apocalypticism in American thinking, stating that the

> ideas and images about the end of the world permeate American popular culture and folklore, as well as popular religion, and are expressed in films, literature, music, poetry, visual arts, dance, theatre, cartoons, comics, humour, and commercial products . . . Today, millions of Americans embrace beliefs about the imminence of societal catastrophe. Apocalyptic thinking is an enormously influential and pervasive means of conceptualizing the world and one's place in it.[16]

Given its long history in American religious life, and the large number of Americans who continue to self-identify as Christian, Christianity is one of the strongest influences shaping the American apocalyptic consciousness. As Christopher Partridge states in his discussion of eschatological re-enchantment in the West, "Christian thought and influence are, in various ways, continuing to inform contemporary Western religion and culture."[17] In his view, Christian eschatology "is informing popular culture and contemporary political and religious thought."[18]

The term apocalypse comes from the Greek word *apokalypsis*, which means an "unveiling" or "revelation," which in the Judeo-Christian tradition refers to things known to God which are revealed as a means of providing comfort and hope of ultimate divine deliverance to a persecuted people. In the Christian tradition, the biblical book of Revelation is most commonly associated with apocalyptic. Although a variety of interpretations have been offered as to how to properly understand this text, in much of Protestant fundamentalism and evangelicalism, as well as rank and file popular culture, the book is read as a prediction of events in the "End Times," the final chapter of disobedient human beings brought about by divine judgment through a series of catastrophes. So while the New Testament apocalyptic material speaks more to the unveiling of divine mysteries (which can include predictions of judgment), it has increasingly been understood as referring to doomsday, and this concept has permeated popular culture to the extent that any number of potential disasters are referred to as apocalyptic.

Part Two: Zombies

As America shifted from the modern to the postmodern, the concept of apocalypse has changed with it. Although the Judeo-Christian apocalyptic continues to be extremely influential, postmodernity puts interesting twists on the concept. Elizabeth Rosen writes that "postmodernists have remained interested in the apocalyptic myth, even as they reject the myth's absolutism or challenge the received systems of morality that underlie it."[19] One of the aspects of the Judeo-Christian apocalyptic rejected by postmoderns is the idea of divine rescue and the resting place in a New Jerusalem for the redeemed. The postmodern apocalyptic is more pessimistic concerning human nature and its chances for surviving the apocalypse. In this scenario, writes Rosen, "[t]he neo-apocalyptic variant assumes that all mankind is beyond renovation, that this degeneracy is so complete that the Ending can only be so, too. There is nothing beyond this Ending, no hope of a New Heaven on Earth, precisely because there is nothing worth saving."[20]

It is in this apocalyptic context that the Zombie Walks can be understood. Zombie films have long depicted the rise of the living dead in end-of-the-world terms, and it is common to hear reference made to "the zombie apocalypse."[21] The father of the contemporary zombie film, George Romero, is one of the strongest influences in this area, having established a strong sense of pessimism[22] and nihilism in his zombie narratives, beginning with *Night of the Living Dead*, although a certain level of optimism is found in his later work, such as *Land of the Dead*, where it is intimated that zombies and humans might be able to co-exist in some fashion (a feature echoed in zombie comedy-horror films like *Shaun of the Dead* and *Fido*). Despite a few instances of more positive zombie films, the majority of them, as well as television programs like *The Walking Dead*, are still largely negative in their depictions of the chances for survival for the human race following a zombie rising, understood in apocalyptic terms. The dominant pessimism in zombie apocalyptic concerning humanity fits well within the "neo-apocalyptic variant" of postmodernity where human beings are beyond saving. The best one can hope for is a "resurrection" from the dead, but one without any divine saving agent, and where no New Jerusalem on a New Heaven and Earth is available, even with the presence of Zombie Jesus. So while the Zombie Walks with Zombie Jesus may be interpreted as reflecting Christian eschatology, it does so in a postmodern fashion where the Judeo-Christian narrative is challenged and combined with the zombie narrative reflecting the pessimism of many of the depictions of the zombie apocalyptic in horror.

In addition to the light shed on Zombie Walks with consideration of the postmodern apocalyptic imagination, Western attitudes toward death and the body are also present, shaped by the history of horror as entertainment, and film in particular, with zombie films making their own unique contribution.

DEATH, HORROR, THE BODY, AND THE SELF

Over the years, many scholars and writers have attempted to explain the appeal of horror. Each has presented their own theories through differing analytical frameworks, and perhaps quite understandably, one of the common explanatory elements for the appeal of horror is the depiction of death. In *The Thrill of Fear: 250 Years of Scary Entertainment*, Walter Kendrick picks up on this idea and explores it as part of his overall thesis in grappling with the appeal of horror as entertainment which he feels is an expression of the "[m]odern fear of deadness."[23]

Kendrick argues that there has been a shift in the way in which death is dealt with in the Western world, going back to the mid-eighteenth century, which saw the beginnings of a repression of death. His historical analysis begins with a group that came to be labeled the "Graveyard School" of poets.[24] These writers, many of them clergymen, came largely from England and their influence spread across Europe as well as to the United States. They would influence the later Gothic and Romantic writers, and the most notable feature of their work was to connect horrific writing about death with Christian spirituality. Although these writers invoked the literary descriptions of the grotesque in connection with death, they pointed beyond it to the promise of an afterlife for the faithful.

That many of the Graveyard School were clergyman, and yet wrote about death and horror in ways that read much like Edgar Allen Poe, should not be surprising, given the historical context in which they wrote. During this period, the reality of death was not far from common experience, and this included the church. Churches were often situated in the middle of cemeteries that included the remains of those that had attended the various congregations.[25] The writings of the Graveyard School served as yet another reminder of the reality and eventuality of death, but did so in ways that functioned as sermons, admonishing the living to consider their spiritual standing before they too rotted in the church graveyard. The thrust of their message was, "The effects of death are horrific, *but* immortality redeems them."[26]

As Kendrick's historical analysis continues, he notes that the close proximity of death disappeared and the suppression of death took its place. Eventually Western culture shifted from a time in which death was an intimate part of daily experience, to the present period, where most people die in sanitized places removed from the presence and experience even of loved ones. Added to this, the way in which the dead are treated attempts to gloss over the effects of death, with funeral homes using embalming fluid and makeup to portray the dead as sleeping, funerals often involving closed caskets, and all of this serving to minimize if not ignore the horrific effects of the process of death and decay. Further, our cultural grieving processes anticipate a relatively short process of recovery, followed by mere memory of the dead, with no sense of an ongoing connection to deceased ancestors found in many non-Western cultures.

At the same time, many in the West are devoted to health and the maintenance of the body. As a result of this state of affairs a curious situation occurs. Many people spend great amounts of time exercising, following careful diets, receiving botox injections, and having plastic surgeries as a means of fighting the signs of aging and death and, in effect, perpetuating the modern fear of deadness. But at the same time, horror films continue to present graphic imagery of death and decay to eager viewing audiences. Kendrick notes this strange situation and writes: "It looks paradoxical at best—psychotic at worst—that one might go from an hour on the Nautilus machines or in an aerobics class, where the body is urged to the acme of aliveness, directly to a screening of *Night of the Living Dead*, which pits animated corpses against the living and lets the corpses win."[27]

Two facets of Kendrick's thesis are important for my analysis of the Zombie Walk. First, in Kendrick's view, horror provides a means whereby the repression of death in societal as well as individual experience can surface through a process that allows the imagery of death to "cavort in the imagination."[28] Zombie films are especially suited to this process as they not only deal in general with death, but also put walking corpses at the center of their narratives. These in turn have influenced Zombie Walks, which then present not only the imagery of death, but also identification with it through its actual embodiment by participants. Secondly,

Kendrick notes that in times past, an intimate connection was drawn between death and the spiritual. The repression of death in the West (including in Christian circles as churches reflect the denial and sanitization of death from the surrounding culture), coupled with skepticism about religion and the possibility of life after death in whatever forms, has in many circumstances only served to heighten our fear. Kendrick writes that, "Our culture's loss of trust in redemption has turned a premodern faith into a nagging modern fear."[29] This then makes a contribution to horror with its depiction of creatures, from vampires to zombies, each possessing the power to overcome the grave. According to Kendrick, "in these and innumerable other forms (all of which are better off dead), the twisted memory of lost faith haunts us still."[30] Gatherings of people in Zombie Walks, particularly with the religious figure of Zombie Jesus, would seem to signal a way in which individuals are grappling with the reality of death, and yet also weaving in aspects of the dominant religious influence of the West in terms of Christianity and its narrative of the resurrection of the dead, however imaginatively this is reinterpreted.

Another discussion with application to the Zombie Walk is found in Linda Badley's work on horror films and the body. In *Film, Horror, and the Body Fantastic*, Badley echoes many of the sentiments of Kendrick in acknowledging the denial of death in the West.[31] But in response to this phenomenon she argues that horror films function as "one of several discourses of the body that use the fantastic—the iconography of the monstrous," to allow us to articulate our anxieties and to "re-project the self."[32] As Badley considers expressions of horror over time she identifies horror films of the 1980s as especially important, particularly for those living in a decade that saw itself as "grotesquely embodied and in transformation."[33] This decade's expression of horror is understood as having special significance in terms of its presentation of the body in connection with concepts of the self. She writes: "In the 1980s horror (whatever the medium) became a spectacle offering not mere transcendence *of* the body but transcendence *through* the body—albeit the body in a recharged, re-gendered, and regenerated sense—through shock, transposition of the senses, intense feeling, and special effects."[34] This perspective is interesting in that through grotesque depictions of the body in horror, and not merely the "body horror" subgenre of David Cronenberg and others, Badley believes that a form of transcendence is achieved. It is a form of transcendence that is achieved both of and through the body. In the Zombie Walk, at times participants in that phenomenon may be understood as enacting some kind of transcendence through the body by adopting the imaginative identity of a living corpse. Death is transcended in that the dead return to "life," and concepts of the body are transcended as well. In regards to the body, as will be discussed below, dualistic concepts of body and soul are set aside in favor of more unitary concepts of the self with an emphasis on the self as body. This includes an embrace of all the visceral aspects that can accompany it.

Related to this, and also in keeping with Kendrick's analysis, Badley sees the influence of the breakdown of traditional religion in culture, and with it a loss of confidence in narratives of an afterlife. These would find expression in new concepts of the self that are informed by horror as they develop new mythologies of the body. Badley suggests, much as Kendrick did before her, that

> The dissolution of the boundaries of death and life has also destroyed any simple concepts of soul as an "eternal" or essential self. Its loss raises disturbing questions about identity that have fostered new mythologies of the body. The monster show of the 1970s and 1980s was like the icons it replaced, a rite of passage and a coping mechanism. It constituted both a denial of and confrontation with the "facts" of death. By the war-starved health and fitness-obsessed consumer culture of the 1980s, the tangible yet mysterious inner spaces of the body had become sites for new mythologies and a location, after the loss of the soul and the psyche, for the self.[35]

It is also worth noting that as she continues to discuss this topic she draws upon the concept and terminology of Christian resurrection and connects it to horror films that portray, in various ways, the dead returning to "life": "As pointed out by the zombie craze—from Romero's *Night of the Living Dead* (1968), to *Pet Sematary* (1989), to *Death Becomes Her* (1992)—death's mystique was linked with a 'resurrectionist' technology intent on manipulating the forces and forms of life."[36] In her follow up volume on this topic, *Writing Horror and the Body*, Badley presses this point slightly further. In a chapter that discusses the horror writing of Stephen King, she once again makes the connection between horror's depiction of the body and its relationship to a perverse form of resurrection in light of the book *Pet Sematary*. For those unfamiliar with the storyline of the book and the film adaptation, *Pet Sematary* tells the story of a family who suffers the untimely death of their young son, Gage. His distraught father decides to disinter his body from the cemetery, and to rebury him in an Indian burial ground, where legend has it that the dead return to life. Unfortunately, they return in a perverse moral and bodily fashion, and Gage is no exception. In light of this form of resurrection the book and film are best known from the resulting tagline: "Sometimes dead is better." Badley describes *Pet Sematary* as "an encounter with mortality," where "[t]he world of religion, myth, and ritual is signified in conspicuous absences or reversals."[37] In this connection, the Christian concept of resurrection, and Christ's resurrection in particular, seem to be in the background. This is confirmed by Badley, who insightfully notes that King's story portrays, "Gage's death and grotesque resurrection [as] occurring sometime around Passover or Easter,"[38] perhaps serving even as a darkly ironic reversal of the New Testament story of the raising of Lazarus.[39]

In light of the preceding discussion about horror and the body, several ideas present themselves with application to an understanding of the Zombie Walk phenomenon.

First, Western culture is involved in a process of the denial of death. This takes place not only through the way in which we deal with the dying and the dead, but also through the modern obsession for countering the effects of aging. At the same time, horror films continue to be popular, and paradoxically present graphic reminders of death and decay for viewers who suppress the idea of death in other aspects of life and culture.

Second, this denial is difficult to sustain completely, and in part horror films represent a "return of the repressed" in their portrayal of death. Horror films provide a forum whereby death surfaces from the depths of the psyche and is allowed to "cavort in the imagination." Zombie films, and television programs as well with AMC's *The Walking Dead*, are especially well suited to this process as risen, shuffling corpses present a graphic reminder of the reality of death. The process whereby Zombie Walk participants dress up as corpses and walk through various cities represents in some sense an acceptance, if not embrace of mortality through imaginative role-play and visceral display.

Third, horror films often deal with the monstrous body, and not only in the "body horror" subgenre. The body in horror films has become a place where the individual not only deals with death, but also explores various concepts of the self. As will be discussed in more detail in the next section on theological analysis, one of those new self concepts is the "enlightened body-self," a spiritual concept that involves a shift away

PART TWO: ZOMBIES

from dualistic anthropologies of body and soul toward more holistic understandings of the self as the body. Dressing up and walking about as the risen dead in Zombie Walks provides a means by which individuals can experiment with and embrace this and other concepts of the self as actors creating new identities shaped and informed by participation in horrific narratives and mythologies.

Fourth, even with a shift from supernatural to more secular approaches to horror, the spiritual dimension is not far from the various manifestations of the genre.[40] This is not surprising, given the long history of cultural dominance and influence from Christianity, but in the post-Christendom and postmodern period it has shifted, as popular culture continues a process of re-enchantment.[41] One example of this comes in the retention of the idea of resurrection in connection with the dead, but this is reconceptualized in ways that reshape Christian dogma. There are various references to "resurrectionist" elements in horror as discussed above, and the Zombie Walk phenomenon can also be understood in this regard, as it puts a postmodern twist on Christian eschatology, particularly when Zombie Jesus is present leading his ghoulish, risen followers.

With these considerations in mind I now move to bringing the pieces together in consideration of the theological meaning and significance of Zombie Walks, a phenomenon that involves not only a challenge and critique to Christian theologians, but also one of opportunity for those able and willing to engage popular culture in this area.

"CAN THESE BONES LIVE?": THEOLOGICAL CONSIDERATIONS OF THE ZOMBIE WALK

The Hebrew prophet Ezekiel had a vision in which he saw a valley of dry bones.[42] As his vision unfolded he asked God whether the bones would live again. God instructed the prophet to speak to the bones with the promise that He would raise them again. After doing as commanded, flesh covered the bones and God breathed life into them, promising further to reach into the graves of the nation of Israel and raise the dead.

The vision of Ezekiel is but one of many instances in the Judeo-Christian scriptural tradition where the idea of the rising dead may be found. Given the prevalence of this idea, and that the resurrection is at the center of Christianity, theological consideration of an aspect of popular culture that incorporates aspects of the rising dead would seem to make it especially relevant for Christian theologians. Yet it must be understood at the outset of such an analysis that it presents both challenges to Christian theology, as well as opportunities for reflection and engagement. Some have interpreted the zombie theme as satire on Christian teaching,[43] and this is especially the case with the Zombie Jesus element discussed above. As a result, while some have been willing to explore more positive possibilities in regards to Christianity and zombies,[44] many theologians are likely to view the topic with disdain, if it is even taken seriously at all. Even so, it is my hope that the elements discussed above provide some initial thoughts about the positive possibilities for theological engagement of this topic, and that these possibilities will be confirmed and expanded in the theological reflection that follows.

In light of the phenomenon of the Zombie Walk, particularly where elements of the Christian tradition are incorporated, I suggest the following elements should be considered in a theological engagement with this aspect of popular culture.

First, *expand concepts of the sacred*. One of the greatest initial challenges theologians may face in considering the Zombie Walk is skepticism concerning its connection to anything religious or spiritual. On the surface it appears to be little more than an aspect of popular culture, and, while this element cannot be denied, I believe that an argument can be made that the Zombie Walk can in some ways be interpreted as an expression of the human quest for the sacred.

When theologians think of religion, the tendency is to think in categories similar to their own religious tradition. Theologians are not the only ones to do this, of course, but religion in our time is broader and more diverse than traditional categories permit. This point has been made by a number of scholars, including Gary Laderman. Laderman is the author of *Sacred Matters*, with the long but telling subtitle of *Celebrity Worship, Sexual Ecstasies, the Living Dead, and Other Signs of Religious Life in the United States*.[45] In an essay in *Religion Dispatches*, he picks up the main thrust of *Sacred Matters*, with the American Religious Identification Survey as the point of departure. He notes how Christianity is prominently featured, with commentators arguing variously about whether that faith is growing or receding in American religious life. But he then argues that these interpretations of American religiosity in the survey miss significant facets of how Americans construct their religious identity and engage in the spiritual quest. Survey takers tend to think of religion in certain traditional categories related to God, Scripture, and

Part Two: Zombies

participation in institutional worship settings. But Laderman suggests this misses a large part of the picture:

> What if there were more to religious life in America than belief in God? More holy possibilities than those outlined in the so-called "Great Religions of the Book"—Judaism, Christianity, and Islam—or other sacred texts like the Upanishads in Hinduism or the Tibetan Book of the Dead in Buddhism?
>
> What if religion is better understood as a ubiquitous feature of cultural life, expressed through and inspired by basic, universal facts of life and fundamentally biological phenomena in human experience: suffering and ecstasy, reproduction and aging, family and conflict, health and death.[46]

For some time now, scholars have recognized a Western shift away from identification with institutional religion, to more personalized forms of spirituality.[47] Laderman suggests that with continued developments in our religiosity, our understanding of this phenomenon needs to be broadened even further. He argues that American religious life is not only confined to the major religious traditions, but also involves expressions of cultural life that may not normally be considered religious, including how we deal with biological phenomena like death and "funereal spectacles."[48] In Laderman's view, having an expanded concept of American spirituality involves understanding what is sacred in contemporary experience. As his essay continues, he states that, "Attention to what is sacred—sacred matters—points instead to robust, thriving forms of religious life, experience, and community that are less about theology and more about anthropology."[49]

Elsewhere Laderman has written on death, and drawn out an interesting observation that connects it to the sacred and to the zombie: "The monsters in [George] Romero's [zombie] film [*Night of the Living Dead*] are the dark side of luminous angels. While angels are eternally alive though disembodied, these zombie cannibals are eternally dead yet fully embodied."[50] In consideration of Laderman's call for an expanded understanding of the sacred in our time, in a theology informed by anthropology, the ways in which human beings deal with death, may be understood as expressions of religious life; the Zombie Walk is one such imaginative way of dealing with death. More directly to the subject matter of this chapter, the zombie can be understood as the dark flipside of angels. Scholars and other cultural observers have long noted the prevalence of angels, surfacing in everything from television programs to lapel pins to bumper stickers. These have rightly been interpreted as a manifestation of pop-religiosity. Previously, scholars such as Douglas Cowan have recognized horror as involving inversion, specifically "the inversion or reversal of accepted religious categories as a means of invoking the horrific."[51] Perhaps the zombie as the inversion of the angelic functions as the "anti-sacred," which can itself serve as a means of representing and attempting to engage the sacred in its own way, embracing elements marginalized or ignored by more mainstream expressions of spirituality. With Laderman's angelic/zombie contrast in mind,, the embrace of the "dark angelic zombie" represents a shift in a symbol of the sacred from the luminous to the dark, the disembodied to the embodied, from the eternally alive to the eternally "living" dead.

Theologians seeking to understand pop-culture events like Zombie Walks will benefit from an expanded concept of the sacred, one that can encompass messy biological phenomena like death and funereal spectacles, and does so with reference to a popular creature from horror.

Next, *recognize new concepts of the body and self*. As discussed above, horror has become a mode of discourse, whereby new concepts of the body and the self—or more precisely, the self through the body—are explored. In the Zombie Walk these are combined as both the body and the self (understood as each intimately connected to the other, if not identified with each other) come into focus.

Although Christianity has tended to promote dualistic understandings of human nature, a unity of an immaterial spirit or soul and with a physical body,[52] there is a strong Western cultural component that rejects this view in favor of a monistic view that identifies the self with the body. This view has been shaped by a number of influences, from Darwinian evolution, to the neurosciences (which has connected many of the phenomena previously identified with the soul to activities in the brain),[53] to metaphysical religion in American popular culture.

I have discussed above the importance of Christianity as an influence upon the Zombie Walk, which should be evident especially when Zombie Jesus is present and some subversion of the Christian concept of resurrection is at play. But another influence may be discerned in the form of American metaphysical religion. In her exploration of this topic, Catherine Albanese argues that many popular histories of American religion are incomplete in that American metaphysical religion has been neglected. One of the more recognizable expressions of this was the New Age movement, but Albanese states that metaphysics should be understood as "a movement much broader than the self-conscious New Age movement,"[54] and that American metaphysics has been and continues to be very influential. In times past in metaphysical religion, the power of the mind played a significant role. But over time new forms of this religion saw the body become an influential element. As Albanese describes it:

> Metaphysical religiosity—in the declining New Age and in the new spirituality that was succeeding it—was different from the metaphysical religion of a century previous[;] . . . the mind had manifestly acquired a body, and the body refused to stay out of metaphysical discourse. It was the enlightened *body*-self that twenty-first-century metaphysicians and their immediate forebears hailed.[55]

Here Albanese not only points out that the body is significant in metaphysical religion and its understanding of the spiritual, but also that this factors into what she calls the "enlightened body-self." Recall the discussion above where Badley suggested that horror and its depiction of the body provides a means whereby individuals can express anxieties and experiment with new concepts of the self, and in so doing achieve transcendence of and through the body. When this idea is connected to the influence of metaphysical religion in American culture, an interesting possibility presents itself. I suggest that the "resurrected" zombie represents a postmodern monist metaphysic in regards to the self and the body. This plays out as an identification of the self with the body that transcends the dichotomy between life and death. In other words, I am not my body, only insofar as it is my container until death; but rather, I am my body in a way that transcends that dichotomy so that my self is constructed by means of (at least in part) body maintenance, development, and change. In short, as I construct my body, so I construct my self, including in ways wherein Zombie Walk participants act out the revival of the body from death. The implication is that the resurrected body as zombie represents a new conception of resurrection, a blending of satire on Christian teaching about the resurrection with metaphysical religion and its enlightened body-self. The result is the resurrected zombie body-self that tells us as much about the construction of the self through the body in life as it does about attitudes toward death and hopes for survival beyond it.[56]

Christian theologians may feel that they have little to contribute to such considerations, but I suggest this is not the case. A trajectory of scholarship exists whose dots can be connected to the concept of the body in the Zombie Walk. This is found in the work of Christian scholars who have brought theology into dialogue with the neurosciences, and this has led toward a reassessment in biblical studies regarding human nature, which in turn has moved "away from notions of body-soul dualism, toward some form of monism."[57] One example of this is found in Nancey Murphy's work, where she has argued for a form of Christian monism that she calls "non-reductive physicalism." In this position, Murphy and like-minded colleagues agree "with the scientists and philosophers who hold that it is not necessary to postulate a second metaphysical entity, the soul or mind, to account for human capacities and distinctiveness.[58] But, as the term indicates, non-reductive physicalism is not reductionistic like purely materialist accounts of human nature, for it allows for free will, morality, and religious awareness.

Monistic concepts of human nature among Christian scholars can inform a variety of disciplines that can also be connected to similar reflections on resurrection in eschatology. More will be said about this below, but here too an emphasis on the body in connection with the concept of the self is found. As physicist and theologian John Polkinghorne has stated,

> there is indeed the Christian hope of a destiny beyond death, but it resides not in the presumed immortality of a spiritual soul, but in the divinely guaranteed eschatological sequence of death and resurrection. Only a hope conceived of in this way can do full justice to human psychosomatic unity, and hence to the indispensability of some form of re-embodiment for a truly human future existence.[59]

So while those participating in the Zombie Walk engage in activities informed by zombie films that express fears, they also allow for experimentation with new concepts of the self, and Christian theologians have something to contribute to this topic as well. It is not only metaphysical religion that allows for the concept of the body-self. Christianity has its own teachings on the importance of the body, both in this life and in the life to come at the *eschaton*. It is here that Christian theologians can not only empathize with the zombie resurrected body-self, but also provide some critique. For the form of resurrection found in the Zombie Walk

Part Two: Zombies

phenomenon misses the important context of "eschatology as transformation" related to the body and the world to come.

To consider this, would then be to address the last point—*To Present an Eschatology of Hope*. Earlier in this chapter I suggested that the Zombie Walk represents an expression of the postmodern eschatological imagination. It draws upon the Christian metanarrative, specifically with reference to eschatology and the resurrection of the dead, but also subverts it. The result is that the dead reanimate, but the form of resurrection is one in which personal identity is lost, the body maintains and continues the process of decay, and the resurrected return to the corrupted world in which they died. The eschatological picture of the Zombie Walk is one of pessimism, and here the Christian theologian can introduce an alternative eschatology of hope.

At the outset theologians must confirm the reasons for pessimism where the human future is concerned. In his helpful book on eschatology,[60] a summary of a much larger book that came about as a result of an interdisciplinary conference on eschatology by Christian scholars,[61] John Polkinghorne sketches the cosmic forces of destruction that have been operative in the past history of the universe and the earth, and the negative implications of what this means for the future in terms of the ultimate death of humanity, the planet, and the universe. But he goes on to discuss human optimism that is often expressed in the face of the certainty of death: "I believe that this intuition of hope is a significant and essential aspect of what it is to be human. It is not just a survival technique for whistling in the dark to keep our spirits up, but it is an encounter with the reality within which we live."[62] He then builds upon this and mentions the inductive theological method of the noted sociologist of religion, Peter Berger. In *A Rumor of Angels*, Berger set forth "an approach to theologizing informed by sociology and anthropology that begins with ordinary human experience," but which, in his view, involved "elements of that experience that point toward a reality beyond the ordinary."[63] He called these elements "signals of transcendence," which allow us to "transcendentalize secularity."[64] Polkinghorne adopts Berger's approach, and mentions an example where Berger references a common event wherein parents calm the fears of a child that awakens from a bad dream and tells him/her everything will be fine. In Polkinghorne's view, this is a conformation of our optimism in the face of death, and a signal of transcendence in that this feeling is rooted beyond the human and cosmic condition.

This can be applied to the Zombie Walk. Some who participate may be expressing, however skeptically, a lingering interest in the survival of the self and the body beyond death. The participation in the Zombie Walk represents a signal of transcendence, and yet one which retains the skepticism of postmodernity. The theologian can draw upon this signal of transcendence in the face of death, and yet also point out that the eschatological context of the Zombie Walk fails to support such optimism. Although "nihilism is in the ascendant in the postmodern West and hope on the way out,"[65] here the theologian can introduce the need for consideration of an "eschatology of transformation," both of the self and the body after death, as well as the environment in which the individual is resurrected, both terrestrial and cosmic. For the individual, this can be seen in the New Testament presentation of Jesus and his resurrection, particularly in Luke-Acts:

> Jesus' disciples did not mistake him for a cadaver brought back to life, a reanimated corpse. Luke distinguishes Jesus' resurrected body from the resuscitated bodies of the widow's son in Nain (7:11–17), Jairus' daughter (8:40–42, 49–56), Tabitha (Acts 9:36–43), and Eutychus (20:7–12). Second, he certifies that neither is Jesus an "immortal soul" free from bodily existence. Jesus is present to his disciples, beyond the grave, as a fully embodied person.[66]

In other words, the body of Jesus is presented in the New Testament as having gone through a process of transformation, one in which his identity was retained and which also saw a new form of embodiment. This involved continuity and discontinuity with the present order. Theologians have also noted that the resurrection of Jesus is connected in New Testament theology to a broader eschatological context: "This in turn means that the resurrection of Jesus as the breaking in of the New Creation is both *continuous* with the present one in which we live and die and yet immensely *discontinuous* with the present one, for it is a world in which death will one day be banished."[67]

CONCLUSION

Understandably, not every theologian will accept this form of addressing postmodern concerns about death or the resurrection of Jesus through a pop-culture phenomenon like Zombie Walks. Most conservative

Part Two: Zombies

theologians will want to stay away from the topic altogether, while more progressive theologians will find any connection between resurrection, Jesus, and zombies absurd. In an example of the latter, an essay in *Religion Dispatches* touched on a controversy between the Vatican and systematic theologian Roger Haight. The Vatican had concerns about some of Haight's views that surfaced as a result of his book *Jesus, Symbol of God* (Orbis, 1999). In order to explore the subject, the author of the essay interviewed Jeremy Kirk, a student of Haight's at Union Theological Seminary, who did his MA on the professor's Christology. One of Haight's controversial views (from the perspective of the Vatican) is his interpretation of the resurrection of Jesus. When asked to describe Haight's views on this topic, Kirk said:

> Haight would affirm that the resurrection was not an historical event that happened physically and empirically in the space-time continuum. When Christians bury a loved one, they put the body in the ground with the faith/hope that the person is resurrected in a way that does not deny the historicity of the physical burial. Haight would state that Jesus' body did not go anywhere; it is not the resuscitation of a corpse. *There was no zombie Jesus.*[68]

Haight misses an opportunity to engage contemporary concerns through a practical theology, by not exploring the zombie Jesus concept in popular culture. This is especially surprising in Haight's case since the essay in *Religion Dispatches* states that "Haight's project was intended for a current intellectual context" that addresses "the postmodern critiques of Christianity."[69] Rather than simply invoking the term "zombie Jesus" in negative fashion, Haight and other theologians might consider exploring the concept in more depth, unpacking its various meanings, engaging in self-critical theological reflection where appropriate, and then engaging those who celebrate the figure of "Zombie Jesus."

END NOTES

1. Associated Press, "Mexico City 'Zombie Walk.'"
2. Subissati, *When There's No More Room In Hell*, 31. See also the "History" section of the Wikipedia entry on "Zombie walks."
3. Jenkins, *Convergence Culture*. Cf. Henry Jenkins, *Fans, Bloggers, and Gamers*.

4. The Philly Zombie Crawl website can be found at http://phillyzombiecrawl.com/crawl_details.html.
5. D'Arbonne, "Zombie Jesus at the Denver Zombie Crawl."
6. *Uncyclopedia*, "Zombie Jesus."
7. One example is the film *Zombie Jesus*, with the tagline, "Zombie Jesus is back, and he's got a taste for the pious." The film's website can be found at http://www.zombiejesusisback.com/. Other examples can be found at YouTube.
8. *Dead Meat Walking: A Zombie Walk Documentary*, directed by Omar J. Pineda (forthcoming 2012), http://www.deadmeatwalkingmovie.com/Home_Page.html.
9. "Church of the Resurrection" entry, Urban Dead Wiki.
10. Van Buren, "Atheists Continue To Disrespect Easter."
11. Zombie Jesus Day website, "About."
12. Jesus Was a Zombie! page: http://www.zombiejesus.com/.
13. Lauro, "Playing Dead: Zombies Invade Performance Art."
14. Subissati, *When There's No More Room In Hell*, 31, 93.
15. Tancons, "Occupy Wall Street: Carnival Against Capital?; "Occupy Las Vegas Holds 'Zombie Walk,'" Daubs, "Zombies and Occupy Toronto."
16. Wojcik, *The End of the World as We Know It*, 2–3.
17. Partridge, *The Re-Enchantment of the West*, vol. 2, 280.
18. Ibid.
19. Rosen, *Apocalyptic Transformation*, xx.
20. Ibid., xv.
21. The notion of a zombie apocalypse is so well embedded in popular culture that in 2011 the Center for Disease Control drew upon the concept in tongue in cheek fashion as a marketing tool to promote interest in disaster preparedness: http://www.cdc.gov/phpr/zombies.htm).
22. This turn to the pessimistic has been amplified in a post-9/11 environment, and can also be seen in the horror genre in general, as well as other related genres like science fiction. See Walliss and Aston, "Doomsday America," 53–64. Cf. Wetmore, *Post-9/11 Horror*.
23. Kendrick, *The Thrill of Fear*, xv.
24. This is a "loose label" applied to a group of writers with no conscious connection as a self-identified movement. Although the roots of literary horror are often traced to the Gothic and Romantic traditions, James Kendrick has argued that we need to go further back to this Graveyard School of poets "whose contributions to the horror genre have been consistently understated, if not ignored." See "A Return to the Graveyard," 147.
25. One is tempted to think of Hebrews 12:1 with its encouragement that the living saint is "surrounded by a great cloud of witnesses," albeit in more gruesome

Part Two: Zombies

fleshly rather than spiritual terms in the context of eighteenth-century churches with surrounding cemeteries.

26. Emphasis in original; *The Thrill of Fear*, 31.
27. Ibid., xvii.
28. Ibid., xvi.
29. Ibid., 32.
30. Ibid.
31. Badley, *Film, Horror, and the Body Fantastic*, 43.
32. Ibid., 3.
33. Ibid., 7.
34. Ibid., 9.
35. Ibid., 24.
36. Ibid.
37. Badley, *Writing Horror and the Body*, 49. Another example of religious reversal in regards to the rising dead is found in the zombie comedy-horror film *Fido*, where special funeral arrangements can be purchased so that the head and body of the deceased are buried in separate caskets, thus preventing zombie resurrection.
38. Ibid.
39. John 11:1–43. The latter idea was suggested by Badley in a personal email to the author from August 19, 2011.
40. Stone, "The Sanctification of Fear." Cf. Kendrick, *The Thrill of Fear*.
41. Partridge, *The Re-Enchantment of the West*, vol. 1.
42. This vision can be found in Ezekiel 37:1–14.
43. Toppe, "Reversing the Gospel of Jesus." Cf. Moreman, "Dharma of the Living Dead," 263–81.
44. Gilmour, "The Living Word Among the Living Dead." This volume considers the Bible as an important influence on the Western cultural imagination and how the biblical material includes a number of aspects related to zombie literature and film. Of particular note are the "fundamental narrative elements" of resurrection and bodily consumption which parallel resurrection and the Eucharist.
45. New York: The New Press, 2009.
46. Laderman, "Sacred & Profane."
47. Fuller, *Spiritual, But Not Religious*.
48. Laderman, "Sacred & Profane."
49. Ibid.
50. Laderman, *Rest in Peace*, 123.
51. Cowan, *Sacred Terror*, 85.

52. Even so, Christians have recognized that there has been and continues to be diversity in the understanding of biblical anthropology, some of which allows for a form of monism. See the discussion of this in Green, *Body, Soul, and Human Life*.
53. Brown et al., *Whatever Happened to the Soul?*
54. Albanese, *A Republic of Mind and Spirit*, 10.
55. Ibid., 514 (emphasis in the original).
56. Thanks to Andrea Rene Jain, Assistant Professor in the Department of Religious Studies at Indiana University-Purdue University of Indianapolis, for our emails and phone discussion on the viability of this idea.
57. Green, *Body, Soul, and Human Life*, 22.
58. Murphy, "Human Nature."
59. Polkinghorne, *The God of Hope*, 108.
60. Ibid.
61. Polkinghorne and Welker, *The End of the World*.
62. Polkinghorne, *The God of Hope*, 31.
63. Berger, *A Rumor of Angels*, 13.
64. Ibid.
65. Soskice, "The Ends of Man and the Future of God," 79.
66. Green, *Body, Soul, and Human Life*, 168.
67. Russell, "Scientific Insights," 242.
68. VonWachenfeldt, "No Zombie Jesus," lines 70–75 (emphasis mine).
69. Ibid., lines 16, 47.

7

When All Is Lost, Gather 'Round

Solidarity as Hope Resisting Despair in *The Walking Dead*

Ashley John Moyse

With this wretched gathering that our planet now is, despair returns to tempt me with the idea that there is no purpose, only petty personal ends for which we fight! We make little revolutions, but there is no goal for mankind. One cannot think of such things. They tempt you incessantly . . . the world seems ugly, bad and without hope. There, that's the cry of despair of an old man who will die in despair. But that's exactly what I resist. I know I shall die in hope. But that hope needs a foundation.

—Jean Paul Sartre[1]

INTRODUCTION

Frank Darabont's adaptation of Robert Kirkman's comic-book series, *The Walking Dead*, introduces us to an ugly, bad, and hopeless world, where the cry of despair, the grieving over all that has been lost, is potent and thick. Yet, throughout the series there seems to be a fragile hope, which undergirds many of the survivors and their labors together. That is, throughout this series one is introduced to a world where the smell of death interrupts and the trauma of loss overwhelms. With every step, one must beware the walkers instinctively seeking flesh—not to mention the other hazards from within and without the group of survivors seeking safety and solace. Episode after episode, we have been confronted with images of death and of grief as the survivors grapple with the trouble of missing friends, dead family members, and the terrific apprehension of the pending zombie rebirth awaiting those exposed to the walkers' bite. This grief is ominous and opaque. It is despair. But such despair is opposed by a hope that may be encountered in the community of humans struggling to flourish in a world-gone-wrong—in a community capable of encountering hope in the joy of mutual service and faithful labor with and for each other.

The purpose of this essay will be to explore the themes of despair and hope as illumined by the post-apocalyptic horror unraveling in *The Walking Dead* television series.[2] Friedrich Nietzsche will serve to instruct on the theme of despair, or the meaninglessness of life. In opposition to the nihilistic over-current in the series narrative—or rather, serving as reconciliatory resistance—the subtle under-current in the narrative, solidarity as hope, will be explored. With this, I will argue that the gathered community, individuals living for others, is what may offer the survivors not only strength but also hope during times of crisis: When all is lost, gather 'round. Thus, I will not negate nihilism, but will offer hope as a counterweight that may overcome it. This argument will be explored through the theological considerations of French philosopher and playwright, Gabriel Marcel, Swiss Reformed theologian, Karl Barth, and German Lutheran pastor, Dietrich Bonhoeffer, who may help us to understand the conditions of and foundation for hopeful communities that are enabled to overcome despair.

PART TWO: ZOMBIES

ALL IS LOST: OBSERVING NOTHINGNESS

You know what's out there. A short, brutal life and an agonizing death.... There is no hope. There never was!

—Dr. Edwin Jenner (Noah Emmerich),
Season 01 Episode 06 (S01E06)

As with the epigraph, the world revealed in *The Walking Dead* may be seen as a wretched gathering where death embodied haunts and despair overwhelmingly tempts the living. The walkers embody the tyranny of death and their resurrected existence interrupts the survivors with an ever-present reminder that the world-as-we-knew-it has passed. It has been replaced by a world of great sorrow and uncertainty, of oppressive grief and nothingness. Oh, wretched world! That has *nothing* in it.[3]

A strong current of nihilism runs over the narrative that drives this series. As the characters discover a world dispossessed of that which they desire and/or once had, the crisis of meaninglessness is encountered.[4] That is, as the incomprehensible dread of despair contaminates the living, the great sense that all is lost becomes overwhelming and the traditional order of things is assaulted by the walking dead. Take, for example, Rick (Andrew Lincoln), enclosed and alone in the tank that is to be his tomb, gun in hand, surrounded by an absurd new world where the dead-resurrected advance on the living; a world where he is alone, without his wife, Lori (Sarah Wayne Callies), and son, Carl (Chandler Riggs). Further, consider Andrea's (Laurie Holden) expressions of despair after the loss of her sister, Amy (Emma Bell), let alone that all once familiar is now lost to the chaos of imminent death and the threat of walkers. She seems, in more than one instance, consoled by the palliative certainty of death at her own willing. Moreover, consider Shane's (Jon Bernthal) progressing anomie and careless aggression as the norms that ordered his existence dissolve and his desires go unfulfilled. His story continues to unravel and his neuroses mature. Finally, the mid-season finale of the second season reveals Dr. Hershel Greene (Scott Wilson) collapsing with exasperated hopelessness during the massacre at the barn. Any hope for recovering his family is now gone in a dizzying flurry of rage and gunfire. Each of these scenes, and many others, provide the evidence that this series narrates the ongoing human struggle to find meaning in a world where great suffering and terrific injustices abound.

The world has been stripped of any meaning and tradition, of normalcy and value. That which formed the social and moral capital in pre-apocalyptic Georgia has been lost, and for the survivors, there is a constant struggle to wrestle with the thought that nothing much matters any more. There is no goal for humanity. Rather, there is only despair over death.

Friedrich Nietzsche articulates his doctrine of nothingness, or nihilism, this way: "A nihilist is a man who judges of the world as it is that it ought not to be, and of the world as it ought to be that it does not exist."[5] It is the belief that existence is meaningless or without value; or, at the very least, it is the idea that meaningful lives are elusive. Accordingly, the crisis of nihilism comes in the form of the question: "Does life have meaning?" Asked another way: "Is life worth living at all?" The response to these questions is the real problem for the survivors struggling not only to exist, but also to find meaning to exist in a world saturated with despair.

Life is meaningful, according to Nietzsche, in relation to something else. These relations, these symbolic associations, are reflective of the values one holds to be true or real. The idea of a meaningful life is constructed about these values that inspire life towards such ends. But what if these values are not realized?

Nihilism, in general contrast, is the recognition that life is without value, possessing no meaning at all. The nihilist ambulates through life, struggling with feelings of valuelessness. Consider Nietzsche's own words:

> What does nihilism mean? *That the highest values devaluate themselves.* The aim is lacking; "why?" finds no answer. . . . The nihilistic consequence (the belief of valuelessness) as a consequence of moral valuation. . . . We see that we cannot reach the sphere in which we have placed our values; but this does not by any means confer any value on that other sphere in which we live: on the contrary, we are weary because we have lost the main stimulus. "In vain so far!"[6]

The crisis, for Nietzsche, is raised as one realizes the ends for which she has struggled are not there—one has aimed but realizes she "aims at *nothing* and achieves *nothing.*"[7]

The movement from an affirmation of life to a repudiation of life is one goaded by a progressive or sudden loss of inspiration. Accordingly, for Nietzsche, the concept of "ideals" is an important one. Ideals delimit the aims that guide human action toward the realization of a meaningful existence. These aims are valued as purpose-giving or meaning-nurturing.

Part Two: Zombies

They represent the goals that, reciprocally, actualize value in and for life. They provide the substance for which one may justify a positive response to the question, "Is life worth living?" However, it may be found that not all of these ideals are achievable and their valuation may recede—these are the very sources of nihilism.[8] The ideals, the constructs, for which human thought and action flourish are proven to be faulty, untrue and/or untenable in the world that stifles ideals. Consequently, the aims for which one strives are considered to be aims of an anti- or un-reality. Reality, rather the no-true-world[9] in which one finds oneself, concludes a different perspective: nothing really matters.

Indeed, it is at the point of realizing that one's ideals are unachievable, valueless, or untrue, that one may actualize despair. As with Sartre's expression in the epigraph, there is no goal but insignificant ends for which we fight. It is a response to an observation that provokes pessimism and cultivates nihilism.[10] Pessimism in this instance means more than a simple turn for the worse but "the world does not have the value that [was] once thought it had.... it seems worth less."[11] Nihilism is just the most extreme form: "the world [is] ugly, bad, and without hope."[12] Nihilism concludes, from the pessimistic logic, that it would be better if the world did not exist. In addition, the nihilist will argue, there is no other world where that which we value (or once valued) may be realized. As defined above, Nietzsche writes: "A nihilist is a man who judges of the world as it is that it ought not to be, and of the world as it ought to be that it does not exist."[13] Nihilism, then, is about the possibility of realizing that which we value—and it may conclude, lamenting, that we cannot, thereby casting one, without reserve, into the pit of despair.[14]

What then does it mean to despair? Despair antagonizes human existence, tempting it incessantly. It tempts one to death. As Gabriel Marcel writes,

> It seems as though it were always capitulation before a certain *fatum* [destiny] laid down by our judgment.... To capitulate, in the strongest sense of the word, is not only, perhaps is not at all, to accept the given sentence or even to recognise the inevitable as such, it is to go to pieces under this sentence, to disarm before the inevitable. It is at bottom to renounce the idea of remaining oneself, it is to be fascinated by the idea of one's own destruction to the point of anticipating this very destruction itself.[15]

Dr. Edwin Jenner serves as an example of one tempted to death. He argues the destruction that the Center for Disease Control (CDC) self-destruct protocol will bring is but the inevitable end. It is an end with neither pain nor sorrow. It is an end to the anguish of existence. It is the end to "everything"—or rather, an end to nothingness. Attempting to console and to convince the others entrapped by the locked doors and barricaded exits, Jenner continues: "You know what's out there. A short, brutal life and an agonizing death.... There is no hope. There never was!" For Jenner, all those petty ends for which one may fight are worthless.

Jenner is a nihilistic apologist who not only grieves the hopelessness of the world but also the hopelessness of the self. That is, Jenner expresses the hopeless conditions the group has faced in the walker-infested world, exposing their own despair that hope is lost and that all aims are in vain. However, his monologue is also a public declaration of his perceived worthlessness, capitulating his destiny to the control of computers. He has no will to fight. For Jenner, even the fight for existence is merely petty. Accordingly, Marcel has written, "Man is capable of despair, capable of hugging death, of hugging his *own* death."[16]

> Pius Ojara comments,

> So long as disease, famine, war, glaring injustices and repression define and characterize the human condition and situation, suffering, loss and pain will always diminish human inner resources, possibilities and potentials. And life becomes visibly unattractive and meaningless.... Captivity in [this] human condition, which is essentially confinement to conditional values, cripples the human being, in his or her individual and social dimensions, in that they devitalize him or her.[17]

Quoting Marcel, Ojara continues: "In all suffering, I risk becoming self-centered and thus locking myself up in despair."[18]

The movement from despairing over the world about you to despairing for the world within, the *self*, should be an expected movement, however. The nihilist posture is that the world is void of meaning and all that exists is but an illusion—there is no real truth, no actual worth, no evident meaning. This logic must turn towards the executer of such judgment—I am meaningless. The nihilistic logic may be argued as follows:

> Everything that exists is meaningless.
> (*Cogito ergo sum* [I think, therefore I am]) I exist.
> Therefore, I am meaningless.

Part Two: Zombies

With such judgment despair crushes self-consciousness, provoking the embrace of self-nothingness. The ontological weight of self may be adjudicated as follows: "I am only what I am worth (but I am worth nothing)."[19] Such a despair of self ensures that one may die in despair, and, "To despair of one's self—is it not anticipating suicide?"[20]

The rejection of existence, in its totality, is not only a valuation of self as being worth less but also a judgment that "I" am worth less for others. It is akin to stating my life is wholly disposable and utterly unworthy of existence. It is the act of denying one's self as being an instrument of hope with and for others. It is the act so dramatically revealed through Noah Emmerich's portrayal of Dr. Jenner in the final episode of season one.

Positively, however, as stated by Gabriel Marcel, "The truth is that there can strictly speaking be no hope except when the temptation of despair exists. Hope is the act by which this temptation is actively or victoriously overcome."[21] That is, one does not have to give up. Rather, one does not have to consent "to be a useless creature which my . . . captivity may finally make of me."[22] Marcel continues, "I shall rise infinitely above this *fatum* to which I have never allowed myself to shut my eyes."[23] Despair is exactly what I resist.

Gather 'Round: Resisting Despair, Encountering Hope

There's always hope! Maybe it won't be you. Maybe not here . . .
But, somebody! Somewhere!

—Rick Grimes (Andrew Lincoln) S01E06

Jean Paul Sartre acknowledges, in the epigraph, that hope needs a foundation. Rick Grimes, in response to Dr. Jenner's despairing appeal, expresses, though with great uncertainty, that hope may be found with someone, somewhere. Founding hope in someone or somewhere will be the focus of the following. That is, throughout the first and second season (through episode 07) the embodied hope—hope founded in someone, somewhere—is what gives the community the strength and power to overcome despair. It is what I call the undercurrent of the narrative being developed in this series. Rick Grime's response to Dr. Jenner is but one that hints at this. Dale Horvath (Geoffry DeMunn), entering into the despair of Lori grieving her pregnancy and the joyless life her child may experience, provides further support of this undercurrent: "We can still find joy!" Dale exclaims (S02E06). He continues, "and we can . . . we can still take strength from each other." As the series has progressed, the promise and power of authentic interpersonal relationships to resist despair has been explored.

Donald MacKinnon has written, considering the dynamics of authentic relationships or communities that may overcome despair in the works of Gabriel Marcel: "human societies [are] enduring spiritual communities from whom individuals could, and indeed must, derive not only their elementary human formation but also a kind of interior strength powerful enough to sustain them in periods of personal disintegration and catastrophe."[24] This is a fitting summary of the philosophy of Marcel, who explored, extensively, through both careful philosophical work and creative play writing, the conditions and characteristics of authentic human relations. The conditions that make such relationships possible are availability, fidelity, and hope.

Availability, as a condition of authentic relations, is a particular posture or perception that the other, who stands before me, is one who has my full attention. The other confronts us with his/her existence, and the presence is "apprehended by the senses and in communication."[25] Such presence may be reciprocated in the relational encounter, yet it requires that I take a radical posture of submission, openness, or availability. This availability obliges me to hear the will of the other and to act responsibly for the other. That is, through the participation of presence, one becomes available to the other. To be present and available means that one is to be at the service of another, to listen and to hear the other in joy and in sorrow.

Karl Barth suggests that since we live and that we live in "indissoluble correlation"[26] to the lives of others, we are commissioned to accept the neighbor as an authority that counsels, corrects, and guides. It requires that we subordinate ourselves to the freedom of the other, so that we might not only hear, but that they might be known. Accordingly, one approaches the other, not as one who seeks to control something (an object), but as one who wills to know someone (a subject). Rick Grimes throughout this series has demonstrated his capacity to listen and to hear. He is clearly committed to being with and for his family—unlike Shane, who only wants Lori and Carl (the source of his failing), Rick's being for them has continued to serve as his vital strength. Such authentic

Part Two: Zombies

relationships, as Kim Paffenroth has noted, "are reliable sources of purpose for the characters and are shown to be capable of withstanding the destructive forces of an undead world."[27] Rick, however, seems to be the one character who is truly available not only for his family but for all whom he encounters, listening to and serving the others by his very posture and presence. Yet, Paffenroth suggests that the pattern of "reaching outside," and "making the newcomer a part of the family," is a common one throughout the series, noting a series of events that provoke one to wonder whether, "In a world where the dead walk, the living find it all the more imperative—and sometimes, ironically, even easier—to love one another."[28]

However, availability also requires fidelity. Availability suggests a radical recognition of the other's presence now. Fidelity, as the second condition of an authentic relationship, offers a promise that I will be here, with you and for you, regardless of what experience may come. It is a weighty act, which anchors a commitment to the other—a commitment that transcends time or place. It is an act of promise, or commitment, shown toward a person ("but never at all to a notion or an ideal"[29]). Moreover, it is an act of promise that is victorious over time: "Fidelity is linked up with fundamental ignorance of the future. A way of transcending time.... In swearing fidelity to a person, I do not know what future awaits us or even, in a sense, what person he will be tomorrow; the very fact of my not knowing is what gives worth and weight to my promise."[30] Accordingly, Marcel suggests that "fidelity is never fidelity to one's self, but is referred to ... the hold the other being has over us.... This hold is the term in relation to which even freedom is ordered and defined."[31] Sarah Katherine Pinnock comments further, "Fidelity is a promise to the [other] who is present, a promise of permanency and the resumption of the [relational encounter] stretching into the future, ... pointing towards a transcendent dimension of intersubjectivity ... beyond death into immortality."[32]

For the survivors gathered together, groping for direction, disturbed by the absence of meaning and purpose, facing a future that has become an option, availability and fidelity are vital. These categories serve as the essential acts that ground community and give it solidarity. That is, *The Walking Dead* television series depicts the despairing lives of many, but the story is much more than a nihilistic narrative. Simultaneously, in opposition, the story portrays a movement toward hope rooted in the response of some to enter the life of their neighbors (their co-survivors) in haste, without want, and out of genuine empathy. The choice to enter into human suffering by submitting to the life of the other and suffering alongside is a potent undercurrent that supports this series in offering a very real depiction of human life, though in quite unreal circumstances.

Rick is the central protagonist who not only demonstrates availability but also fidelity. Time and again Rick expresses the seriousness and permanency of his promise. He is revealed to be a partner and friend to Shane, a husband to Lori, a father to Carl, and the leader of the survivors. In each encounter, Rich seeks to enter into authentic relationship demonstrating a capacity not only to listen and to hear but also to offer himself as one whom the others may trust. We see this, for example, in his fierce defense of the survivors against all that may harm them including harm from within the group. We see this in his willingness to put himself at risk for the sake and safety of the others. We see this in his decision to leave guns and ammunition with Guillermo and the Vatos at the elderly care facility. We see this in his continued endeavors to leave radio messages for Morgan and his son, Duane. We see this in his wisdom to mediate the wants and needs of the two communities forced together on the farm—even when the decisions he makes are not well received. However, Rick's posture of availability and promise of fidelity is particularly evident in his relationships with Lori and Shane. He is living for them, in haste and without want, choosing to forgive even their lies, deception, and infidelity.

By way of contrast, Shane has consistently demonstrated a lack of availability and fidelity. We know this from the first season as we discover that he left Rick in the hospital to die. We see it again as he advances on Lori in the CDC bunker. We see it again and again. But the story of Shane's self-centeredness and failing to resist despair is revealed early in the second season as he begins to make plans to leave the group as contempt for Rick grows and as desires for Lori and affection toward Carl are stifled. However, authenticity as a man-for-others is most profoundly devastated by the violence at the school, where Shane takes Otis' life while fleeing the walkers—deceiving the others about heroics and sacrifice. After this event, Shane embodies despair changing his appearance as he shaves his head reflecting the new man that he has become—a man for himself enraged by the walkers' existence and desirous of that which he cannot have.

Indeed, many people do lose themselves in the abyss of nothingness because nobody is waiting on the other side of today. But Shane has lost himself because he alone sees no one to wait for. He seeks to satisfy only himself. However, Rick seems to wait with and for everyone. Accordingly, it is the call of Marcel's availability and fidelity to enter into the void of loneliness and despair so that the other, one's neighbor, may know that someone is waiting with and for her. The phrases, "I will wait with you," and, "I am here for you," are expressions of solidarity, which break through the nothingness of despair, overcoming its looming shadow. It is here the unconditional promise, the expression of solidarity by the one who hears and waits, may break the bonds of hopelessness and restores meaning—not meaning through ideals, but through authentic relationships among persons. The critical point is that one must become involved in the lives of others. Solidarity, in this way, also liberates the one who hears and waits. This is the strength that liberates Rick to make the tough choices and continue to lead the others in service and sacrifice.

Availability and fidelity, then, are not only essential acts for the other, but also liberating for the self. Consider Marcel's play, *Un Homme de Dieu* [A Man of God]. This is a play centered around the life of a pastor despairing of his own life as the world about him has fallen to ruin. He is a man, not too dissimilar from Dr. Jenner above—seemingly gripping on to death. But despair is overcome as he confronts the needs of another. He allows himself not only to hear of the needs of, but also to wait with an elderly woman for whom he bears certain pastoral obligations. Though the obligation is small, seemingly insignificant, "he comes to realize that his personal disintegration does not bring the world to an end."[33] Rather, as MacKinnon comments, "the world goes on curiously oblivious to the turmoil raging within his spirit, taking notice of him only as a man with particular responsibilities that it presumes he will (health and other circumstances permitting) fulfill in the usual way."[34] That is, one might suggest that the meaninglessness or absurdity of the world about us will continue, but the movement to participate in, with, and for the life of another may be the essential move to resist despair.

Put another way, the world where the dead walk seems ugly, bad, and without hope. But that's exactly what Rick resists. Though he knows he will die, he will die in hope. But, as Sartre stated above, that hope needs a foundation. As I have argued above, the foundation of hope rests in the responsibility to be with and for the ever-present other—to become the wounded co-sufferer, whose embodied presence and promise is hope. This posture of hearing and waiting, of availability and fidelity, for people who suffer (and as people who suffer) serves to catalyze the movement toward hope—it catalyzes Rick's continued labor with and for the survivors.

THE THEOLOGICAL FOUNDATION OF SOLIDARITY: CHRIST, MAN FOR HUMANITY

In his March 4, 1949 poem, Dietrich Bonhoeffer asks the question, "Who am I?" He weaves together a series of thoughts about who he has pretended to be, but feels he is not. The response he gives is one not too dissimilar from that of Dr. Jenner above—alone he is none of these illusions of being. He closes the piece, though with these words, "Who am I? They mock me, these lonely questions of mine. Whoever I am, Thou knowest, O God, I am Thine."[35] This conclusion is deeply rooted in Bonhoeffer's Christology, but it also grounds his humanism. That is, in the desperate search for meaning amidst great trial and suffering, turmoil and absurdity, the incarnation for Bonhoeffer is central to understanding not only his humanism but also his rich and guiding social theory. Specifically, Bonhoeffer's Christology illumines his "affirmation of life in its fullness amidst struggle and suffering."[36] Indeed, as John de Gruchy notes, human dignity takes centre stage, though that stage is built upon the incarnation and cross. In this place, one is directed toward God's "No," which is known only in light of God's "Yes" that surrounds it, in Jesus Christ. Here, he affirms that Bonhoeffer's humanism is richly constructed from this pattern where the Divine "Yes," affords an understanding of creation, becoming, honor, and flourishing, in contrast to and in opposition against death, suffering, degradation and resignation.[37]

In Bonhoeffer's own words,

> God did not become an idea, a principle, a program, a universally valid belief, or a law. God became human. That means ... Christ does not abolish human reality in favor of an idea that demands to be realized against all that is real. Christ empowers reality, affirming it as the real human being and thus the ground of all human reality.[38]

Indeed, these words oppose the vision of an unrealized, untrue, and unsatisfactory human existence founded upon the failure to actualize certain ideals, or the devaluation of values, as the nihilist would argue. Rather, in suffering, frailty, and limitedness—in every noble and ignoble part of the human being—Bonhoeffer argues that Christ reveals an all-embracing humanism.[39]

Christ is really human. He is not a projected ideal or reinterpretation of Nietzsche's *Übermensch* (overman, superman). The incarnation defines God's relation to the world; such that, in Christ, "the reality of God encounters the reality of the world and allows us to take part in this real encounter."[40] That is, "[Jesus] is not *a* human being, but *the* human being. What happened to him happens to human beings. It happens to all and therefore to us."[41] In an act of solidarity, God occupies time and space, vindicating human existence as authentic, real, and good. Consequently, for Bonhoeffer, authentic human life means being human in the gratuitousness of Christ's life, death, and resurrection—"The message of God's becoming human attacks the heart of an era when contempt for humanity or idolization of humanity is the height of all wisdom."[42]

Karl Barth agrees:

> [I]f the humanity of Jesus is originally and totally and genuinely fellow-humanity this means that He is man for other men in the most comprehensive and radical sense. He does not merely help His fellows from without, standing alongside, making a contribution and then withdrawing again and leaving them to themselves until further help is perhaps required. . . . [Rather] It means that He interposes Himself for them, that He gives Himself to them, that He puts Himself in their place, that He makes their state and fate His own cause, so that it is no longer theirs but His, conducted by Him in His own name and on His own responsibility.[43]

Barth considers Jesus to be so radically for humanity that he is "fully claimed and clamped by His fellows, by their state and fate, by their lowliness and misery; to have no other cause but . . . to live and work for His fellows and their salvation."[44]

Thus, nothingness, as described above, is very real for both Barth and for Bonhoeffer. However, in His act of availability and fidelity, "God Himself willed to become a creature in the creaturely world, yielding and subjecting Himself to [despair] in Jesus Christ in order to overcome it."[45] The pattern of this peculiar theological foundation, God-for-us in Jesus Christ, has profound implications, for it has the capacity to fashion a Christian humanism that may "struggle for truth and justice against dehumanizing power [against nothingness], . . . always affirming human goodness against perversity, hope against despair, and life against death."[46]

Accordingly, from the theological model that Bonhoeffer and Barth illumine, the following may serve as a summary of their work: from Christ everything has its being, and to Christ everything will return, including the becoming human who, in participation with Christ, living with and for others, may become truly human. The responsibility, as humans, is to "belong together—irrevocably and undividedly."[47] Thus, solidarity (availability and fidelity), considered in the theology of Barth and Bonhoeffer, alike, indicates that human persons, individuals to be sure, come into being and flourish in community. Accordingly, *being-in-community* demands humility, as one encounters the other who ought not to be conceived as "the other" to be opposed, but as the one whom we are commissioned, in participation with Christ, to live with and for.

Therefore, the embodied act of solidarity, the task of hearing and waiting, finds its foundation in Christ, who hears and waits. Such embodied solidarity results in a conformation with Christ that may reorient one's existence, one's very being-in-action, "toward the actual lives and needs of [the other]."[48] That is, the doctrine of incarnation articulated by both Barth and Bonhoeffer may serve as the reorienting narrative, which provokes responsibility to follow after Christ with the simultaneous responsibility to be one-for-the-other—and this is our hope. Rather, "Jesus Christ is our hope."[49]

SOLIDARITY IS OUR HOPE

Gabriel Marcel writes, "[Hope] is really a prophetic power. It has no bearing on what *should* be or even what *must* be; it just says, 'This will be.'"[50] But, *what* will be?

It is vital to recognize that not just any sort of hope is an authentic, valid, or true hope. "After all," as argued above, "pessimism is partially fuelled by increased disillusionment with previous dominant [hopes]."[51] But, as founded above, the sort of hope, of which I am now speaking, is the hope embodied and enacted in Christ. It is the sort of hope in which we participate. It is the sort of hope that transforms—or rather, transfigures—our despairing existence, to one of mutual service and faithful labor toward the open, yet reconciled, future. However, as John C. McDowell

Part Two: Zombies

has commented on Barth's theology of hope, "the future being 'open' ... is not 'open' in the sense of being neutral or indeterminate, a nothingness waiting to be filled by human acts."[52] Rather, McDowell explains, considering Karl Marx's (and by proxy Barth's own) understanding of hope's regulative function, "the Future casts its shadow over all contemporary contexts ... redirecting the vision of those alienated from the products of their labor, each other, and themselves."[53]

The vision which Christ embodies, offers a very real vision of hope overcoming despair. In this, in Him, one is redirected to consider hope as an ethics, which "seeks to liberate humanity from all things that dehumanize it, act against needless suffering, and participate in God's 'de-demonising' of the world."[54] With this, Gabriel Marcel may be correct to suggest that reflecting on the tenuous fragility of existence as well as those conditions that tempt toward despair is critical for the formation of hopeful action—for a hope that "always has to do with the restoration (transfiguration) of a certain living order."[55]

Consequently, it is essential that one not only acknowledges the world as it is but accepts it.[56] Moreover, it is critical that one, in waiting, does not sit in contentment or consternation, but hastens to human action: to live for the world, to suffer with the world, and to protest, quite candidly, about its need, while simultaneously proclaiming the joyful hope of its being overcome.[57] Acceptance *and* reconciliation, acknowledgement *and* protest—such is the characteristic reality of hope, embodied in Christ.

This is the simple wisdom of the theology of Dietrich Bonhoeffer and Karl Barth (and Gabriel Marcel, in his own way). The point of being for the world, being with and for the other in radical solidarity, is to afford a vision of reality, a timeless and authentic reality, which finds rest in Jesus Christ, reconciler of all. It is a vision that has the strength to overcome despair for the present situation—which, no matter how intolerable, is not, and cannot be final. Solidarity is hope for humanity.

The embodiment of hope may be theologically rooted and may find its foundation in Christ, as argued above. People may participate in Hope as they are directed and formed by His act of solidarity, to embody and perform similar acts towards the liberation and redemption of the world—or rather, for the liberation of a broken world and for the broken individual.

In this television series, Dale Horvath has been a character who has embodied solidarity as he has taken up the task of hearing and of waiting—living with and for those gathered by the despair of life and undeath.

We are introduced to Dale in the second episode of the first season as he stands, in typical posture, atop the motor home. Lori gives word to Dale that she is wandering off and he is to watch after Carl. Dale offers a word of caution and of care, "Don't wander too far. . . . And, if you see anything, holler. I'll come runnin." Lori replies, "Yes, Mom."

The term, "Mom," here may be appropriate for it provides a clue as to how Dale is perceived in the camp. He is the one who, ever vigilant with unconditional concern, as mothers often are, has invested in the lives of the others: they are his family for whom he lives. "I'll come running," is the promise of fidelity. With this expression, Dale serves to remind Lori that he is there, regardless of what experience may come. Though this scene is very brief, Dale's character is revealed and his story of availability, fidelity, and hope begins to unfold.

His most profound exercise of solidarity, however, may be his willingness to wait with Andrea in the CDC, which is soon to be annihilated. This expression of solidarity, this embodiment of fidelity unto death, also liberates Andrea from her despair, if only for a moment, serving her with the strength to flee the grip of death. The scene is a memorable one as Dale responds to Andrea's cry of despair: "If you're staying, I stay, too. He's right, we know what's waiting for us out there. I don't want to face it alone. . . . I'm staying! The matter is settled."

For Dale, the matter is settled. At some time, as this group of survivors came together, Dale submitted himself to Andrea, choosing to care for her as his own. As such, he has embodied not only an availability to be responsible for her but has expressed, with certainty, that he is there for her—regardless of what may come. "I'm staying! . . . The matter is settled." In his practice of hope, Dale puts himself in Andrea's place, offering to share her state and fate as his own. He enacts radical availability and timeless fidelity as he sits alongside and proclaims, "If you're staying, I stay too. . . . The matter is settled." This enactment is in fact the embodiment of solidarity, which is our hope. It is the very act which, as a participation in the solidarity of Christ (God-for-us), grounds a hope "that can fragilely (since it is perennially prone to failure, weakness, and ideology), and humbly (no thoughts and actions are identical with, while they may have a certain analogy to, those of God), live even through and after the horrors of [*The Walking Dead*]."[58]

Part Two: Zombies

However, Dale may not offer the most consistent example of solidarity as hope. We see Dale continue to be with Andrea. However, his methods of nurturing their relationship seem to become much more emotionally manipulative. It leaves room to question whether or not he is *for* her. That is, during the second season, one might question Dale's authenticity.

Nevertheless, another expression of solidarity as hope may be seen in the way Dr. Hershel Greene responds to the walkers. Particularly, Greene serves to offer a character radically committed to see through death, and undeath, the timelessness of fidelity. He is the embodiment of hope for those for whom existence is in question, as he continues to proclaim, in his continued expression of solidarity, that you are not without value: here hope rages against despair. Yet, there are certain conditions that continue to tempt Dr. Greene.

We learn in the fifth episode of the second season, that the barn is home to a horde of walkers. In the following episode, Dale, responsibly, confronts Dr. Greene regarding the secret; Dale expresses how those he has cared about have died and come back as walkers—no longer people. The conclusion one might draw here, is that his responsibility to live for those he cares does end. His expression of fidelity may not transcend (un)death. In contrast, Dr. Greene responds that those in the barn remain his family: they remain, whatever their state, those he intends to be with and for. Similarly, the action of others throughout the series demonstrate a higher regard for the undead. Rick, for example, says to the torso-zombie dragging her gray and colorless body across the lush green grass of a city park, "I am sorry this has happened to you." This expression of profound regret precedes Rick's action intending to allay her torment.

However, the knowledge that the walkers are contained in the barn unsettles the entire camp. It also unsettles Dr. Greene. In fact, Greene seems conflicted throughout the second season as his commitment to be for the other is tested by their encounter with the outside group. Though it seems quite radical for Dr. Greene to continue to demonstrate fidelity to his family (and even other walkers they encounter), it may in fact be more difficult for him to demonstrate the same type of availability, fidelity, and embodied hope to those he holds with eminent suspicion—Rick, Shane, and the others.

The flurry of gunfire and hastened rage which closes the seventh episode of the second season only adds to the developing storylines of despair and of hope. I am left wondering, will the relationships dissolve and despair overwhelm? Or, will despair find right resistance, in solidarity as hope.

CONCLUSION

As argued above, two overlapping storylines are being drawn out as we journey with those who have survived the zombie-apocalypse. The first is the story of increasing sorrow and the oppressive torment of despair. It is one that reflects a great deal on real life, though in quite unreal circumstances here, and with episodic tensions. We are incessantly plagued with the great terrors of our day and the absurdities of violence and warfare, of injustice and hate, of all that which seems ugly and bad and without hope.

However, there is the second storyline, which must be considered: this is one of embodied hope and the encounter with the other that fosters authentic relationships that grant meaning to existence, in spite of and in resistance to the pressing despair. It is a story that may reflect, in a strange way, where and in whom one may encounter hope—challenging hopes that escape this life, thereby offering an enduring hope, founded upon the relational encounter. It is a hope that allies itself with life, in all its noble and ignoble expressions, creating communities whose embodied solidarity may keep hope alive. In this, the expression of Christian hope for Christ's future, which he brings to us in his incarnation, death, and resurrection, may be an appropriate guide as we continue to invest our times and our thoughts in this ongoing television series, *The Walking Dead*.

Thus, it may be wise to continue to keep our attention on Rick Grimes who may serve as the key to this reading of *The Walking Dead*. He is certainly the one who has consistently, though not necessarily clemently, embodied hope as he navigates through life with and for the others—as the embodiment of hope that may resist against despair.

END NOTES

1. An interview of Jean Paul Sartre by Benny Levy was published in the 25 March 1980 edition of *Le Nouvel Observateur*. The epigraph is a translation of some of Sartre's final thoughts. He died one month following. Translations of the interview may also be found in the 1980 editions of *Telos* (Summer) and *Dissent* (Fall). However, for a masterful translation of the interviews, see Sartre and Levy, *Hope Now*, 109–10.

Part Two: Zombies

2. *The Walking Dead* television series is broadcast via the American Movie Classics (AMC) cable channel, which is a subsidiary of AMC Networks™.
3. A play on Shakespeare's phrase from *The Tempest*: "Oh, Brave New World! That has such people in it"; Shakespeare, *The Tempest*, 62. However, some may be familiar with this phrase, which John the Savage repeated in Huxley's *Brave New World*. See Huxley, *Brave New World*, 209.
4. Nietzsche, *The Will to Power*, 12–13, 22, 36.
5. Ibid., 318. One may explore nihilism further in the great writings of many thinkers, including but not limited to Baruch Spinoza, Immanuel Kant, G. W. F. Hegel, Jean Paul Sartre and Gilles Deleuze. Conor Cunningham has written a superb though challenging book entitled, *Genealogy of Nihilism*, where he walks the reader through these and many others who have contributed to the ongoing dialogue about nothing. See Cunningham, *Geneology of Nihilism*.
6. Nietzsche, *The Will to Power*, 9, 11. Emphasis in the original.
7. Ibid., 12. Emphasis in the original.
8. Reginster, *The Affirmation of Life*, 25: "The meaning of [an agent's] life, the point of living, so to speak, depends not just on his being committed to certain values or ideals, but also on the belief that the world is hospitable to their realization."
9. Nietzsche, *The Will to Power*, 14.
10. Reginster, *Affirmation of Life*, 29–30.
11. Nietzsche, *The Will to Power*, 22.
12. Sartre, *Hope Now*, 110.
13. Ibid., 318.
14. Nietzsche, *Thus Spoke Zarathustra*, 228: "It's not worth it anymore to live, all is the same, all is in vain."
15. Marcel, *Homo Viator*, 37–38.
16. Marcel, *Being and Having*, 104. Emphasis in the original.
17. Ojara and Madigan, *Marcel, Girard, Bakhtin*, 22.
18. Ibid.
19. Marcel, *Being and Having*, 104.
20. Ibid., 80.
21. Marcel, *Homo Viator*, 36.; Marcel, considering hope and despair, writes on December 9th 1931, "I return to the problem of hope. It seems to me that the conditions that make it possible to hope are strictly the same as those which make it possible to despair. Death considered as the springboard of an absolute hope. A world where death was missing would be a world where hope only existed in the larval stage" (*Being and Having*, 93).
22. Marcel, *Homo Viator*, 38.
23. Ibid.

24. MacKinnon, "Drama and Memory (1984)," 182.
25. Pinnock, "Existential Encounter with Evil, 30.
26. Barth, *Ethics*, 263–64.
27. Kim Paffenroth, "For Love Is Strong as Death," 226.
28. Ibid.
29. Marcel, *Being and Having*, 96.
30. Ibid., 47.
31. Ibid., 46, 54.
32. Pinnock, "Existential Encounter," 31.
33. MacKinnon, "Drama and Memory (1984)," 182.
34. Ibid.
35. Bonhoeffer, *Letters and Papers*, 348.
36. Zimmerman and Gregor, *Being Human*, 17.
37. Ibid., 18.
38. Bonhoeffer, *Ethics*, 99.
39. Zimmerman and Gregor, *Being Human*, 27.
40. Bonhoeffer, *Ethics*, 159.
41. Ibid., 85.
42. Ibid. "Only because God became human it is possible to know and not despise real human beings. Real human beings may live before God, and we may let these real people live beside us and before God without either despising or idolizing them. This is not because of the real human being's inherent value, but because God has loved and taken on the real human being. The reason for God's love for human being does not reside in them, but only in God. Our living as real human beings, and loving the real people next to us is, again, grounded only in God's becoming human, in the unfathomable love of God for us human beings" (Bonhoeffer, *Ethics*, 87).
43. Barth, *Church Dogmatics*, §45, 9.
44. Ibid., III.3 §45, 12, 13.
45. Ibid., III.3 §50, 16.
46. Zimmerman and Gregor, *Being Human Thought*, 24.
47. Ibid., 64.
48. Ibid., 188.
49. Barth, *Credo*, 120.
50. Marcel, *Being and Having*, 79. Emphasis in the original.
51. McDowell, "For What May We Hope?," 2. As I have alluded to in this essay, Shane had anchored his hope upon filling his partner's shoes as the provider and protector of Lori and Carl. Additionally, he was regarded as the leader of the group. His hopes were founded on position and an idea of family. The death

Part Two: Zombies

of these with the resurrection of Rick from the dead may, in fact, be that which is fueling Shane's nihilistic turn and moving him towards even more profound acts of self-service and violence.

52. Ibid., 3.
53. Ibid.
54. Ibid., 3–4.
55. Marcel, *Being and Having*, 75. Rick wrestles with despair as his son, Carl, clings to life. He wrestles with his choice to bring Carl along in the search for Sophia Peletier (Madison Lintz). He argues, in concert with Shane, whether it was the right decision to search after the lost girl. He continued to repeat the imperative, "When a girl goes missing, you search for her." In this, he is trying to determine, once again, the order of things, wrestling with despair to determine the way of the future.
56. "There is no part of the world, no matter how lost, no matter how godless, that has not been accepted by God in Jesus Christ and reconciled to God. Whoever perceives the body of Jesus Christ in faith can no longer speak of the world as if it were lost, as if it were separated from God; they can no longer separate themselves in clerical pride from the world. The world belongs to Christ, and only in Christ is the world what it is . . . Christ has died for the world, and Christ is Christ only in the midst of the world" (Bonhoeffer, *Ethics*, 67).
57. Karl Barth praises Christoph Blumhardt's capacity to proclaim Christ as our hope in the afterword of Blumhardt's *Action in Waiting*. He writes of Blumhardt, "On the one hand he has insight into the needs of the world, and on the other hand he possesses the joyful hope of its being overcome" (Blumhardt, *Action in Waiting*, 191).
58. McDowell, "For What May We Hope?," 4.

8

Apocalyptic Images and Prophetic Function in Zombie Films[1]

KIM PAFFENROTH

THIS ESSAY WILL EXAMINE how current zombie films—although they depict the apocalypse in outwardly secular terms as a mass plague, usually with no explicit mention of God—nonetheless frequently use that apocalypse to pass judgment on current American society and sinfulness, often sounding much like Old Testament prophets in their decrying of sins and announcement of judgment.[2] The essay will focus on the films of George Romero, whose *Night of the Living Dead* (1968) defined the current zombie genre, taking the monster from its roots in magic and transforming it into a peculiarly modern scourge. As will be shown, the resulting films are recognizably biblical in their apocalyptic imagery, and their prophetic denunciation of the society in which their creator and audience lives.

First, one should probably note the sheer ubiquity of the humble zombie today. Until Stephenie Meyer's *Twilight* series (2006 and following), it was as though vampires had disappeared from popular culture, and only the zombie remained as the chief representative of the undead. The zombie had always appeared in films, at least as far back as *White Zombie* (1932), but the new millennium saw many more of these than previous decades. It also saw a diversification among the various films, from the straightforwardly horrific depictions of George Romero (*Land*

145

Part Two: Zombies

of the Dead [2005] and *Diary of the Dead* [2007]) and his followers like Zack Snyder (*Dawn of the Dead* [2004]) and Danny Boyle (*28 Days Later* [2002]), to comedies like *Shaun of the Dead* (2004), *Fido* (2006), and *Zombie Strippers* (2008). Zombies are favorite targets in video games, led by the *Resident Evil* franchise, which spun off into films (2002, 2004, and 2007). They have also increasingly shambled on to the printed page, either in comic book or graphic novel form, as with the immensely popular *Walking Dead* series (2003 and following)—which has now given us the first zombie hit television series; or in novels and short stories, most notably with the hugely successful *World War Z* (2006) by Max Brooks. Though Brooks is the best known author in this genre, many other writers now exploit the narrative possibilities of the zombie, including Brian Keene (e.g., *The Rising* [2003] and *City of the Dead* [2005]), David Wellington (the *Monster Island* trilogy [2004–2006]), and even the author of this essay (*Dying to Live* [2007], *Dying to Live: Life Sentence* [2008], and *Dying to Live: Last Rites* [2011]). As with the films, the literary world of zombies has expanded and diversified, and now includes such highbrow parody as Seth Grahame-Smith's *Pride and Prejudice and Zombies* (2009), and the romantic comedy of S. G. Browne's *Breathers* (2009).

The "rules" of zombies have been fairly consistent throughout all these works, building on the depiction first put forward by Romero in his movie *Night of the Living Dead* (1968).[3] These are not Haitian or voodoo zombies, animated by magic and under the control of a summoner's will.[4] Instead, they are a recognizably modern monster, their magical or supernatural elements rationalized to fit contemporary sensibilities. Zombies in these current depictions are either living people infected with some virus (*28 Days Later*), or people killed by a virus that then causes their bodies to reanimate (Romero's more "traditional" zombie, now called by many fans, simply "Romero zombies" or zombies that follow the "Romero rules"). They are not afraid of garlic, holy water, crucifixes, or any other talisman. They can not be killed by running water or sunlight or a stake through the heart, but only with the very brutal act of destroying their brains, usually with a spectacular head-shot, decapitation, or a beating that reduces their skulls to broken, bloody piles. They cannot fly or turn into a bat; they have average strength and way below-average intelligence, speed, and coordination. When pursuing live humans, they are as likely to stumble off a cliff or stagger into a whirling blade or electrified fence, as they are to succumb to the counterattacks of the living. So weak are they, zombies only pose a threat when attacking as a mob. Zombies are overwhelmingly ordinary, which is to say, they are terribly and fully human. This ultimately, I think, is their appeal, for they seem so much more "real" to us than more superhuman monsters, such as vampires and werewolves.

It should be noted, however, that the "scientific" explanation offered in the current mythos is so mysterious as to be functionally equivalent to "magic": the disease works with a speed unknown among any terrestrial disease ever before seen, killing in seconds in some films, and it is not only 100% fatal, but also has the power to reanimate a human body with at least limited motor skills and memory—and apparently, also to keep the body from noticeably decaying way past its normal "shelf life," as some of the stories take place years or even decades after the initial devastation. The virus is pretty clearly functioning to serve the narrative needs of the story, which is to fill the world with walking corpses, and watch how the characters react.[5] The characters themselves seem to strain against the "scientific" framework that is imposed on them, and sometimes give what almost seems the more plausible explanation—that this is a curse or judgment from an angry God (*Dawn of the Dead* [both 1978 and 2004]), something akin to many of God's statements in the book of Ezekiel: "Thus says the Lord God: Disaster after disaster! See, it comes. An end has come, the end has come. . . . My eye will not spare; I will have no pity. . . . The sword and is outside, pestilence and famine are inside; those in the field die by the sword; those in the city—famine and pestilence devour them" (Ezek 7:5, 9, 15).

However the process got started, zombies rapidly increase their numbers by attacking and killing uninfected people, who then die and become zombies themselves. The particularly horrible addition made by Romero is that zombies partially eat their victims. This not only enables the film-maker or author to create scenes of grotesque cannibalism and dismemberment, but it also raises the symbolic stakes of the zombie. Unlike the seductive vampire, who often bites his/her victim on the neck in a very erotic, sensuous embrace, the zombie tears people limb from limb, savagely flinging a bloody barrage of intestines and organs all over, while greedily stuffing some morsels into its snarling mouth. There is nothing attractive or sensual about a zombie attack—it is animalistic and sickening. But since zombies look exactly like living human beings, their cannibalism also brings out the image of humanity preying on itself—the self-destructive and sadistic elements of all people, which have been seen on killing fields all across the "real" world, even without a zombie virus to excuse the behavior. One of the more artful uses of this parallelism is found in the framing of *Land of the Dead*, which begins with a brutal massacre of zombies by gleefully laughing humans, and ends with a zombie feeding frenzy on the hapless human population. Human violence reaps what it sows; the fiction of zombies just makes this more graphic.

Because the zombie hordes multiply so rapidly, the outcome in almost all zombie fiction and films is an apocalypse, an end of the world as we know it: an end of "civilized" life and the ushering in of an indeterminately long age of barbarism, terror, and violence—or perhaps, even, a nihilistic end to all movement on the planet's surface, should the zombies devour everything and leave themselves with nothing left to eat or do. Also, in the original meaning of "apocalyptic," the cataclysm of murderous corpses also "reveals" terrible truths about human nature, existence, and sin, since the zombies are themselves only human. This apocalyptic aspect of zombies is made perhaps the most explicit in the *Dawn of the Dead* (2004) remake, which uses the haunting, apocalyptic Johnny Cash song, "The Man Comes Around," for the opening credits.[6] On the one hand, it is the most brutally and universally hopeless song imaginable: it ends with death and hellfire engulfing the entire earth at God's instigation. In that sense, it is the perfect choice for the movie, as ultimately all the characters are horribly killed. But in apocalyptic—whether it is the Bible's or Cash's or *Dawn of the Dead*'s interpretation of it—there is always some sense that choices still matter, that how we live our lives is important, even if the same horrible, inevitable, and equalizing death awaits each of us. In the song this is expressed in several lines, especially in the assurance that different groups of people receive very different treatment on the Judgment Day. Such reestablishment of righteousness is seriously undermined in much current horror, which is often nihilistic, and depicts everything as ultimately meaningless and random. Such a dismal evaluation is seen in Romero's earlier films, especially *Night of the Living Dead*, but here in the *Dawn* remake a sense of justice reappears, not just in the song, but in how the characters behave and how they die.[7] The ignoble characters die without any pity from us, even with a sense of our approval. And though the noble characters are also dead by the end, they die with our compassion and admiration. Exactly as in Revelation, where many of the elect die, this film shows that biological death (or life) should not be our only focus and is not the source of value in our lives.

Whether or not zombie films have a full sense of apocalypse—both as end of the world and as vindication of the just—and despite their eschewing a supernatural cause for the outbreak, one way in which they consistently resemble the biblical prophets is the strong sense of moral outrage and condemnation of the society in which the film-maker or prophet lives. This has been a visible, even blatant component of Romero's work throughout his career; it is what distinguishes his work from many of the lesser luminaries working in the horror genre.[8] The Hebrew prophets are known for railing against the moral deficiencies and sinful excesses they saw in contemporary Israel and Judah. The prophet Amos is particularly well-known for his denunciation of the economic disparity between rich and poor: "Therefore because you trample on the poor and take from them levies of grain, you have built houses of hewn stone, but you shall not live in them; you have planted pleasant vineyards, but you shall not drink their wine" (Amos 5:11). Another favorite target of the prophets' ire was the smug complacency and reliance on the people's "chosenness" as somehow insulating them from possible misfortune, rather than demanding a higher level of ethical commitment and devotion to justice: "Its [Israel's] rulers give judgment for a bribe, its priests teach for a price, its prophets give oracles for money; yet they lean upon the Lord and say 'Surely the Lord is with us! No harm shall come upon us'" (Mic 3:11; cf. Matt 3:9; Luke 3:8). Romero repeatedly returns to the current versions of those sins in modern America,[9] usually presented as consumerism (not just the hoarding of wealth, but the definition and valuation of oneself as a consumer of goods), and racism (which may well include nationalism, similar to Israel's discounting of other peoples as somehow less in God's eyes, but with the added animosity and oppression of racial minorities within the United States). I will consider these two elements of social criticism in three of the five Romero zombie films, produced between 1968 and 2005.[10]

Romero's first zombie film, *Night of the Living Dead* (1968), which has virtually defined the depiction of the undead since, also established—albeit in a muted and indirect manner—the films' tradition of critiquing a society they depict as lost and unfaithful to its calling as a force for justice in the world. Romero's critique is perhaps most similar to that of the prophet Jeremiah, who depicted his people as faithlessly turning from the higher purposes they had been given by God: "How can you say, 'We are wise, and the law of the Lord is with us,' when, in fact, the false pen of the scribes has made it into a lie? The wise shall be put to shame, they shall be dismayed and taken; since they have rejected the word of the Lord, what wisdom is in them?" (Jer 8:8–9). Given its time, the appearance of a

Part Two: Zombies

black protagonist in the film could not help but be remarked on by many viewers and critics, even though the race of the protagonist, Ben, is never noted or mentioned by the characters in the movie.[11] It is hard for viewers sometimes not to "read" back into the film a reaction that is not there, and even critics have asserted that the antagonist, Harry Cooper, is a racist or bigot,[12] but there is no real hint of this in the film itself. But even though the posse that kills Ben at the end makes no remark about his race (they may not even be able to tell his skin color when they shoot him through a darkened window at a great distance), Romero seems to go out of his way to surround the posse with imagery that makes it nearly impossible to overlook their similarity to an American lynch mob—a crowd of exclusively white men, only loosely governed by governmental authorities, with guns and barking dogs, killing everything in their path.[13] Moreover, in their role as protectors and re-establishers of societal order—which is to say, white, American, capitalist order—against the zombies' chaos, the posse's killing of a black man may be meant to equate him with the zombies, as a perceived threat to that order.[14] If racism is not explicitly raised by the film, many of the trappings of it are used as background, subtly hinting at its presence in contemporary American society—and with the film's violent, nihilistic ending, hinting at racism's catastrophic results to the health of our country.

Romero's second zombie film, *Dawn of the Dead* (1978), begins with a much more blatant and explicit depiction of racism in the United States. At the very beginning of the film, a SWAT team storms a zombie-infested apartment building, inhabited by blacks and Latinos. Before the siege begins, one police officer expresses the stereotypical, white American rant against government aid to minorities, by claiming that the housing project is an unfair handout and waste: "Shit, man, this is better than I got!" He then begins gleefully and indiscriminately shooting both living and undead people in the head. The transition from a fairly commonly-heard rant against government assistance, immediately into a murderous rampage, seems a pretty pointed criticism of those who use such rhetoric: if societal rules and restraints were to break down, Romero implies, some in the United States would quickly escalate from racist rhetoric to racist violence. Comments made by a United States congressman after hurricane Katrina would tend to make one believe Romero's cynicism was not misplaced or overstated: the congressman joked that the storm—whose official death toll was 1,844—had "finally cleaned up public housing in New Orleans."[15] In this sense, the congressman is following what seems one of the less helpful tendencies of apocalyptic—its tendency toward sectarianism and an "us versus them" mentality (in this case, "us" as the wealthy, white, and in power; "them" as the unruly minorities and poor),[16] while Romero's vision is closer to Old Testament prophecy with its warnings against self-righteousness and a feeling of moral or ethnic superiority.

But *Dawn of the Dead* moves on to consider more positive relations between the races. The most endearing and frequent image is that of a deep friendship between Roger (white) and Peter (African-American).[17] Their rapport begins under fire, highlighting how the shared experience of suffering and horror often brings people together and transcends their differences. Like other famous film and literary couples or trios, they are complementary, completing each other's thoughts and actions.[18] Roger spends a good deal of the movie on his deathbed after a zombie attack; the scenes between them are touching, as two very macho and laconic characters try not to express their feelings. Peter is also entrusted with shooting his friend before he can rise as a zombie. Again, enacting what rites seem appropriate to his macho demeanor, Peter drinks a toast at his friend's grave. The whole relationship seems quite believable, and their differing races are never mentioned: they are simply and sincerely friends, because fate has brought them together under the horrible circumstances that it has.

Dawn of the Dead goes further, however, than the relatively safe subject of an interracial friendship, daring to tread into what is still mostly taboo in mainstream films—an interracial, heterosexual couple of Peter, a black man, and Fran, a white woman. The film's end is utterly ambiguous as to the couple's ultimate fate, but what is clear is that the future of humanity—whether it is measured in minutes or centuries—will be based on this interracial couple.[19] Whether their life together will be happy—leaving aside the problems of the undead for a moment—is unknown, but how they might relate to each other with a new and better respect, overcoming racial and sexual tensions and expectations, is hinted at earlier in the film. Of all the male characters, Peter is the most polite and respectful towards Fran. He expresses this at their first meeting, even though Fran has just insulted him by objecting to his escaping with them in a helicopter. This is made more awkward, with the two sitting next to each other, but Peter effectively defuses it in the following exchange.

Part Two: Zombies

> Peter (nodding toward Steve): "He your man?"
>
> Fran (laughing nervously): "Most of the time."
>
> Peter (smiling): "I just like to know who everybody is."
>
> Fran (smiling): "Me too."

Besides doing the socially graceful thing of overlooking her rudeness and "breaking the ice," Peter also phrases the relationship between Fran and Steve in a revealing way. He seems to show her respect, by implying that Steve might belong to Fran, rather than her belonging to him. Fran welcomes this rapport, just as Roger had responded to Peter's friendly camaraderie earlier. Fran and Peter show here and throughout the film that they have better skills in dealing with people and relationships than do Roger or Steve—Roger being stubborn and headstrong, Steve being envious and insecure. It may not be too farfetched to posit that such a rapport between Peter and Fran stems in part from their similar experiences of being belittled and pushed aside in a racist, sexist America.

Peter subsequently is the first one to agree with Fran that she should have a say in their plans, and should be armed and able to protect herself from now on.[20] Peter is also the only one who welcomes and encourages Fran to learn to fly the helicopter, and her newly acquired skill is the only thing that saves them at the end of the film. When they fly off, he is much more beholden to her and reliant on her than she on him. She has saved Peter from Steve's foolish attempt to defend the mall, and she is now literally in the driver's seat. Given their personalities, we have some reason to think that Peter is more comfortable with this situation vis-à-vis a woman, than Steve could have been.[21] Perhaps even more importantly, we have to remember that Fran is pregnant with Steve's (white) child, not Peter's. Whatever their relationship may develop into, Peter's first role will be as a stepfather to another man's child, the very un-stereotypical situation of a child of one race, born to an interracial couple. It is a strange permutation of the Adam and Eve roles that we might expect at the end of such a movie, but oddly hopeful in its own way. Given Peter's kind, generous, and respectful attitude throughout the story, we have some confidence that he will fulfill such an awkward and demanding role better than most men. It also presents us with a potential future in which the significance of race is seriously undermined, if not totally abolished. But Romero implies that more hopeful future will only be realized when the mindless zombie hordes devour the old, corrupt, racist, capitalist regime under which we now live.

Besides continuing and making more explicit the theme of American racism, the second film adds what would become perhaps Romero's best-known image: zombies stampeding through a mall as a parody of rampant, American consumer culture. The image has become so much a part of the modern definition of the zombie that there are now mass zombie walks in malls all over, often to gather blood for blood drives, or food for local charities, and usually staged around Halloween or (more blasphemously) Easter.[22] The final image in *Dawn of the Dead*—in which zombies stagger around the mall, mesmerized by the products there, while an absurd tune called "The Gonk" plays on the Muzak system—is perhaps its most iconic, and later films can evoke and pay homage to the whole Romero corpus just by playing Muzak as their characters flee the living dead.[23] Romero's prophetic use of the image is to show that it is not the zombie's bite that turns us into monsters, but materialism and consumerism that turn us into zombies, addicted to things that satisfy only the basest, most animal or mechanical urges of our being.[24] This is repeatedly shown throughout *Dawn of the Dead* in the behavior of both the zombies and the human characters.

With the zombies, it is shown by their monomaniacal obsession with getting into the mall, even if it means their destruction. Sheer, unthinking tenacity or the search for prey cannot explain why the zombies pick *this* place as the one they feel they must occupy, over any other, and at any cost or risk. Though we will never know for sure, one can reasonably infer, based on Romero's depiction, that in a zombie-infested world, the former churches, libraries, and classrooms are not nearly as crowded with the undead as are the malls. (Even, one could reasonably suspect, conventionally sinful places like casinos, bars, and brothels would not be as crowded with the eager undead as the shopping malls, for materialism and constant, mindless consumption are not just tolerated, but enthusiastically encouraged in our society, while these other sinful behaviors are still regarded as slightly embarrassing and furtive.) Steve interprets the zombies' behavior very accurately when they first land on the roof of the mall: to Fran's question of, "Why do they come here?" he answers, "Some kind of instinct. Memory. What they used to do. This was an important place in their lives." This raises and complicates the horror of the living dead: not just that one will be torn to pieces and eaten alive—bad enough, surely—but that one will join the undead as an eternal mall-goer, never again able to conceive of anything higher or more interesting to do than wander about with a vacuous look of contentment, punctuated by longing, lustful stares at racks and displays full of useless, worthless stuff.

Peter will infer this eternal judgment of the zombies and themselves later in the film, as the human survivors again ponder the zombie hordes that are so eagerly and tenaciously trying to break in to their fortified mall, even though the humans have just finished slaughtering hundreds of them to secure it: "They don't know why, they just remember they want to be in here," to which Fran asks, "What the hell are they?" and Peter replies, "They're us, that's all. . . . When there's no more room in hell, the dead will walk the earth." It is the most chilling line in a chilling movie, repeated in the remake in a cameo appearance by Ken Foree, who played Peter in the original. With this statement, Peter rightly judges both zombies and humans as damned to repeat their trivialities and mistakes for all eternity, never again with the possibility of learning from them or improving, because such education and improvement were so consistently spurned in life, and such trivial sinfulness was so enthusiastically embraced. Though people usually use the word "Dantean" to describe the horrible grotesquery and torture in a movie like *Dawn of the Dead*, it is really more applicable to a vision like this. For Dante's depiction of sin is that it is exactly like an addiction, as depicted here—one that is willingly embarked on in life, and hopelessly and eternally repeated in death: "I learned that to this place of punishment all those who sin in lust have been condemned, those who make reason slave to appetite."[25] When they had reason and could think of better things to do than go to the mall, the people who would become mall zombies did not. Instead, they enslaved and finally killed their reason with their mundane and trivial appetites, thereby dooming themselves to repeat their sinful actions forever, never able to correct or extricate themselves from their sinful mistake. If you "shop till you drop," you will drop very far indeed, and will be condemned to shop forever.[26]

Romero has increased the relevance and discomfort of his prophetic critique by showing how the live humans are no less obsessed with getting into and staying in the mall than are the zombies. The plot of the movie is consistently driven by the survivors' lust to acquire and possess, especially predominant in the male characters. Roger, Steve, and many of the bikers who attack their mall/fortress are killed for their mad, foolish lust for possessions, but all the characters succumb to it at one point or another. The bikers, comically portrayed as the least thoughtful among the characters, are even more obsessed with possessions and indiscriminate in acquiring them than our protagonists, killing and dying just to grab any old thing in sight.[27] Steve and Peter steal paper money and then play poker with it, even though it's completely worthless now. Steve also epitomizes the attitude that possession is nine tenths of the law, and nine tenths of the value he puts on his life, apparently, when he snarls, "It's ours! We took it!" and madly sacrifices his life to die in his consumerist prison rather than give it up without a fight. Earlier, his only consolation to Fran when she was attacked and nearly killed by a zombie was to reassure her, "You should see all the great stuff we got. . . . This place is terrific, it really is. It's perfect!" Roger, in his final, dying delirium, must be comforted by Peter that his sacrifice was worth it, but we know that this is simply and pathetically not so. When the four of them survey their "victory" over the undead for which Roger has sacrificed himself, Romero dresses them up in enormous, poofy fur coats, in what can only be described as the fashion choice of a pimp—gaudy, tasteless, flamboyant, androgynous, and utterly unnecessary in their climate-controlled fortress/prison.[28] Even Peter, who seems the most enlightened and thoughtful of the men, is in fact the first to utter a cry of delight at what they variously call their newfound "kingdom" and "gold mine": to Roger's objection that they are now cut off from Fran and Steve and trapped inside JC Penney's, Peter shouts, "Who the hell cares?! Let's go shopping!" From beginning to end, the film is full of men killing themselves and others to get and hold on to things that they do not really need, and which do not even make them happy. It is one of the saddest and most damning critiques of consumerism imaginable.

After Roger's death, the survivors' consumerist glee turns even more sour. As the saying goes, they no longer own their possessions, their possessions own them. The especially poignant aspect of this is how corrosive it is to their relationships, especially the romantic and sexual relation between Fran and Steve. The scene of Steve's marriage proposal is the most obvious example of this.[29] Although I strongly suspect that it is another ploy of our consumerist society to persuade men that they *have* to spend two months' salary on an engagement ring, it would also seem true that all of the romance and attraction is lost if one could just walk into a jewelry store and grab anything one wanted for free, as Steve has done with Fran's ring. Such a "gift" is not real, for it costs the giver nothing in a world where everything is simply lying around, worthless and unappreciated (even as it is ironically pursued and grabbed with such murderous zeal). Indeed, after their initial slaughter to take over the mall, our protagonists need make no effort for anything, and they settle into a smothering ennui, disinterested in everything, even sex. At one point, Steve is shown in his fancy bed and silk sheets, sullen and bored, and the camera pulls back to reveal Fran right next to him: they could be making love or cuddling or talking or even just playing checkers, but instead they are utterly miserable and alone together in their gilded prison.

Even Fran, although she seems ten times more perceptive and resistant to the mall's supposed charms than her male companions, is shown briefly succumbing to some kind of consumerist fantasy late in the movie. She sits at an enormous vanity mirror, made up with so much make-up that it is clownish and grotesque, not sexy or attractive. She tries to strike seductive or suggestive poses with a pearl handled pistol, like Bonnie in *Bonnie and Clyde* (1967), though it all seems quite unnecessary and absurd, for Fran is a very pretty woman, allowing for the clothes and hairstyles of the 70s, and this hideous posturing is clearly no improvement. Whatever the reasons for or content of her fantasy, it is already going badly enough, when the mall loudspeakers issue a call, "Attention shoppers!" The illusion of glamour and beauty is completely shattered by the loudspeakers' offer of a free bag of cheap candy with every purchase—when now every purchase is free. Following this wakeup, Fran seems more disgusted than ever, this time with herself as well.[30] She realizes the mall is hypnotizing them and making them as fake as it is, with its faux foliage in planter boxes, one of which now unceremoniously serves as a tomb for Roger; its hollow, toyland-like clock tower, chiming hours in a land where time certainly does not matter anymore;[31] and its mannequins with painted tans and grins, in a world where there is no sun, and very little at which to smile. The mall is also making them as dead and numb as the other zombies that ravenously and impotently paw and slobber at its outside doors: they are trapped outside, and our three survivors are trapped inside.

As with biblical prophecy, however, the point of the movie is not simply to announce doom and judgment, but to issue a warning that its audience might actually act upon: "Hear the word of the Lord, O nations, and declare it in the coastlands far away; say, 'He who scattered Israel will gather him, and will keep him as a shepherd a flock.' . . . Indeed, I heard Ephraim pleading: 'You disciplined me, and I took the discipline; I was like a calf untrained. Bring me back, let me come back, for you are the Lord my God'" (Jer 31:10, 18). Right up until the death rattle or disembowelment that will make one permanently and irrevocably a zombie, one can make choices that matter. Fran takes responsibility for herself, not blaming the situation or others, when she confronts the men: "What have we done to ourselves?"[32] That question is really the fundamental one from a Christian perspective, much more so than the question of theodicy (i.e., "Why is God doing this to us?"), that one usually expects in an apocalyptic scenario.

Land of the Dead (2005) returns to these themes of racism and consumerism with less humor and more action. The zombie hordes are not the real villains of this installment. That role is fulfilled by a power-hungry and power-mad capitalist, Kaufman, providing another pointed and memorable part of Romero's critique of current society. Kaufman seems to be a combination of capitalist robber-baron, mad Roman emperor, and organized crime king-pin.[33] His name means "trader" or "merchant," as though that were the essence of his character. To have the new ruler of the only remaining human society be named "merchant," shows how Romero believes that commerce is the highest form of power in the old, pre-zombie human society. In this chilling, cynical, but uncomfortably realistic view, it is not the military, government, or church that exercises real power, but the wealthy, who may use these other institutions as proxies or fronts for their selfish machinations. According to Romero, the White House, the Pentagon, and the Vatican do not run or exploit the world, Wall Street does—a dire prophetic warning he'd make three years before the global economic crisis of 2008, a crisis which has shown the very limited power of world governments over their economies.

Played by Dennis Hopper with more restraint than he often exercises, and therefore much more effectively, Kaufman is positively Satanic in the absurd and sadistic lengths to which he will go in order to perpetuate his reign, as the reviewer for the *New York Times* noted: "With this new movie, we jump straight to the ninth circle, where Satan is a guy in a suit and tie who feasts on the misery of others, much as the dead feast on the living."[34] Kaufman is one of the few, perhaps the only one of the characters in any of the films, to note how the zombie menace fundamentally changes all human interactions, and does so to his advantage: when informed that he's in "trouble," Kaufman quite correctly responds that, "In a world where the dead are returning to life, the word 'trouble' loses much of its meaning." Only the raiders in *Dawn of the Dead* would perhaps share Kaufman's preference for life in a world overrun by zombies, but the raiders were crude, disorganized, and comical amateurs compared to Kaufman. Again, *Land of the Dead* teases us with the idea that it is not the

Part Two: Zombies

leather-clad, tattooed biker, or the big, scary black man who will do us harm, but the well-dressed, well-mannered, sinister, and well-organized banker and businessman who is the real threat to our well-being.

While others in the movie long to return to "normal" life, Kaufman sees how "good" life can be in a zombie-infested world, for it not only removes all restraints on him, it even lets him set up a hellish society based on his values of greed, envy, vice, and cruelty.[35] We see this when he explains his own version of "civic duty" at one point: according to him, he has a great and noble "responsibility" for his fellow citizens, because he "kept people off the streets by giving them games and vices." Like Milton's (1608–74) Satan more than Dante's, Kaufman believes that it is, "Better to reign in Hell, than serve in Heav'n."[36] And while he's mixing in various classic depictions of Satan, Romero is, of course, not above the burlesque version of Goethe's (1749–1832) Mephistopheles, having Kaufman say, as probably only Hopper could pull it off, while picking his nose (!), "Zombies, man, creep me out!"

The fantasy of what Satan/Kaufman tempts us with is graphically shown in the advertisements and reality of Fiddler's Green, the safe tower in the middle of Kaufman's city. It is a place where "Life goes on!" as before, undisturbed by the miseries of others, or by the inevitable specter of (un)death. The ground floor of Fiddler's Green resembles a much more upscale mall than that depicted in the original *Dawn of the Dead*,[37] now made more horrible and wretched by its opulence, and by the fact that it is not just zombies and biker gangs that are being kept out, but sick and starving children. All attempts to dress the fantasy up as anything other than crass and cannibalistic consumption has finally been stripped away by the exigencies of a zombie-infested world. The inner sanctum of consumption and exclusion is not named something bellicose like The Citadel, or patriotic, like Freedom Tower: instead, it's got one of those generically happy-sounding names like the $1.5 million condos with 24-hour fitness centers, climate control, and security, cocooned in shining glass and steel towers and advertised in the back of in-flight magazines. It is an image of privileged irresponsibility in the face of suffering, like "fiddling while Rome burns."[38] Apparently the name even comes from an old Irish legend of where happy fishermen go when they die, a place where, "There's pubs and there's clubs and there's lassies there too. And the girls are all pretty and the beer is all free. And there's bottles of rum growing on every tree."[39] It is an adult version of Pleasure Island in *Pinocchio* or Neverland in *Peter Pan*, but it is no more mature, and no more real. The cut scene of a suicide (now available on the DVD version) makes the fantastical and unsatisfying aspect of such an existence painfully clear: surrounded by comfort and ease, some people find their life so empty and meaningless that they kill themselves and become zombies, who at least have a lot more drive and ambition. And even if they don't avail themselves of suicide, zombie-hood is where they are all headed anyway, but before they get there, they have the added damnation of being the docile and cooperating thralls of Kaufman/Satan.

The reality of the hellish kingdom over which Kaufman rules is indelibly impressed on our imaginations by the view from his office, which is as Dantean and apocalyptic as anything else presented in the films. As far as the eye can see is a grey, blighted, lifeless urban moonscape that might as well be Hiroshima or Auschwitz, it is so dead and demoralizing, yet it represents the best view in Fiddler's Green, one for which Kaufman is eager to kill, protecting it and keeping it away from the "common" folk who dwell below, or from the hungry undead outside the walls. Twice, as the zombies are attacking his kingdom, he cries out, "You have no right!" when, of course, Kaufman based his kingdom on ignoring others' rights and acting like a terrorist and a criminal. His evil reign is not based on any "right" other than "might makes right" and if the zombie hordes now possess more might, than they are the rightful rulers.

Besides making a capitalist robber-baron the villain, Romero increases the social criticism of this film with his choice of who leads the zombie army against Kaufman. The smartest zombie in this film, the one who thinks to launch a counterattack against the sadistic humans, and who thinks of various ways around the obstacles in getting there, is a black gas station attendant whose name tag reads "Big Daddy." One reviewer rightly noted that Big Daddy and Riley (the main human protagonist) are the only two sympathetic characters in the film, and even went as far as to say that Big Daddy is Riley's "zombie alter ego."[40] At the end of the movie, with Kaufman killed and his city in ruins, Big Daddy and Riley look at one another from a distance and seem to declare some truce—Big Daddy shambling off without further attacks, as the intelligent zombie Bub had done at the end of *Day of the Dead*. The films had begun with a black man lying dead at the hands of a white posse sent out to impose order on society; *Land of the Dead* ends with a black zombie bringing about the end of a corrupt, violent human society and then seemingly ceasing his own rampage. If the former was a potent and uncomfortable indictment of 1960s America with its racism and pointless overseas wars in places like Vietnam, the new installment is a sobering implication of how it might end—with an army of those exploited rising up against the oppressors who have based their affluent and wasteful lifestyle on the toil and suffering of others.[41]

Modern Christians in the West often seem as smug as any caricature of the ancient Israelites to whom Amos prophesied. We too often assume our way of life will continue as it is now, maintaining our level of affluence and consumption indefinitely, even though such extravagance is at the expense of other people and the environment and will inevitably run out. Further, whether or not we espouse something as explicit as a "prosperity gospel," many seem to take it for granted that our material well-being is a good thing, ordained and approved by a God whom we have pleased through our behavior. Zombie movies stand as a stark, sobering, even terrifying counterbalance to such a vision of modern Christianity. They instead offer us Amos' bitter, disillusioned criticism of our wealth and skewed values, couched in the horrifying, monstrous terms of Ezekiel, and leading to the ultimate destruction and judgment of Revelation. The compatibility between zombie films and the biblical tradition seems to me irrefutable and compelling, and therefore their relevance to Christians—or, indeed, any religious or humanist person who seeks to expose the sinful, misguided excesses of the modern world—seems equally certain.

END NOTES

1. This essay originally appeared in *Reel Revelations*, 6–24; it has also been reprinted in *Light Shining in a Dark Place*.

2. The discussion here is an expansion on points from my book, *Gospel of the Living Dead*. All biblical quotations are NRSV.

3. Romero's depiction of zombies or "ghouls" has some precedent in the vampires of Richard Matheson's novel, *I Am Legend*, adapted several times into films. See Waller, *The Living and the Undead*, 275: "But by far the most important antecedent for *Night of the Living Dead* is *I Am Legend*. On various occasions Romero has acknowledged that the original idea for his film was 'inspired' by Richard Matheson's novel, and the resemblance between the two works is striking." Pirie, *The Vampire Cinema*, 141, also notes *I Am Legend* as the inspiration for Romero.

4. Though these too may have a "rational" explanation: see Davis, *The Serpent and the Rainbow*; ibid., *Passage of Darkness*.

5. On the uselessness of explanations, cf. Waller, *Living and the Undead*, 275–76: "To assert that 'mysterious radiation' in some unexplained way causes the dead to roam the land in search of human flesh is finally little better than no explanation at all (especially since this is a quasi-official explanation and therefore likely in *Night of the Living Dead* to be a lie, distortion, or cover-up). . . . Ben and the other people trapped in the isolated house do not have the time to search for explanations, which would make little difference in any case."

6. In an otherwise negative evaluation of the film, Russell, *Book of the Dead*, 185, notes the aptness of this choice of music.

7. In this sense, the film returns to a more classical, pre-Romero vision of horror movies, as described by Fraser, "Watching Horror Movies," 39–54, esp. 47: "And once the possibility of splatter effects had been opened up, an interesting tension was established wherein one partly *wanted* horrible things to happen, for their shock effect, and yet at the same time did not want them to happen to everyone. So that one stayed alert for possible clues as to who in some sense 'deserved' to become victims."

8. This may be true of "great" horror movies in general: see Britton, "The Devil, Probably," In *American Nightmare*, 34–42, esp. 41: "The great American horror movies . . . seem to me to be characterised not so much by ambivalence—a phenomenon discernible in such eminently mediocre and objectionable works as *The Texas Chainsaw Massacre*—as by the use of the monster as the focus, or the catalyst, for the critical analysis of everything that 'normality' represents."

9. On American society in zombie movies, cf. Waller, *Living and the Undead*, 280: "Perhaps the monstrous creatures in *Night of the Living Dead*, the 'things' that are somehow still men, are the projection of our desire to destroy, to challenge the fundamental values of America, and to bring the institutions of our modern society to a halt."

10. *Day of the Dead* (1985) takes quite a different approach than the other films, returning us to the claustrophobia of the first film, but not making the sweeping social criticism of the second, focusing instead on more general observations of human nature, rather than society. And though I was not as disappointed with *Diary of the Dead* (2007) as some fans, the main target of its satire is our media culture (a self-referential target already at the periphery in *Night* and *Dawn*). While certainly timely in a world where the apocalypse will not just be televised, but will be blogged and tweeted and podcast every moment, it is harder to tie it in to broader critiques in the other films, or to the biblical critiques of similarly bad habits. As for non-Romero zombie films, they have tended to dilute his message (as with Snyder's remake, though it is an exciting action film), or simply take over the brains and intestines for shock value.

11. See Hutchings, *The Horror Film*, 112: "the hero's racial identity is never referred to by any of the characters in the film"; Wood, "Apocalypse Now," 93: "The film has often been praised for never making an issue of its black hero's colour (it is nowhere alluded to, even implicitly)." Dillard, "*Night of the Living Dead*,

Part Two: Zombies

14–29, gives an optimistic interpretation of this, esp. p. 19: "Perhaps the only unusual thing about them is that no one of them ever comments about one of their numbers being black, especially in the light of his assuming a natural leadership. But even that lack of race prejudice in a tight situation may be more ordinarily American than we might suspect."

12. E.g., Pirie, *Vampire Cinema*, 143, calls Cooper a "bigot."
13. Cf. Hutchings, *Horror Film*, 112: "More than one critic has seen references here to lynching"; Waller, *Living and the Undead*, 295, who to some extent must rely on the second film: "Though the posse cannot see that Ben is a black man, this murder evokes American racism at its deadliest and most virulent, a topic Romero will return to in the opening sequences of *Dawn of the Dead*."
14. The analysis of Wood, "Apocalypse Now," 93: "It is the function of the posse to restore the social order that has been destroyed; the zombies represent the suppressed tensions and conflicts—the legacy of the past, of the patriarchal structuring of relationships, 'dead' yet automatically continuing—which that order creates and on which it precariously rests."
15. Source for the death toll is the website of the National Weather Service—http://www.hpc.ncep.noaa.gov/tropical/rain/katrina2005.html (accessed June 26, 2009). The comments were made by Representative Richard Baker (R - La.), as reported in the *Washington Post*, http://www.washingtonpost.com/wp-dyn/content/article/2005/09/09/AR2005090901930.html (site visited June 26, 2009).
16. The sectarianism of Jewish apocalypticism reaches a highpoint with the Qumran community: see Regev, *Sectarianism in Qumran*, which also includes consideration of later movements such as the Anabaptists and the Shakers.
17. See Wood, "Apocalypse Now," 96, for the possible homosexual overtones of the friendship.
18. On their relationship, cf. Waller, *Living and the Undead*, 304: "Peter and Roger are a confident, effective team who speak the same language, share ideas, and perfectly complement each other."
19. On the failure of traditional relationships and the formation of a new, see Wood, "Apocalypse Now," 96: "In place of *Night*'s dissection of the family, *Dawn* explores (and explodes) the two dominant couple-relationships of our culture and its cinema: the heterosexual couple (moving inevitably towards marriage and its traditional male/female roles) and the male 'buddy' relationship with its evasive denial of sexuality"; and Waller, *Living and the Undead*, 321: "The couple that survives in *Dawn of the Dead*—a black man and a pregnant white woman—is not the traditional heterosexual couple (Fran and Stephen come closest to filling the role of the new Adam and Eve) or the pair of male buddies (like the team of Roger and Peter), but potentially a new type of partnership."
20. Cf. Wood, "Apocalypse Now," 96: "But in the course of the film she progressively assumes a genuine autonomy, asserting herself against the men, insisting on possession of a gun, demanding to learn to pilot the machine."

21. On their possible future relationship, see Wood, "Apocalypse Now," 96: "Instead of the restoration of conventional relationship-patterns, we have the woman piloting the helicopter as the man relinquishes his rifle to the zombies"; and Waller, *Living and the Undead*, 321–22: "Fran—carrying within her the prospect of new life—has been the most perceptive of the group, and Peter has been the most skillful and the most inclined to regard her as an equal.... Perhaps since Fran is piloting the helicopter and Peter has left behind his rifle, this couple is also escaping from the limiting roles fostered by a racist and sexist society that has now been destroyed."
22. "Zombie walk" now has its own Wikipedia page, as well as a website at zombiewalk.com, which offers a forum for enthusiasts to keep informed of upcoming events. Though most are in the USA, the site lists walks in Canada, the UK, Europe, and South America.
23. Romero does this himself in *Day of the Dead*. It is also done in the *Dawn of the Dead* remake and in *Shaun of the Dead*.
24. For a scholarly analysis of consumerism in the film, see Loudermilk, "Eating dawn in the dark," 83–108. For a sociological application of the image of "living dead," but without reference to the film, see Ritzer, "Islands of the Living Dead," 119–36.
25. Dante, *Inferno*, 5.37–39.
26. The consumer motto is invoked similarly in Skal, *The Monster Show*, 376: "Ellis' world of blood-soaked designer labels recognizably upgrades the voracious mall zombies in *Dawn of the Dead*: they shop till they drop, eat your brains, then shop some more"
27. On the comparison of the bikers with our protagonists, see Wood, "Apocalypse Now," 96: "The motorcycle gang's mindless delight in violence and slaughter is anticipated in the development of Roger; all three groups are contaminated and motivated by consumer-greed (which the zombies simply carry to its logical conclusion by consuming *people*)"; and Waller, *Living and the Undead*, 317, who notes that "their looting of the mall is a parodic repetition of Fran, Stephen, Peter, and Roger's shopping spree."
28. The fur coats are also other corpses with which they surround themselves: cf. Waller, *Living and the Undead*, 311: "The mall—refuge or promised land or prison—belongs to the living. However, in making it safe and habitable, they have, figuratively at least, closed themselves in and surrounded themselves with corpses."
29. On the scene, see Wood, "Apocalypse Now," 96: "The pivotal scene is the parody of a romantic dinner, the white couple, in evening dress, cooked for and waited on by the black, with flowers and candlelight, the scene building to the man's offer and the woman's refusal of the rings that signify traditional union."
30. Cf. Waller, *Living and the Undead*, 314: "Striking 'provocative' poses with a six-gun, Fran resembles a painted mannequin or a poor imitation of a gangster's moll or a child costumed as an adult. Over the mall's loud-speakers, a voice

Part Two: Zombies

calls all 'shoppers' to pay attention, and Fran looks up as if she realizes the extent to which she has become the willing, predictable 'shopper'—the prisoner who can no longer see the bars of her prison."

31. Waller, *Living and the Undead*, 320, observes this of the very end of the movie: "Ironically, the mall's clock chimes over and over, marking the hour for a crowd of shoppers who will never again worry about the passage of time."

32. Cf. Waller, *Living and the Undead*, 314–15: "For unlike the automatistic zombies who still fill the parking lot and press against the entrances of the mall, the well-fed, safe, comfortable human beings inside this fortress have the freedom to choose."

33. Cf. Klawans, "Alien Nation," 41–44, esp. 44, where he calls Kaufman "an all-purpose realtor, corporate czar and crime boss." Russell, *Book of the Dead*, 190, makes the reference much more explicit and historically-contextualized: "Presenting Kaufman as a composite of George W. Bush and Defense Secretary Donald Rumsfeld, Romero makes his criticism of the regime more than transparent."

34. Dargis, "Not Just Roaming,".

35. Cf. Russell, *Book of the Dead*, 186: "What was threatened before in Romero's series has finally come to pass: the living are now more like monsters than the living dead."

36. Milton, *Paradise Lost*, 1.263.

37. Cf. Russell, *Book of the Dead*, 189: "With the apartments of Fiddler's Green a more luxurious take on the shopping mall enclave from *Dawn of the Dead*, it's obvious that Romero has lost none of his anti-consumerist fervour even when taking a major Hollywood studio's dollar."

38. The connection suggested by Russell, *Book of the Dead*, 189.

39. I was first alerted to this by the "Trivia" section for *Land of the Dead* on the Internet Movie Database site: http://www.imdb.com/title/tt0418819/ (site visited November 14, 2005). The lyrics are from "Brobdingnagian Bards," http://www.thebards.net/music/lyrics/Fiddlers_Green.shtml (accessed June 28, 2009).

40. Dargis, "Not Just Roaming."

41. Cf. Degiglio-Bellemare, "*Land of the Dead*," 7: "Romero's new film offers a very important statement on the reality of 'lockdown America,' with its gated communities, its stark class divisions, and its racial demarcations."

9

Negotiating (Non)Existence
Justifications of Violence in Robert Kirkman's *The Walking Dead*

J. RYAN PARKER

"I'm addicted to murder, and that's about the nicest way I can put it. You might say that's not technically true, that since they're already dead I'm not really killing. Horseshit; it's murder, and it's a rush like nothing else."

"Who can get a rush anymore from pulling a trigger? It's gotta be hard, dangerous, and the more Gs you gotta take on, the better. Of course, sooner or later there's not gonna be any of them left. And when that happens..."

—T. SEAN COLLINS IN MAX BROOKS'S *WORLD WAR Z*[1]

INTRODUCTION

In the Clinical Research section of the website zombiedefense.org, visitors can access a discussion on "The Ethics of Zombie Destruction." The author of the statement asks, "[Is] it morally justifiable to destroy a zombie?" Utilizing rule utilitarianism, the author concludes that it is indeed morally justifiable and, moreover, imperative to destroy all zombies in order to remake and improve the world of a post-zombified-apocalypse.

Part Two: Zombies

The author argues that because zombies are no longer human (they lack collective memories, consciousness, and the identity of their former selves), their utility should not be considered, and, as a result, humans have a moral duty to "re-kill each and every one of them."[2]

This bit of armchair philosophy finds its way into most, if not all, zombie narratives; however, these narratives and the contributors to zombiedefense.org fail to consider the ways in which such violent reactions to zombies affect the human survivors of their respective zombie apocalypses. Few characters illustrate the lingering emotional and psychological effects of zombie extermination quite as succinctly as T. Sean Collins, a mercenary hired to protect celebrities in Max Brooks's *World War Z*. What Brooks does on a small scale with T. Sean, Robert Kirkman takes to another level with his post-zombie apocalypse narrative, *The Walking Dead*. Unlike so many other zombie writers or directors, Kirkman is less concerned with the origins of the zombie plague (he currently has no plans to reveal said origins) than he is with how the survivors react to the undead. Kirkman writes:

> *The Walking Dead* is not an action zombie romp with intense gore and paper-thin characters meant only as cannon fodder. ... [It's] a gripping tale of survival set against the most horrific worldwide tragedy one could think of, the dead walking and devouring the living. *The Walking Dead* is something sad and tragic, a story that puts its characters through the wringer and sticks around to see what comes out the other end.[3]

Kirkman's comic book series, which has inspired AMC's critically acclaimed television adaptation, provides Kirkman with ample space to play with these human survivors. Given the series' (both print and television) popularity, his story is here to stay.[4]

Despite my love of the television series and its popularity, for the purposes of this chapter, I will limit my discussion to Kirkman's books. The comic book series, currently on its 92nd issue with 15 trade paperbacks, numerous re-issues, and a first volume compendium, gives us more material with which to work as it has progressed further along in Kirkman's vision, introducing scenarios and characters that may never see the small screen or will take several more seasons to arrive. The print series is, I believe, closer to Kirkman's vision, most specifically in its depiction of violence, the centerpiece of my discussion here. Finally, as a unique art form, comics make demands on and implicate the reader in ways that film and television do not. While film scholars have discussed the ways in which directors implicate the audience in the events of a film, film viewers are always being led along by that director.[5] On the other hand, comics and their creators allow readers to make choices that affect their experience. In comics, readers can make the choice to move the story along or to move back and forth between panels. Moreover, because comic book artists cannot depict every event that takes place in the narrative, the reader must co-create with the writers and artists to fill in those in between spaces. In his foundational study of comics, *Understanding Comics: The Invisible Art*, Scott McCloud writes, "The comics creator asks us to join in a *silent dance* of the *seen* and the *unseen*. The *visible* and the *invisible*. This dance is *unique* to comics. No other artform gives so much to its audience while asking so much *from* them as well.... What happens between these panels is a kind of magic *only* comics can create."[6] This is especially important when the narrative discussed is as violent as Kirkman's *The Walking Dead*.

Without a doubt, Kirkman puts the survivors of his zombie apocalypse through the wringer like few other directors or writers have. Like most survivors, these characters persevere through the violent extermination of their zombie "enemies." However, James Lowder points out a key difference between *The Walking Dead* and its zombie peers. In his essay, "In Medias Apocalypsis," Lowder notes, "Unlike so many serial narratives, where the heroes are fixed points, unaffected by the furious adventures spinning around them, *The Walking Dead* features protagonists who are most assuredly altered by their experiences."[7] While the appearance of zombies does influence these changes, I would also argue that the ways in which these characters choose to react to the zombies and, more importantly, to one another do so more extensively.

In this chapter, I consider the (non)violent ways in which survivors of the zombie apocalypse negotiate (non)existence, both the zombies that plague them and the competing survivors that endanger them. Just as important for this discussion are the ways in which these survivors justify these actions, employing a host of techniques that find real-world parallels. In the end, I argue that the survivors pose a far greater risk to one another and their potential futures than the zombies ever could and provide a mirror for the ways in which we negotiate perceived threats in our own experiences. In the real world, where unthinkable acts of violence (and violent reactions to them) are often cloaked in moral/religious/theological armor, Kirkman's dark narrative sheds light on the hypocrisy of one

Part Two: Zombies

individual or group claiming superiority over another, even if that other happens to be a zombie.

The Walking Dead rises above its undead counterparts, *True Blood* and the *Twilight* series, for example, in a variety of ways. It pulls no punches: these zombies don't sparkle and the characters' sex appeal is the furthest thing from the creators' and audiences' minds. That Kirkman's series is a straightforward zombie narrative no doubt accounts for much of its success. The series follows law enforcement officer Rick Grimes and a diverse group of survivors that includes his wife Lori and son Carl. They wander throughout the southeastern United States in search of safe havens from the zombies that roam this increasingly deserted wasteland. Along the way, they encounter both friendly and threatening individuals and groups of fellow survivors with whom they cooperate or against whom they fight in order to stay safe. We can divide their journey into five broad time frames: life in a camp just outside Atlanta shortly after the outbreak of the zombie plague, life on Hershel's farm, life in a prison compound, life on the road after fleeing the zombie-infested prison, and life in a walled-in community in Alexandria, Virginia.

The strength of Kirkman's series is that his characters are not cardboard cutouts or overly chiseled heroes or buxom heroines. These characters feel real, as do their struggles, hopes, fears, and relationships even as they take place against a literally impossible setting. Though W. Scott Poole is writing about a second season episode of the television series, his assessment applies equally to Kirkman's books: "It's a *cri de coeur* from the post-apocalyptic landscape, all supports gone, monsters walking the world threatening to rend and tear the physical self to bits. And isn't that us and the pre-apocalyptic world we live in? Aren't we, really, the walking dead?"[8] Along with a host of other themes, *The Walking Dead*'s overriding question asks what it means to be human, and in Kirkman's world, to be human is to be violent and to employ an arsenal of justifications for that violence.

A NOTE ON VIOLENCE

"Acts of violence are germane to the story itself—this *is* a zombie apocalypse, after all.... The mayhem is quite necessary for the tale that's being told."

—VINCE A. LIAGUNO[9]

Many people steer clear of zombie narratives because of their inherent gore and violence. To be sure, *The Walking Dead* is not for the squeamish or faint of heart. However, it is important to note that no matter how intense Kirkman's use of violence may be, it is never gratuitous. In fact, Kirkman and artists Tony Moore, Charlie Adlard, and Cliff Rathburn employ a black-and-white aesthetic that effectively decreases the shock value of their work while still managing to convey the brutality of human-on-zombie and human-on-human violence. Kirkman writes:

> There's a lot of horrendous stuff happening on the page. If you were seeing that in color, it would be that much more offensive. ... But you can't really do a story like this without the gore. By doing it in black and white, the gore recedes into the background so it isn't quite as jarring and doesn't really take center stage as much as it would if the book were in color.[10]

Kirkman et al. employ gore and violence not to shock the reader but to heighten the series' primary function as a character study. In his essay on violence and viscera in *The Walking Dead*, Vince A. Liaguno writes, "The violence *is* important because it frames the narrative in such unyieldingly bleak and punishing circumstances, which only makes the human interaction, action, and reaction to the unfolding events all the more pronounced, ultimately heightening the audience's response to and expectations of the show's characters."[11]

It is also important to note that the world of *The Walking Dead* was violent well before the zombies stumbled on the scene. A shoot-out with a fleeing criminal puts Rick in a coma from which he awakens to a zombie-infested world. Carol, one of the members of the first community, hints that her husband abused her. Dexter, one of the prison inmates, confesses to killing his wife's boyfriend. Most disturbing of all, however, is the news story that Douglas, the leader of the community in Alexandria, shares with Rick:

Part Two: Zombies

> A man in Florida, Fort Lauderdale if I recall correctly, was on a drug of some kind. I don't remember which—some type of hallucinogen, I would assume. While under the influence of these drugs . . . he—he *ate* his four year old son's eyeballs. Just ate them right out of his head. Aside from the story in general being just . . . *horrific*, the thing that really stuck with me, that sends shivers down my spine to this very day . . . was a quote from the son. "Daddy ate my eyes." [. . .] I don't tell that story to offend you, I know you have a young son. *The point is that there is* **evil** *in the world . . . always was, long before it came in the undead variety.* If anything . . . things only got *worse* after the collapse. People who were keeping themselves in check, living by society's rules . . . they no longer had any checks and balances. The crazy, free to roam, unchecked—a world gone *mad*.[12]

It is in this unchecked world, in what David Hopkins calls "the impossible ethical situations of a cruel world," that Kirkman plays out his allegory of the human condition.[13]

ZOMBIE KILLERS . . . RUN, RUN, RUN AWAY

> "Okay, it's pretty obvious what we're doing here, people—if it's dead—*fucking kill it!*"
>
> —Abraham

The survivors of the zombie plague do not immediately understand what is happening around them. We do not hear the undead referred to as zombies until a few issues into the series, and it is not until the group occupies the prison that they realize that a bite does not immediately infect or necessarily kill the victim. The first thing that the survivors realize is that, "A good blow to the head will take 'em out." Though the survivors may be slow to learn how the zombies operate (primarily through senses of smell and sound), they prove to be adept at dispatching their undead counterparts, re-killing them in just about every way possible from a bullet to the brain to running them over with an RV. It is clear, however, that as these survivors dispatch the zombies, they are also exercising their own demons of pent up fears, aggression, or hostility. While some survivors have other opinions on how to deal with the zombies (more on that later), the majority opinion is to attack with extreme prejudice. Of course, who can blame them when their very lives are at stake?

Nevertheless, the human/zombie conflict raises ethical questions that reach beyond zombiedefense.org's discussion and provide an avenue for the discussion of justifiable violence. From an ethical perspective, deontology seems to wrap it up quite nicely. In his essay, "Justifications for Violence," Kevin Magil writes, "Deontologists typically take the view that, other than in circumstances of war, the only acceptable justification for violence is that of self-defense or defense of others from wrongful attack. Persons have moral rights not to be wrongfully injured or killed and, consequently, they have the right to defend themselves against wrongful physical attack."[14] In *The Walking Dead*, the human survivors justify their (mis)treatment of zombies from this perspective, along with a host of others from sympathy (putting them out of their misery) to morality and biology (zombies are sub-human and thus less valuable). However, in his discussion of deontology and violence, Magil offers a caveat: "We can only be justified in using as much violence against an attacker, however, as is required to defend ourselves."[15] As the narrative progresses, the survivors cease rationalizing their treatment of the zombies and begin to mow through them with the same mindlessness with which the undead devour the living. Of course, they don't *have* to do this, as I will later discuss alternative ways in which some of Kirkman's characters deal with the zombies. For the time being, it is impossible to ignore the reality that this violent behavior towards the zombies negatively affects the ways in which the surviving humans treat one another. With shocking speed, the survivors begin to turn on each other . . . as if the threat of being eaten alive by the undead is not enough to worry them.

Part Two: Zombies

HUMAN KILLERS ... RUN, RUN, RUN AWAY

"When it begins, when the killing starts, don't let their appearance deceive you. You will see women—children even, but I assure you these people are *beasts*, no different than the biters we kill without a second thought. Life out here—it's changed them, twisted them into creatures who kill without a second thought—with no regard for human life. They don't deserve to live."

—The Governor

Zombies are not people. Zombies are a life-consuming, greedy, aggressive horde that will stop at nothing to get at the things they crave the most. Well, maybe there are more similarities between humans and zombies than meets the eye. As far as Kirkman has taken his audience in *The Walking Dead*, it is difficult to remember a time when the survivors (or most of them) were not cold-blooded killers. Surprisingly, there was such a time. Rick sheds a tear as he kills the remains of a zombie on the side of the road when he leaves for Atlanta. When the zombies first attack the camp just outside of Atlanta, Jim is bitten. Jim asks Donna to leave him in the woods, but she responds, "No ... we can't do that to you. You could start getting *better*. This would be *murder*." Jim counters, "Donna ... you don't understand. I can *feel* it coming. This—you gotta do this. I ..." Donna, like the rest of the survivors, clings to this notion that killing someone else, even someone bitten and infected with a virus is wrong.

Along with their rapidly evolving skills of zombie extermination, these survivors learn how to handle potential human enemies as well. The narrative moves from the *almost* harmless to the horrific. In the first issue, Duane Jones hits Rick on the head with a shovel and says, "He was *going* to try to *eat us*, Dad," mistaking Rick for a zombie. At the outbreak of the zombie plague, humans began to turn on each other. When Rick learns more about Tyreese, an ex-football player wandering around with his daughter and her boyfriend, Tyreese tells Rick that he beat to death a man that attempted to rape his daughter. Tyreese tells Rick, "I'm beating myself up because I don't feel **bad** about doing it. Yeah—the end of the world changed *him* ... but look at how it changed *me*." Unlike his peers, Tyreese seems to understand that, on one level, all violence is the same.

In the midst of all the chaos throughout the series, three events summarize the breakdown of society and the survivors' turn to violence. In a variety of ways, all other acts of violence are derivative of these three events. In the first instance, when the survivors take refuge in the prison compound after ridding it of zombies, everything seems fine until Hershel's daughters are found beheaded. The group immediately suspects Dexter, who had confessed to having been imprisoned for killing his wife and her boyfriend. When they later learn that the unassuming Thomas actually killed them, Rick freaks out and almost beats him to death. As he beats Thomas, Rick yells: "*You!* It was *you* who *killed* them!! *Wasn't it?!* You *sick* fuck! *You killed them!* They were just *little girls*! They didn't do *anything* to you! *Nothing!* [. . .] He deserves *every bit* of this, Lori. Don't you?! *You psycho son of a bitch!* Don't you deserve this?! [. . .] He *killed* them, Tyreese. He *killed* a couple of *helpless* little girls!" When Rick finally stops beating Thomas, his hand is an almost irreparable gnarled mess of broken bones, blood, and teeth.

When Rick tells everyone that he will kill Thomas as punishment, Lori responds, "We've got a chance to *change* things, Rick. We've got a chance to break the cycle. *No killing* means *no killing*. If we kill him—we're no better than *he* is." When Tyreese suggests that they make rules for this sort of thing, Rick quickly responds with a blanket proclamation, "You kill? You *die*. It's as simple as *that*." Later Rick adds, "We have to make an *example* of Thomas—we have to make the statement *once* and for *all*—we do not kill. We *do not* tolerate it. We *will not* allow it. *That* is our rule—our pledge. You kill. You die. No exceptions." Originally sworn to uphold the law, Rick has fallen victim to the lawlessness of his surroundings. Thomas will have no trial, no judge, no jury. Despite Rick's pronouncement of hanging, Maggie shoots Thomas when he tries to escape.

It takes no time at all for Rick to break his own commandment, setting up the second important event. The group releases Dexter from his cell after wrongfully "imprisoning" him for the beheading of Hershel's daughters, and he soon foments revenge with fellow inmate Andrew. When he threatens Rick, and by extension the group, Rick knows that Dexter will be a problem. When Andrew and Dexter accidentally release zombies from an unexplored wing of the prison, a shootout starts. In the chaos, Rick shoots Dexter in cold blood and kills him. Rick, rather unconvincingly, blames it on a stray bullet. When things calm down, Tyreese tells Rick, "I think you did the *right* thing. The way things were looking that fool was going to attack *us* as soon as the roamers were cleared out, anyway. Who knows *who* he would have *killed*. *Fuck* him, y'know. Still, kinda throws the whole '*You kill, you die*' thing out the window, huh? Maybe you should *rethink* your 'no killing' stance." From this point until

Part Two: Zombies

his arrival at the Alexandria community, Rick ceases to justify an increasingly violent existence and takes a "whatever-it-takes" approach to his and his family's survival.

The final instance of violence involves one of the series most notorious characters. During their stay in the prison, Rick, Glen, and Michonne meet the Governor, the "ruler" of the nearby Woodbury community. The Governor is most likely the most violent villain in the entirety of the zombie genre and will certainly pose countless problems for the FCC should he make the television adaptation cut. The Governor rules over his community of survivors and pacifies them by staging routine fights between survivors in cages with imprisoned zombies. To keep the zombies calm, the Governor tells Rick, "Well, *stranger*. We're feeding them *strangers*."

In order to find out where Rick, Michonne, and Glen come from, the Governor cuts off Rick's left arm, tortures and rapes Michonne, and emotionally tortures Glen. When the three manage to escape Woodbury, Michonne stays behind to return the favor and enacts stomach-turning revenge, most often reserved for Asian shock films. She nails his penis to the floor, anally probes him with a spoon, drills a hole into his shoulder, rips his fingernails out one by one, cuts off half his arm and burns the wound to cauterize the bleeding, scoops an eye out with a spoon, and finally cuts off his penis. The Governor survives this torture and after healing and biding his time, mounts an offensive against the inhabitants of the prison. In the chaotic battle between Rick's group of survivors and the Governor's "soldiers," the latter, in his rage, rams his tank into the fences surrounding the prison, inadvertently allowing the zombies to overrun it and making it uninhabitable for any group of survivors. This event reveals the depths to which the characters sink in harming one another while also revealing the self-destructiveness of that violence.

As the series progresses, all other instances of violence echo these events. Rick is almost always the first to step up and address a problem—or kill it. In Alexandria, Rick accuses Jessie's husband Pete of beating her and their son and attacks him in a fit of rage. The cannibals that Rick, Abraham, and Andrea find on the way to Alexandria are immediately tortured and killed. That Kirkman refuses to show this revenge, but focuses instead on Father Gabriel Stoke's horror at what happens before him, allows the readers to fill in the horrific blanks with the worst they can imagine. Carl's murder of Ben, one of Allen and Donna's twin sons, echoes Rick's murder of Dexter. Carl, like Rick did with Dexter, recognizes that Ben will forever be a threat to the group and must be dealt with definitively.

THE ZOMBIE MADE ME DO IT

"I do bad things ... a lot of *bad* things, to help you and all the other people in our group. And as you grow up, you'll probably have to do that too. That's the world we live in now [...]."

—Rick Grimes to son Carl

Just as interesting as the violence in *The Walking Dead*, although perhaps much less entertaining, are the survivors' explanations for and defense of their violent actions. In many ways, these parallel studies of the justification of violence like Albert Bandura's discussion of mechanisms of moral disengagement in terrorism. Bandura highlights a variety of ways in which terrorists morally disengage from the violence that they enact against others. He writes, "Self-sanctions can be disengaged by reconstruing conduct as serving moral purposes, obscuring personal agency in detrimental activities, disregarding or misrepresenting the injurious consequences of one's actions, and blaming and dehumanizing the victims."[16] All of these are at play in *The Walking Dead*, but before discussing them, I want to highlight a couple of points about each mechanism. No matter the mechanism, it is important to note that one does not become a terrorist, or a competent zombie killer, overnight. Bandura writes, "Intensive psychological training in moral disengagement is needed to create the capacity to kill innocent human beings as a way of toppling rulers or regimes, or accomplishing other political goals."[17]

It is interesting to note the complex ways in which moral reconstrual takes place. Bandura writes, "Through moral sanction of violent means, people see themselves as fighting ruthless oppressors who have an unquenchable appetite for conquest, protecting their cherished values and way of life, preserving world peace, saving humanity from subjugation to an evil ideology, and honoring their country's international commitments."[18] Moral justification requires nonviolence to have been deemed ineffective while also outweighing potential suffering over actual inflicted suffering. Of course, the more outrageous the comparison, the easier it is to enact violence. Bandura concludes, "After destructive means become invested with high moral purpose, functionaries work hard to become proficient at them and take pride in their destructive accomplishments."[19]

Along with morally reconstruing violence, individuals can displace responsibility by either referring to the dictates of authority figures or

Part Two: Zombies

mob mentality. Along with authority figures, Bandura argues, "Group decision-making is another common bureaucratic practice that enables otherwise considerate people to behave inhumanely, because no single individual feels responsible for policies arrived at collectively. Where everyone is responsible no one is really responsible."[20] Finally, individuals morally disengage from violence by dehumanizing the other. Perhaps most importantly for our discussion here, Bandura writes:

> To perceive another as human enhances empathetic or vicarious reactions through perceived similarity. [. . .] As a result, it is difficult to mistreat humanized persons without risking self-condemnation. Self-sanctions against cruel conduct can be disengaged or blunted by divesting people of human qualities. Once dehumanized, they are no longer viewed as persons with feelings, hopes, and concerns but as subhuman objects. [. . .] Subhumans are regarded as insensitive to maltreatment and capable of being influenced only by harsh methods.[21]

In the end, Bandura concludes with an observation that is strongly supported by the events in *The Walking Dead*. He writes, "It requires conducive social conditions rather than monstrous people to produce heinous deeds. Given appropriate social conditions, decent, ordinary people can be led to do extraordinarily cruel things."[22] When reading Bandura's essay, it is tempting to think of terrorists as an easily defined "other" like Al Qaeda; however, it is important to recognize the ways in which our own political leaders employ these mechanisms when choosing to go to war with said recognizable terrorists.

The survivors of the zombie apocalypse in Kirkman's narrative employ Bandura's mechanisms, and then some. Rick's justifications are the most interesting because he is, at first, an officer of the law, a fact to which he occasionally refers at the beginning of the series. In trying to explain his treatment of Thomas to Lori, he tells her, "I'm an officer of the *law*. I may not have anyone to *answer* to anymore—but these people look to me to keep them *safe*. I *owe* it to them to do everything in my power to do so." In the same scene, he tells Carl, "But if we're going to keep him from killing anyone *else*, we're going to have to kill *him*. Do you understand, Carl?" Rick is clearly engaging in the moral negotiation of an immoral act.

Characters frequently displace responsibility for violent actions throughout *The Walking Dead*. They primarily blame their zombie-plagued surroundings for forcing them into violent behavior. Even the

Governor, the most irrational, ruthless character in the series, justifies his behavior. In explaining the fights that he organizes for the people of Woodbury, he tells Rick, "There's a *lesson* there. You gotta keep people *occupied* or they'll *turn* on you. *Reading* and *fucking* will only keep people busy for *so long*. Eventually there's gotta be something *else*. Hence our little sporting event here." Of course, we can hear echoes of displaced responsibility in Rick's statements to Lori and Carl in the previous paragraph.

Of the three mechanisms highlighted in this section, the dehumanization of the other is obviously the most prevalent. We have seen that the extermination of the zombies depends on this mechanism. Despite their shared conflict, the survivors of the zombie apocalypse still feel the need to dehumanize one another. When Rick realizes that Martinez, a Woodbury resident, has fled the prison to lead other members of Woodbury back to the prison, he chases him down, runs him over with Dale's RV and strangles him. As they wrestle with one another, they have this exchange:

> Martinez: My people *deserve* to be *safe*, too.
>
> Rick: *You people* are a *poison*—a plague *worse* than the dead! You stage *fights*—people die for your *amusement*! You're animals! [. . .] You're not *getting* it Martinez! Don't *you know what people are capable of*?!
>
> Martinez (as he is choking to death): "I'm starting— . . . I'm—I think I'm getting—the idea.

Ignoring his own brutal treatment of strangers (and even members of his own community), the Governor dehumanizes human threats to his survival. The quote in the previous section testifies to his attitude, and when he prepares his community to invade the prison, the Governor refers to Rick and his group in this way: "These savages know where we live! They know what we have! They know our strengths and they know our weaknesses! I say we strike at them before they have a chance to come at us."

Despite all the violent posturing of most of the survivors who dehumanize potential threats in order to rally the troops or settle their conscience after violent attacks, few characters evidence the effects that such an environment and mechanisms of dealing with it have on the survivors as succinctly as Rick's wife Lori. After the Thomas debacle, Lori confesses to Rick, "I can't get it out of my head, Rick, I can't stop *dwelling* on it. Those monsters outside are one thing but any of the people in here *with*

PART TWO: ZOMBIES

us could cause us just as much harm any time." Again, this is where Kirkman helps drive home the point that violence threatens us from within our own communities just as often as it does from without.

TRAUMA ZOMBIES

"What's happening to us? It's never going to be the *same* again. We're *never* going to be normal ... just *look* at us."

—LORI

If Bandura can speak about the long-term effects of sustained training to develop a terrorist, then we can certainly think in similar terms about the effects of the zombie apocalypse on Rick and the other survivors. When the group confronts Rick about killing Dexter in cold blood, he admits to doing it for the good of the group—to keep everyone safe. When Rick regains consciousness after a brutal fight with Tyreese, he addresses the group and gives what is perhaps the central speech of the series. It is worth quoting at length:

> Rick: The *world* has changed—and we're going to have to change *with* it. Understand? [. . .] If you still think things are going to go back to the way they *were—stop!* They're *not! Nothing will ever be the way it used to be. Ever!* [. . .] You can sit around *trying* to follow every retarded little *rule* we *ever* invented to make us feel like we *weren't* animals—*and you can die!* We will *change!* We will *evolve*. We'll make *new* rules—we'll still be *humane* and *kind* and we'll still *care* for each other. But when the time comes—we *have* to be prepared to do *whatever* it takes to *keep* us *safe. Whatever it takes!* "You kill—you *die*." That was probably the most naïve thing I've *ever* said. The fact is—in most cases, *now*, the way things are—you kill—you *live*.
>
> Tyreese: We don't *want* to become *savages*, that's what you don't *get*.
>
> Rick: It's *obvious* now that I'm the only *sane* one here! We *already are* savages, Tyreese. *You* especially! The *second* we put a bullet in the head of one of these undead monsters—the *moment* one of us drove a hammer into one of their faces—or cut a head off. We became what we *are!* [. . .] You see them out there. You

know that when we die—we *become* them. You think we hide behind walls to protect us from *the walking dead*. Don't you *get it*? We ARE *the walking dead!* We are the walking dead.

In other words, Rick and the others have become what Nick Muntean calls "trauma zombies."

Though it is not a zombie film, Muntean argues that the plot of *On the Beach* (1959) provides us with another class of zombies, "trauma zombies." Muntean observes that in the film's post-nuclear apocalyptic setting, "the characters' psychic annihilation precedes their physical destruction, and life itself becomes a state of walking death [. . .] as their normal symbolic processes of meaning-making (that is to say, ideology) are so disrupted that they are unable to maintain a coherent identity and thus enter a muted, dazed state of being not unlike that of the traditional zombie." As a result, Muntean concludes that death becomes a state that these characters inhabit within their own earthly vessels, something they become, rather than somewhere they go.[23] Paralleling Bandura's discussion of the power of dehumanizing the other, Muntean is aware of the self-dehumanization that helps create a trauma zombie. He adds, "The most despairing element of the trauma zombie, then, is its own inability to recognize itself as being human, a negative feedback loop of dehumanizing anguish and alienation."[24] While the trauma zombies in *On the Beach* suffer from mental and emotional despair and shuffle about more akin to their truly undead counterparts, the humans-cum-trauma-zombies in *The Walking Dead* are far more dangerous.

The anger with which these trauma zombies terminate the undead has a deleterious effect on their possibility of survival. Steven Schlozman notes the harmful effects of unleashing anger and violence on an undead threat. He writes, "There is neither empathy nor wrath among the adversaries of those who survive the zombie apocalypse. So what do we do? We take all that wrath, all that emotion that we'd expect back from something that appears to hate us so much that it would eviscerate us without a second thought, and we direct it toward one another."[25] With echoes of Frantz Fanon's observations on colonial violence between the oppressed and their oppressors, the survivors' violence, with nowhere to go, simply infects the community and undermines its ability to stay safe(r) in the zombie apocalypse.

PART TWO: ZOMBIES

Much like T. Sean Collins in *World War Z*, Tyreese recognizes the ways in which the survivors' violent behavior can infect them like a poisonous disease. In an argument with Rick, Tyreese tells him:

> You had the group's best interests in mind?! *Bullshit!* Maybe at *first*—yes, but I see it written all over your *face!* This shit you've been through—the stuff you've done to *survive*—killing Dexter especially—it's given you a bloodlust! You're starting to *enjoy* the things you do. You're always the first one ready to act when anything goes wrong. I've seen it in your *eyes*—I saw it when you *mutilated* Allen. *You enjoyed it!!*

Tyreese recognizes that so much killing has become a part of who Rick is. His assertion that Rick enjoys it might not accurately describe the situation, but he does recognize that it has become a need that Rick must fill. As a result, Rick might have much more in common with the Governor than he would dare to admit. Dr. Stevens, Woodbury's resident physician and court doctor to the Governor, provides an assessment of the Governor that could easily apply to Rick:

> He did what had to be done, what needed to be done to keep people *safe*. After a while, it was clear to some of us that he was doing this more out of enjoyment than the need to protect us. It was clear he was little more than an evil bastard. [. . .] What do you think he'd *do* to anyone who opposed him? I hate the son of a bitch but I can't *do* anything. Whatever else he *does . . .* he keeps these people *safe*. That's *enough* for most people. As long as there's a wall between them and the biters they're not too concerned with who's with them on their side of the wall.

Along with displacing responsibility for the atrocities that happen in Woodbury onto the Governor, Dr. Stevens also recognizes that he and the other residents of Woodbury have become trauma zombies as well, accepting their impotent and tortured lot in life.

After Rick and the group leave the prison, he encounters a man named Abraham, another survivor who has done whatever was necessary to protect himself and those he loved. Abraham also recognizes that something foundational has changed in himself and among his fellow survivors. Abraham tells Rick about the time his neighbors tried to rape his daughter at the outbreak of the zombie plague:

> Abraham: I hadn't realized—hadn't noticed how much people had *changed*. Some people—was like a *fucking* switch went off in

them. One day they were nice, law-abiding folks, the next—they
were animals. Some of the animals stayed back at the grocery
that day. Don't know what happened to set them off... I'll never
know. Maybe they just thought this was their last chance to have
a woman—so they'd take it. My son tried to fight them. They
held him down—made him watch. Hundreds of those flesh-
eating fucks out there—never thought I'd locked up my family
with something worse. [. . .] So I found out. I found out and I
did things to those people. I had help, but I did the worst of it
to be sure. I did things I never though I'd be able to . . . things I
wouldn't have thought possible. Six men, pulled apart with my
bare hands, mostly. I went fucking crazy—practially turned one
boy inside out. Was a good kid . . . mowed my lawn a few times
when he was younger.

Rick: You did what you had to—.

Abraham: No. I did what I *wanted* to do. They saw it all. My family *saw* me do everything. That's not what they wanted. It *scared*
them. I scared them. I scared them so they *left*.

Abraham understands that, to his family at least, he became just as scary as, or scarier than, the zombies that plagued them. Oblivious to the implications of the story that Abraham shares, Rick presses on in his "for-the-greater-good" fashion and reassures Abraham, "You and me—our switches flipped. We're doing whatever it takes—*whatever* it takes to survive and to help those around us survive. The people without the switch—those who weren't able to go from law-abiding citizens to stone-cold killers . . . those are the ones shambling around out there—trying to eat us."

In one of the more recent issues of the series, Rick and his group have been welcomed into a community in Alexandria, Virginia. He is quickly nominated to security detail and begins supervising the community much like he has his own group up to this point. Some members of the community resent his leadership and the effects other new arrivals like Glenn and Michonne are having on the community. Nicholas, a long-standing member of the Alexandria community, violently confronts Rick, but Rick calms him down and reassures him that he is only interested in the good of the entire group. Later, after the altercation, Rick tells Andrea:

Andrea, I need to tell someone . . . I . . . I wanted to kill him. That
man today—Nicholas. [. . .] No, you don't get it. I didn't *need* to.

Part Two: Zombies

> I *wanted* to kill him—I even thought, when I was talking to him, how much easier it'd be if I just killed him, right then and there. I wanted to kill him because of how *pathetic* he is ... like he holds no value. I've done it so many times, it's ... it's something I *casually* think about when someone comes into conflict with me, killing them. That's fucked up—I mean ... that's *terrifying* ... right?

This is indeed terrifying, especially when it comes from someone who has been entrusted with the responsibility of protecting the community. However, nothing signifies the depths to which Rick has fallen than his statement to Jessie. As a horde of zombies invades the Alexandria community and in the chaos that ensues, Rick and Jessie consider fleeing with their children to resume a life on the run. When Jessie asks about taking other children with them, Rick tells her, "The thing to keep in mind ... about other people's children ... they're not our children."

PACIFISM IN THE ZOMBIE APOCALYPSE

> "I'm sorry—there has to be another answer—this—this is *unacceptable*. I just, I can't think of any way to justify ... *this.*"
>
> —Father Gabriel Stokes

That Rick and the others indiscriminately kill zombies in order to survive is understandable. That Rick and his group engage in violent conflict with competing survivors is also understandable, but deeply unfortunate. Throughout *The Walking Dead*, however, I believe that Kirkman implicitly asks us to consider if another way of being in the zombie apocalypse exists. Is violence the only option? In raising this question, and as some of the examples will show below, Kirkman is also drawing on a minor, but important, feature of some zombie narratives that can be traced back to the foundational work of Romero.[26]

Unlike the creators of most other zombie narratives, Kirman and his artists take great care to individualize each zombie, which is no small feat given the number of them that roam abandoned cities and the desolate countryside.[27] Only when Adlard and Rathburn draw them from a distance do the zombies appear to be an undistinguishable mass of roving flesh eaters. Zombie scholar Kyle William Bishop notes, "[The] zombies are also carefully depicted in an empathetic light, and this empathy invariably draws viewers back to the plight of the human characters. [. . .] *The Walking Dead* presents its feckless monsters as victims, beings that were once human themselves."[28] While our chief concern will lie with the safety and well-being of the human survivors, in a genre in which "the other" is used as nothing more than target practice, that Kirkman and his team present the zombies in this fashion should give us pause. His brief reminders of the zombies' former identities lend an emotional gravity to the narrative often absent in other iterations of the genre.

Though the central group of survivors is a thrown-together, rag-tag lot, there are features about the group that set them apart from other zombie apocalypse survivors. In his essay, "'For Love is Strong as Death:' Redeeming Values in *The Walking Dead*," Kim Paffenroth points out alternatives to the violence and gore that attract so many fans. He recognizes that the zombie genre requires certain elements and writes, "[A] world overrun by zombies may be almost unbearably violent and sad, but it need not be unholy and meaningless. The living can choose to honor the dead and respect whatever remains of their humanity, just as they can choose to love one another and find purpose in that love."[29] For Paffenroth, a chief redemptive value in *The Walking Dead* is love, particularly familial love. This is essentially what helps communities of survivors persevere. Paffenroth adds, "First, the love that family members have for one another several times expands to include others—either reaching outside the original family unit or making the newcomer a part of the family."[30] Though these elements are fleeting, Paffenroth argues that they are not futile and may, in fact, prove salvific.[31]

In fleeting moments throughout *The Walking Dead*, we see survivors combat the violent treatment of zombies with reactions from sympathy to familial love. Again, in the first issue, before Rick can leave his small town for Atlanta, he returns to the half zombie crawling on the side of the road and shoots it in the head, shedding a tear in the process. It is impossible to imagine Rick shedding a tear for a zombie in issue 91. The familial love about which Paffenroth writes finds its chief example in Hershel and his family. Living on a farm outside Atlanta, they have remained somewhat immune to the chaotic violence that enveloped Atlanta and other big cities. Hershel's medical training has influenced his views of the zombies, as he sees them suffering from a potentially curable disease. Hershel keeps zombies, some of which are family members, in his barn. Opposing Rick's "we-kill-them-before-they-kill-us" plan, Hershel tells

Part Two: Zombies

him, "We're keeping them in the barn until we can figure out a way to *help* them. What have *you* been doing with them? [. . .] *Killing them?!* You've just been *killing them?!* [. . .] You don't know *why!* You don't even know what's *wrong* with them. *Nobody* does. We don't know a *damn* thing about what happened or what's going on. [. . .] My *son* is in there, *god dammit!*" When Rick tries to tell Hershel that the zombie in the barn is no longer his son, Hershel explodes:

> Not my son?! What made *you* such a *goddamn expert?!* I don't know about *you* but the zombies around *here* didn't come with a fucking *instruction manual*! We don't know a *goddamn thing* about them. We don't know what they're *thinking*—what they're *feeling*. We don't know if it's a *disease* or side effects of some kind of chemical warfare! We don't know *shit*! For all *we* know these things could wake up *tomorrow*, heal up, and be completely *normal* again! We just don't *know*! You could have been *murdering* all those people you "put out of their misery." [. . .] Rick, *listen*. These things could be in the early stages of *recovery*. They could be *healing* . . . and that's why things aren't working right. This is all completely *unknown* to us. We've got no clue how to handle this. I don't want to have *blood* on my hands if we find out these people *are* alive.

Hershel's reluctance to mindlessly attack the zombies should also give us pause. While his view of the zombies changes when he and his children are attacked by the very zombies he has been saving, Hershel never seems to be as enthusiastic about exterminating zombies as Rick, Tyreese, or Michonne frequently are.

Like Hershel, other characters attempt to keep zombies alive. Michonne shows up with two jawless zombies on a leash, her boyfriend and his best friend. However, since she's detached the lower half of their jaws to keep them from biting her, they would not fare well should Hershel ever find a cure for the plague. Both the Governor and Morgan keep their children alive after they fall victim to the zombie plague. Though Morgan's relationship is less disturbing than the Governor's relationship with his daughter, the two both kill other survivors in order to feed their children.

Other characters' reactions to the zombies, if only in passing, contrast greatly with Bandura's discussion of the dehumanization of the other as a way of aiding in their destruction. Through Sophia, one of the youngest characters in the series, Kirkman provides a non-violent, far less angry reaction to the zombie threat. Playing in the prison yard, Sophia and Carl look through the fences at a group of zombies stumbling in the field. They discuss:

> Carl: You—are you still *scared* of them?
>
> Sophia: I was. I *used* to be. I still don't like the *sounds* they make, but I'm not *scared* of them anymore. Mostly I just feel sorry for them.
>
> Carl: You feel *sorry* for them? Why?
>
> Sophia: Because they look so sad. Don't they look *sad* to you?

In the same setting, Axel, a former prison inmate, works in the garden with Hershel. He takes a break from his work and, looking out at the surrounding zombies, says:

> I think about them [the zombies] all the time. Who they were—what they did before they died—all kinds of stuff. I think about what jobs they had. Or if they had any family, and if so, where they went or what happened to them. Are any of them family members who have stuck together? Any of them out there know each other before they died? I mean, those things all used to be people. Every single one of them had lives. [...] You don't wonder about that? What kind of people they were before they died and decided to try and eat us. I bet most of them were good people, like you or me—or well, you. [...] I wonder what it felt like when they died. I wonder what it was like to start turning into one of them—to come back. I wonder if it hurts. I bet it hurts real bad. That's why they moan so much. You gotta ask yourselves these questions. I mean, odds are we'll all be like that before long. Odds are.

These are important viewpoints in a zombified post-apocalypse, but unfortunately, they have little effect on the people who prefer more violent approaches. One long-standing member of Rick's group does represent a non-violent model for his peers.

Few characters embody an alternative means of existence in the zombie apocalypse as clearly as Dale, an older man who only kills out of necessity. His presence in the group does have an effect on his more violent counterparts. Dale has been through the wringer like few other characters. He lost his wife to the plague, was bitten by a zombie, lost a

Part Two: Zombies

leg in the process, was captured and partially eaten by cannibals, and eventually killed himself when he was too sick to carry on. Standing over his grave, Rick reflects on the choices that Dale made throughout their ordeal compared to his own:

> Dale has me rethinking a lot of things. He resisted things that I deemed necessary. He wouldn't allow himself to be completely changed by his surroundings. I thought that made him *weak*, but maybe I was wrong. Maybe he was strong to resist those urges. Maybe he was stronger than any of us to hold on to his humanity and refuse to let it go. What *we've* done to survive... sometimes I feel like we're no better than the dead ones.

In similar fashion, Morgan, despite the violent lengths to which he has gone to protect Duane, gives some dying advice to Carl... even though he thinks he is talking to his son Duane. Morgan says that he can tell that Carl cares about people and encourages him to remember that this is what matters in life. He reminds Carl, "[We] stop caring about other people. Maybe it's what we have to do to get by... but it takes away a piece of your soul... every time."

In the 86th issue of the series, it seems that Rick finally figured out that in their current situation a good defense might be the best offense. Though fans of the series are well aware that anything can happen under Kirkman's direction, Rick does seem to be shifting from a more aggressive stance to one that could be considered more truly protective. As he settles into the community in Alexandria and survives the largest zombie attack yet, he realizes something. Rick tells Andrea:

> The things I did... the moves I made. I justified it by saying it was for the good of my family... but really, I was overlooking the most important part of survival in this world. *Community.* Protecting the group protects Carl in a better way than I ever realized. It's like this new barrier we're talking about outside the fence. Protect the fence and make it that much more secure by design. That's the key... *that's* how we're going to survive in this world.

CONCLUSION

"The thing you have to realize is that they're just *us*—they're no different. They want what they *want*, they *take* what they *want* and after they *get* what they *want*—they're only content for the *briefest* span of time. Then they want more."

—The Governor

So what does all of this have to do with religion and theology? Though it has not been integral to my discussion here, Kirkman is not unaware of the effects that zombie narratives can have on God talk. Hershel's conversations with Maggie and the introduction of Father Gabriel Stokes open up opportunities for religious discussion. Hershel uses the zombie apocalypse to prove Scripture:

> Depending on your interpretation this could be proof of the Bible being *right*. [. . .] The dead walk? This could be the resurrected dead—during the rapture, we could be in the seven years of tribulation . . . being tested and strengthened. I'd have to ask why *we* weren't called up, good people that we are—but maybe something got lost in the translation along the way. It's all about *faith*, honey. My faith ain't never been *stronger*.

Kirkman also takes advantage of the science vs. faith possibilities inherent in *The Walking Dead*. Later in the series, science teacher Eugene calls Father Gabriel's beliefs absurd, to which the minister responds, "Are they? You are a man of science, and so I'm sure there was a time not too long ago when you would have told me how it was physically impossible for the dead to walk . . . and yet, here we are."

Such exchanges in *The Walking Dead* are far more entertaining than they are informative, even though they could potentially open up avenues for further reflection. Far more important, for the purposes of our discussion, are the theology- and religion-laden conversations that the series engenders around topics of human identity and spirituality. In a couple of places, John W. Morehead has asked whether or not zombies can be spiritual or if we can have a zombie theology.[32] In his blog post on the religious implications of the contemporary zombie craze for the Religion Blog at CNN.com, John Blake provides two competing reactions to zombie narratives from David Murphy and Rebecca Borah. The former argues that the genre reveals how we can appeal to a "higher spirit" to prevent us from eating one another, whereas the latter argues that when it comes down to it, we must tap into our baser natures to ward off the zombies lest we be infected too.[33]

The implication of such approaches to the zombie genre seems to be that they appeal to us because they show us what we *might* be or what we *could* become. I believe that *The Walking Dead* is so popular and has helped resurrect and breathe new life into the zombie genre because it shows us what we already are. When Rick screams at his fellow survivors, "We are the walking dead," he might as well be speaking for the reader too. Kevin Boon echoes this sentiment in his essay, "The Zombie as Other: Mortality and the Monstrous in the Post-Nuclear Age," when he writes, "The proliferation of the zombie mythology into mainstream culture during the past three decades has established the zombie as the predominant symbol of the monstrous other. [. . .] The increased appeal of the zombie in the later twentieth century is linked to the mythology's ability to stir existential anxieties about our own mortality within the larger context of cultural attitudes about the nature of self."[34]

While the zombie perseveres and appeals as that monstrous other, perhaps it also lingers in the pop culture conscience because we know and fear it as our own self. Zombie-satirist Scott Kenemore notes that one of the many strengths of *The Walking Dead* is its portrayal of guilt, innocence, and responsibility. Kenemore concludes, "For humans to survive in the apocalyptic wasteland, they must become killers—at least of zombies and probably also of other humans. That is, there are no longer any innocents. Nobody who has made it this far has done so without blood on his or her hands."[35] The actions of these survivors, however, are not just about survival but the ability to maintain some sort of (positive?) identity as well. In his discussion of personhood in *The Walking Dead*, Brendan Riley argues that human identity is situated and adds that the "surviving humans work very hard to define themselves in ways that maintain their sense of humanity, even at the cost of dehumanizing others."[36] As I have already shown, Riley also claims that human survivors employ similar strategies towards one another in times of trouble, again blurring the lines between humans and zombies.[37]

Our world might not be an apocalyptic wasteland that is the backdrop for *The Walking Dead*, although I imagine for many it is. Yet like the characters in Kirkman's zombie narrative, we kill for survival, and none of us are innocent. In the process, we embrace a host of mechanisms to cope with the atrocities of which we are guilty, devaluing nature and dehumanizing the other in the process from outsourced labor to the death penalty. We develop elaborate biological or economic arguments to defend our behavior, all in an effort to preserve our self-delusions of humanness while keeping our monstrous natures at bay. At the same time, we are a fearful and often confused people struggling to negotiate a multitude of existences and the ever-looming possibility of non-existence. We are afraid of being undead, yet unalive, of being caught in those places where life has no meaning and experience is rote or exploitative. In reality, we might be more like Dale than any other character in the series—trying to minimize the death and destruction around us while also harboring the virus against which we are fighting.

And this is, at its core, the brilliance of *The Walking Dead*—the both/and identity of its characters. Adlard and Rathburn's most thrilling artwork often involves pages and panels in which the survivors undertake a mass slaughter of invading zombies. In these panels, the artists juxtapose agonizing zombies with enraged humans, and it takes a second look to distinguish between the two. In a very real way, Rick is right. He and his fellow survivors are all the walking dead, not because of the zombies that lurk around whatever safe haven they think they have found or created, but because of the ways in which they treat one another. Over the course of the series, Rick, as Jonathan Maberry puts it, "decides to take back the world. Or, looked at another way, Rick decides to *conquer* the world."[38] Unfortunately, Rick's old world ways (i.e., violence) break him and the very world he is trying to reclaim. Maberry adds, "At the worst, Rick may become so thoroughly damaged that he might not be a fit member for the new society he creates."[39] As it has with the survivors in *The Walking Dead*, the logical reasoning and the psychological and emotional defenses for the (mis)treatment of the other chip away at our ability to feel compassion and sympathy for one another and blind us to the realities of our existence.

No doubt, there will be a host of potential viewers and readers that brush off *The Walking Dead*, the zombie genre, and books like this one. This is an unfortunate reaction, given the number of fans that rush to the series, and a potentially fatal mistake given what the series has to tell us about ourselves. Critics might dismiss all of this because of its sheer fantastical nature and the pure impossibility of it all. Hopkins' assertion that the events in *The Walking Dead* are "[the] impossible ethical situations of a cruel world" works on two levels.[40] They are impossible because we know that the dead do not rise to feed on the living. On the other

Part Two: Zombies

hand, they are impossible because there is no right answer to them. And it is on this second level that the series functions best as a mirror for the impossible ethical situations that plague our own experiences. The value of Kirkman's work, and narratives like it, lies in this very impossibility, for if we can navigate the (non)existence in the pages of *The Walking Dead*, then surely we can navigate our own.

END NOTES

1. Brooks, *World War Z*.
2. www.zombiedefense.org.
3. Kirkman, "Introduction," 10.
4. AMC's television adaptation garnered 5.2 million viewers in its first season and reached 7.3 million viewers with the first episode of its second season. Licensed products, like action figures and T-shirts, spin-off literature, and a video game that is currently in development have made *The Walking Dead* a pop culture phenomenon. See "AMC's 'The Walking Dead' Delivers," and Goldberg, "TV Ratings: 'The Walking Dead.'"
5. E.g., Mulvey, *Visual and Other Pleasure*, and Clover, *Men, Women, and Chain Saws*.
6. McCloud, *Understanding Comics*, 89, 92. Please note that the use of bold font throughout this chapter is an attempt to accurately quote the original comic book and/or graphic novel text.
7. Lowder, "In Media Apocalypsis," xv.
8. Poole, "Praying to the Zombie Jesus."
9. Liaguno, "Happy (En)Trails," 124.
10. Robert Kirkman quoted in Ruditis, *The Walking Dead Chronicles*, 20, 23.
11. Liaguno, "Happy (En)Trails," 125.
12. Italics mine.
13. Hopkins, "The Hero Wears the Hat," 209.
14. Magil, "Justifications for Violence," 1086.
15. Ibid., 1086.
16. Bandura, "Mechanisms of Moral Disengagement, 161.
17. Ibid., 163.
18. Bandura, "Mechanisms of Moral Disengagement," 164.
19. Ibid., 172.
20. Ibid., 176.
21. Ibid., 181.
22. Ibid., 182.

23. Muntean, "Nuclear Death, 82, 83.
24. Ibid., 96.
25. Schlozman, "Feel Better," 170.
26. See Paffenroth, *Gospel of the Living Dead*.
27. Paffenroth, *Gospel of the Living Dead*, 69, also points out that a similar kind of individualization of the zombie is at work in some of Romero's films, particularly *Dawn of the Dead*.
28. Bishop, "The Pathos of the Walking Dead," 11.
29. Paffenroth, "'For Love is Strong as Death,'" 229.
30. Ibid., 226.
31. Ibid., 230.
32. See Morehead, "Can Zombies Be Spiritual?," and Morehead, "Toward a Zombie Theology."
33. Blake, "The zombie theology behind the walking dead."
34. Boon, "The Zombie as Other," 50.
35. Kenemore, "A Zombie Among Men," 193.
36. Riley, "Zombie People, 89.
37. Ibid., 90.
38. Maberry, "Take Me to Your Leader," 30.
39. Ibid., 32.
40. Hopkins, "The Hero Wears the Hat," 209.

PART THREE

Other Undead

10

When You're Undead, the Whole World is Jewish

Arnold T. Blumberg

INTRODUCTION

When the subject of the living dead arises, one question often comes up: Why are there no Jewish zombies (apart from a certain carpenter)? That is, there are certainly a few; with over 600 zombie movies in existence, to say nothing of comic books, novels, television shows, games, and other media, we can be quite sure that a few Jews have joined the ranks of the undead at some point, even if we don't know exactly who they are. But the question is of a more abstract nature: Where is the comparable Jewish cultural tradition for all the other creatures that roam the dark corridors of our subconscious? There is one in fact, and it occupies a unique position in that it is truly "undead" in a way none of those other monsters are. It was never really alive, never really dead, and now trapped between those states in a grotesque parody of both. It is the Golem.

Part Three: Other Undead

ORIGIN STORY

The Golem, a figure most often found in the Ashkenazic Jewish traditions of Eastern Europe rather than those of the Sephardic/Mediterranean strain, is an artificial creature fashioned from earth or clay and imbued with a semblance of life via mystical means. Although many sources credit the Kabbalistic *Sefer Yetzirah* (*Book of Creation*) as playing a role in the legend—it includes instructions for making a Golem of your very own—the stories of the Golem rarely rely on the use of that text for the creature's manufacture. Most tales involve a Rabbi shaping a humanoid form from clay and then raising it via various methods including combinations of inscription, incantation, and physical gestures.

Although it is not a human being, we may be more closely related to the Golem than we think. Genesis 2:7 tells us that Adam—the first man himself—was shaped out of clay or dust. In Hebrew, *'adam* is a variation of *'adamah*, the word for "earth." The word Golem itself turns up first in Psalm 139 in what Talmudic scholars suggest may be the equivalent of a journal entry from Adam discussing his "unformed" limbs. The Talmud later ruminates on this and sets the time at which the first man was merely a "shapeless mass" or Golem at his third hour of existence. By the sixth, he was imbued with a soul and became a living, sentient being. Other sources claim that he was without a soul for the first twelve hours of his life; but no matter which schedule you go by, Adam was for a short time the world's first Golem.

In creating a Golem, a person must engage in the ultimate hubris by assuming the role of the divine and creating his or her very own "man." Since we cannot create a life equal to that which God can create, the results are inherently limited. The Golem usually does not speak and certainly has no soul, no free will or sentience, and is no more than a puppet to be directed by its master. As zombie aficionados are fond of pointing out, their metaphorical potency lay in the fact that they are, essentially, us; by looking at the Golem from the context of humanity's own creation, it too shares that status, and like a zombie the Golem is a mere shadow of humanity, a funhouse mirror reflection with lots of symbolic potential. We also have to wonder exactly how this animation of the Golem works. If they are creatures without a soul, then what is it providing the spark of life after the incantations and inscriptions are accomplished? Is it God responding to a Rabbinical request, reaching out and offering a tethered

Soul Lite™[1] for temporary use, ready to yank it back when that letter is erased?

God's possible direct role in the process also brings up another intriguing link with the zombie mythos from a theological perspective. All of those rotting re-animated corpses shambling toward you might paradoxically be the harbingers of good news. After all, if you're in a reality where the zombie apocalypse has come about not by scientific or other natural, human means, but through some mysterious supernatural universal switch being thrown, doesn't that inherently confirm the existence of God? Well, maybe, and in the case of the Golem the confirmation of a reality complete with supreme deity seems even more certain.

Another point of connection with zombies is that the Golem shares with its maker a similar relationship to that of the Voudoun practitioner or *bokor* and a zombie. If we consider the supernatural interpretation of the process, the *bokor* calls upon the powers of the Loa (Voudoun gods) to help in the creation of the zombie subject as a Rabbi calls upon God to imbue his Golem with lifelike existence, but the similarities stop at the surface. *Bokors* are considered to be corrupt or evil versions of the *houngan* and *mambo* priests and priestesses that practice what the Western world calls Voudoun, or more popularly, "voodoo," while a zombie is often the product of a dark, selfish desire to enslave someone for the uses of the *bokor* or a paying customer. A Rabbi is, of course, representative of Jewish devotion to God, the Torah, and scholarship, and a Golem's creation is only possible through the use of and belief in the mystical power that comes from dedication to God as well as for the purpose of protection of the Jewish people in times of crisis. Selfish motivations would theoretically prevent a successful animation. Even the divine forces involved in both processes differ drastically, since at least one Loa—Baron Samedi—is said to engage in questionable if not offensive behavior that in no way correlates with what humanity has come to expect from the Judeo-Christian God.

Given this comparison, it's interesting to note that while hubris is a primary theme in many Golem tales, the creation of one is more in accordance with respect for God than it might seem. The commandment prohibiting any graven images would seem to rule out the creation of a Golem, but perhaps its intended role nullifies that directive. Its purpose is noble—to protect and serve the Jews in times of crisis—and in some stories there is the implication of a divine order to make the creature in the first place. Defiance of the divine would supposedly make a Golem

Part Three: Other Undead

impossible to make, and since it's not technically crafted from a human being like a zombie, it also cannot be construed as violating one of Judaism's cherished principles, that of *K'Vod HaMes* or "respect for the dead." As with other religious traditions, Judaism has a system for dealing with the dead that is part codified religious law, part tradition, and part cultural imperative. *K'Vod HaMes* could be why Jewish culture lacks more of an undead mythology, but as we'll see later, a modern mutation of the Golem brings this issue into shocking relief.

While the Golem is largely represented as a lumbering muscle man, a glorified bouncer standing at the symbolic gates of the Jewish community to keep the peace and protect its charges, there are tales that give the creature a few other powers. A Golem sometimes has the ability to turn invisible, either on its own or via the use of a talisman, while some are described as burning the unrighteous with a fiery touch. Any Marvel Comics fans that remember the Man-Thing and its catch-phrase—"Whosoever knows fear burns at the Man-Thing's touch"[2]—might find this more than a little intriguing. At times a Golem can even serve as a conduit to the afterlife, drawing back the souls of the dead for a star witness appearance if crucial testimony is required to accuse and condemn those that threaten the Jews. Ultimately, the Golem is most often depicted as a protector of the Jews, but in its unusual creation also lay a danger to its maker and those under its protection as well.

THE GOLEM OF PRAGUE AND OTHER ASTOUNDING TALES

The most famous version of this legend concerns the Golem of Prague, supposedly created by Rabbi Judah Loew ben Bezalel in the sixteenth century. At a time when accusations from Christian leaders concerning "blood libel"—that Jews used the blood of Christian children in rituals and for baking *matzah* bread—were common, Polish Jews lived in a constant state of fear. The danger of recurring *pogroms*—violent mob-led attacks on Jewish people and property owned by Jews—and rampant anti-Semitism as well as the looming threat of expulsion or execution of all Jews by order of the Holy Roman Emperor inspired Loew, the "Maharal," to seek an answer via mystical means. Loew took clay from the Vltava riverbank, fashioned an inanimate figure, and inscribed the Hebrew word *'emes* ("truth") on its forehead. The Golem awakened, "alive" if not truly sentient, to serve as a protector for the Jews of Prague. Alternate versions of this and other tales include different methods for animating a Golem, such as inscribing the Rabbi's name in blood on a rolled parchment similar to a *mezuzah*, an encased parchment inscribed with the prayer *Shema Yisrael*, affixed to the right side of doorways in a Jewish home in observance of a *mitzvah* referred to in Deuteronomy 6:9. Another eschews the use of the word *'emes* but merely employs one Hebrew letter, *shin*, which represents God.

In all versions of the story, however, the result is the same—as the Golem continued to exist, its actions became more violent and erratic, threatening the lives of Gentiles and possibly even the Jews he was created to protect. Even the Emperor himself was terrified and pledged to leave the Jews alone if Loew called off his earthen automaton. Loew removed the first letter of the word on its forehead, an *aleph*, leaving the Hebrew word for death, *Mes*. Apart from the clever word play, *aleph* has added significance as the first Hebrew letter; it represents the beginning, and the most significant beginning for our purposes is that of Creation itself. The notion that the Golem is brought to life by a word and the act of writing in this story is also profound, given the value placed by Jewish culture on scholarship and the power of words. That a simple word can carry such power, and lead to things both wondrous and woeful, also captures another snippet of Jewish wisdom imparted to us by none other than living legend and *lantzman* Stan Lee: "With great power comes great responsibility."[3]

Bringing the discussion back to Prague, when Loew rendered the Golem inanimate once again, it was supposedly stored in the local synagogue's *genizah* or attic storeroom. No concrete evidence has ever been found to substantiate the Loew tale, with most documentation not turning up until accounts published in the early 1800s, although there are still adherents in the Orthodox Jewish community that believe the Golem of Prague did indeed walk—and it might not have been alone.

Tales of the Golem do crop up in material that pre-dates the Prague story. In addition to the Talmudic discussion of Adam's earthy origins, there is a reference to the Babylonia-based Abba ben Joseph bar Hama or "Rava" creating a non-speaking man-like being and sending it to a colleague that correctly identified its origins and consigned it to the dust from whence it came. Prior to Prague, the most significant Golem adventure took place in the Polish city of Chelm, where, according to several accounts, Rabbi Eliyahu created a muddy manservant, with one version moving the word *'emes* from the forehead to a medallion around its neck.

PART THREE: OTHER UNDEAD

Another version of the story suggested that the creature was physically growing in size, threatening to tower over the entire community before Eliyahu at last ripped the medallion from it—or erased the *aleph* on its forehead—and rendered it inanimate, but not before it attacked and left its mark on Eliyahu's face as a reminder of his presumption. In a variation on this tale told about a different Rabbi, the Golem topples over and crushes its creator in a tragic if poetic finale.

POP CULTURE IN CLAY

It isn't entirely fair to claim that the Golem is overlooked, at least not in a grander pop culture sense. True, many ignore the Golem's relationship to its undead brethren, but the clay automatons do occasionally turn up in the media when other more familiar monsters are exhausted. Anthology series like *The X-Files* are particularly prone to featuring the Golem eventually if they run long enough,[4] and there have been a few genuinely significant adaptations of the legend in popular film and literature.

The Golem's pop culture credentials were first established in the early twentieth century through a trilogy of German silent films, only one of which still exists today. With a stiff pageboy helmet, ersatz five-pointed "Star of David" embedded in his chest, and earthen complexion, Paul Wegener—who also served as co-director and co-writer—appeared as the titular terror, an iconic image that earned a permanent place in virtually every horror movie coffee table book ever published. The surviving film, *The Golem: How He Came into the World*, is a 1920 adaptation of the Loew/Prague tale as well as a 1915 novel by Gustav Meyrink, and it still packs a stone-powered punch today.[5] The sight of a little girl offering fruit to the towering monster in one oft-printed image is one that would resonate later in horror fare like the 1931 *Frankenstein*; but I'm getting ahead of myself. Another cinema incarnation appeared in *It!*, a 1966 film alternately titled *Curse of the Golem*. The movie adapted the Prague tale by transplanting it to the modern era and casting Roddy McDowall as a museum curator that reanimates Loew's preserved creation. With overtones of *Psycho* and a pointy-headed title creature, *It!* is a memorable but not especially faithful rendition of the legend.[6]

In the print world, Marvel Comics has featured a handful of Golem characters (the aforementioned Man-Thing may have borrowed a Golem skill but was an otherwise unrelated swamp creature), including one that had his own series of stories in the *Strange Tales* anthology. The Golem, as he was unimaginatively named, housed the consciousness of a human Rabbi and battled alongside S.H.I.E.L.D. in all his purple glory. Yes, purple: gray was presumably too boring a color for a Golem superhero.[7] There was also "It! The Living Colossus," an animated statue that was a hybrid Golem/robot motivated by the consciousness of a wheelchair-bound master.[8] Not to be left out, DC Comics recently featured a heroic Golem called "The Monolith," controlled by a Jewish girl recovering from drug addiction.[9] If we want to stretch the point, the entire modern comic book superhero era technically started with a Golem. Many comic book historians interpret the creation of Superman by Cleveland-based Jewish teenagers Jerry Siegel and Joe Shuster as akin to crafting a Golem that could protect the helpless. With a letter inscribed on his chest, he crusades for justice while paralleling the Jewish immigrant experience as an outsider disguising his identity and assimilating into American culture. Comic book creator and novelist Michael Chabon acknowledged and endorsed this interpretation in his novel *The Amazing Adventures of Kavalier & Clay*, which featured fictionalized versions of Siegel and Shuster.[10]

THE GOLEM MADE FLESH

While it still may be persuasively argued that the Golem is at best a peripheral if not merely honorary member of the army of the undead, a more modern variation on the theme links the legend much closer to its undead cousins and provides a whole host of those Jewish zombies everybody's been asking about. They are called Flesh Golems, and for this we largely have to thank Mary Shelley.

Some believe Shelley was partly inspired by the Golem legend when fashioning her own undead creature, the part-work monster stitched together from bits and pieces of dead human remains by mad but brilliant Dr. Frankenstein in *Frankenstein: or, The Modern Prometheus* (1818). Some have even tried to draw the threads tighter by claiming that Frankenstein is supposed to be Jewish, but that's not remotely suggested in the book. Frankenstein is actually Swiss, and the "stein" in his surname is a common Germanic construction that doesn't necessarily imply a Jewish heritage.[11] But whether Shelley knew anything of the Golem legend or borrowed from it to shape her own work, what is certain is that although the idea of the Flesh Golem had existed prior to Shelley's landmark novel, it was forever after defined by her work and the 1931 Universal Pictures adaptation that sent children to bed with nightmares about a flat-topped Boris Karloff lumbering about in size 100 boots.[12] Once again, we see hubris rear its presumptuous head as the DNA of the Golem myth is woven into other cautionary tales about the forces with which humanity was not meant to meddle.

The Flesh Golem has mutated into an apparition that is truly nightmarish, leaving behind the humanoid familiarity of the Golem proper and Frankenstein's Monster to become a bloated, misshapen, hodgepodge of dead body parts like some work of unholy art. Now firmly ensconced in the realm of the living dead, these creatures shatter any illusion of adherence to the principle of *K'Vod HaMes* and therefore challenge the very essence of that deeply held Jewish belief. In one of the more prominent explorations of the Flesh Golem concept in pop culture, twentieth-century Frankenstein wannabe Dr. Herbert West takes his experiments in creating zombies from the 1985 film *Re-Animator* to the next level in its sequel, 1990's *Bride of Re-Animator*. West brings "unlife" to separate body parts stolen from a nearby cemetery and fuses them together into twisted creations that pile up until they angrily rebel in the film's apocalyptic climax. In the movie's most telling moment, West rails against the notion of blasphemy, suggesting that he has merely collected God's cast-offs and improved on nature. Before everything goes almost literally to Hell, West proclaims: "I will not be shackled by the failures of *your* God!" When the cemetery walls come tumbling down and the monsters try to tear their maker to pieces, there can be no better expression of the theme of hubris.[13]

Players of the online MMORPG (massively multiplayer online role-playing game) *World of Warcraft*, its print predecessor *Dungeons & Dragons*, or any of hundreds of other derivative games, are well acquainted with similar monsters that are not only composed of dead human body parts joined in inventive and infernal ways, but some that even blend pieces of other species into their "bodies." The less said about those the better, but surely the foreboding nature of presuming to play God can only be heightened by crossing the line into the animal kingdom—as if desecrating human graves wasn't bad enough. It's worth noting that many credit *Dungeons & Dragons* with playing a huge role in increasing the Golem's pop culture market share, introducing it to a much broader audience beyond scholars and those familiar with Jewish mythology via their 1977 *Advanced Dungeons & Dragons Monster Manual*, which was the first *D&D* source to feature Golems in clay, iron, stone, and flesh.[14]

The Flesh Golem represents the core horror of the legend taken to its ultimate organic extreme, but the Golem also branched off in a more metallic direction via the many robot monsters that also reflect the theme of hubris in their shiny surfaces. It's perhaps significant that although the robot as pop culture figure is a subject for other books, its name was first coined in Karel Capek's 1921 play, *R.U.R.: Rossum's Universal Robots*, which was written in Prague.[15] Hmmm. The emergence of science fiction storytelling that focuses on rampant robots usurping human authority and A.I.s asserting themselves over us—our own inanimate creations turning into threats to our very survival on this planet—reflects a technological adaptation of the Golem legend into something less specifically Jewish and more universal in its meaning and appeal. Was Isaac Asimov thinking of his own heritage and the dangers of a Golem run amok when he first wrote his carefully considered Laws of Robotics to rein in the metal Golem of the future?[16]

A KINDER, GENTLER GOLEM

Now that we're scared, it's time to calm down a bit. As with any other embodiment of our fears in the horror genre, the need to keep the Golem close whenever we might need that cathartic hit has also spawned a few cute-and-cuddly incarnations to soothe our souls when the darkness lifts. In the case of the Golem, the potential for a friendly interpretation is deeply embedded in the original legend itself since the creature is supposed to serve as a protector and sentinel despite the possibility of mischief and mayhem.

Although I do not define myself as a Jew by religious observance, but rather through heritage and family tradition, I did attend a Jewish private school as a child. Part of the process was a semi-annual trip to the local Hebrew book store for the year's relevant texts, and on one occasion I was surprised to discover that the Orthodox community had finally decided to try to employ more media-savvy means to inform and entertain—some might say indoctrinate—young students. There amid the Talmudic volumes and Old Testament tomes were some of my favorite things—comic books!

Part Three: Other Undead

These comics didn't feature Spider-Man, the Fantastic Four, or Batman however, but a little Jewish boy named Mendy Klein and his best friend, a rather gray, blocky fellow who was so tall that his head never fit into the frame and left him visible only from the neck down. This was Sholem the Golem, a benign buddy that Mendy found stored in a synagogue (did Sholem know Rabbi Loew?) and that accompanied Mendy on a series of morally-themed adventures in what was subtitled "the world's only Kosher comic book."[17] The 1980s series lasted only a short while, and a twenty-first-century revival employed the talents of veterans from Archie and Marvel Comics.[18]

If you want to see the Golem rearing its head pop culturally in the unlikeliest places, look no further than one of the cute and cuddliest seasonal tales of all time, "Frosty the Snowman." First shuffling his snowy form into our hearts via the 1950 Walter Rollins/Steve Nelson Christmas song recorded by the previous year's "Rudolph the Red-Nosed Reindeer" vocalist, Gene Autry,[19] the undead ice sculpture was immortalized by one of those ubiquitous Rankin/Bass animated television specials that still runs every year at holiday time.[20] With a magical hat that brings his otherwise inanimate form to life, Frosty has been labeled a "Snowlem," and he's not alone. Although Frosty himself always seems benign, fearsome and more threatening versions of the Snowlem have turned up in everything from movies like *Jack Frost*[21] and science fiction novellas like *Doctor Who: Time and Relative*.[22] Little Calvin of the classic comic strip *Calvin & Hobbes* even tried to animate his own frightening snowmen but with no success. The world can rest easy.[23]

Written by Pete Hamill and published in 1997, *Snow in August* was not the first retelling of the Loew/Prague story relocated to a modern setting, in this case Brooklyn in 1947, but one of the more endearing. Focusing on the inspirational, empowering aspects of the tale, the book centered on the growing friendship between an Orthodox Rabbi and a comic book-reading Irish boy that must confront the threat of post-war anti-Semitism by making their very own hero.[24] A 2001 film adaptation of the novel starring Stephen Rea as Hirsch went mostly unnoticed but remains a sweetly understated version of this venerable legend.[25] The Golem even turned up in a Halloween episode of *The Simpsons*. Voiced by Jewish comedian Richard Lewis, a dead ringer for Wegener's Golem (although this time sporting the correct six-pointed star) runs amok and is then married off to a Play-Doh girl voiced by Fran Drescher; surely a fate worse than undeath.[26]

WHITHER THE GOLEM?

It's taken a while but today the Golem has finally permeated pop culture with a plethora of appearances in film, television, novels, comics, cartoons, games, and even academia through the peer-reviewed Internet publication titled *GOLEM: Journal of Religion and Monsters*.[27] With the Golem myth's relationship to Jewish scholarship and the power of words, it's particularly appropriate that the term has now been employed in this manner. Ironically, Mishnah passages sometimes referred to simpler-minded people that lacked a scholar's clarity or discipline to be a "Golem." Perhaps building on that usage, "Golem" in Yiddish became an insult meaning "stupid" or "empty-headed." With the term becoming associated with cogent analysis of a monster's place in a world of spiritual traditions, and with an improved cultural profile, perhaps now the Golem can get a little respect.

Why has it taken so long for the Golem to assume a more prominent place in the annals of undead media, even given its somewhat shaky membership qualifications? Perhaps the most significant factor is its perceived limited thematic potential. After all, the real power of the zombie is its capacity to evolve with every new generation and reflect any anxiety currently pervading the world in which it shambles (or sprints). From Western civilization's demonization of Haitian religious traditions to paranoia about Communist infiltration of American home life to widespread fears of terrorist attack, biochemical warfare, or global disease outbreaks, the zombie is endlessly applicable as a media monster for any occasion. Vampires too have a powerful role to play in the public discourse as the embodiment of a cultural tug of war between spirituality and sexuality. Once loathsome monsters often equated with anti-Semitic depictions of Eastern European Jews and symbolic of everything from sexual repression to spiritual corruption and virulent disease, they have become in modern times more alluring, tragic figures of dark romantic longing and the conflict between conservative morality and wanton desire.

But with the Golem, many storytellers stick with only a few options. There is the ever-present theme of hubris as well as the juxtapositioning of the fleshier Golems with *K'Vod HaMes*. But where else can it go? Surely the Golem, a sculpture shaped by the hand of humanity and built quite literally from the ground up, has as much if not more potential than the zombie or the vampire? There have been attempts to test that versatility.

Part Three: Other Undead

A Christian re-interpretation of the Golem has emerged over the years, with some likening its "immaculate conception" and almost invariable tragic end to that of Jesus, but it seems to be the more familiar version of the Golem steeped in its Jewish roots that has legs, so to speak. In fact, after commenting briefly on some of the ways in which the Golem has reared its stony head in all manner of recent media, there is one category in which the future of the legend may be forged. Where would that be? Look no further than the young adult section of any bookstore—if you can find a bookstore, that is. Never mind, there's always Amazon.

The Golem's greatest growth area in popular media today is in children's literature. Elie Wiesel once wrote a book about the Golem of Prague intended for all-ages readers,[28] but here in the twenty-first century Golems of various sizes and shapes are spreading across the pages of novels for children and young adults as quickly as in your average zombie apocalypse. Interestingly, it is in these explorations of the myth that we may find more potential for the Golem to find more thematic meaning than it ever has in past media outings. With stories that blend a child's investigation of their own identity, the Golem becomes an avatar for young and undisciplined intellects seeking answers about the deeper meaning of life, their place in the world, and their spirituality. There is even the profound correlation to be drawn between today's increased awareness of bullying in schools with the role of the Golem as a protector. From the Caldecott Medal-winning *Golem* by David Wisniewski[29] to the dystopian fantasy of Chris Wooding's *Storm Thief*,[30] young readers of all grade levels can have a clay automaton of their very own. And yes, in a category of popular literature that seems obsessed with attaching yearning teen romance to every genre under the sun, young adult shelves now feature Nina Malkin's novel *Swoon*, which you might call a "girl creates boyfriend" story.[31] Go figure.

SET IN STONE

Search through Greek, Norse, and other cultural mythologies, and you will find many other variations on the clay, stone, or metal automaton that walks like a human being but lacks a soul. Striding ahead of them all is the Jewish Golem, a creature that simultaneously symbolizes humility and pride, nobility and corruption, security and menace, unlife and undeath. Whether formed from clay, a mud man parodying his human creator in shape and action, or sewn together into a grotesque flesh puppet dancing on psychic strings wielded by a living master, or gently melting in the December sun as he leads a parade of children down the streets of town,[32] the Golem is one of the more complex if often marginalized members of the menagerie of undead monsters lurking in our collective cultural consciousness. As we've seen, there are also opportunities to freshen up that dusty complexion and bring new meaning to an old icon. A more modern interpretation of the Golem might cast it as a metaphor for our current American dilemma of freedom versus security. What are we willing to risk or to sacrifice in order to protect ourselves? Can there be a limit to how much self-determination we are willing to relinquish in the face of threats from outside, and what happens when the solution becomes a greater danger than the problems it's created to solve? The Golem may have a lot more work to do in the twenty-first century.

So when considering the threat of the living dead and barricading yourself in your house, you might want to spare a moment of thought for the Golem, the oft-forgotten Jewish cousin of the re-animated zombie. You might even consider making one to help protect you from the hordes beyond the door, or maybe just nail up a few extra boards for good measure. *Zei Gezunt.*[33]

END NOTES

1. This is just a joke, of course; they haven't trademarked it yet.
2. The Man-Thing first appeared in *Savage Tales* #1, May 1971, Marvel Comics.
3. This is the valuable lesson learned by Peter Parker in the very first story about the Amazing Spider-Man, appearing in *Amazing Fantasy* #15, Marvel Comics, August 1962.
4. "Kaddish," by Howard Gordon, *The X-Files* (FOX Network, 16 February 1997). This episode was analyzed in depth by Koven in his article, "Have I Got a Monster for You!," 217–30.
5. *Der Golem (The Golem: How He Came into the World)*, directed by Carl Boese, Paul Wegener (UFA, 1920).
6. *It!* Directed by Herbert J. Leder. Warner Bros., 1966.
7. "The Golem," *Strange Tales* (Marvel Comics, 1974), issues 174, 176–77.
8. "It! The Living Colossus," *Astonishing Tales* (Marvel Comics, 1973–1974), issues 21–24.
9. *The Monolith* (DC Comics, 2004–2005), 12 issues.
10. Chabon, *The Amazing Adventures.*

Part Three: Other Undead

11. Shelley, *Frankenstein*.
12. *Frankenstein*, directed by James Whale (Universal Pictures, 1931).
13. *Bride of Re-Animator*, directed by Brian Yuzna (Wild Street, 1990).
14. Gygax, *Advanced Dungeons & Dragons*.
15. *R.U.R.: Rossum's Universal Robots*, by Karel Capek (premiered 1921).
16. Asimov's Three Laws of Robotics, which first appeared in the 1942 short story, "Runaround," included in the *I, Robot* anthology, are as follows: 1) "A robot may not injure a human being or, through inaction, allow a human being to come to harm;" 2) "A robot must obey the orders given to it by human beings, except where such orders would conflict with the First Law;" 3) "A robot must protect its own existence as long as such protection does not conflict with the First or Second Laws."
17. *Mendy and the Golem* (Mendy Enterprises, 1981–85), 19 issues.
18. *Mendy and the Golem* (The Golem Factory, 2003–2005), 6 issues.
19. Walter Rollins and Steve Nelson, "Frosty the Snowman." LP. Columbia Records, 1950.
20. *Frosty the Snowman*, directed by Jules Bass and Arthur Rankin Jr. (Rankin/Bass, 1969).
21. *Jack Frost*, directed by Michael Cooney (Moonstone, 1997).
22. Newman, *Doctor Who*.
23. Watterson, *Calvin & Hobbes*.
24. Hamill, *Snow in August*.
25. *Snow in August*, directed by Richard Friedenberg (Showtime, 2001).
26. "Treehouse of Horror XVII: You Gotta Know When to Golem," by Peter Gaffney, *The Simpsons* (FOX Network, 5 Nov. 2006).
27. http://www.golemjournal.org.
28. Wiesel, *The Golem*.
29. Wisniewski, *Golem*.
30. Wooding, *Storm Thief*.
31. Malkin, *Swoon*.
32. You caught this? Yes, it's a reference to the lyrics to "Frosty the Snowman," Columbia Records, 1950, by Walter Rollins and Steve Nelson.
33. Basically, Yiddish for "Be well."

11

"Eat of My Body and Drink of My Blood"
Johannine Metaphor, Gothic Subculture, and the Undead

Beth M. Stovell

INTRODUCTION

The conceptual metaphor theory of George Lakoff and Mark Johnson has demonstrated that the metaphors we use impact the way we view the nature of reality.[1] Scholars have often noted the themes of inclusivity and exclusivity in the book of Revelation and in the Johannine corpus more broadly, but few have explored how these themes are realized through the metaphors of Revelation and how this impacts the modern and ancient readers' perspective of their place as "insiders" or "outsiders" to the text and its world. This essay will examine these themes of inclusion and exclusion by analyzing three ways metaphors are used in Revelation: 1) as a reaction against mainstream culture; 2) as a reaction against exploitation; and 3) as a form of paradox and irony that subverts expectation. This essay will then analyze the similar use of metaphors in subcultures by focusing on the use of apocalyptic metaphors in Goth subculture. This essay will assert that Revelation's use of metaphors creates an inside group, while rejecting the culture of its time, and this lends itself to the cultural critique prevalent in modern subcultures, especially within the Goth subculture. Just as the ancient early Christians found solace in Revelation's themes of inclusion codified in metaphor, modern Goths use these apocalyptic metaphors to question today's society and create a community of insiders. Through a close examination of the use of apocalyptic imagery in Goth music, movies, and writings, this essay will provide a new way of reading and re-reading Revelation that also allows for the reading (and re-reading) of today's society.

Towards this end, this essay will begin by examining the uses of metaphor in Revelation and in apocalyptic literature, noting the sociopolitical implications of these metaphors in their ancient contexts. After introducing these elements in Revelation, this essay will provide a brief introduction to Goth subculture and point to the recent trends of popularization of elements of Goth subculture and the horror genre. This essay will then examine how these metaphors of Revelation are re-interpreted through modern examples of "undead" literature, films, and music. These findings have important implications for understanding the role of Revelation in modern culture and for re-reading Western society in light of these Gothic interpretations.

METAPHORS OF INCLUSION AND EXCLUSION IN THE BOOK OF REVELATION

While the genre of apocalyptic literature, its function(s), and its sociological setting(s), are all hotly debated in scholarly circles,[2] to varying degrees many scholars have pointed to alienation, oppression, and injustice as key themes in the apocalyptic worldview.[3] Stephen O'Leary argues that anthropologically speaking the theme of theodicy is key to the construction of an apocalyptic mindset both in ancient and modern contexts.[4] Grappling with alienation, oppression, and injustice and re-affirming God's place amidst the problem of evil in the world also sets the groundwork for differentiation of insiders from outsiders in both the book of Revelation specifically and apocalyptic literature more broadly. Further, scholars widely agree that some sort of persecution existed, whether actual or perceived, that caused the author of Revelation to create strong boundary lines between his community and the broader outside world, effectively creating a community of insiders.[5] This section will briefly address four ways scholars have noted that Revelation uses metaphors that provide a framework for a later discussion on Goth interpretation.

First, Greg Carey has argued that the book of Revelation represents a form of resistance literature. Carey describes Revelation as "a sort of introversionist identity politics" and states, "Revelation struggles to identify a movement by constructing its identity over against neither a church or a foreign power, but against the dominant culture of its own time and place."[6] Carey points to four "symptoms of resistance" in Revelation: markers of identity, internal division, discursive hybridization, and re-inscription of "other" discourses. As examples of these "symptoms," Carey points to several metaphors, including repeated reference to Babylon and the Beast. Carey explains that these two symbols especially demonstrate "strict communal boundaries" of Revelation that create identity markers, "the discursive hybridization" in the "parody of Rome's pretensions to glory, as well as its imperial cult," and the "reinscription of 'others' discourses" in the promises of wealth (Babylon) and peace (Beast), characterized as gaudiness and war.[7]

Second, viewing Revelation as a form of resistance literature often means that its metaphors stand in contrast not only to the dominant culture generally, but its practices of oppression and exploitation. Though several metaphors could be included in this category, the figure of Babylon is perhaps the most prominent. While some feminist scholars like Tina Pippin and Susan Garrett have pointed to Babylon herself as an oppressed figure,[8] the work of Elisabeth Schüssler Fiorenza and Richard Bauckham in different ways provide insight into ways that Revelation uses the figure of Babylon to deconstruct the discourses of power used for oppression. Schüssler Fiorenza argues that, while a "gender reading does not destabilize but rather literalizes the gender inscriptions of Revelation," a critical-systemic political analysis provides a more nuanced lens for reading the "multiplicative structures of domination engendered by Roman imperialism" that "[point] to four areas of ideological struggle over the meaning of gender in Revelation."[9] Bauckham's close examination of the products of Rome in comparison to the spoils of Babylon provides a similar insight into the depiction of Babylon as the Roman imperial figure of oppression and injustice. When addressing the question of why the merchants' lament at Babylon's fall is included and almost sympathetic, Bauckham suggests that in the mixed audience hearing Revelation, some with ties to Rome would be forced to rethink whether they would wail with the merchants at her demise and, thus, change their position in relation to Roman oppression. As with Schüssler Fiorenza's account of Babylon, Bauckham demonstrates that the author of Revelation is writing a form of resistance against the imperial power of Rome and the injustice of her practices, which powerfully calls its readers to re-examine their position in relation to the lies of the empire.[10]

Third, as Richard Bauckham and Steven Friesen have demonstrated in their work, Revelation uses parody, sarcasm, and irony to subvert the expectations of readers for rhetorical purposes. Along these lines, Bauckham points to Nero as the beast as a parody of Christ and to the ironic use of the figure of the Lamb as military leader.[11] Friesen provides a series of examples of Revelation's use of irony, satire, and sarcasm throughout with a particular focus on their use in Revelation 2-3. In each of these cases, these forms of irony,[12] by subverting expectation, draw their reader into new configurations of symbolic understanding. The use of irony allows for the critique of society to provide a sharper contrast, through its pairing of similarity and dissimilarity in surprising ways.

Each of these elements contributes to the creation of an "insiders" versus "outsiders" mentality in Revelation. As Carey has pointed out, a key "symptom of resistance" in Revelation are "markers of identity," which set John's community apart from the "dominant" (or as Goths would call it, "mainstream") world of his time. Adela Yarbro Collins provides further insight into this tension between insiders and outsiders by attributing the use of vilification in Revelation as a strategy for establishing the group and for maintaining it. In a similar way as will be noted with Goth subculture, the outsiders in Revelation are vilified through derogatory labels in order to define the boundaries where insiders are positioned.[13] Thus, the boundary lines dividing insiders versus outsiders are often drawn through the use of metaphor, including metaphors that resist the mainstream culture, metaphors that oppose the injustice of society, and metaphors (and other figurative language) that are parodic, sarcastic, satirical, ironic, or even vituperative.

Dualism is a fourth characteristic of apocalyptic literature that often functions in forming community identity in similar ways. Scholars have also described dualism as an important characteristic in apocalyptic literature. One may describe the types of dualism in three main categories: temporal, spatial, and ethical. Temporal dualism distinguishes this present age from the age to come, usually emphasizing the negative elements in this present age and the expectation of a better "age" in a future time. Spatial dualism differentiates this world from the "other" world. At times, this dualism will lead to a similar negative estimation of earthy existence, favouring a heavenly "other" world. Ethical dualism also contrasts negative against positive elements, but in terms of ethical characteristics. This may include distinguishing between the righteous and the wicked or the good and the evil, at times using the metaphors of light and darkness to represent these opposing forces, whether human or otherwise.[14] As will be described in the discussion below, each of these forms of dualism have a correlation within Goth subculture and within the horror genre.

THE BASICS OF GOTH SUBCULTURE

With these elements of apocalyptic literature (and John's Apocalypse specifically) in mind, this section attempts to provide a framework for understanding the origins and basic tenets of both the Goth subculture broadly and the Goth Christian subculture specifically in order to understand how and why Goths re-interpret apocalyptic metaphors within their particular community.

Often traced to the sounds and images of the band Bauhaus, particularly their song "Bela Lugosi's Dead" released in 1979, Goths emerged in Britain in the early 1980s as punk, glam rock, and new romantic merged with other elements to form a new and distinctive music and fashion style. The music of the Goth scene was often described as "dark, macabre, and sinister."[15] In describing their style of fashion, Hodkinson uses the three major headings of "the sombre and the macabre," "femininity and ambiguity," and "fragments of related styles," to describe the focus on various kinds of darkness, the femininity and androgyny of Goth styles for both men and women, and the interrelatedness between Goth and other types of styles.[16] Hodkinson is careful to point out repeatedly that a key facet of Goth subculture is the tension between creative individuality, which is of high value among Goths (and is even a form of "social capital"), and dressing and listening to music within certain proper boundaries to identify oneself as part of the Goth community and maintain one's position as an insider.[17]

Though Paul Hodkinson rightly warns against drawing too strong a dichotomy between "subculture" versus "mainstream" culture (as older, traditional models of cultural studies would), Hodkinson, along with several other scholars, have pointed to the markings of resistance within the Goth subculture as important elements in constructing Goth identity.[18] Those things that the "mainstream" culture of America (and other parts of North America and Western Europe) tells us to deny, Goths instead

Part Three: Other Undead

openly embrace. For example, Carol Siegel traces the development of the Goth subculture to the time of "unprecedented despair" among the young in Western culture of the late 1970s and early 1980s. Siegel asserts that Goth's darkness was not only a result, but an answer to these dark times, providing a response to

> the dominant discourses of a culture that is in the process of failing its most vulnerable members.... [I]n place of the denial of the future that characterizes mainstream American life, Goth offers a very special kind of masochistic delight in knowing the worst[;] ... a way of generating affects that can stand against State institutions of control and the discourses of power they authorize. Goth cannot tell us how to live both darkly and against fascism, but it can show us.[19]

One distinctive of Goth subculture is the desire of Goths to put the darkness on the outside where everyone can see it, rather than keeping it hidden. Goth author Voltaire explains that he believes Goths are hated by the mainstream because of the Goth willingness to "assume the appearance of 'the unknown'" while those in mainstream culture "don't dare to look into the pit of their own souls for fear of what they might find. The truth of the matter is that everyone is evil. And everyone is good. In varying degrees, we are all a mixture of the two."[20] This hidden inner evil causes evil that extends to the rest of the world, impacting society, religion, and the environment. As Voltaire explains:

> mundanes keep their creepiness hidden, employing their socially acceptable pretences as a disguise. Their world is populated by "respectable" CEOs who pay themselves millions while laying off thousands and embezzling the pensions of their employees; "spiritual" people who go to church every Sunday but live lives full of hate and bigotry; ... countless "upstanding" corporations that knowingly kill our planet to save an extra cent on the dollar ..."[21]

This indictment against the rich oppression of the poor, the hypocrisy of the religious, and the destruction of the environment for the sake of business also resonates in the music of artists like Nine Inch Nails, Siouxsie and the Banshees, and Laibach.[22]

While Goths value an awareness of designating who are among the "mundane" and "normal" and therefore, are also an outsider, equally important is the awareness of who *is* included in Goth subculture over against the mainstream culture. In fact, within Goth subculture, the norms of society are often intentionally inverted. In the ideal of Goth subculture, the alienated, the marginalized, and the oppressed are all provided a place.[23] However, as Hodkinson correctly points out, while the Goth intention is towards tolerance, its practice of tolerance is by no means without its own blind spots and its own forms of exclusion alongside inclusion.[24]

One form of inclusion and solidarity within Goth culture comes directly from the choices within Goth fashion. As noted previously, for Goths, style evokes substance.[25] Dunja Brill argues that the androgyny of male Goth styles "open themselves up to quasi-sexist and homophobic abuse[;] . . . their style can be seen as deliberate appropriation of the marginalised position assigned to women and gay men in our culture."[26] In this way, Goths can stand in solidarity with the oppressed by *becoming* the oppressed themselves. Thus, the Goth subculture does allow for new ways to stand in solidarity with those marginalized by mainstream society.

Another distinctive trait of Goth subculture is its willingness to face that life includes pain and suffering in comparison to mainstream's denial. Goths will often note that mainstream culture unreasonably expects everyone to put on a happy face. In contrast, Goths at times argue that the Goth willingness to acknowledge the sadness, suffering, and evil present in the world and within themselves can actually allow for more happiness in their lives.[27] This also demonstrates an important difference between the perception of Goth subculture by outsiders versus the actual experience of Goths within the subculture. As noted above by Hodkinson, outsiders to Goth subculture confuse the appearance of sombreness within Goth subculture, and the themes of death and suffering within some Goth music, to mean that all Goths are depressed. The majority of Hodkinson's Goth respondents were resistant to aggression and depression, "regarding them . . . as a misplaced negative stereotype of Goths held by outsiders."[28]

Michael du Plessis argues that "Goth melancholia" is similar to Julia Kristeva's definition of melancholia in her work *Black Sun*.[29] Du Plessis notes that this melancholic signature is also key to the subculture's cohesiveness and to the Gothic ability to do "Goth damage" to "what is conventionally understood as sexuality and gender."[30] Thus, the Goth acknowledgement of suffering and pain in life through dramatic melancholic symbolic signification allows for the breakdown of typical modes of seeing the world and, thus, greater levels of tolerance, inclusiveness, and, some Goths would argue, happiness.[31]

Many who study the Goth subculture have noted that "style-as-substance" is a key characteristic.[32] Within Goth Christian circles, the style of Goth as representing oneself as "already dead" is writ large in strikingly theological terms. The Goth "undead" style in Goth Christian circles represents one's death to self so that Christ might live within the believer. While examples are plentiful, we will focus on two striking examples. First, among the Christian ministries ministering to Goths, the First Church of the Living Dead gains its nomination and its self-description from this concept of the mutual elements of life and death existing simultaneously in every Christian, crucial to the already/not yet eschatology of first century Christians. As Paul says, "I have been crucified with Christ and I no longer live, but Christ lives in me" (Gal 2:20); the white faces, black lips, eyes, and fingernails echoing the bodies of the dead act as a physical representation of this sentiment within the Goth Christian community.[33] This acknowledgement of the reality of death and the emphasis on *not* denying death in Goth subculture more broadly is given theological meaning through identification with Christ's death and its redemptive and healing power within Goth Christianity. Whereas death is simply unavoidable in Goth subculture, it is the gateway to new life in Goth Christianity. This will have important implications for Goth Christian readings of the book of Revelation.

This identification with the death of Christ within Goth Christianity leads to explicit emphasis on some of the more gruesome aspects of Christ's passion and its haunting and often challenging metaphorical use in the New Testament.

One Goth Christian website called "Blood God" centers its overall framework around the sacrifice of Christ as a "blood bath." Taking the idea of being "washed in the blood of the Lamb" in Rev 7:14 to its macabre metaphorical extreme, this website uses the language of horror films to subvert expectations about Christianity and encourage its users to become closer to "the Blood God" through a personal relationship with Jesus, who cleanses them through his "blood bath."[34] This re-reading of the Lamb's sacrifice in the terms of Gothic entertainment provides an ironic means of engaging with the average Goth, while re-interpreting traditional Christian metaphors with fresh eyes.

Caitlin Moran points to a similar re-working in Goth Christian ministries in the U.K. Moran in her article for *The Times* made the following comment on the unique intertwining of Goth with Christianity (particularly in the Goth Eucharist in Cambridge): "church services are all about a misunderstood man who got nailed to a cross. They are held in a looming, bell-towered, candle-lit edifice in the middle of a graveyard. Indeed if you go catholic, you get to burn incense and drink blood, as well."[35] Moran's comment identifies how certain forms of Christianity allow a natural bridge for Gothic sensibilities. Particularly interesting is Moran's comment concerning the Eucharist itself. The Goth perspective provides a new way to appropriate traditional symbols of Christianity.

In a similar vein, a Goth Christian video called "Night of the Living Bread" depicts "zombies" finding Jesus hanging on the cross. As they begin to devour his flesh, it becomes the bloody bread of the sacrament. These "zombies" are transformed back into real humans by their cannibalistic ingestion. The movie ends with two passages from John's Gospel (John 6:53 and 6:51) that describe Jesus' flesh as the bread of life which must be eaten to gain eternal life.[36] In the more watered down versions of the Eucharist in mainline Protestant churches, Jesus' words about eating his flesh and drinking his blood lose their provocative and frighteningly cannibalistic overtones.[37] Goth Christianity's dramatic uses of conventions of horror, combined with its penetrating gaze into the reality of suffering in the Passion of the Christ and the Eucharist, provides modern Christianity with a helpful reminder of why ancient Romans believed early Christians to be scandalous cannibals.[38]

GOTH AND HORROR RE-INTERPRETATIONS OF APOCALYPSE

In light of the description provided above of both Goth subculture general and Goth Christianity in specific, this section will focus on how these Goth tenets impact Goth interpretation of particular texts and re-interpretation of key metaphors in Revelation.

While some Goths' hopes for the end of the world have positive overtones when connected to the love and sacrifice of Christ, the end of the world can also point to destruction for those who have oppressed Goths and performed broader injustices on the world. At times, Goth Christian band Saviour Machine's interpretation of Revelation moves in more traditionally Dispensationalist directions, including depicting important roles for Islam, the Middle East, and Israel in the final judgement, describing the "rapture," and focusing on the ultimate destruction of those who have sinned against God. These depictions can be intensified through metaphorical extension of Goth subculture and its use of the horror genre.

For example, Saviour Machine's focus on the Beast as Anti-Christ follows in the lines of Revelation's use of the metaphor in creating the Anti-Christ as a parody of Christ, which plays upon the ironic tenor of Goth discourse.[39] In "Ten-The Empire," Saviour Machine speaks of the coming Anti-Christ, and invents a parody of the Lord's prayer, asking that the Anti-Christ's will be done on earth "as it is in hell."[40] Saviour Machine's depiction of Gog also intertwines traditional Dispensationalism with a twist of the dark, macabre of Goth sensibility.[41] In their depiction of Gog, the indictment against "coveting hands" and the cannibalistic response are sharply in focus and these two elements represent some overlap with other Gothic indictments against oppressors and a Gothic openness surrounding horror. This description of cannibalizing the dead as a "sacrificial feast" builds on Revelation's original creation of social boundaries as resistance literature while adding a flare of the horrific that intensifies the vilification and differentiations of the oppressor as an outsider deserving of wrath.

As noted in the earlier sections on inclusion and exclusion in the metaphors of Revelation, the figure of Babylon plays a crucial role in depicting the exploitation, oppression, and injustice in the imperial context of ancient Roman rule. Thus, the fall of Babylon embodies the ultimate destruction of all evil economic powers that set themselves up against God. The re-interpretation of Babylon within Goth subculture mirrors many of these anti-imperial sentiments, placing them in modern contexts. Therefore, the figure of Babylon in Goth subculture may at times be identified with the United States or Western culture more broadly.

One important re-interpretation of the imagery of Revelation comes in the figure of Babylon. In many ways, the ancient depiction of Babylon as the Roman imperial power representing social injustice, exploitation, and oppression finds its parallel in the Goth interpretation of the United States of America as Babylon. For many Goths, the tendency to "rage against the machine" and question the duplicitous nature of Western society (often deemed "the system") goes hand in hand with interpreting Babylon in terms of the misdeeds of America specifically. One such example (though there are quite a few) is the song "American Babylon" by Saviour Machine. Written shortly after the destruction of the

Two Towers at 9/11, the lyrics equate the fall of Babylon with America "dying."[42] While these lines depict the "fall" of America in terms similar to the fall of Babylon, other lines point to the reason for this analogy. Forces of "fascism" and "tyranny," directed by Satan himself, are placed close beside the language of liberty and light, demonstrating the distinction between appearances and reality, which has caused the ultimate fall of America, according to Saviour Machine. The speaker of the song appears to be familiar with this picture of Babylon's fall, but without an expectation that all the injustices would eventually lead this far. Thus, like Babylon herself who rode the Beast believing her power was secure, Saviour Machine depicts the bloody shift in America's sense of security post-9/11. Here prophecy is fulfilled in the figure of America as Babylon already, particularly in light of 9/11 (as Saviour Machine here displays), and yet another Day of Judgment appears also to be awaited.

Besides these re-interpretations of the book of Revelation, Goth subculture and undead literature more generally also re-interpret the dualism of apocalypticism. Voltaire's work points to the dualism within Goth subculture in which Goth insiders positively compare themselves to the "normals" or "mundane" world. Voltaire clarifies that while Goths are spooky, they are not creepy. Instead Voltaire asserts what Goths find truly creepy are those within the "mundane world": "The mundane world is a place that endeavors to maintain a bright, cheery, and optimistic appearance. Just under the surface, however, there are truly dark and very real forces at play that put to shame anything a Goth could come up with!"[43]

While Hodkinson rightly warns against oversimplifying the great complexity of dynamism and diversity within Goth subculture, Voltaire's insider description of the perceived difference between the Goth world vs. the world of the "mundanes" and the distinction between "spooky" vs. "creepy" points to the insider vs. outsider dualism that can exist within Goth subculture. Scholars have pointed to dualism as a characteristic of the apocalyptic mindset. These apocalyptic dualities of chronological and spatial dimensions have parallels in the Goth imagination and are particularly demonstrated in Goth movies and within the horror genre more broadly.

Many Goths claim Tim Burton's movies as "Goth" or at least acknowledge his work among their favorites. This may be because of Tim Burton's love of the dark and eerie, or as Gavin Baddeley would say about Goths, Burton "uses darkness to illuminate"; one might even go so far as to say that Burton focuses on "the unholy, the uncanny, the unnatural."[44]

Part Three: Other Undead

A common theme in Tim Burton's movies is the two natures of the world or two worlds: the normal world, sometimes characterized as the suburban world as in *Edward Scissorhands,* or the Victorian world in *Corpse Bride* or *Alice in Wonderland,* and the "other world". In *Nightmare Before Christmas* and *Corpse Bride,* this "other" world is characterized by death, and is, in a sense, more real than our normal world. Thus in *Corpse Bride* the black and white and generally dismal everyday world is contrasted with the color and music of the Underworld; in *Edward Scissorhands,* new life and excitement accompanies Edward's arrival and forms of abuse are removed; in *Nightmare Before Christmas,* joy and love are emphasized amidst the horror of Halloween land; and in *Alice In Wonderland,* it is only through acknowledging the reality of "Underland" that Alice finally has the ability to slay dragons. Through this acknowledgement she sets life aright within the Underland itself and these actions propel her forward into a positive change in the normal world when she returns. Thus, while Burton follows the apocalyptic pattern of making the supernatural world the more positive world, he does this while also emphasizing that the "other" world is the world of darkness and even death.

Another element of Tim Burton's movies that relate to the Goth subculture and the apocalyptic genre is the theme of inclusion and exclusion consistent with the dualism noted above. Film scholars have noted that Burton's work focuses on the outsider. Jenny He notes,

> Edward Scissorhands, Jack Skellington, Ed Wood, and Ichabod Crane—variations on a theme—represent a central figure in Burton's filmic universe: the "misunderstood outcast." . . . Edward [Scissorhands] is Burton's most literal Frankenstein's monster. Clad in a stitched-together leather body suit and unable to touch others with his razor-sharp fingers, he is the physical manifestation of isolation, one of Burton's predominant themes.[45]

He notes that part of Edward's position as an outsider is because of his willingness to point to the exploitation of others. "At first superficially accepted by the neighbors, they inevitably turn on Edward when he rebukes their exploitation.[46] Despite narrative attempts to the contrary, Burton never diminishes Edward's outsider persona."[47]

Similarly the undead figure of Emily in Burton's *Corpse Bride* represents an outsider from the perspective of the Victorian mundane world, yet Victor is the outsider in her world of the Underworld. In *Corpse Bride,* it is exploitation that creates the "other"ness that Emily experiences through her abuse and murder at the hands of the fiendish Lord Barkis Bittern. The revelation of this exploitation and murder create an important climax to the movie, eventually resulting in Emily's liberation from her somewhat purgatorial state in the Underworld. In this way, the spatial dualism of the other world and our present reality and the ethical dualism of the pure versus the wicked (equated with the insider and the outsider) are themes in Burton's highly Gothic work.

In the Goth cult classic *The Crow*, the figure of the crow functions as an otherworldly messenger that, in a sense, inverts the usual structure of the apocalyptic. In most apocalyptic literature, the mundane figure is taken into the heavenly realms or given a glimpse into the "other" world. In *The Crow*, this otherworldly figure comes from the "other" world to enter into the "normal" world in order to effect change, namely to restore justice. This vision of the "living dead" existing in the "normal" world, which *The Crow* envisions, is a key factor to the self-identification of Goths. In Revelation, the addresses to the churches provide a similar framework. As some have noted, the book of Revelation connects the present situation of these churches with the "other" world, where justice will be finally served, though at the moment all that is visible to the people is the destruction and martyrdom of this world. Several elements corresponding with apocalyptic dualism arise here, including the transport between the two worlds for the purpose of setting things right; apocalyptic overtones to the earthly destruction of the fire setters; Beast and Babylon figures as the sister-brother at the centre of the injustice; and the evil Beast-like figure seeking power, domination, and chaos.

Described by *Entertainment Weekly* as the "best bloodbath" and the "New American Gothic," Season 4 of *True Blood* brings to the forefront a question repeatedly asked throughout the show, "Who is truly evil?"[48] From the outset of the show, characters frequently speak of the dual natures of good and evil, within humans and vampires alike.[49] In Season 4, the war between the Wiccan medium Marnie Stonebrook and the vampires combines several dualisms found within apocalyptic literature: a) the ethical dualism of good versus evil; b) the temporal dualism of past and present (through Marnie's possession by Antonia); and c) the spatial dualism of this world and the "other" world displayed in Antonia's ghost and in the ghosts in the Season 4 finale.[50] These elements of dualism further resonate with the language of Revelation as the punishment of the vampires is described as "resurrection."[51] The use of the term "resurrection" plays on the apocalyptic expectation of the universal resurrection of the dead in Revelation 20, but *True Blood* provides a Gothic twist by making this universal resurrection not of the dead, but of the *undead*. It is the action of "resurrection" that draws lines firmly between those who side with the vampires and those who side with Marnie and the Wiccans. Thus, social boundaries of inside-outside are drawn sharply by Marnie's chosen form of vengeance. These dualisms and the language of resurrection from Revelation 20 sharply focus in the Season 4 finale on the issue of how power can be abused and thus cause suffering to the innocent and the guilty alike. As in other works within the Goth subculture, *True Blood* challenges the notion of total vengeance and the pursuit of ultimate power, resisting common mainstream cultural assumptions. The use of the term "resurrection" and the implications of universal resurrection in connection to Revelation 20 provides an interesting correlation as this passage, like *True Blood*, demonstrates a picture of ultimate justice, but, unlike *True Blood*, places this justice in the hands of the Lamb who was slain.

CONCLUSION: LIVING DEAD OR WHITE-WASHED TOMBS?

The Significance of Gothic Apocalyptic Interpretation

In her book, *Apocalyptic Bodies*, Tina Pippen compares the book of Revelation to the horror genre, using the classic horror film *The Blob* as an analogy and showing how the responses to some of Revelation's more apocalyptic elements are akin to contemporary mixed feelings about such horror films.[52] While one may agree or disagree with Pippin's view of the violence in Revelation, Goth interpretations of Revelation equally press their readers towards seeing with squeamish eyes the vivid, even horrific metaphors used in Revelation to depict the reversal of mainstream expectations. Using the conventions of horror, Goth readings challenge their readers to question whether they, like the merchants wailing at Babylon's fall, have bought into the lies offered by today's society, particularly the lies of wealth, empty happiness, and false righteousness so prevalent in much of Western culture. Through parody and irony, Goth readings subvert the expectations of their readers, surprising them and moving them towards deeper questions of inclusion and exclusion, of center and margin. The various types of dualism present in Goth films allow for the imaginative reinterpretation of a fallen world, where another world offers a place for the marginalized and oppressed, where truth may be revealed and a quest for understanding God's role in the evil of the world may find some resolution, and where justice may be gained by otherworldly means.

In examining the metaphors of Revelation and their re-interpretation in the Goth subculture and in undead literature and film more generally, the theme of inclusion and exclusion has proved important to the creation of community identity. Revelation itself and Gothic interpretations of Revelation force readers to rethink their place in relation to mainstream culture, in relation to the oppression and exploitation happening every day (whether seen or unseen), and in relation to the Church. The use of inversion of symbolic frameworks of imperialism and the dualism inherent in apocalyptic literature and within Goth subculture leads to a choice that each reader must make that is radical and even dangerous, for choosing to align oneself with those on the "inside" means choosing to stand in solidarity with the oppressed and potentially become the oppressed because of this choice. The value of Goth readings of Revelation is the new configuration of this symbolism as culturally relevant to today's world. If America is truly Babylon, how might one "come out of [her]," while still living in her?[53] Perhaps Goth Christians provide at least one way to reside in this tension.

END NOTES

1. See Lakoff and Johnson, *Metaphors We Live By*.
2. For varying introductions on the genre of apocalyptic literature, see Aune, "Apocalypse Renewed," 43–70; Barr, "Beyond Genre," 71–90; Linton, "Reading the Apocalypse," 9–42.
3. Aside from the scholars listed, one can also see this trend in Sanders, "The Genre of Palestinian," and Meeks, "Social Functions of Apocalyptic," 447–60 and 687–706 respectively; and the works of Collins, including Collins, *Apocalypse*; Collins, *The Apocalyptic Imagination*. Unlike Sanders and Meeks who seek a specific social background for the genre of apocalypse as a whole, Collins deals with the various aspects as dealt with in diverse ways through the imagination in different times and different places.
4. O'Leary, "When Prophecy Fails," 341–62. Likewise, Paolo Sacchi has pointed to the problem of evil in the earliest apocalypse as important to a diachronic view of the apocalyptic genre. See Sacchi, *L'apocalittica Giudaica*.
5. While for a long period of time scholars assumed that the crisis and persecution experienced by the recipients of the book of Revelation was widespread

Part Three: Other Undead

Roman persecution of Christians, some more recent scholarship has suggested that this crisis was actually only a "perceived" crisis rather than a real crisis. Among the scholars holding this position of perceived crisis is Adela Yarbro Collins. See Collins, *Crisis and Catharsis*, esp. 84–110.

6. Carey, "Symptoms of Resistance," 174–79.
7. Ibid.
8. See Garrett, "Revelation," 469–74; Pippin, *Death and Desire* and Pippin, "Reading for Gender," 193–210. Schüssler Fiorenza provides these two examples and critiques them.
9. Schüssler Fiorenza, "Babylon the Great," 259.
10. See Bauckham, *Climax of Prophecy*, 338–83, "The Economic Critique."
11. Bauckham, *Climax of Prophecy*, 384–452 and 174–98, "Nero and the Beast," and "The Lion, the Lamb, and the Dragon."
12. Friesen groups his headings of satire and sarcasm under the broader heading of "irony." One might argue that parody could function along the same lines. See Friesen, "Sarcasm in Revelation 2–3," 127–44.
13. Collins, "Vilification and Self-Definition"; and Collins, "Insiders and Outsiders," 187–218.
14. See Collins, *The Apocalyptic Imagination*.
15. This description is largely a summary of Hodkinson's description of "Goth as a Subcultural Style." See Hodkinson, *Goth: Identity*.
16. Hodkinson, *Goth: Identity*, 41–58.
17. Ibid., 41–58.
18. See especially the first chapter of Hodkinson, *Goth: Identity*.
19. Siegel, *Goth's Dark Empire*, 25.
20. Voltaire, *What is Goth*, 76.
21. Ibid., 83.
22. Examples include Nine Inch Nails' groundbreaking album *Pretty Hate Machine* with its critique of the unscrupulous businessman in "Head Like a Hole," and the lament of religiosity in "Terrible Lie"; "Cities in the Dust," and "Hong Kong Garden," of Siouxsie and the Banshees, both included on their *Best of Siouxsie and the Banshees* CD (Polydor/Geffen Records, 2002); and Laibach's "B Maschina" from their album *WAT* (Mute, 2003).
23. Hodkinson, *Goth: Identity*, 77.
24. Ibid., 73–83.
25. Hodkinson explains that many Goths he interviewed "felt there was some sort of link between their style and certain general qualities they shared with other Goths, including individuality, creativity, open-mindedness, and commitment" (ibid., 62).
26. Brill, "Gender, status and subcultural capital," 111–25, esp. 123. However, Brill does not glorify this trait in Goth subculture. Arguing against the "fantasy

of genderlessness," Brill asserts that such a sense of subcultural capital is not equally available to female Goths and, therefore, a "better than" view can develop around Goth men's ability to transgress social boundaries through androgyny in ways that Goth women cannot. Thus, Goth women's value can be somewhat muted compared to their male counterparts, according to Brill.

27. See Montenegro, "The World according to Goth." This interaction with the teen Goth was in a personal e-mail to Montenegro on December 2, 2001.
28. Hodkinson, *Goth: Identity*, 47.
29. Du Plessis, "Goth Damage," 160.
30. Ibid., 166.
31. Du Plessis cites an excellent example of this happiness in their melancholy representation in the lyrics of a song by The Sisters of Mercy called "Lucretia My Reflection" for their album *Floodland* (Merciful Release/Elektra Records, 1987): "We got the kingdom, we got the key,/We got the empire, now as then,/ We don't doubt, we don't take direction./Lucretia my reflection, dance the ghost with me." See Du Plessis, "'Goth Damage,'" 168.
32. See Siegel, *Goth's Dark Empire*, esp. 25.
33. Galatians 2:20 is used both as the central verse on their website and is printed on T-shirts for the church. See http://www.thefirstchurchofthelivingdead.com, (accessed 10 November 2010). In a similar vein, the Goth Christian website called "Blood God" uses the metaphor of the "walking dead" to speak about true Christianity, stating: "The walking dead have been set free from the lies and complexities of hopeless religion by choosing to be covered from head to toe in BLOOD. It is only by being covered in blood that you can escape the pain, misery and hopelessness of this life and walk in the reality of a personal relationship with BLOOD GOD." Online at http://bloodgod.org/the_walking_dead.htm, (accessed 11 November 2010).
34. On the home page of the website, users are encouraged to explore sections entitled "Chamber of Torments," "The Walking Dead," "Bathed in Blood," and "Death to Religion."
35. Quoted by Ramshaw, "Being Christian and Being Goth."
36. Revo O'Ohay and Steven Leath, directors, "Night of the Living Bread," online at http://www.Gothicchristianity.com/galleries/art_livingbread.html (accessed 11 November 2010).
37. Serving grape juice in place of wine can cause further problems in this direction as its nearness to the color and consistency of blood is further muddied.
38. I am indebted to Jon Stovell for the insight in private correspondence that early Romans in this area actually understood the scandalousness of the implications of Jesus' words more than modern Christians do today. For more on Roman rumors of Christian cannibalism, see McGowan, "Eating People," 413–42.
39. Bauckham's article entitled "Nero and the Beast" is informative here. See Bauckham, *The Climax of Prophecy*, 384–452.

Part Three: Other Undead

40. Saviour Machine, "Ten-The Empire," *Legend Part 1*, MCM Music/Massacre Records, 1997.
41. Saviour Machine, "Gog: The Kings of the North," *Legend Part 1*, MCM Music/Massacre Records, 1997.
42. Saviour Machine, "American Babylon," *Legend Part 1*, MCM Music/Massacre Records, 1997.
43. Voltaire, *What is Goth?*, 82–83.
44. Baddeley and Woods, *Goth Chic*, 19.
45. He, "Inhabiting Tim Burton's Universe," lines 5–14.
46. He notes "Joyce, a randy neighbor attracted to Edward, attempts to seduce him; and Jim, Kim's boyfriend, coaxes Edward to commit petty larceny" (Ibid., footnote 3).
47. Ibid., lines 27–30.
48. Rice, "The Best Bloodbath"; and Rice, "The New American Gothic."
49. For example, in Episode 3 of Season 2, "Scratches," of *True Blood*, Sookie Stackhouse says to Bill Compton: "I used to get so mad when people judged vampires just for being different. It's like they were judging me too. I told myself their fear was nothing but small mindedness. But maybe that's what I wanted to believe. 'Cause the more open my mind gets, the more evil I see." Bill responds: "Sookie, most of us, vampire, human or otherwise are capable of both good and evil. Often simultaneously."
50. "When I Die," Season 4 Finale, *True Blood*.
51. In "The Cold Grey Light of Dawn," Season 4 Episode 43, *True Blood*, Luis whispers "resurrection" before staking himself and in the remainder of the episodes the spell to force the vampires to walk into the sun is referred to as "resurrection."
52. See Tina Pippen's "Prequel, or Preface" in Pippin, *Apocalyptic Bodies*, x.
53. As Greg Carey notes, this cry in Revelation represents "a call for the most radical of sectarian practices, an absolutely negative stance toward society at large, against the empire and its inhabitants." See Carey, "Symptoms of Resistance," 173.

12

Fire, Brimstone, and PVC
Clive Barker's Cenobites as Agents of Hell

Andrea Subissati

In this modern technological age, we are constantly bombarded with headlines about atrocities happening all over the globe, and thanks to technological advancements we can access this information from every direction imaginable. It would seem that evil is something humanity must live with, but how is one to lead a meaningful life amidst all the chaos, conflict, and violence? For the answers to questions like these, we turn to mythmaking. Imagery of the devil has fascinated humanity for centuries because it inspires our darkest imaginings of evil, giving it a face, a voice, and a story. Tales of the devil and his continuing mission to lure immortal souls to the eternal torment of hell have long been used to frighten us into good behavior, and for good reason; our stay on Earth seems relatively short when compared to the eternity of the afterlife. Hell has captured the imagination of artists, poets, and scholars in ways the heavens could not aspire to, possibly because it is more relatable to us earthlings who know far more of suffering than of paradise.

In Clive Barker's novella *The Hellbound Heart*,[1] Frank Cotton's search for carnal pleasure beyond the earthly realm leads him to the Lament Configuration, a puzzle box which is the key to opening a gateway to hell. Hell, as described in Barker's book and depicted in the subsequent film franchise, is occupied by a unique variety of demonkind, and their mythology speaks to a modern understanding of post-mortal punishment. Concepts of sin and torment are also redefined, while still maintaining a binary between the mortal body and immortal soul. The demons who govern Barker's hell are called cenobites, a term literally defined as members of a religious community who live a communal life. Unlike the traditional horned and hooved devil of folklore who goes out of his way to tempt the innocent into evildoing, these demons are content to stand by and wait to be summoned by those who seek out their special gifts and talents. Barker's cenobites and their unique motivations and methods represent a new spin of the classic Faustian devil compact, where those whose desires transcend the earthly realm must be willing to pay a great cost for satisfaction.

The first part of this chapter delves into the analytical depths of hell with a view to providing comparison between the ways in which Barker's hell differs and engages with more classical conceptions of the less-fortunate afterlife. Talk of judgment and punishment must necessarily engage with talk of sin, and of which sins merit the harshest sentences. The second portion will revisit the cenobites and discuss their relationship to their demonic predecessors including the myths of Lucifer and Satan. Overall, this chapter argues that changed times have called for altered mythologies of hell and devilry in order to stay relevant to contemporary society and to maintain their role as deterrent for sin and immorality. Barker's novella and resulting film franchise have provided us with a modernized spin on familiar themes of sin, desire, torment, and salvation.

ABANDON ALL HOPE, YE WHO ENTER HERE

Throughout history, the integration of religious faith and political power among Christian nation states has played a great role in the maintenance of social order. By combining the threat of immediate corporeal punishment by legal means with the threat of eternal torment of the immortal soul in the afterlife, crime and sin were taken quite seriously. At the blackest of times, between the fall of the Roman Empire and the Renaissance, when disease was rampant and daily life was already replete with suffering, threats of bodily torture and imprisonment were no longer sufficient to maintain social order, and the punishment of an eternity in hell for sinners was a far more powerful deterrent from crime. At times like these, it was understood that our time on Earth is short as compared to the eternity we will spend in the afterlife, and the suffering of our mortal coil is of little concern when compared with the possible bliss our immortal soul could enjoy. Unsurprisingly, the grislier our descriptions of hell, the more powerful it became as a preventative measure, making it fertile ground for elaborate description in art, literature, and countless church pulpits. As feudal life trudged slowly toward modernity and modernity hurtled into the current postmodern condition, our stories of hell and its ruler have evolved accordingly to accommodate emergent conceptions of evil, sin, and punishment.

The most common secular understanding of hell in the Western world is that it is one of two possible destinations after death, the other being heaven. Hell is considered the polar opposite of heaven, a site of suffering is experienced either temporarily (as in cyclic religions—where hell is a rite of passage between incarnations) or for eternity. Apart from the conceptual polarization of the two possible sites for the recently deceased, hell and heaven differ significantly in how they are talked about. Heaven is almost automatically understood as a metaphor, because it is infinitely more difficult to imagine the mysterious bliss of God's presence. Hell, on the other hand, is talked about with nonchalance almost as often as it is talked about it gravity. Perhaps this is another result of modernization processes, where the virtuous life seems all the more distant and unattainable: Western nation states have become keenly aware that our abundance of wealth and luxury comes at great cost elsewhere in the world. We know our sneakers are made by children and that our livestock suffer tremendously before winding up on our dinner plates, but we resign ourselves to live as best we can under these circumstances.

The idea of an eternity of hell as punishment for a sinner's immortal soul is a Christian one, but it is interesting that the term was never explicitly described as such in the Old or New Testaments of the Bible. The Zoroastrian tradition had enormous influence on early Christianity, introducing the main tenets of a dualistic religion where a force of good is pitted against evil, a conflict upon which all life on Earth is based. Zoroastrianism also described judgement that occurred after death, based on listing one's good deeds and misdeeds in a ledger, and then comparing them for numbers before being sentenced in one direction or the other.[2] For Abrahamic traditions, there is a common belief that the hell myths we know today began in the New Testament with mention of a site called Gehenna. Gehenna (or the Valley of Hinnom) was an immense garbage dump located outside of Jerusalem where corpses, animal carcasses, and garbage were collected and burned in a huge perpetually burning pyre.[3] The mention was intended to illustrate the dominant Christian teaching of the soul which may live forever in paradise as distinct from the deceased body which became unclean upon death and would inevitably wind up in a garbage dump.[4] Despite the prevalence of this belief, scholars like George Beasley-Murray have noted that "the notion, still referred to by some commentators, that the city's rubbish was burned in this valley, has no further basis than a statement by the Jewish scholar Kimchi made about A.D. 1200; it is not attested in any ancient source." From here, the idea of good souls ascending from the pyre while evil ones continued to burn in it developed into the mythos of the fiery furnace we know today. The idea of hell being located deep below the Earth's surface came about as the opposite pole to the idea of heaven as a place of ascension (presumably in the sky), near to God and his chosen. Hell is thus a human construct, not a divine or holy one, which is what makes it so adaptable and also especially fascinating.

Hell has been described, cautioned against, and elucidated upon in countless pulpits, but the most illustrious of the literary elaborations of hell appear in Dante Alighieri's *Divine Comedy*.[5] The epic poem, famed for its political allegory and its graphic and imaginative depiction of the afterlife, tells the story of author's own travels through hell, heaven, and purgatory with his guide Virgil (writer of the *Aeneid*, another Roman tome containing elaborate descriptions of the underworld). Alighieri was a prominent political figure of Florence in his time but scandals involving church and government corruption forced his exile from 1308 to 1321, whereupon he wrote the *Divine Comedy*. His political frustrations are evident in the poem with political figures found in various levels of punishment for crimes committed while on Earth, but the figurative tale remains the most celebrated and cited account of the medieval Christian worldview of the afterlife. Most importantly, the *Divine Comedy* describes a multi-tiered structure of heaven and hell where souls are judged and assigned their fate according to a certain hierarchy. The punishments do seem harsh, even for what would be considered slight infractions today: those who were unable to commit to a life of good or evil, for example, were doomed to the Ante-Inferno, where they must run in a futile chase for eternity while being stung by hornets.[6] The first circle of hell houses the pagans and great historical writers, poets, and philosophers whose only sin was living in ignorance of Christ.[7] The more grievous sins are punished deeper in hell, with the lowest depth of hell being the site where those who betrayed their benefactors are subject to the worst possible torment.[8] The *Divine Comedy* is an important cultural text for a number of contextual reasons, including the political element of Alighieri's decision to write the epic poem in the language of the people as opposed to Latin, but its significance for our purposes lies in the conception of a hierarchical hell, where different sins are punished differently and at varying levels of severity. As such, Alighieri's work represents an important stage of development of hell mythology between the vague all-encompassing inferno of Gehenna to Barker's hell of sensory and psychological torture.

In *The Hellbound Heart*, Frank Cotton is not looking for hell; in fact, he is seeking his vision of paradise. He has lived a life of hedonism that has only slaked his thirst for pleasure while dulling his capacity for satisfaction, and his search for new plains of experience brings him to the Lament Configuration. He decides to summon the cenobites because he was told that they were a collective of like-minded hedonists, unrivalled experts in the topics of pain and pleasure, among whom he would finally be "exalted by his lust, instead of despised for it."[9] Lemarchand's Box was rumored to be the conduit to the cenobites; the mysterious "theologians of the Order of the Gash,"[10] and the promise of boundless pleasure was enough for Frank to cast aside all fear and set about opening the gateway into hell.

In the novella, we are offered only brief glimpses of hell when the doorway is opened for the cenobites to enter our realm. The gateway (referred to throughout the book as the Schism) can be opened anywhere as needed, through brick and mortar if necessary. From Frank's perspective, the cenobites emerge from a frenzied void, a "panic-filled darkness,"[11] where a tempest whirled in madness, full of "broken things that rose and fell and filled the dark air with their fright."[12] Upon arrival, the cenobites confirm that they are capable of offering him sensation beyond his wildest dreams, that "There are conditions of the nerve endings the like of which your imagination, however fevered, could not hope to evoke."[13] They choose their words carefully, using "experience" where Frank would imagine "pleasure," and true to their word, the experience they offer Frank causes him to relive every bodily sensation he had ever experienced in his life with twenty times the intensity; both erotic and agonizing. He can smell the long-dried paint in the walls and ceilings, the sap in the wooden floorboards, and a thousand dins in his ears. When he recovers, he is left alone with a single terrifying cenobite sitting upon a pile of rotting human heads. He thinks, "There was no pleasure in the air; or at least not as humankind understood it,"[14] and we don't hear from him again until he is partially revived by his brother Rory.

Classic Christian wisdom describes two principal ways of suffering the torment of hell, both in the corporeal and incorporeal senses. *Poena sensus* refers to the torment of fire; a metaphor for physical agony that is inflicted upon the disembodied soul.[15] The torment of fire is meant to refer to the tangible pain of hell, a sensory experience of perpetual agony. Sins of flesh and activity are punished more harshly in the *Divine Comedy*, implying that they are somehow more grievous than cognitive or emotional infractions. This line drawn between impure intentions and maleficent activity is also reflected in the current legal system where *actus reus* (Latin for "guilty act") is more harshly punished when paired with the allegation of *mens rea* (the "guilty mind"). The cenobites ask Frank to verbally affirm his desire to partake of the cenobites' offering and he agrees. It is hard to say what might have happened if he declined at the last minute out of fear, but Barker returns to this theme later when Rory's friend Kirsty (his daughter in the movie) unknowingly summons the cenobites from her hospital room. Initially, the cenobites tell her that "There's no help for it. No way to seal the Schism, until we take what's ours,"[16] but they do strike a deal with her to spare her in exchange for Frank. As such, we can be sure that there are no innocents suffering in hell and while Frank may not have known what he was getting into, he was punished for what he was looking for.

The second pain of hell is called *poena damni*, considered the more dreadful of the two *poenas*, referring to the pain of being permanently separated from God and his presence.[17] Before Frank is able to reanimate, he remembers lingering in the wall, incorporeal, for what seemed like eons. The initial torture at the hands of the cenobites was a great overdose of experience and sensitivity, but once he is torn apart, he find there was also a long-term element to their torture, a sophisticated and psychological one "devised by a mind that understood exquisitely the nature of suffering."[18] In the moments between the cenobites exercise of "pleasure," Frank was imprisoned the room he had once occupied, incorporeal and immaterial, looking in on the living and unable to share their freedom. He endured torture unimaginable without knowledge of a possibility of escape, and this was the worst of it: "What punishment could be meted out worse than the thought of pain without hope of release?"[19] His torment is thus reminiscent of *poena damni*; in addition to the destruction of his body, he is doomed to spend eternity watching the lives of others continue, knowing what he could never have back. Barker's hell, then, is less a geographic space than a state of being: a state of being in pain, specifically, in both physical and psychological ways. In this, we see Barker's hell as a fusion of the *peonas* of classical belief and the current state of law and order wherein sin comprises both the desire and the deed, and so does the punishment.

The novella and the first film of the series describes hell as experienced both physically and incorporeally, with the body pushed to sensory extremes and the mind doomed to madness. The second film in the series, *Hellbound: Hellraiser II*, has Barker credited only for the story, which follows Kirsty to an institution where her physician, the cult-obsessed Dr. Channard, shares Frank's proclivities and curiosities about pleasure. This time, Kirsty is deceived by Frank into entering hell to look for her father, and she wanders through a labyrinthine corridor with stone walls that break into Daliesque catacombs of staircases. Tiffany, another mental patient at the hospital where Kirsty is imprisoned, is also lost in hell and finds a funhouse where her mother appears to her in the house of mirrors and a clown juggles with his own eyes. When Kirsty tells Pinhead she has come for her father, he replies that her father is in his own hell, as she is in hers. This hell, then, is one that caters specifically to the anxieties of the subject in question: a maze for Kirsty who searches for her father and a hall of illusions for the confused and lost Tiffany. The idea of hell being one's personal tailor-made torment speaks to the merging of individualism with the rise of consumer culture, where people identify strongly with material goods and seek to define themselves with as much specificity as possible. In other words, these characters do not simply experience hell as passive subjects; they are complicit in its reality. Just as Dante envisioned a hell segregated by typology of sin, Barker's hell is specialized even further, to the level of the individual.

Thus far I have sought to illustrate the development of hell mythology from the broadest metaphor for a garbage pyre, to a tiered hell based on grievousness of sin to a personal hell, tailor-made just for you. The significance of this shift is in its alignment with Western modernization processes and its relevance to the changing psycho-spiritual needs of this generation. In the remainder of the chapter I will look at how Barker's conception of the cenobites can be said to represent a similar developmental stage in devil mythology: from the traditional legends of Satan and Lucifer to the emergence of the Faustian contract as a literary trope for the unfulfilled desires of humanity.

THE DEVIL WE KNOW

In every story, there is a hero and a villain. As God personifies goodness and glory, he needs an adversary; someone to stand for evil and sin. Many cultures develop some form of a personification of evil: Rudwin identifies Lucifer's opposition to God as analogous to Vrita and Indra in Hindu mythology, Ahriman and Ormuzd in Persian mythology, Set and Horus in Egyptian mythology, and Prometheus and Zeus of Greek mythology.[20] In ancient Greece, love, war, death, and wisdom each had a god or goddess to represent it, and when something defied explanation, it was simply the will of that particular deity at the moment. In addition, the Greeks did not hold their gods or goddesses to particularly noble or holy behavior: they understood their gods to act out of fear, jealousy, rage or boredom just as likely as they would out of virtue. This system helped the populous to cope with the inconsistencies of life that they could not explain or understand. As discussed earlier with regard to hell, the devil we know makes scant direct appearances in the Bible (save for possible fleeting mention in the Old Testament) and the legend of Lucifer does not appear at all, and so the bulk of devil mythos comes from ancient folklore and common knowledge.[21] The remaining portion of this chapter will discuss the classic conceptions of the devil with reference to how the cenobites in Barker's novella engage with them.

The names Lucifer and Satan are often used interchangeably when referring to the overlord of the underworld, but Rudwin argues that the legends have been conflated as the result of a biblical misinterpretation by the church.[22] As far as folklore goes, Lucifer is described as a terribly beautiful angel, so lovely and favored by God as to have been given the seat at his left hand. By this, Lucifer was overcome by ambition and conceit and was cast from heaven by the archangel Michael for trying to take the holy throne.[23] Satan, on the other hand, is believed to have been charged with envy of humanity, and it was this jealously that compelled him to go to the Garden of Eden in the form of a serpent and tempt Eve with forbidden fruit.[24] In both cases, the myth of the fallen angel serves to construct the devil as a tragic being who knew the paradise of heaven and must now endure the torment of being separated from it (*poena damni*).

Common portrayals of the devil relate to this fallen-angel status: he is often depicted as a winged creature, but with pointed bat-wings instead of an angel's soft feathers. He is occasionally portrayed as monstrous and ugly, with features borrowed from animals and other creatures from non-Christian (ergo unholy) mythologies and is also known to be carrying a pitchfork; a nod at Poseidon's trident, the symbol of skill and prowess.[25] In the Romantic era, the devil was often personified in a pointed beard and an opera cape to allude to his talents of seduction and persuasion.[26] Contemporary cinematic depictions of the devil are as varied as his many names (see Rudwin for an exhaustive list of his numerous monikers) and his appearances range from an unseen force of malevolent possession (*The Exorcist*), a shameless comedic hedonist (*Little Nicky*), an erotic tempter/ess (*End of Days, Bedazzled*) and, perhaps most interestingly for our era, a ruthless business executive (*The Devil's Advocate*). Unlike the Christian God who insists upon faith for salvation while remaining unseen, the devil celebrates those who doubt his existence and relishes his skills at seducing the souls of believers and unbelievers alike. The only way to guard against the devil's influence is to live virtuously and take comfort in what comforts are available to us within the earthly realm, which is easier for some than others.

Frank Cotton is a textbook hedonist whose offenses range from sexual to criminal and beyond, and as a result of a lifetime of indulgence, he had become beyond satisfaction. Barker writes at length on Frank's misery and how he contemplated suicide before discovering Lemarchand's Box. While undoubtedly the villain of the tale, Barker is notably sympathetic to both Frank and his accomplice Julia, humanizing her through their misery and desperation until she resorts to the unforgiveable by helping reanimate Frank's body. These two are no angels, but it is noteworthy that their later misery is born of their attempts to escape their prior misery: the misery of dissatisfaction is described as wretchedly as the misery of bodily torture. In the film *Hellraiser*, Pinhead describes his cohort of cenobites as "Demons to some, angels to others," hinting at both the subjective line between pleasure and pain but also between good and evil. Faust of German legend was a highly successful scholar, who grew bored of his many books made a pact with the deal to exchange his soul for unlimited knowledge. The story was published later by German author Johann Wolfgang von Goethe as a play, which complicated the simple Christian moral of the story to include a caveat in the story where the devil agreed to leave Faust with his powers until he had reached the utmost zenith of human happiness. Prior to summoning the cenobites, Frank has been told by Kircher (the man who sold him the box) that they were "theologians of the Order of the Gash. Summoned from their experiments in the higher reaches of pleasure, to bring their ageless heads into a world of rain and failure."[27] This description rings of theology directly but also of science; a combination of faith-based knowledge and objective inquiry. This duality is affirmed by the cenobites' leader Pinhead, who calls his brood explorers in the furthest regions of experience. The cenobites are equally driven by curiosity and the desire to fully know the furthest reaches of sensory experience. Science and religion are often pitted as irreconcilable enemies, as oppositional and antagonistic as God and the devil, and their conflict appears to be timeless as evidenced by the popularity of Faust's deal with the devil as a literary trope. The cenobites and their devotion to empirical research in the realm of experience transcend this duality, bridging the gap between the spiritual with the sensory while walking the thin line between pleasure and pain.

In the *Hellbound Heart*, the cenobites are monstrous by virtue of their scarred and disfigured appearance, with flesh that has been "cosmetically punctured and sliced and infibulated, then dusted down with ash."[28] Their clothing is not explicitly described in the book, but in the *Hellraiser* film series they are dressed in dark, dramatic garments that combine elements from religious vestments, butchery smocks, and sadomasochist fetish apparel. The association between the cenobites and the S&M community is likely enough; a lifestyle built around a fetish for receiving sexual pleasure through pain or humiliation is heavenly to some and hellish to others. Both the cenobites and the S&M subculture thrive in the underworld, so to speak, concealing their taboo proclivities from the mainstream, but while the fetish community does so to avoid judgement, the cenobites are themselves the adjudicators. Questions of safety and consent are of paramount importance to sex play involving BDSM, and the cenobites also require the explicit verbal consent of their prisoners when they are summoned. The saying "the devil must have his pay" speaks to the devil's reliability as a debt collector, but the devil is sometimes described as a cheat and a liar in his own right, and is just as likely to change the deal or alter it to suit his purposes. When Kirsty strikes a deal with the cenobites to spare her life in exchange for turning in their prize escapee, Frank, they keep their word, allowing her to flee as soon as they had their escapee in hooks. Though it might seem counter-intuitive that such horrific demons would spare Kirsty's soul, their actions correspond with a sense of law and fairness that permeates their activities; a certain code by which they adhere. Consent is required for the cenobites to take, but once given, cannot be retracted. The devil may only punish the deserving, and cenobites are equally uninterested in the innocent.

The cenobites contribute a modernized take on traditional devil folklore in that they do not actively recruit their victims. They must be summoned in order to appear, and their reputation for expertise in pleasure has a further reach than their malevolent proclivities. Among the real effects of globalization on culture is a heightened awareness of what the world has to offer: technology has increased the speed of information flow exponentially, and for those of us with the privilege of access, anything we want is just a few clicks away. The byproduct of this is increased capacity for desire due to such overstimulation and abundance. The more we have, the more we want, and this is increasingly evident in emergent consumer culture. As such, the cenobites represent the potential evils of modernity, representations of what can happen when too much is not enough. As a literary trope, this theme is nothing new: Icarus melted his wings when he flew too close to the sun and even Lucifer was cast out of heaven as the result of his own ambition. Frank is both villain and victim in this fairy tale, and the cenobites represent antiheroes who have the power to both punish the gluttonous deserving while reinforcing the virtues of humility.

CONCLUSION

For as long as humanity has occupied the Earth, it has been keenly aware of the presence of evil and the effort to understand that evil is part of what inspires theological inquiry into the fantastical. Humankind has a long-standing custom of using stories and mythology to come to grips with that which cannot be easily explained and although we live in an age where faith is often pitted against reason, we have only to look at our fiction to realize that we are still telling stories that inform our understanding of right and wrong and what it means to be human. Evil still exists in the world as much as it ever has but now we no longer speak of it as lurking around the corner to seduce a soul and drag it off to hell. Perhaps the devil has learned that he need only wait, and those who grow weary of the overstimulation of modern life will willingly seek him out.

Part Three: Other Undead

The *Hellbound Heart* is a contemporary example of how the human imagination seeks to get a grasp on the darkness of the unknown by twisting and mutilating the familiar into something new and hideous. The stories that remain relevant to us are the ones that are able to adapt with the times, and Clive Barker's reimagining of hell and the devil speak to the modern social context. Modernization processes have redefined rationality and community and a new emphasis on the individual is reflected in the fact that the final judgements of the cenobites are made based on individual desires and sinners are sent to their personal hells. Far from any argument that Barker is the harbinger of a new religious persuasion, this chapter has sought to illuminate the ways in which his conception of hell and the demons that inhabit it represent the human necessity to describe evil in ways that are most meaningful for the time and cultural climate. While creationism and evolution are often pitted against one another as competing ways to understand and explain life on Earth, Barker's reimagining of hell and the devil proves that the two can come together to create a new mythology, one that can speak to a new era in human existence while reminding us that evil is just a puzzle box away.

END NOTES

1. Barker, *The Hellbound*.
2. Turner, *The History of Hell*, 17.
3. Thayer, *The Origin and History*.
4. Ibid.
5. Alighieri, *The Divine Comedy*, Canto III.
6. Ibid., Canto IV.
7. Ibid., Canto XXIV.
8. Barker, *The Hellbound*, 9.
9. Ibid., 4.
10. Ibid., 6.
11. Ibid., 12.
12. Ibid., 6.
13. Ibid., 11.
14. Ibid., 19.
15. Hontheim, "Hell."
16. Barker, *The Hellbound*, 134.
17. Hontheim, "Hell."

18. Barker, *The Hellbound*, 62.
19. Ibid., 63.
20. Rudwin, *The Devil in Legend*, 2.
21. Ibid., 1.
22. Ibid., 3.
23. Ibid, 6.
24. Russell, *The Devil*, 8.
25. Wilson, *The Devil*, 10.
26. Ibid., 10.
27. Barker, *The Hellbound*, 4.
28. Ibid., 7.

Bibliography

Abbot, Stacy. *Celluloid Vampires: Life after Death in the Modern World*. Austin, TX: University of Texas Press, 2007.
Albanese, Catherine L. *A Republic of Mind and Spirit: A Cultural History of American Metaphysical Religion*. New Haven: Yale University Press, 2007.
Ali, Tariq. *The Coming British Revolution*. London: Jonathan Cape Ltd., 1972.
Alighieri, Dante. *The Divine Comedy*. Bloomington, IN: Indiana University Press, 1996.
———. *Inferno*. Translated by Mark Musa. New York: Penguin, 1984.
Altick, Richard D. *To Be In England*. New York: Norton, 1969.
AMC Press Release. "AMC's 'The Walking Dead' Delivers the Strongest Telecast for Any Drama in Basic Cable History against Key Demos." October 17, 2011. Online: http://www.amcnetworks.com/release_release_press.jsp?nodeid=6428.
Anonymous. "About." Zombie Jesus Day website. Online: http://www.zombiejesusday.org/About.aspx.
———. "Church of the Resurrection." Urban Dead Wiki. Online: http://wiki.urbandead.com/index.php/Church_of_the_Resurrection.
———. "The First Church of the Living Dead." Online: http://www.thefirstchurchofthelivingdead.com/.
———. "The Golem." *Strange Tales*. Marvel Comics, 1974. Issues 174, 176–77.
———. "It! The Living Colossus." *Astonishing Tales*. Marvel Comics, 1973–74. Issues 21–24.
———. *Mendy and the Golem*. Mendy Enterprises, 1981–85. 19 issues.
———. *Mendy and the Golem*. The Golem Factory, 2003–2005. 6 issues.
———. *The Monolith*. DC Comics, 2004–2005. 12 issues.
———. "Occupy Las Vegas Holds 'Zombie Walk' to Protest Corporate Greed." *Avax News*, 1 November 2011. Online:http://avaxnews.com/fact/Occupy_Las_Vegas_Holds_Zombie_Walk_To_Protest_Corporate_Greed.html.
———. "The Walking Dead." Online: http://bloodgod.org/the_walking_dead.htm.
———. "Zombie Jesus." Uncyclopedia. Online: http://uncyclopedia.wikia.com/wiki/Zombie_Jesus.
———. "Zombie walks." Wikipedia. Online: http://en.wikipedia.org/wiki/Zombie_walk.
Arthur, Paul. "The Heath Government and Northern Ireland." In *The Heath Government, 1970–1974*, ed. by Stuart Ball and Anthony Seldon. London: Longman Press, 1996.
Asimov, Isaac. *I, Robot*. New York: Gnome, 1950.
Asma, Stephen. *Stuffed Animals and Pickled Heads: The Culture and Evolution of the Natural History Museum*. New York: Oxford University Press, 2003.
Associated Press, "Mexico City 'Zombie Walk' Hopes to Break World Record (PHOTOS)." *The Huffington Post*, 27 November 27, 2011. Online: http://www

Bibliography

.huffingtonpost.com/2011/11/27/mexico-city-zombie-walk-record_n_1114724.html.

Auerbach, Nina. "My Vampire, My Friend: The intimacy Dracula destroyed." In *Blood Read: The Vampire as Metaphor in Contemporary Culture*, edited by Joan Gordon and Veronica Hollinger, 11–16. Philadelphia: University of Pennsylvania Press, 1997.

———. *Our Vampires, Ourselves*. Chicago: The University of Chicago Press, 1995.

Augustine. *The City of God*. Edited and translated by Marcus Dods. Peabody, MA: Hendrickson, 2009.

———. *The Confessions of St. Augustine*. Translated by J. K. Ryan. Garden City, NY: Doubleday, 1960.

Aune, David Edward. "Apocalypse Renewed: An Intertextual Reading of the Apocalypse of John." In *The Reality of Apocalypse: Rhetoric and Politics in the Book of Revelation*, edited by David L. Barr, 43–70. Atlanta: Society of Biblical Literature, 2006.

Baddeley, Gavin, and Paul Anthony Woods. *Goth Chic: A Connoisseur's Guide to Dark Culture*. London: Plexus, 2002.

Baddeley, Gavin. *Lucifer Rising: Sin, Devil Worship and Rock and Roll*. London: Plexus Publishing, 2006.

Bader, Christopher D., F. Menken, and J. D. Baker. *Paranormal America: Ghost Encounters, UFO Sightings, Bigfoot Hunts and other Curiosities in Religion and Culture*. New York: New York University Press, 2010.

Badley, Linda. *Film Horror, and the Body Fantastic*. Contributions to the Study of Popular Culture. Westport, CT: Greenwood, 1995.

———. *Writing Horror and the Body*. Westport, CT: Greenwood, 1996.

Bandura, Albert. "Mechanisms of Moral Disengagement in Terrorism." In *Origins of Terrorism: Psychologies, Ideologies, Theologies, States of Mind*, edited by Walter Reich, 161–91. Washington, DC: The Woodrow Wilson Center, 1998.

Barber, Paul. *Vampires, Burial and Death: Folklore and Reality*. New Haven: Yale University Press, 1988.

Barker, Clive. *The Hellbound Heart*. New York: Harper, 1986.

———. *Hellbound: Hellraiser II*. New World Pictures, 1988.

———. *Hellraiser*. New World Pictures, 1987.

Barkun, Michael. *A Culture of Conspiracy: Apocalyptic Visions in Contemporary America*. Berkeley: University of California Press, 2003.

Barr, David L. "Beyond Genre: The Expectations of Apocalypse." In *The Reality of Apocalypse: Rhetoric and Politics in the Book of Revelation*, 71–90. Atlanta: Society of Biblical Literature, 2006.

———. "The Lamb Who Looks Like a Dragon?: Characterizing Jesus in John's Apocalypse." In *The Reality of Apocalypse: Rhetoric and Politics in the Book of Revelation*, edited by David L. Barr, 205–20. Atlanta: Society of Biblical Literature, 2006.

Bartal, Inbal, Jean Decety, and Peggy Mason. "Empathy and Pro-Social Behavior in Rats." *Science* 9 (2011) 1427–30.

Barth, Karl. *The Christian Life: Church Dogmatics IV.4. Lecture Fragments*. Translated by Geoffrey W. Bromiley. Grand Rapids: Eerdmans, 1981.

———. *Church Dogmatics*. Edited by Geoffrey W. Bromiley and Thomas F Torrance. Translated by T. F. Torrance. Study ed. London: T. & T. Clark, 2009.

———. *Credo*. Translated by James Strathem. London: Hodder & Stoughton, 1936.

———. *Ethics*. Edited by Geoffrey W. Bromiley and Dietrich Braun. New York: Seabury, 1981.

———. "Rudolph Bultmann—An Attempt to Understand Him." In *Kerygma and Myth: A Theological Debate, Vol. II*, translated by Reginald Fuller, edited by H. Bartsch, 83–132. London: SPCK, 1972.

Bass, Jules, and Arthur Rankin, Jr., directors. *Frosty the Snowman*. Rankin/Bass, 1969.

Bauckham, Richard. *The Climax of Prophecy: Studies on the Book of Revelation*. Edinburgh: T. & T. Clark, 1993.

Beal, Timothy K. *Religion and Its Monsters*. New York: Routledge, 2002.

Beasley-Murray, George. R. *Jesus and the Kingdom of God*. Grand Rapids: Eerdmans, 1988.

Bebbington, D. W. *Evangelicalism in Modern Britain: A History from the 1730s to the 1980s*. London: Hyman, 1989.

Beeson, Trevor. *Priests and Prelates: The Daily Telegraph Clerical Obituaries*. New York: Continuum International Publishing Group, 2006.

Benefiel, Candace R. *Reading Laurell K. Hamilton*. Santa Barbara: Libraries Unlimited. 2011.

Beresford, Matthew. *From Demons to Dracula: The Creation of the Modern Vampire Myth*. London: Reaktion, 2008.

Berger, Peter L. *The Heretical Imperative: Contemporary Possibilities of Religious Affirmation*. Garden City, NY: Anchor, 1979.

———. *A Rumor of Angels: Modern Society and the Rediscovery of the Supernatural*. Garden City, CA: Anchor, 1969.

———. *The Sacred Canopy: Elements of a Sociological Theory of Religion*. Garden City, NY: Anchor, 1969.

Bishop, Kyle William. "The Pathos of the Walking Dead: Bringing Terror Back to Zombie Cinema." In *Triumph of the Walking Dead: Robert Kirkman's Zombie Epic on Page and Screen*, edited by James Lowder, 1–14. Dallas: BenBella, 2011.

Blake, John. "The Zombie Theology behind The Walking Dead." CNN.com. Online: http://religion.blogs.cnn.com/2010/12/20/the-zombie-theology-behind-the-walking-dead/.

Block, Ned. "Are Absent Qualia Impossible?" *Philosophical Review* 89 (1980) 257–74.

Blumhardt, Christoph. *Action in Waiting*. Rifton, NY: Plough, 1969.

Boese, Carl, and Paul Wegener, directors. *Der Golem (The Golem: How He Came into the World)*. UFA, 1920.

Bohm, Anton Wilhelm. "Universal love the surest way to advance the interest of religion, and unite the several contending parties about it. In a letter to a friend." London: Downing, 1709. Online: http://catalogue.nla.gov.au/Record/4868310?

Bonhoeffer, Dietrich. *Ethics*. Vol. 6, Dietrich Bonhoeffer Works. Minneapolis: Fortress, 2005.

———. *Letters and Papers From Prison*. Edited by Eberhard Bethge. London: SCM, 1971.

Boon, Kevin. "The Zombie as Other: Mortality and the Monstrous in the Post-Nuclear Age." In *Better Off Dead: The Evolution of the Zombie as Post-Human*, edited by Deborah Christie and Sarah Juliet Lauro, 50–65. New York: Fordham University Press, 2011.

Brill, Dunja. "Gender, Status and Subcultural Capital in the Goth Scene." In *Youth Cultures: Scenes, Subcultures, and Tribes*, edited by Paul Hodkinson and Wolfgang Deicke, 111–25. New York: Routledge, 2007.

Bibliography

Britton, A. "The Devil, Probably: The Symbolism of Evil." In *American Nightmare: Essays on the Horror Film*, edited by R. Wood and R. Lippe, 34–42. Toronto: Festival of Festivals, 1979.

Brooks, Max. *World War Z: An Oral History of the Zombie War*. New York: Crown, 2006.

———. *The Zombie Survival Guide: Complete Protection from the Living Dead*. New York: Three Rivers, 2003.

Brown, Warren S., Nancey Murphy, and H. Newton Maloney, editors. *Whatever Happened to the Soul?: Scientific and Theological Portraits of Human Nature*. Minneapolis, MN: Fortress, 1998.

Browning, John Edgar, and Caroline Joan Picart, editors. *Draculas, Vampires, and Other Undead Forms: Essays on Gender, Race, and Culture*. Lanham, MD: Scarecrow, 2009.

Bundtzen, Lynda K. "Monstrous Mothers: Medusa, Grendel, and Now Alien." In *The Gendered Cyborg: A Reader*, edited by Gill Kirkup, 101–9. London: Routledge, 2000.

Bussee, Kristina. "Crossing the Final Taboo: Family, Sexuality, and Incest in Buffyverse Fan Fiction." In *Fighting the Forces: What's at Stake in Buffy the Vampire Slayer*, edited by R. V. Wilcox and D. Lavery, 207–17. Lanham, MD: Rowman & Littlefield, 2002.

Capek, Karel, director. *R.U.R.: Rossum's Universal Robots*. Premiered 1921.

Carey, Greg. "Symptoms of Resistance in the Book of Revelation." In *The Reality of Apocalypse: Rhetoric and Politics in the Book of Revelation*, 169–80. Atlanta: Society of Biblical Literature, 2006.

Carrasco, David. *Religions of Mesoamerica: Cosmovision and Ceremonial Centers*. Long Grove, IL: Waveland, 1998.

Carter, Margaret. "Lust, Love, and the Literary Vampire." *Strange Horizons* (22 July 2002). Online: http://www.strangehorizons.com/2002/20020722/vampire.shtml.

Cavanaugh. William. *Being Consumed: Economics and Christian Desire*. Grand Rapids: Eerdmans, 2008.

Chabon, Michael. *The Amazing Adventures of Kavalier & Clay*. New York: Random House, 2000.

Chalmers, David. *The Conscious Mind: In Search of a Fundamental Theory*. Oxford: Oxford University Press, 1996.

Christie, Deborah, and Sarah Juliet Lauro, editors. *Better Off Dead: The Evolution of the Zombie as Post-Human*. New York: Fordham University Press, 2011.

Clifton, Jacob. "Showing the Scars." In *Ardeur: 14 Writers on the Anita Blake, Vampire Hunter Series*, edited by Laruell K. Hamilton and Leah Wilson. Dallas: BenBella, 2010.

Clover, Carol. *Men, Women, and Chain Saws: Gender in the Modern Horror Film*. Princeton: Princeton University Press, 1992.

Cohen, Nick. "The Eurozone: Its Pyrrhic Victory for the Euroskeptics." In *The Observer* (August 13, 2011).

Collins, Adela Yarbro. *Crisis and Catharsis: The Power of the Apocalypse*. 1st ed. Philadelphia: Westminster, 1984.

———. "Vilification and Self-Definition in the Book of Revelation." *Harvard Theological Review* 79 (1986) 308–20.

———. "Women's History and the Book of Revelation." *SBL Seminar Papers* 26 (1987) 80–91.

———. "Insiders and Outsiders in the Book of Revelation" in *"To See Ourselves as Others See Us": Christians, Jews, "Others" in Late Antiquity*, edited by Jacob Neusner and Ernest S. Frerichs, 187–218. Chico, CA: Scholars, 1985.

Collins, John Joseph. *Apocalypse: The Morphology of a Genre*. Semeia 14. Missoula, MT: Scholars, 1979.

———. *The Apocalyptic Imagination: An Introduction to Jewish Apocalyptic Literature*. Grand Rapids: Eerdmans, 1998.

Cooney, Michael, director. *Jack Frost*. Moonstone, 1997.

Cowan, Douglas E. *Sacred Terror: Religion and Horror on the Silver Screen*. Waco, TX: Baylor University Press, 2008.

Cuneo, Michael W. *American Exorcism: Expelling Demons in the Land of Plenty*. New York: Doubleday, 2001.

Cunningham, Conor. *Genealogy of Nihilism: Philosophies of Nothing and the Difference of Theology*. Radical Orthodoxy Series. London: Routledge, 2002.

Curran, Andrew, and Patrick Graille. "The Faces of Eighteenth Century Monstrosity." *Eighteenth-Century Life* 21.2 (1997) 1–15.

d'Arbonne, Jess. "Zombie Jesus at the Denver Zombie Crawl." Examiner.com, 23 April 2011. Online: http://www.examiner.com/zombie-in-denver/zombie-jesus-at-the-denver-zombie-crawl-picture.

Dargis, M. "Not Just Roaming, Zombies Rise Up." *New York Times*, 24 June 2005. Online: http://movies.nytimes.com/2005/06/24/movies/24rome.html.

Daubs, Katie. "Zombies and Occupy Toronto Protesters March through City." thestar.com, 22 October 2011. Online: http://http://www.thestar.com/news/article/1074563--zombies-and-occupy-toronto-protesters-march-through-city.

Davis, W. *Passage of Darkness: The Ethnobiology of the Haitian Zombie*. University of North Carolina Press, 1988.

———. *The Serpent and the Rainbow*. New York: Simon & Schuster, 1985.

Demson, David E. "The Advantages and Limits of Irregular and Regular Dogmatics— Political Responsibility according to Lehmann and Barth." In *Explorations in Christian Theology and Ethics: Essays in Conversation with Paul L. Lehmann*, edited by Philip G. Ziegler and Michelle J. Bartel, 79–100. Burlington, VT: Ashgate, 2009.

Dennison, Michael J. *Vampirism: Literary Tropes of Decadence and Entropy*. New York: Lang, 2001.

Dillard, R. H. W. "*Night of the Living Dead*: It's Not Like Just a Wind That's Passing Through." In *American Horrors: Essays on the Modern American Horror Film*, edited by G. A. Waller, 14–29. Urbana, IL: University of Illinois Press, 1988.

Dillon, Martin. *The Enemy Within: The IRA's War against the British*. London: Doubleday Press, 1994.

Du Plessis, Michael. "'Goth Damage' and Melancholia: Reflections on Posthuman Gothic Identities." In *Goth: Undead Subculture*, edited by Lauren M. E. Goodlad and Michael Bibby, 155–68. Durham, NC: Duke University Press, 2007.

Ellington, Devon. "Ardeur's Purpose." In *Ardeur: 14 Writers on the Anita Blake, Vampire Hunter Series*, edited by Laurell K. Hamilton and Leah Wilson, 105–20. Dallas: BenBella, 2010.

Ellis, Bill. *Raising the Devil: Satanism, New Religions and the Media*. Lexington, KY; University Press of Kentucky, 2000.

Bibliography

Erickson, Gregory. "'Sometimes You Need a Story': American Christianity, Vampires, and Buffy." In *Fighting the Forces: What's at Stake in Buffy the Vampire Slayer*, edited by Rhonda V. Wilcox and David Lavery, 108–19. Lanham, MD: Rowman & Littlefield, 2002.

Fingeroth, Danny. *Superman on the Couch: What Superheroes Really Tell Us about Ourselves and Our Society*. New York: Continuum, 2004.

Fiorenza, Elisabeth Schüssler. "Babylon the Great: A Rhetorical-Political Reading of Revelation 17–18." In *The Reality of Apocalypse: Rhetoric and Politics in the Book of Revelation*, edited by David L. Barr, 243–60. Society of Biblical Literature Symposium Series. Atlanta: Society of Biblical Literature, 2006.

Flanagan, Owen, and Thomas Polger. "Zombies and the Function of Consciousness." *Journal of Consciousness Studies* 2 (1995) 313–21.

Fondren, Natasha. "The Domestication of a Vampire Executioner." In *Ardeur: 14 Writers on the Anita Blake, Vampire Hunter Series*, edited by Laurell K. Hamilton and Leah Wilson, 89–104. Dallas: BenBella, 2010.

Fraser, J. "Watching Horror Movies." *Michigan Quarterly Review* 24.1 (1990) 39–54.

Friedenberg, Richard, director. *Snow in August*. Showtime, 2001.

Friesen, Steve. "Sarcasm in Revelation 2–3: Churches, Christians, True Jews, and Satanic Synagogues." In *The Reality of Apocalypse: Rhetoric and Politics in the Book of Revelation*, edited by David L. Barr, 127–44. Atlanta: Society of Biblical Literature, 2006.

Fuller, Robert. *Spiritual, But Not Religious: Understanding Unchurched America*. New York: Oxford University Press, 2001.

Gaffney, Peter. "Treehouse of Horror XVII: You Gotta Know When to Golem." *The Simpsons*. FOX Network, 5 November 2006.

Garrett, Susan. "Revelation." In *The Women's Bible Commentary*, edited by Carol A. Newsom and Sharon H. Ringe, 469–74. Louisville, KY: Westminster/John Knox, 1992.

Gasser, George, editor. *Personal Identity and Resurrection: How Do We Survive Our Death*. Aldershot, UK: Ashgate, 2010.

Giddens, Anthony. *Modernity and Self-Identity: Self and Society in the Late Modern Age*. Stanford, CA: Stanford University Press, 1991.

Gilmour, Michael J. "The Living Word among the Living Dead: Hunting for Zombies in the Pages of the Bible." In *Zombies Are Us: Essays on the Humanity of the Walking Dead*, edited by Christopher M. Moreman and Cory James Rushton, 87–99. Jefferson, NC: McFarland, 2011.

Glinert, Lewis. "Golem! The Making of a Modern Myth." *Symposium* 55.2 (2001) 78–94.

Goldberg, Lesley. "TV Ratings: 'The Walking Dead' Midseason Finale Tops Season 1 Closer." The Hollywood Reporter, November 28, 2011. Online: http://www.hollywoodreporter.com/live-feed/tv-ratings-walking-dead-midseason-finale-266631.

Gordon, Howard. "Kaddish." *The X-Files*. FOX Network, 16 February 1997.

Graham, Billy. *Angels: God's Secret Agents*. Nashville, TN: W. Publishing Group, 1994.

Green, Joel B. *Body, Soul, and Human Life: The Nature of Humanity in the Bible*. Grand Rapids: Baker Academic, 2008.

Griffin, Susan M. *Anti-Catholicism and Nineteenth-Century Fiction*. Cambridge: Cambridge University Press, 2004.

Bibliography

Guiley, Rosemary, and J. B. Macabre. *The Complete Vampire Companion*. New York: Macmillan, 1994.
Guran, Paula. "Playing with Plenty of Imaginary Toys." *Publisher's Weekly*, 24 March 2003, 63. Online at http://www.publishersweekly.com/pw/print/20030324/26290-playing-with-plenty-of-imaginary-toys.html (accessed 27 June 2011).
Gygax, Gary. *Advanced Dungeons & Dragons Monster Manual*. Wisconsin: TSR, 1977.
Hallab, Mary Y. *Vampire God: The Allure of the Undead in Western Culture*. Albany, NY: SUNY, 2009.
Hamill, Pete. *Snow in August*. New York: Little, Brown & Co., 1997.
Hamilton, Laurell K. *Blood Noir*. New York: Jove, 2008.
———. *Bloody Bones*. New York: Jove, 1996.
———. *Blue Moon*. New York: Jove, 1998.
———. *Bullet*. New York: Berkley, 2010.
———. *Burnt Offerings*. New York: Jove, 1998.
———. *Cerulean Sins*. New York: Jove, 2003.
———. *Circus of the Damned*. New York: Jove, 1995.
———. *Danse Macabre*. New York: Jove, 2006.
———. *Guilty Pleasures*. New York: Jove, 1993.
———. *The Harlequin*. New York: Jove, 2007.
———. *Hit List*. New York: Berkley, 2011.
———. *Incubus Dreams*. New York: Jove, 2004.
———. *The Killing Dance*. New York: Jove, 1997.
———. *The Laughing Corpse*. New York: Jove, 1994.
———. *The Lunatic Cafe*. New York: Jove, 1996.
———. *Micah*. New York: Jove, 2006.
———. *Narcissus in Chains*. New York: Jove, 2001.
———. *Obsidian Butterfly*. New York: Jove, 2000.
———. *Skin Trade*. New York: Jove, 2009.
Hamilton, Laurell K., and Leah Wilson, editors. *Ardeur: 14 Writers on the Anita Blake, Vampire Hunter Series*. Dallas: BenBella, 2010.
Handlen, Zack. Review of "Pretty Much Dead Already." *A.V. Club* (blog), 27 November 2011. Online: http://www.avclub.com/articles/pretty-much-dead-already,65692/.
He, Jenny. "Inhabiting Tim Burton's Universe." Curatorial Essay for the Museum of Modern Art's Tim Burton Exhibit. Online: http://moma.org/interactives/exhibitions/2009/timburton/includes/pdf/films.pdf.
Hearn, Marcus. *The Art of Hammer*. London: Titan Books, 2010.
Heldreth, Leonard G., and Mary Pharr. *The Blood Is the Life: Vampires in Literature*. Bowling Green, OH: Bowling Green State University Popular Press, 1999.
Hodkinson, Paul. *Goth: Identity, Style, and Subculture*. New York: Routledge, 2002.
Hontheim, Joseph. "Hell." In *The Catholic Encyclopedia*. Vol. 7. New York: Appleton, 1910. Online: http://www.newadvent.org/cathen/07207a.htm.
Hopkins, David "The Hero Wears the Hat: Carl as 1.5-Generation Immigrant and True Protagonist." In *Triumph of the Walking Dead: Robert Kirkman's Zombie Epic on Page and Screen*, edited by James Lowder. 201–15. Dallas: BenBella, 2011.
Hunt, Arnold. "Moral Panic and Moral Language in Media." *British Journal of Sociology* 48.4 (Dec. 1997) 629–48.
Hutchings, P. *The Horror Film*. New York: Longman, 2004.
Huxley, A. *Brave New World*. Bath, UK: Lythway, 1932.

Bibliography

Internet Movie Database. "*Land of the Dead.*" Online: http://www.imdb.com/title/tt0418819/.

Introvigne, Massimo. "Satanism Scares and Vampirism from the 18th Century to the Contemporary Anti-Cult Movement." Paper presented at the World Dracula Conference, Los Angeles, 1997. Online: http://www.cesnur.org/testi/vampires_wdc.htm.

Jenkins, Henry. *Convergence Culture: Where Old and New Media Collide*. Rev. ed. New York: New York University Press, 2008.

———. *Fans, Bloggers, and Gamers: Media Consumers in a Digital Age*. New York: New York University Press, 2006.

Johannes, Paulus, Jenny McPhee, and Vittorio Messori. *Crossing the Threshold of Hope*. New York: Knopf, 1994.

John Paul II. *Love and Responsibility*. San Francisco: Ignatius, 1981.

Kearney, Richard. *Strangers, Gods, and Monsters: Interpreting Otherness*. London: Routledge, 2003.

Kendrick, James. "A Return to the Graveyard: Notes on the Spiritual Horror Film." In *American Horror Film: The Genre at the Turn of the Millennium*, edited by Steffen Hantke, 142–58. Jackson, MS: University of Mississippi Press, 2010.

Kendrick, Walter. *The Thrill of Fear: 250 Years of Scary Entertainment*. New York: Grove Press, 1991.

Kenemore, Scott. "A Zombie among Men: Rick Grimes and the Lessons of Undeadness." In *The Triumph of the Walking Dead: Robert Kirkman's Zombie Epic on Page and Screen*, edited by James Lowder, 185–99. Dallas: BenBella, 2011.

Kirk, Robert. "Zombies v. Materialists." *Proceedings of the Aristotelian Society* 48 (1974) 135–52.

———. *Zombies and Consciousness*. Oxford: Clarendon, 2005.

Kirkman, Robert. "Introduction." In *The Walking Dead Chronicles: The Official Companion Book*, by Paul Ruditis, 8–11. New York: Abrams, 2011.

Klawans, S. "Alien Nation." *Nation* 281.4 (2005) 41–44.

Koven, Mikel J. "Have I Got a Monster for You!: Some Thoughts on the Golem, The X-Files and the Jewish Horror Movie." *Folklore* 111.2 (2000) 217–30.

Kristeva, Julia. *Black Sun: Depression and Melancholia*. European Perspectives. New York: Columbia University Press, 1989.

Laderman, Gary. *Rest in Peace: A Cultural History of Death and the Funeral Home in 20th Century America*. New York: Oxford University Press, 2003.

———. "Sacred & Profane: ARIS Survey Gets 'Religion', Misses Boat." *Religion Dispatches*, 11 March 2009. Online: http://www.religiondispatches.org/archive/atheologies/1209/sacred%26profane%3A_aris_survey_gets_%E2%80%98religion%E2%80%99%2C_misses_boat.

Laibach. *WAT*. Mute Records, 2003.

Lakoff, George, and Mark Johnson. *Metaphors We Live By*. Chicago: University of Chicago Press, 1980.

Laycock, Joseph. *Vampires Today*. Westport, CT: Praeger, 2009.

Leder, Herbert J., director. *It!* Warner Brothers, 1966.

Leggett, Paul. *Terence Fisher, Horror, Myth and Religion*. Jefferson, NC: McFarland Press, 2003.

Bibliography

Liaguno, Vince A. "Happy (En)Trails: Violence and Viscera on *The Walking Dead*." In *Triumph of the Walking Dead: Robert Kirkman's Zombie Epic on Page and Screen*, edited by James Lowder, 115–26. Dallas: BenBella, 2011.

Linton, George. "Reading the Apocalypse as Apocalypse: The Limits of Genre." In *The Reality of Apocalypse: Rhetoric and Politics in the Book of Revelation*, edited by David L. Barr, 9–42. Atlanta: Society of Biblical Literature, 2006.

Lloyd-Jones, D. Martin. *The Christian's Warfare*. Grand Rapids, MI: Baker Books, 2003.

Loudermilk, A. "Eating *Dawn* in the Dark: Zombie Desire and Commodified Identity in George A. Romero's *Dawn of the Dead*." *Journal of Consumer Culture* 3.1 (2003) 83–108.

Lowder, James. "In Media Apocalypsis." In *Triumph of The Walking Dead: Robert Kirkman's Zombie Epic on Page and Screen*, edited by James Lowder, xiii–xvii. Dallas: BenBella, 2011.

Luther, Martin. "Address to the Christian Nobility of the German Nation." Online: http://history.hanover.edu/texts/luthad.html.

Maberry, Jonathan. "Take Me to Your Leader: Guiding the Masses through the Apocalypse with a Cracked Moral Compass." In *The Triumph of the Walking Dead: Robert Kirkman's Zombie Epic on Page and Screen*, edited by James Lowder, 15–34. Dallas: BenBella, 2011.

MacKinnon, Donald. "Drama and Memory (1984)." In *Philosophy and the Burden of Theological Honesty: A Donald Mackinnon Reader*, edited by John C. McDowell, 181–88. London: T. & T. Clark, 2011.

Magil, Kevin. "Justifications for Violence." In *Encyclopedia of Violence, Peace, & Conflict*, edited by Lester Kurtz, 2:1085–97. Oxford: Elsevier, 2008.

Malkin, Nina. *Swoon*. New York: Simon-Pulse, 2010.

Maple, Eric. *The Dark World of Witches*. New York: Castle Books, 1964.

Marcel, Gabriel. *Being and Having*. Translated by Katherine Farrer. Westminster, UK: Dacre, 1949.

———. *Homo Viator: Introduction to a Metaphysic of Hope*. Translated by Emma Craufurd. Chicago: Regnery, 1951.

Marsden, George. *Fundamentalism and American Culture: The Shaping of Twentieth Century Evangelicalism, 1870–1925*. New York: Oxford University Press, 1982.

Maximus the Confessor. *On the Cosmic Mystery of Jesus Christ: Selected Writings from St. Maximus the Confessor*. Edited by Paul M. Blowers and Robert Louis Wilken. Crestwood, NY: St. Vladimir's Seminary, 2003.

McClelland, Bruce. *Slayers and Their Vampires: A Cultural History of Killing the Dead*. Ann Arbor, MI: University of Michigan Press, 2006.

McCloud, Scott. *Understanding Comics: The Invisible Art*. New York: HarperCollins, 1993.

McDonald, Beth. *The Vampire as Numinous Experience: Spiritual Journeys with the Undead in British and American Literature*. Jefferson, NC: McFarland, 2004.

McDowell, John C. "For What May We Hope? Karl Barth's 'Theology of Hope.'" *Whitefield Briefing* 5.5 (2000) 1–4.

McGowan, A. "Eating People: Accusations of Cannibalism against Christians in the Second Century." *Journal of Early Christian Studies* 2 (1994) 413–42.

Meeks, Wayne. "Social Functions of Apocalyptic Language in Pauline Christianity." In *Apocalypticism in the Mediterranean World and the Near East*, edited by David Hellholm, 687–706. Tübingen: Mohr, 1989.

Bibliography

Meikle, Denis. *A History of Horrors: The Rise and Fall of the House of Hammer*. Lanham, MD, & London: The Scarecrow Press, Inc., 1996.
Melton, J. Gordon. "Christianity and Vampires." In *The Vampire Book: The Encyclopedia of the Undead*, edited by J. Gordon Melton, 117–21. Detroit: Visible Ink, 1999.
———. *The Encyclopedia of Religious Phenomena*. Detroit: Visible Ink, 2007.
Milton, John. *Paradise Lost*. Edited by C. Ricks. New York: Signet, 1968.
Min-woo, Hyung. *Priest. Genesis. Vols. 1–3*. Translated by Jake Forbes. Los Angeles: Tokyopop, 2011.
Montenegro, Marcia. "The World according to Goth." *The Christian Research Journal* 29.1 (2006). Online: http://journal.equip.org/articles/the-world-according-to-goth-.
Morehead, John W. "Can Zombies Be Spiritual?." Theofantastique.com. Online: http://www.theofantastique.com/2011/03/10/can-zombies-be-spiritual.
———. "Toward a Zombie Theology." ReligionDispatches.org. Online: http://www.religiondispatches.org/dispatches/guest_blogger/3871/toward_a_zombie_theology/.
Moreman, Christopher M. "Dharma of the Living Dead: A Mediation on the Meaning of the Hollywood Zombie." *Studies in Religion/Sciences Religieuses* 39.2 (2010) 263–81.
Morgan, Kenneth O. *Britain Since 1945: The People's Peace*. London: Oxford University Press, 2004.
Mulvey, Laura. *Visual and Other Pleasures*. New York: Palgrave MacMillan, 2009.
Muntean, Nick. "Nuclear Death and Radical Hope in *Dawn of the Dead* and *On the Beach*." In *Better off Dead: The Evolution of the Zombie as Post-Human*, edited by Deborah Christie and Sarah Juliet Lauro, 81–97. New York: Fordham University Press, 2011.
Munz, Philip, et al. "When Zombies Attack!: Mathematical Modelling of an Outbreak of Zombie Infection." In *Infectious Disease Modelling Research Progress*, edited by J. M. Tchuenche and C. Chiyaka, 133–50. Hauppauge, NY: Nova Science, 2010.
Murphy, Colette. "Someday My Vampire Will Come? Society's (and the Media's) Lovesick Infatuation with Prince-Like Vampires." In *Theorizing Twilight: Critical Essays on What's at Stake in a Post-Vampire World*, edited by Maggie Park and Natalie Wilson, 56–69. Jefferson, NC: McFarland, 2011.
Murphy, Nancey. "Human Nature: Historical, Scientific, and Religious Issues." In *Whatever Happened to the Soul?: Scientific and Theological Portraits of Human Nature*, edited by Warren S. Brown, Nancey Murphy, and H. Newton Maloney, 1–30. Minneapolis, MN: Fortress, 1998.
Murray, Iain H. D. *Martin Lloyd-Jones: The Fight of the Faith*. Edinburgh: Banner of Truth Press, 1990.
Newman, Kim. *Doctor Who: Time and Relative*. London: Telos, 2001.
Newsom, Carol A., and Sharon H. Ringe. *The Women's Bible Commentary*. Louisville, KY: Westminster/John Knox, 1992.
Nickelsburg, George. "The Apocalyptic Construction of Reality in 1 Enoch." In *Mysteries and Revelations: Apocalyptic Studies Since the Uppsala Colloquium*, edited by John Joseph Collins and James H. Charlesworth, 51–64. Sheffield, UK: JSOT, 1991.
Nietzsche, Friedrich. *Thus Spoke Zarathustra*. Translated by Adrian Del Caro. Edited by Adrian Del Caro and Robert B Pippin. Cambridge Texts in the History of Philosophy. Cambridge: Cambridge University Press, 2006.

Bibliography

———. *The Will to Power*. Translated by Walter Kaufmann and R. J. Hollingdale. Edited by Walter Kaufmann. New York: Vintage, 1968.
Ojara, Pius, and Patrick Madigan. *Marcel, Girard, Bakhtin: The Return of Conversion*. European University Studies. Bern: Lang, 2004.
O'Leary, Stephen. "When Prophecy Fails and When It Succeeds: Apocalyptic Prediction and the Re-Entry into Ordinary Time." In *Apocalyptic Time*, edited by Albert I. Baumgarten, 341–62. Leiden: Brill, 2000.
O'Ohay, Revo, and Steven Leath, directors, "Night of the Living Bread." Online: http://www.gothicchristianity.com/galleries/art_livingbread.html; Accessed: November 11, 2010.
Paffenroth, Kim. "For Love Is Strong as Death: Redeeming Values in *The Walking Dead*." In *Triumph of the Walking Dead*, edited by James Lowder, 217–30. Dallas: Ben Bella, 2011.
———. *Gospel of the Living Dead: George Romero's Visions of Hell on Earth*. Waco, TX: Baylor University Press, 2006.
Partridge, Christopher. *Re-Enchantment of the West: Alternative Spiritualities, Sacralization, Popular Culture and Occulture Vols. 1 and 2*. London: T. & T. Clark, 2006.
Pegg, Simon, and Edgar Wright. *Shaun of the Dead*. Directed by Edgar Wright. Universal Pictures, 2004.
Pinnock, Sarah Katherine. "Existential Encounter with Evil: Gabriel Marcel's Response to Suffering as a Trial." In *Beyond Theodicy: Jewish and Christian Continental Thinkers Respond to the Holocaust*, 23–38. Albany, NY: State University of New York Press, 2002.
PiPaoulo, Mark. "Vampires." In *Encyclopedia of Religion and Film*, edited by Eric Michael Mazur, 443–49. Santa Barbara, CA: ABC-CLIO, 2011.
Pippin, Tina. *Apocalyptic Bodies: The Biblical End of the World in Text and Image*. New York: Routledge, 1999.
———. *Death and Desire: The Rhetoric of Gender in the Apocalypse of John*. Louisville: Westminster/John Knox, 1992.
———. "Reading for Gender in the Apocalypse of John." *Semeia* 59 (1992) 193–210.
Pirie, D. *The Vampire Cinema*. New York: Crescent, 1977.
Playdon, Zoey-Jayne. "What You Are, What's to Come: Feminism, Citizenship and the Divine in Buffy." In *Reading the Vampire Slayer: The New, Updated, Unofficial Guide to Buffy and Angel*, edited by R. Kaveney, 156–94. London: Tauris Parke, 2007.
Pohle, Joseph. "The Real Presence of Christ in the Eucharist." NEW ADVENT: Home. Online: http://www.newadvent.org/cathen/05573a.htm. Accessed 23 July 2011.
Polkinghorne, John. *The God of Hope and the End of the World*. New Haven, CT: Yale University Press, 2002.
Polkinghorne, John, and Michael Welker, editors. *The End of the World and the Ends of God*. Harrisburg, PA: Trinity, 2000.
Poole, W. Scott. "Praying to the Zombie Jesus." ReligionDispatches.org. 28 October 2011. Online: http://www.religiondispatches.org/archive/culture/5324/praying_to_the_zombie_jesus%3A_the_spirituality_of_horror/.
———. *Satan in America: The Devil We Know*. Lanham, MD: Rowman & Littlefield, 2009.
Porterfield, Amanda. *The Transformation of American Religion*. New York: Oxford University Press, 2001.

Bibliography

Powell, Anna. "God's Own Medicine: Religion and Para-Religion in U.K. Goth Subculture." In *Goth: Undead Subculture*, edited by Lauren M. E. Goodlad and Michael Bibby, 357–74. Durham, NC: Duke University Press, 2007.

Ramshaw, Marcus. "Being Christian and Being Goth: A Challenge for the Churches." Online: http://www.st-edwards-cam.org.uk/bcg.html.

Ratzinger, Cardinal Joseph. "Receiving the Tradition: Concerning the Notion of Person in Theology." *Communio* 17 (1990) 439–54. Online: http://http://www.communio-icr.com/articles/PDF/ratzinger17-3.pdf.

Regev, E. *Sectarianism in Qumran: A Cross-Cultural Perspective*. Religion and Society 45. Berlin: de Gruyter, 2007.

Reginster, Bernard. *The Affirmation of Life: Nietzsche on Overcoming Nihilism*. Cambridge: Harvard University Press, 2006.

Rice, Lynette. "The Best Bloodbath." *Entertainment Weekly*, 3–10 June 2011.

———. "The New American Gothic." *Entertainment Weekly*, 24 June 2011.

Riley, Brendan. "Zombie People: The Complicated Nature of Personhood in *The Walking Dead*." In *The Triumph of the Walking Dead: Robert Kirkman's Zombie Epic on Page and Screen*, edited by James Lowder, 81–97. Dallas: BenBella, 2011.

Ritzer, G. "Islands of the Living Dead: The Social Geography of McDonaldization." *American Behavioral Scientist* 47.2 (2003) 119–36.

Rollins, Walter, and Steve Nelson. "Frosty the Snowman." Columbia Records, 1950.

Rosen, Elizabeth K. *Apocalyptic Transformation: Apocalypse and the Postmodern Imagination*. Lanham, MD: Lexington, 2008.

Ruditis, Paul. *The Walking Dead Chronicles: The Official Companion Book*. New York: Abrams, 2011.

Rudwin, Maximilian. *The Devil in Legend and Literature*. Chicago: Open Court, 1931.

Russell, D. S. *Divine Disclosure : An Introduction to Jewish Apocalyptic*. Minneapolis: Fortress, 1992.

Russell, J. *Book of the Dead: The Complete History of Zombie Cinema*. Surrey, UK: FAB, 2005.

Russell, Jeffrey Burton. *The Devil: Perceptions of Evil from Antiquity to Primitive Christianity*. Ithaca, NY: Cornell University Press, 1977.

Russell, Robert John. "Scientific Insights into the Problem of Personal Identity in the Context of a Christian Theology of Resurrection and Eschatology." In *Personal Identity and Resurrection: How Do We Survive Our Death*, edited by George Gasser, 241–58. Aldershot, UK: Ashgate, 2010.

Sacchi, Paolo. *L'apocalittica Giudaica E La Sua Storia* Biblioteca Di Cultura Religiosa 55. Brescia, Italy: Paideia editrice, 1990.

Saintcrow, Lilith. "Ambiguous Anita." In *Ardeur: 14 Writers on the Anita Blake, Vampire Hunter Series*, edited by Laurell K. Hamilton and Leah Wilson, 25–40. Dallas: BenBella, 2010.

Sanders, E. P. "The Genre of Palestinian Jewish Apocalypse." In *Apocalypticism in the Mediterranean World and the Near East*, edited by David Hellholm, 447–60. Tübingen: Mohr, 1989.

Sargent, Tony. *Gems from Martyn-Lloyd Jones: An Anthology of Quotations from "The Doctor."* Exeter, UK: Paternoster Press.

Saviour Machine. *Legend Part 1*. MCM Music/Massacre Records, 1997.

Schindler, Dorman T. "Underworld seductress." *Publisher's Weekly*, 20 Sept. 2004. Online: http://www.publishersweekly.com/pw/print/20040920/35185-underworld-seductress-.html.

Schlozman, Steven C. "Feel Better: The Uncaring Science of *The Walking Dead*." In *The Triumph of the Walking Dead: Robert Kirkman's Zombie Epic on Page and Screen*, edited by James Lowder, 159–72. Dallas: BenBella, 2011.

———. *The Zombie Autopsies: Secret Notebooks from the Apocalypse*. New York: Hachette, 2011.

Schmitz, Kenneth L., and John M. Grondelski. *At the Center of Human Drama: The Philosophical Anthropology of Karol Wojtyła/Pope John Paul II*. Washington, DC: Catholic University of America, 1993.

Schneider, Peer. "IGN: An Interview with Joss Whedon." IGN Movies: Trailers, Movie Reviews, Pictures, Celebrities, and Interviews. Online: http://movies.ign.com/articles/425/425492p2.html.

Schüssler Fiorenza, Elisabeth. "Babylon the Great: A Rhetorical-Political Reading of Revelation 17–18." In *The Reality of Apocalypse: Rhetoric and Politics in the Book of Revelation*, edited by David L. Barr, 243–69. Atlanta: Society of Biblical Literature, 2006.

Scott, Ridley. "Joss Whedon Says Serenity Was Firefly Season 2 : SCI FI PI // SCI FI Channel." Home of SCI FI on FOXTEL & AUSTAR // SCI FI Channel. Online: http://www.scifitv.com.au/Blog/2010/08/joss-whedon-says-serenity-was-firefly-season-2/.

Sellars, J., editor. *Light Shining in a Dark Place: Discovering Theology through Film*. Eugene, OR: Pickwick, 2012.

Shakespeare, William. *The Tempest*. Edited by A. Durband. London: Hutchinson, 1985.

Shelley, Mary. *Frankenstein: or, The Modern Prometheus*. London: Lackington, Hughes, Harding, Mavor & Jones, 1818.

Shtulman, Andrew. "Variation in the Anthropomorphization of Supernatural Beings and Its Implications for Cognitive Theories of Religion." *Journal of Experimental Psychology: Learning, Memory, and Cognition* 34.5 (2008) 1123–38. Online: http://psycnet.apa.org/journals/xlm/34/5/.

Siegel, Carol. *Goth's Dark Empire*. Bloomington, IN: Indiana University Press, 2005.

Siouxsie and the Banshees. *Best of Siouxsie and the Banshees*. Polydor/Geffen Records, 2002.

The Sisters of Mercy. *Floodland*. Merciful Release/Elektra Records, 1987.

Skal, D. J. *The Monster Show: A Cultural History of Horror*. Rev. ed. London: Faber & Faber: 2001.

Soskice, Janet Martin. "The Ends of Man and the Future of God." In *The End of the World and the Ends of God: Science and Theology on Eschatology*, edited by John Polkinghorne and Michael Welker, 78–87. Theology for the 21st Century. Harrisburg, PA: Trinity, 2000.

Stanley, John. *Creature Features: The Science Fiction, Fantasy and Horror Movie Guide: Updated Edition*. New York: Berkeley Boulevard Books, 2000.

Stoker, Bram. *Dracula*. 1897. Reprint. New York: Puffin, 2009.

Stone, Bryan. "The Sanctification of Fear: Images of the Religious in Horror Films." *The Journal of Religion and Film* 5.2 (2001). Online: http://www.unomaha.edu/jrf/sanctifi.htm.

Bibliography

Stott, John. "The Message of Second Timothy." In *The Bible speaks Today*, p. 126. Downer's Grove: InterVarsity Press, 1973.

Stuart, Alasdair. "The Other Side of the Street: Anita Blake and the Horror Renaissance." In *Ardeur: 14 Writers on the Anita Blake, Vampire Hunter Series*, edited by Laurell K. Hamilton and Leah Wilson, 79–88. Dallas: BenBella, 2010.

Subissati, Andrea. *When There's No More Room In Hell: The Sociology of The Living Dead*. Saarbrücken, Germany: Lambert Academic, 2011.

Szerszynski, Bronislaw. *Nature, Technology, and the Sacred*. Oxford: Blackwell, 2005.

Tancons, Claire. "Occupy Wall Street: Carnival against Capital? Carnivalesque as Protest Sensibility." e-flux Journal #30 (December 2011). Online: http://www.e-flux.com/journal/occupy-wall-street-carnival-against-capital-carnivalesque-as-protest-sensibility/.

Thayer, Thomas B. *The Origin and History of the Doctrine of Endless Punishment*. Boston: Universalist, 1855.

Toppe, Jana. "Reversing the Gospel of Jesus: How the Zombie Theme Satirizes the Resurrection of the Body and the Eucharist." In *Roman Catholicism in Fantastic Film: Essays on Belief, Spectacle, Ritual and Imagery*, edited by Regina Hansen, 169–82. Jefferson, NC: McFarland, 2011.

Turner, Alice K. *The History of Hell*. Boston: Haughton Mifflin Harcourt, 1995.

Van Buren, Derek. "Atheists Continue to Disrespect Easter with Zombie Jesus Jokes, Photographic Sacrilege." Christwire.org. 4 April 2010. Online: http://christwire.org/2010/04/atheists-continue-to-disrespect-easter-with-zombie-jesus-jokes-photographic-sacrilege/.

Van Henten, Jan Willem. "Dragon Myth and Imperial Ideology in Revelation 12–13." In *The Reality of Apocalypse: Rhetoric and Politics in the Book of Revelation*, edited by David L. Barr, 181–203. SBL Symposium Series 39. Atlanta: Society of Biblical Literature, 2006.

Victor, Jeffrey S. *Satanic Panic: The Creation of a Contemporary Legend*. Chicago: Open Court, 1993.

Voltaire. *What is Goth?* Boston: Weiser, 2004.

VonWachenfeldt, Jason. "No Zombie Jesus: The Vatican and Roger Haight." *Religion Dispatches*, 1 April 2009. Online: http://www.religiondispatches.org/archive/atheologies/1318/no_zombie_jesus%3A_the_vatican_and_roger_haight.

Waller, G. A. *The Living and the Undead: From Stoker's Dracula to Romero's Dawn of the Dead*. Urbana, IL: University of Illinois Press, 1986.

Walliss, John, editor. *Reel Revelations: Apocalypse and Film*. Bible in the Modern World 31. Sheffield, UK: Sheffield Academic Press, 2010.

Walliss, John, and James Aston. "Doomsday America: The Pessimistic Turn of Post-9/11 Apocalyptic Cinema." *The Journal of Religion and Popular Culture* 23.1 (2011) 53–64.

Watterson, Bill. *Calvin & Hobbes*. 1985–95. Universal Press Syndicate.

Weiner, Robert G. "Marvel Comics and the Golem Legend." *Shofar: An Interdisciplinary Journal of Jewish Studies* 29.2 (2011) 50–72.

Wetmore, Kevin J. *Post-9/11 Horror in American Cinema*. New York: Continuum, 2012.

Whale, James, director. *Frankenstein*. Universal Pictures, 1931.

Whedon, Joss. "Joss Whedon: Atheist & Absurdist—YouTube." YouTube—Broadcast Yourself. Online: http://www.youtube.com/watch?v=EReyF2ZzXGA.

Bibliography

Wheen, Francis. *Strange Days Indeed: The 1970s: The Golden Age of Paranoia.* New York Public Affairs, 1970.

Wiesel, Elie. *The Golem: The Story of a Legend.* New York: Summit, 1983.

Wilcox, Rhonda. *Why Buffy Matters: The Art of Buffy the Vampire Slayer.* London: I. B. Tauris, 2006.

William of Newburgh. *Historia Rerum Anglicarum* (History of English Affairs) c. 1198. In *The Church Historians of England, Prereformation Series*, Volume IV, Part II. Translated by Joseph Stevenson, 657–61. London: Seeleys, 1861. (Latin text = *Historia Rerum Anglicarum*, Vol. II. Edited by H. C. Hamilton, 185–90. London: Sumptibus Societatis, 1858.)

Wilson, Amelia. *The Devil.* London: PRC, 2005.

Wisniewski, David. *Golem.* New York: Clarion, 1996.

Wojcik, Daniel. *The End of the World as We Know It: Faith, Fatalism, and Apocalypse.* New York: New York University Press, 1997.

Wood, R. "Apocalypse Now: Notes on the Living Dead." In *American Nightmare: Essays on the Horror Film*, edited by R. Wood and R. Lippe, 91–97. Toronto: Festival of Festivals, 1979.

Wooding, Chris. *Storm Thief.* New York: Orchard, 2006.

Worley, Lloyd. "Anne Rice's Protestant Vampires." In *The Blood Is the Life: Vampires in Literature*, edited by L. G. Heldreth and M. Pharr, 79–94. Bowling Green, OH: Bowling Green State University Press, 1999.

Yuzna, Brian, director. *Bride of Re-Animator.* Wild Street, 1990.

Zimmerman, Jens, and Brian Gregor, editors. *Being Human Becoming Human: Dietrich Bonhoeffer and Social Thought.* Princeton Theological Monograph Series. Eugene, OR: Pickwick, 2010.

Zizek, Slavoj. "Fantasy as a Political Category: A Lacanian Approach." In *The Zizek Reader*, ed. Elizabeth Wright and Edmond Wright, 91. Oxford: Blackwell, 1999.

Index

9/11, 121, 219
28 *Days Later* (2002) (film), 146

Abbot, Stacey, 19, 33, 241
Abraham (character), 170, 174, 180, 181
Abraham (religious figure), 229
Acts (Bible),103, 119
Adam (religious figure), 152, 196, 199
Adams, Douglas, 55
Adlard, Charlie, 169, 182, 189
Advanced Dungeons & Dragons Monster Manual (1977), 203, 208
Aeneid, 230
Afterlife, 107, 109, 110, 117, 198, 227–30
Aging, 108, 111, 114
Ahriman, 234
Al Qaeda, 176
Albanese, Catherine, xii, 115–16, 123, 241
Aleph, 199, 200
Alexandria, Virginia, 168, 169, 174, 181, 182, 186
Alice (character), 66
Alice in Wonderland (film), 220
Alien(s), 19, 22, 28, 32, 55, 63, 71
  Abduction by, 55, 71
Alien(film), 28, 33
Ali, Tariq, 241
Alighieri, Dante, 154, 158, 159, 163, 230, 231, 233, 238, 241
Allatius, Leo, 34

Allen (character), 174, 180
Altick, Richard D., 73, 241
Amazing Adventures of Kavalier & Clay, The (book), 201
Amazon, 206
AMC, xii, 79, 111, 166, 241
"American Babylon" (song), 218
Amos (Bible), 149, 160
American Religious Identification Survey, 113
Ante-Inferno, 230
Amy (character), 126
Anabaptists, 162
Anarchy, 60
"Ancient Booer" of Florin (character), 95
Andrea (character), 126, 139–40, 174, 181, 186
Andrew (character), 173
Anglican, 61
Angel(s), 20–23, 29, 71, 114–15, 234, 235
  Of mercy, 29
Angel (character), 43, 44
Angel (television show), 36
Anger, Kenneth, 64, 66
Anita Blake, Vampire Hunter, x, 5–16
Anomie, 21, 30, 126
Anthropology, xix, 46, 114, 118
Antonia (character), 221
Anti-Christ, 218
Anti-Semitic / Anti-Semitism, 198, 204, 205

257

Index

Apocalypse, xiii, xvii, 41, 79, 84, 102–6, 141, 145, 148, 165–67, 169, 176–79, 182, 183, 185, 187, 197, 206, 210, 212, 213, 219–23
Apocalyptic Bodies, 222
Aquinas, Thomas, 25
Archie (comics), 204
Aristotle, 25
Ardeur, 17
Armageddon, 43
Art, 105, 189, 227, 229
Arthur, Paul, 75, 241
Asimov, Isaac, 203, 208, 241
Asma, Stephen, 76, 241
Associated Press, 120, 241, 242
Aston, James, 121
Atheist / Atheism, 34, 65, 103
"Attacked by the Devil" (sermon), 59
Attire, 23, 215, 216
Atlanta, Georgia, 172, 183
Auerbach, Nina, 17, 241, 242
Augustine, Saint, 26, 33, 46, 53, 242
Aune, David, 223, 242
Autry, Gene, 204
Auschwitz, 159
Availability, 131–34, 136, 137, 139, 140,
Axel (character), 185

Babylon, 199, 211, 218, 219, 221–23
Baddeley, Gavin, 74, 219, 226, 242
Bader, Christopher D., 71, 76, 242
Badley, Linda, xii, 109–11, 116, 121, 242
Baker, J. D., 242
Baker, Richard, 162
Bandura, Albert, 175, 176, 178, 179, 184, 190, 242
Barber, Paul, 55, 73
Barker, Clive, xiv, xv, 227, 228, 231–35, 238, 239, 242

Barker, Leslie, 61, 62
Barkun, Michael, 33, 242
Barr, David L., 223, 242
Bartal, Inbal, 242
Barth, Karl, xii, xiii, 79, 83–88, 90, 92–94, 96–100, 125, 131, 136–38, 143, 144, 242, 243
Bass, Jules, 204, 243
Batman (character), 204
Bauckham, Richard, 211, 212, 224, 225, 243
Bauhaus, 213
BDSM, 10, 236
Beal, Timothy, 30, 33, 243
Beasley-Murray, George, 230, 243
Beast, the (character), 211, 218, 219, 221
Bebbington, D. W., 73, 74, 243
Bedazzled, 235
Beeson, Trevor, 74, 243
Beggars Banquet (album), 64
"Bela Lugosi's Dead" (song), 213
Bell, Emma, 126
Ben (character), 150, 174
Benedict XIV, Pope, xi, 24, 35, 45–47
Benefiel, Candace R., 17, 243
Beresford, Matthew, 4, 17, 243
Berger, Peter, 21, 30, 32, 33, 118, 123, 243
Bernthal, Jon (actor), 126
Bible, 58, 59, 80, 101, 105, 148, 187, 229, 234
"Big Daddy" (character), 159
Bishop, Kyle William, 182, 191, 243
Bittern, Lord Barkis (character), 221
Black Hat (character), 20, 22, 23, 29, 30, 31, 33
Black Sun, 215
Blake, Anita (character), x, 5, 11, 16
Blake, John, 187, 191, 243
Blake, William, 64
Blue Moon, 6

Blob, The (film), 222
Block, Ned, 97, 243
Blood, 7, 14, 21, 27, 30, 40, 43, 54, 55, 63, 66, 80, 92, 102, 103, 146, 147, 153, 173, 184, 188, 198, 199, 216, 217, 219, 221
Blood (video game), 23
Blood oath, 7, 14
Blumberg, Arnold T., xiv, xvii, 195
Body, xi–xiii, xv, 7, 37–39, 41, 49, 80, 86–88, 93, 94, 102, 107–12, 115–19, 202, 228, 230, 233
Boese, Carl, 243
Bohm, Anton Wilhelm, 243
Bokor, 197
Bonhoeffer, Dietrich, xiii, 125, 135–38, 143, 144, 243
Boon, Kevin, 188, 191, 243
Bonnie (character), 156
Bonnie and Clyde (1967) (film), 156
Book of Common Prayer, 58
Borah, Rebecca, 187
Boyle, Danny, 146
Breathers (book), 146
Brettany, Paul (actor), 20
Bride of Frankenstein, The (film), xv
Bride of the Re-Animator (1985) (film), 202, 208
Brill, Dunja, 215, 224, 225, 243
Britton, A., 161, 244
Brooklyn, 204
Brooks, Max, 98, 146, 165, 166, 190, 244
Brown, Warren S., 123, 244
Browne, S. G., 146
Browning, John Edgar, 33, 244
Buddhism, 6, 80, 114
Buffy (character), 35–45, 48
Buffy the Vampire Slayer (television show), xi, 19, 32, 34–53
Bullet, 15, 18
Bundtzen, Lynda K., 33, 244
Burnt Offerings, 5, 11, 17
Burton, Tim, 219–21

Bush, George W., 164
Bussee, Kristina, 52, 244

Callies, Sarah Wayne (actress), 126
Calvin and Hobbes, 208
Cambridge, 217
Camping, Harold, 104
Cannibalism, xiii, 114, 147, 158, 174, 186, 217, 218
Capek, Karel, 203, 244
Capitalism, 3, 150, 153, 157, 159
Calvin (character), 204
Calvin &Hobbes, 204
Cameron, James, 33
Carey, Greg, 211, 212, 224, 244
"Carmilla," 12
Carrasco, David, 33, 244
Carreras, James, 63
Carter, Margaret, 4, 17, 244
Cartesianism, 46
Carol (character), 169
Cash, Johnny, 148
Catholicism, 35, 36, 50, 51
Cattle mutilation, 55
Catastrophes, 104–5
Cavanaugh, William, 53, 244
Cecily (character), 39, 40, 42, 52
Celluoid Vampires,
Cemetery, 54–56, 67, 68, 70, 110, 202
Cenobites, xiv, xv, 227, 228, 231–38
Center for Disease Control, 121, 128, 139
Cerulean Sins, 8, 17
Chabon, Michael, 201, 244
Chalmers, David, 97, 244
Channard, Dr. (character), 233
Charles V of Spain, 29
Chelm, Poland, 199
Christ, 35, 41, 44, 45, 49, 87, 94, 101, 103, 111, 135–39, 141, 212, 216, 230
  Second Coming of, 104
Christie, Deborah, 244
Christmas, 31, 67, 204

259

Index

Christian in Compleat Armor, The, 60
Christian Warfare, The, 59
Christianity, xii, 5, 29, 36, 49, 52, 60, 80, 88, 93, 96, 101–3, 105, 109, 111–15, 117, 118, 120, 135, 141, 157, 160, 198, 206, 210, 216, 217, 228, 229, 235
Church, 6, 7, 8, 13, 36, 55, 58, 59, 61, 62, 64, 65, 66, 70, 80, 108, 109, 153, 157, 211, 214, 217, 221, 223, 229, 230, 234
Church Dogmatics, 83
Church of England, 61
Church of the Living Dead, 216
Church of the Resurrection, 103
City of the Dead (2005) (film), 146
Clay, 196, 198, 200, 203, 206
Clergy, 25–27, 31, 61, 107
Clifton, Jacob, 17, 244
Clover, Carol, 190, 244
CNN, 187
Cohen, Nick, 75, 244
Collins, Adela Yarbro, 212, 224, 244, 245
Collins, John J., 223, 245
Collins, Sean T. (character), 165, 166, 180
Comic, 105, 189, 201, 203
Commercial products, 105, 153, 155, 156, 233
Communion, 27, 28, 30, 61, 69, 72
Compton, Bill (character), 29
Confession, 27, 28
Constantine (film), 22
Cooney, Michael, 245
Cooper, Harry (character), 150, 162
Corpse Bride (film), 220
Cosplay, 102, 103
Cotton, Frank (character), xiv, xv, 227, 231–33, 235–37
Courtly, Lord (character), 66

Cowan, Douglas, 21, 22, 29, 30, 33, 115, 122, 245
Crane, Ichabod (character), 220
"Cremation of Sam McGee, The," 96
Cronenberg, David, 109
Cross / Crucifix, 5, 6, 13, 14, 19, 20, 23, 24, 25, 36, 65, 80, 135, 217
Crow, the, 221
Crowley, Aleister, 64, 66
Cruise, Tom (actor), 28
Cullen, Edward (character), 29
Cult, 55
Culture, 101, 105, 109, 110, 112, 195, 231, 233, 234, 237
  Ashkenazic, 196
  Babylonian, 199, 211
  British, 55–58, 59, 60, 61, 62, 63, 64, 65, 66, 67, 107, 213, 216
  Bulgarian, 31, 55
  Canadian, 91
  Eastern European, 31, 54, 55, 195, 205
  Egyptian, 234
  European, 55, 107, 213
  German, 200, 235
  Greek, 105, 206, 234
  Haitian, 146
  Mayan, 104
  Mediterranean, 196
  Norse, 206
  North America, 57, 213
  Persian, 234
  Polish, 198, 199
  Sephardic, 196
  Serbia, 55
  Swiss, 201
  United States of America, 55, 58, 61, 62, 63, 104–6, 113, 114, 145, 149, 150–51, 153, 201, 207, 213, 214, 218, 219, 223
  Western, ix, xi, 55, 101, 105, 107–9, 111, 114, 115, 119,

Index

Culture, Western (cont.), 160, 205, 214, 218, 222, 229, 233
    Yiddish, 205
Culture of Conspiracy, A, 28
Cuneo, Michael W., 74, 245
Cunningham, Conor, 142, 245
Curran, Andrew, 76, 245
Curse of Frankenstein, The (film), 63
Curse of the Golem (1966) (film), 200
Cushing, Peter (actor), 64

Danse Macabre, 13, 17, 18
Darabont, Frank, 97, 99, 124
D'Arbonne, Jess, 121, 245
Dargis, M., 164, 245
Dark Shadows, 19
Darkness, ix, xii, 8, 9, 15, 16, 21, 23, 26, 37, 39, 43, 54, 60, 67, 71, 72, 81, 91, 95, 96, 111, 114, 115, 118, 195, 197, 203, 205, 213, 214, 218–20, 227, 231, 236, 238
Darwinian / Darwinism, 115
Daubs, Katie, 121, 245
Davis, W., 160, 245
Dawn (character), 41
Dawn of the Dead (1978) (film), xiii, 147, 148, 150–51, 153, 154, 158, 161–64
Dawn of the Dead (2004) (film), 146–48, 154, 157
Day of the Dead (film), 159, 161, 163
DC Comics, 201
De Civitate Dei, 26
De Sade, 64
Dead Meat Walking: A Zombie Walk Documentary (film), 103
Death, xii, xiv, 16, 21, 30, 31, 35, 37, 41, 62, 66, 80, 86–89, 94, 95, 102, 103, 107–11, 114–19, 125–29, 132, 134–37, 139–41, 148, 154, 156, 158, 172, 173, 177, 179, 189, 199, 215, 216, 220, 229, 230, 234
    Repression of, 107–9, 111, 216
Death Becomes Her (film), 110
Decay, 96, 102, 108, 111, 118, 147
Decety, Jean, 242
DeCou, Jessica, xii
Deleuze, Gilles, 142
Demon / Demonic, xi, xii, xv, 4, 19, 20, 30, 31, 36–38, 40, 41, 49, 54, 57, 59, 61–63, 65, 71, 72, 131, 170, 228, 235, 236, 238
Demson, David E., 99, 245
DeMunn, Geoffry (actor), 130
Dennison, 17, 245
Despair, xiii, 95, 124–34, 136–41, 179, 214
Dexter (character), 169, 173, 174, 178, 180
Deuteronomy (Bible), 199
"Devil and the Nations, The" (sermon), 59
Devil's Advocate, The, 235
Diary of the Dead (film), 146, 161
Dillard, R. H. W., 161, 162, 245
Dillon, Martin, 75, 245
Dispensationalist, 217, 218
Divine, ix, xii, 5, 14, 30, 35, 38, 44, 46, 80, 84, 86–88, 91–94, 96, 105, 106, 117, 135, 196, 197, 230
Divine Comedy, 230–32
Dixon, Daryl (character), 79
Doctor Who: Time and Relative (book), 204, 208
Doomsday, 86, 104, 105
Donna (character), 172, 174
Dracula, 4, 12, 23, 24, 33, 35, 50, 73
Dracula, Count (character), 33, 54, 63, 65, 66

261

Index

Dracula Has Risen from the Grave (film), 64, 65, 67
Dracula 2000 (film), 24
Dredd, Judge (character), 24
Drescher, Fran (actress), 204
Drusilla (character), 39, 40
Dualism, xi, 4, 5, 12, 19, 23, 51, 87, 110, 112, 115, 117, 212, 213, 219–23, 229, 236
Dumpster-Geek (character), 85, 89, 90, 95
Dungeons & Dragons, 202
Du Plessis, Michael, 225, 245
Dusk till Dawn, 28
Dying to Live (book), 146
Dying to Live: Last Rites (book), 146
Dying to Life: Life Sentence (book), 146

Earth, 61, 71, 88, 106, 118, 148, 154, 196, 218, 227, 229, 230, 235, 237, 238
Easter, 103, 111, 153
Ecclesiastes (Bible), 95
Edward Scissorhands (film), 220
Eighteenth century, 34, 107, 199
Eliot, George, 55
Ellington, Devon, 17, 245
Ellis, Bill, 56, 57, 61, 62, 67, 68, 70, 73–76, 245
Eliyahu, Rabbi, 199, 200
'emes / truth, 198, 199
Emily (character), 220, 221
Emmerich, Noah (actor), 126, 130
End of Days, 235
Enlightenment, 27
Entertainment Weekly, 221
Entropy, 3, 4
Ephesians (Bible), 59–60
Erickson, Gregory, 34, 50, 246
Ernst, Monsignor (character), 64
Eschatology, xii, 102, 105, 106, 112, 117–19, 216

"Ethics of Zombie Destruction, The," 165
Eucharist, 49–50, 217
Eugene (character), 187
Eutychus (character), 119
Evangelical, xii, 58, 60, 61, 105
Eve (religious figure), 152, 234
Evil, xi, 3, 5, 6, 12–14, 16, 20, 22, 23, 35, 37, 40, 42, 44, 45, 49, 50, 54, 56, 59, 60, 62, 64, 66, 95, 159, 170, 175, 180, 197, 210, 213–15, 218, 221, 223, 227–30, 234, 235, 237, 238
Of Demons, xi, 20, 59, 60, 66, 234
Of Humans, 6, 95, 159, 170, 180, 227
Of Vampires, 5, 6, 16, 20, 40, 44
Evolution, 58, 115, 178, 205, 229, 238
Exclusion, xiv, 48, 158, 209, 210, 215, 218, 220, 222, 223
Existentialism, 36, 44, 49, 101, 188
Exorcist, The, 235
Ezekiel (Bible), xiii, 112, 122, 147

Faith, xii, 5, 6, 8, 12, 13, 20, 21, 26, 32, 36, 37, 43, 65, 71, 72, 81, 84, 94, 95, 107, 109, 113, 120, 125, 137, 149, 187, 228, 235–37
Family, 10, 24, 41, 42, 66, 92, 114, 131, 132, 139, 140, 174, 183, 185, 186, 203
Family Radio, 104
Fanon, Frantz, 179
Fantastic Four (character), 204
Farrant, David, 56, 67, 68
Faust (character), 228, 234–36
Fear, 4, 7, 8, 11, 14, 21, 25, 26, 28, 31, 68, 107–9, 117, 118, 168, 170, 188, 189, 198, 203–5, 214, 231, 232, 234
Fee, Gordon, xii

Index

Female behavior, 12, 35, 63, 152, 211, 213
Fey, 7
Fidelity, 131–34, 136, 137, 139, 140
Fido (film), 106, 146
Film, 105, 107, 108, 110, 111, 195
Film, Horror, and the Body Fantastic, 109
Fingeroth, Danny, 24, 33, 246
Fiorenza, Elizabeth Schussler, 211, 246
First Church of the Living Dead, 216
Flanagan, Owen, 97, 246
Flash mob, 102, 103
Flesh Golems, 201–3
Flirt, 13
Fondren, Natasha, 17, 246
Foree, Ken (actor), 154
Forsaken, The (film), 24
Fort Lauderdale, 170
Fran (character), 151–57, 162, 163
Frankenstein, Dr. (character), 63, 201, 202, 220
Frankenstein (film), 63, 200, 208
Frankentein: or, The Modern Prometheus, 201, 208
Fraser, J., 161, 246
Free will / lack of, 41, 42, 44, 47, 117, 196
Friedenberg, Richard, 208, 245
Friesen, Steven, 212, 224, 246
From Demons to Dracula: The Creation of the Modern Vampire Myth, 4
Frosty (character), 204
"Frosty the Snowman" (song), 204, 208
Fuller, Robert, 122, 246
Fundamentalism, 58
Funeral, 83, 108, 114, 115
Funeral homes, 108

Gaffney, Peter, 208, 246
Gage (character), 110, 111

Galatians (Bible), 216, 225
Garden of Eden, 234
Garrett, Susan, 211, 224, 246
Gasser, George, 246
Gehenna / Valley of Hinnom, 229, 231
Genesis (Bible), 196
Gentiles, 199
Georgia, 126
Giddens, Anthony, 33, 246
Giger, H. R., 28
Giles, 41
Gilmour, Michael J., 122, 246
Gilpin, Vicky, x
Glenn (character), 174, 181
Glinert, Lewis, 246
Glorificus (character), 37
God, xi, xiv, xv, 5, 8, 13–16, 19–23, 26, 27, 29, 30, 35–38, 42, 44–51, 60, 65, 71, 80, 84, 86–88, 92, 93, 95, 97, 101, 105, 112–14, 135, 136, 138, 139, 145, 147–49, 156, 157, 160, 187, 196, 197, 199, 202, 210, 218, 223, 229, 230, 232, 234–36
Goethe, Johann Wolfgang von, 158, 235
Goldberg, Lesley, 190, 246
Golem (book), 206, 208
Golem (character), xiv, 195–207
Golem: How He Came into the World, The (1920) (film), 200, 207
GOLEM: Journal of Religion and Monsters, 205, 208
Golem of Prague (character), 198, 199, 200, 204, 206
"Gonk, The" (song), 153
Goodness, xi, 5, 7, 8, 10, 15, 16, 20, 22, 35, 37, 41, 44, 45, 49, 60, 136, 137, 181, 185–87, 213, 214, 221, 227, 229, 230, 233–35
Gordon, Howard, 207, 246

263

Index

Gothic, xiv, 23, 27, 31, 63, 107, 209, 210, 212–23
    Literature, 31, 107, 219
Governor, The (character), 172, 174, 177, 180, 184, 187
Graham, Billy, 76, 246
Grahame-Smith, Seth, 146
Graille, Patrick, 76
Grave, 5, 30, 42, 54, 55, 67, 79, 80, 87, 91, 92, 108, 109, 112, 119, 151, 186, 202, 217
    Desecration of, 61, 62, 64, 66, 70
Graveyard School, 107, 121
Green, Joel B., 123, 246
Greene, Dr. Hershel (character), 80, 81, 98, 99, 101, 126, 140, 168, 173, 183–85, 187
Gregor, Brian, 143
Grief / Grieving process, 41, 42, 94, 108, 124–26, 129, 131
Griffin, Susan M., 33, 246
Grimes, Carl (character), 80, 126, 131, 133, 139, 168, 174–77, 185, 186
Grimes, Lori (character), 126, 131, 133, 139, 168, 173, 176–78
Grimes, Rick (character), 80, 81, 126, 130–35, 140, 141, 168, 169, 172–75, 177–86, 188, 189
Gruchy, John de, 135
Guiley, Rosemary, 33, 247
Guillermo (character), 133
Guilt, 9, 38, 84, 179, 188, 222, 232
Guilty Pleasures, 7
Guran, Paula, 247
Gurnell, William, 60
Gygax, G., 208, 247

Haight, Roger, 120
Hallab, Mary Y., 4, 17, 65, 73, 75, 247
Halloween, 153, 204, 220
Hamill, Pete, 204, 247

Hamilton, Laurell K., x, 3, 5, 9, 11, 12, 17–18, 246, 247
Hammer Horror, xi, 54, 57, 62–66, 72
Hampstead and Highgate Express, 54, 67
Handlen, Zack, 247
Happiness, 9, 11, 13, 49, 88, 89, 93, 151, 155, 158, 215, 216, 222, 236
Harker, Jonathan (character), 50
Harlequin, The, 13, 14, 17, 18
Hatcher, Lint, 50
He, Jenny, 220, 226, 247
Hearn, Marcus, 75, 247
Heaven, xv, 13, 42, 212, 221, 227, 229, 230, 234, 236, 237
Hebrew, xiii, 112, 149, 196, 198, 199, 203
Hebrews (Bible), 121
Hedonist, 231, 235
Hegel, G. W. F., 142
Heidelberg Catechism, 83
Heldreth, Leonard G., 33, 247
Hell, xiv, xv, 41, 43, 84, 94, 154, 158, 159, 202, 218, 227–34, 236–38
Hellbound Heart, The, xiv, 227, 231, 236, 238
Hellbound: Hellraiser II (film), 233
Hellraiser (film), 22, 235, 236
Henry, Carl F. H., xii
Heteronormative behavior, 8, 10–12, 14
    As good, 14
    Decline of in the twenty-first century, 11, 12
Hicks (character), 22, 25, 26, 31
Highgate, 54–57, 61, 62, 64, 65, 67, 68, 70, 72
Hinduism, 114, 234
Hiroshima, 159
Hirsch (character), 204
Hitchhiker's Guide to the Galaxy, 55

Hit List, 18
Hodkinson, 213, 215, 219, 224, 225, 247
Holden, Laurie (actress), 126
Holy Roman Emperor, 198, 199
Hontheim, Joseph, 238, 247
Hope / Lack of hope, xii, xiii, xv, 12, 37, 45, 79, 87, 92, 94–97, 102, 105, 106, 116–20, 124–32, 134, 135, 137–41, 148, 152, 154, 168, 228, 176, 217, 231, 232
Hopkins, David, 170, 189–91, 247
Hopper, Dennis, 157, 158
Horror, xi–xiii, xv, 20–22, 27, 28, 30, 32, 35, 54, 56, 57, 64, 72, 103, 106–12, 115, 116, 125, 139, 148, 149, 151, 153, 174, 200, 203, 210, 213, 216–20, 222
Horror of Dracula(film), 63
Horus, 234
Horvath, Dale (character), 81, 130, 131, 138–40, 177, 185, 186, 189
Houngan, 197
Hubris, 196, 197, 202, 203, 205
Humanity / Humans, ix–xii, xiv, 19, 20, 22–24, 27, 28, 31, 32, 47, 65, 79, 81, 84, 86–90, 92, 93–97, 106, 114, 118, 124, 127, 129, 131, 135, 136, 138, 151, 172, 183, 188, 189, 196, 202, 205, 213, 221, 227, 230, 232, 234, 237, 238
   Creation of, 196, 199
   Existence, 5
   Inhuman and, 84, 86, 88, 93, 94, 189
   Journey(s) of
      Psychological, x, 5, 83, 95, 186, 189, 233
      Spiritual, x, 5, 6, 8–11, 13, 14–15, 20, 38, 46, 94–95, 108, 113, 233
   Nature, 117
   Self-reflection, 6, 9, 10, 11, 16, 102, 109, 110, 111, 115, 116, 119, 129, 188
   Survival, 85, 93, 95–96, 104, 106, 118, 119, 131, 132, 186, 188, 189
   Violence, xiv, 148, 167, 185, 186, 188, 189
Hunt, Arnold, 76, 247
Hutchings, P., 161, 162, 247
Huxley, Aldous, 142, 247

Icarus, 237
Idol, Billy, 39
Inclusion, xiv, 209, 210, 215, 218, 220, 222, 223
Incubus Dreams, 17
Individualists, 104
Indra, 234
Inferno, 163
Interview with the Vampire, 28
Introvigne, Massimo, 33, 248
Irony, xiv, 209, 212, 222
Islam, 114, 217
Israel, 84, 112, 149, 156, 160, 217
Isaacs, Ivan (character), 23
It! (1966) (film), 200, 207, 248
"It! The Living Colossus," 201, 207
Italian, The, 27
Immortality, 38, 86, 87, 108, 117, 119, 132, 227–29
Incubus Dreams, 6, 10, 13, 15
Internet, 103, 205

Jack Frost (film), 204, 208
Jagger, Mick, 64, 66
Jain, Andrea Rene, 123
Japan, 102
Jean-Claude (character), 5, 7–9, 11, 12, 14, 15

Index

Jenkins, Henry, 120, 248
Jenner, Dr. Edwin (character), 126, 128–30, 134, 135
Jeremiah (Bible), 149, 156
Jerusalem, 25, 230
Jessie (character), 174, 182
Jesus, 80, 87, 103, 119, 120, 135, 206, 216, 217
Jesus, Symbol of God (book), 120
Jesus Was A Zombie! 103
Jim (character), 172
Johannes, Paulus, 248
Johannine corpus, xiv, 209
John (Bible), 98, 103, 122, 217
John (religious figure), 212, 213
John Carpenter's Vampires (film), 19, 22, 24
John Paul II, Pope, xi, 35, 47–48, 49, 53, 248
Johnson, Mark, 209, 223
Jones, Duane (character), 133, 172, 186
Jones, Morgan (character), 133, 184, 186
Joyce (character), 40
Judah (religious character), 149
Judaism, xiv, 101, 114, 195–99, 201–7, 230
Judeo-Christian, ix, 105, 106, 112, 197
Judgment, 105, 128–30, 145, 147, 149, 154, 156, 160, 228
Judgment Day, 148, 219
Julia (character), xv, 235

Kabbalah, 196
Kant, Immanuel, 142
Karloff, Boris, 63, 202
Karma, 5
Kaufman (character), 157–59, 164
Kearney, Richard, 33, 248
Keene, Brian, 146
Kendrick, James, 121, 248

Kendrick, Walter, xii, 107–10, 121, 122
Kenemore, Scott, 188, 191, 248
Killing, 5, 10, 25, 29, 31, 39, 43, 44, 56, 80, 81, 85, 90, 91, 93, 147, 150, 155, 159, 165, 166, 169, 170, 172–76, 178, 180–85, 188, 214
Killing Dance, The, 7, 14
Kimchi, 230
King James Bible, 60
King, Stephen, 110, 111
Kircher (character), 236
Kirk, Jeremy, 97, 120, 248
Kirkman, Robert, xiii, 97, 98, 120, 124, 165–72, 174, 176, 178, 182, 183, 184, 186, 187, 188, 190, 248
Kirsty (character), 232, 233, 236
Klawans, S., 164, 248
Klein, Mendy (character), 204
Knights Templar, 25
Knowledge, 46, 70, 88, 94, 140, 232, 234–36
Koven, Mikel, 207, 248
Kristeva, Julia, 215, 248
K'Vod HaMes (respect for the dead), 198, 202, 205

Laderman, Gary, 113–15, 122, 248
Laibach, 214, 248
Lakoff, George, 209, 223, 248
Lamb, the (character), 212, 216, 222
Lament Configuration, 227, 231
Land of the Dead (2005) (film), xiii, 106, 148, 157, 159, 164
Lantzman, 199
Laughing Corpse, The, 9, 17
Lauro, Sarah Juliet, 244
Laws of Robotics, 203, 208
Laycock, Joseph, xi, 67, 71, 73, 75, 76, 248
Lazarus (character), 111

Index

Leath, Steven, 225
Leder, Herbert, 207, 248
Lee, Christopher (actor), 54, 63, 65, 66
Lee, Stan, 199
Leggett, Paul, 74, 248
Legion (film), 20–22
Le Manoir du Diable (film), 19
Lemarchand's Box, 231, 235
Leviticus (Bible), 27
Lewis, C. S., 58
Lewis, Richard, 204
Liaguno, Vince A., 169, 190, 249
Lincoln, Andrew (actor), 126, 130
Linton, George, 223, 249
Literature, ix, 105, 212, 229
Little Nicky, 235
Lloyd-Jones, D. Martin, 58–62, 72–74, 249
Loa (religious figure / Voudoun god), 197
Loew ben Bezalel, Rabbi Judah (character / religious figure), 198–200, 204
Longbons, Jarrod, xi
Longbons, Junie, 50
Loudermilk, A., 163, 249
Louis (character), 36
Love, x, 3, 9–16, 39, 40, 42, 43, 45–48, 67, 80, 81, 92, 93, 132, 183, 217, 219, 220, 234
    As power, 11, 14, 15
    Friendship, x, 11–12, 14, 15, 37, 44, 49, 151
    Maternal, 11
    Protection, 12–14
    Religion and, 14, 46
    Sexual, 12, 43, 48
    Vampires lack of understanding of, 11
Lovecraft, H. P., 28
Lowder, James, 167, 190, 249
Luke (Bible), 48, 119, 149
Lust, 12, 14, 15, 43, 154, 180, 231

Differing from love, 11–12, 15
Evil and, 14
Luther, Martin, 27, 33, 125, 249

Maberry, Jonathan, 189, 191, 249
Macabre, J. B., 33
MacKinnon, Donald, 131, 134, 143, 249
Madigan, Patrick, 142
Maggie (character), 173, 187
Magic, x, 7, 11, 15, 37, 41, 45, 57, 64–66, 68, 72, 145–47, 167, 204
    Black magic, 57, 64–66, 68
Magil, Kevin, 171, 190, 249
Malcolm (character), 6–8, 13–15
Malkin, Nina, 206, 249
Mambo, 197
"Man Comes Around, The" (song), 148
Man-Thing (character), 198, 200, 207
Manchester, Sean, 54, 56, 67, 68
Maple, Eric, 66, 75, 249
Marcel, Gabriel, xiii, 125, 128–32, 134, 137, 138, 142–44, 249
Marsden, George, 74, 249
Martinez (character), 177
Marvel Comics, 198, 200, 204
Marx, Karl, 55, 138
Mary (character), 65
Mason, Peggy, 242
Matheson, Richard, 160
Matrix, The (film), 25
Matthew (Bible), 149
Maximus the Confessor, 51, 249
McClelland, Bruce, 31, 33, 249
McCloud, Scott, 167, 190, 249
McDonald, Beth, 4, 17, 249
McDowall, Roddy (actor), 200
McDowell, John C., 137, 138, 143, 144, 249
McGowan, Andrew, 225, 249
McPhee, Jenny, 247

Index

Media, ix, 57, 67, 68, 195, 203, 205, 227
Meeks, Wayne, 223, 249
Meikle, Denis, 63, 74, 75, 250
Melies, George, 19
Melton, J. Gordon, 33, 50, 250
Menken, F., 242
Mes (death), 199
Messiah, 30, 41, 44, 45
Messori, Vittorio, 247
Metaphysics / Metaphysical, 115–17
Mexico City, 102
Meyer, Stephanie, 145
Meyrick, Gustav, 200
Mezuzah, 199
Mic 3:11 (Bible), 149
Michael, Barkun, 28
Micheal (archangel / religious figure), 20, 234
Michonne (character), 174, 181, 184
Middle Ages, 26, 34
Middle East, 217
Milton, John, 60, 158, 164, 250
Min-woo, Hyung, 23, 33, 250
Mishnah, 205
Mitzvah, 199
MMORPG (massively multiplayer online role-playing game), 202
Molay, Jacque de, 25
Monk, The, 27
"Monolith, The" (character), 201
Monster (character), 63
Monster Island trilogy (books), 146
Montenegro, Marcia, 225, 250
Moore, Tony, 169
Morality, xii, 6, 8, 9, 16, 20, 48, 57, 60, 84, 117, 165, 175, 189, 212, 213
Moran, Caitlin, 216, 217
Morehead, John W., xii, xiii, 187, 191, 250

Moreman, Christopher M., 122, 250
Morgan, Kenneth O., 76, 250
Mortality, 111, 171, 188, 228
Moyer, Stephen (actor), 29
Moyse, John Ashley, xiii
Mulvey, Laura, 190, 250
Mummy, the (character), 63
Muntean, Nick, 179, 191, 250
Munz, Philip, 99, 250
Murder, 80, 165, 172, 188, 221
Murphy, Collette, 17, 250
Murphy, David, 187
Murphy, Nancy, 117, 123, 250
Murray, Iain H., 73, 250
Music, 105, 213
Mythology, xi, xii, xiv, 106, 110–12, 202, 205, 206, 227, 228, 231, 233–35, 237

Narcissus in Chains, 9, 11, 12, 17
National Weather Service, 162
Native Americans, 29
Neil-Smith, Christopher, 62, 64
Nelson, Steve, 204
Nero (character), 212
Neuroscience, 115, 117
New Age, 115, 116
New Creation, 119
New Heaven, 106
New Jerusalem, 106
New Orleans, 51
New Spirituality, 104
New Testament, 47, 103, 105, 111, 119, 229
New York Times, 157
Newman, Kim, 208, 250
Newsom, Carol A., 250
Nicholas (character), 181
Nickelsburg, George, 250
Nietzsche, Friedrich, xiii, 125, 127, 128, 136, 142, 250, 251
Night of theLiving Dead (1968) (film), 106, 108, 110, 114,

Index

Night of theLiving Dead (cont.), 145, 146, 148, 149, 160, 161, 217
Nightmare Before Christmas (film), 220
Nihilism, xiii, 45, 49, 102, 106, 119, 125–29, 132, 148, 150
Nine Inch Nails, 214, 224
Nineteenth century, 27, 28, 55, 62
Non-reductive physicalism, 117
Non-violence, 185
Normalcy, 126, 127, 158, 178, 214, 219, 220, 221
    Fetishization of, 9
Nun, 28

Occult, 64
Occupy Movement, 104
O'Hara, Scarlett (character), 95
Ojara, Pius, 129, 142, 251
Old Testament,145, 203, 229, 234
O'Leary, Stephen, 210, 223, 251
On the Beach (film), 179
O'Ohay, Revo, 225, 251
Order of the Gash, 231, 236
Orelas, Monsignor, 24, 27, 32
Ormuzd, 234
Orthodox Jews, 199, 204
Orwellian, 27
"Otherness," 4, 5, 7, 29
Otis (character), 133
Otto, Rudolf, 4, 9, 30
Our Vampires, Ourselves, 3, 17

Paffenroth, Kim, xiii, 132, 143, 183, 191, 251
Paganism, 26
Pain, xv, 232, 233, 235, 236
Paradise Lost, 164
Parker, J. Ryan, xiii
Parker, Peter (character), 207
Parody, xiv, 103, 212, 218, 222
Partridge, Christopher, 76, 105, 121, 122, 251

Passion of the Christ, 217
Passover, 111
Paul (religious figure), 65, 97, 216
Pegg, Simon, 98, 251
Pentagon, 157
Pentecostalism, 61
Pessimism, 106, 107, 118, 128
Pet Sematary (film), 110
Peter (character), 151, 152, 154, 155, 162, 163, 174
Peter Pan, 158
Pharr, Mary, 33
Phil (character), 89, 90, 95
Philip IV, King, 25
Picart, Caroline Joan, 244
Pinhead (character), 233, 235, 236
Pinnock, Sarah Katherine, 132, 143, 251
Pinocchio, 158
PiPaoulo, Mark, 33, 251
Pippin, Tina, 211, 222, 224, 226, 251
Pirie, D., 160, 162, 251
Pitt, Brad (actor), 28
Plato, 87
Playdon, Zoe-Jane, 36, 51, 251
Pleasure, xiv, xv, 231, 232, 235–37
Plessis, Michael du, 215
Poe, Edgar Allen, 107
Pogroms, 198
Pohle, Joseph, 251
Polger, Thomas, 97
Polkinghorne, John, 117, 118, 123, 251
Politics, ix, 28, 60, 228, 230
Pontiff, 48
Poole, W. Scott, xi, 168, 190, 251
Pop culture, ix–xv, 56, 57, 101–3, 112, 115, 119, 120, 188, 200, 202, 203, 205, 223
Porterfield, Amanda, 17, 251
Poseidon, 235
Possession, 55, 66
Post-apocalypse, 185

269

Index

Postmodern, 102, 106, 107, 112, 119, 120
Powell, Anna, 252
Power, x, 4, 7, 8, 11, 14–16, 20, 37, 199
Prague, 198–200, 203, 204
Pretorius, Dr. (character), xv
Pride and Prejudice and Zombies (book), 146
Priest (comic), 23
Priest (film), xi, 19–32
Priest, The (character), 20–27, 29–31
Priestess, The (character), 24, 25, 27
Priests, 25, 27, 197
Priests (character), 19, 20, 22–24
Priestess, 25, 197
Prometheus, 234
Propaganda, 26
Prophecy, The (film), 22
Prophet, xiii, 104, 149
Protection, 12–14, 22, 186, 197, 198, 206
Protestant, 105, 217
Psalm 139 (Bible), 196
Psycho (film), 200
Punishment, 232, 233
Purgatory, 230
Puritan, 58

"Questions and Answers on Healing and Demon Possession" (sermon), 59
Qumran, 162

Rabbi, 196–201, 204
Racism, 150–53, 159
Raising the Devil: Satanism, New Religions and the Media, 57
Ramshaw, Marcus, 225, 252
Rankin, Arthur, Jr., 204, 242
Rapture, 218
Rathburn, Cliff, 169, 182, 189

Ratzinger, Joseph, 52, 252
Rava / Abba ben Joseph bar Hama, 199
Re-Animator (film), 202
Rea, Stephen (actor), 204
Redemption, 43, 44, 49, 87, 88, 91, 94, 109
Reformation, 36, 51
Regev, E., 162, 252
Reginster, Bernard, 242, 252
Relationship, xi, xiii, 132, 133, 151, 152
Religion, x, 3–5, 7, 105, 110, 111, 187, 236, 238
  View of "the other," ix, 5
Religion and Its Monsters, 30
Religion Blog, 187
Religion Dispatches (essay), 113, 120
Renaissance, 228
Renfield (character), 33
Resident Evil, 146
Resident Evil (films), 146
Resurrection, xii, 41, 42, 45, 87, 93, 101, 103, 106, 109–12, 115, 116, 118, 120, 125, 136, 141, 187, 221, 222
Revelation (Bible), xiii, 25, 105, 148, 209–12, 216–19, 221–24, 226
Rice, Anne, 4, 28, 36, 50, 51
Rice, Lynette, 226, 252
Richards, Keith, 64
Riggs, Chandler (actor), 126
Riley (character), 159
Riley, Brendan, 188, 191, 252
Rising, The (film), 146
Ritual, 27, 31, 55, 62, 66, 111
Ritzer, G., 163, 252
Robot, 201, 203
Roger (character), 151, 152, 154–56, 162
Rolling Stones, the, 64
Rollins, Walter, 204, 252

Roman Empire, 26, 217, 218, 228
Romans (Bible), 59, 96, 97
Romantic / Romanticism, 107, 235
Rome, 211, 230
Romero, George, xiii, 106, 110, 114, 145–50, 153, 154, 157–61, 163, 164, 182
Rosen, Elizabeth, 106, 121, 252
Rossetti, Christina, 55
Rory (character), 232
Ruditis, Paul, 190, 248, 252
Rudwin, Maximilian, 234, 235, 239, 252
"Rudolph the Red-Nosed Reindeer" (song), 204
Rumor of Angels, A (book), 118
Rumsfeld, Donald, 164
R.U.R.: Rossum's Universal Robots (1921), 203, 208
Russell, J., 161, 164, 252
Russell, Jeffrey Burton, 239, 252
Russell, Robert John, 123, 252

Sabbath, 49
Sacchi, Paolo, 223, 252
Sacramento, 102
Sacred, xi, 30, 113–15
Sacred Matters (book), 113
Sacred order, 30
Sacred Terror: Religion and Horror on the Silver Screen, 21
Sacrifice, 25, 41, 155, 217, 218
 Self-sacrifice, 41, 43, 87
Saintcrow, Lilith, 252
Samedi, Baron (religious figure / voudon god), 197
Sanders, E. P., 223, 252
Sargent, Tony, 74, 252
Sartre, Jean Paul, 124, 141, 142
Satan / Satanists, 35, 54, 55, 57, 59–62, 64, 65, 157–59, 219, 228, 233, 234
 Devil, xi, xii, xv, 62, 65–67, 227, 228, 234–38

 Fall, 60
 Lucifer, 60, 234, 237
 Possessed, 66
 Prince of Darkness, 61
 Satanists, 54
 Ritual, 55, 66
 Satantic Panic, 57
 Satanic Rites of Dracula, The (film), 57
Satire / Satirical, xii, 103, 112, 116, 188, 212
Satre, Jean-Paul, 32, 124, 128, 130, 134
Sauron (character), 60
Saviour Machine, 217–19, 226, 252
Schindler, Dorman, 17, 253
Schism, 231, 232
Schlozman, Steven, 98, 179, 191, 253
Schmitz, Kenneth L., 38, 51, 253
Schneider, Peer, 253
Schüssler Fiorenza, Elizabeth, 224, 253
Science, xi, 147, 187, 197, 236
Scripture, 46, 113, 187
Scoobies, The (character), 36, 37, 40–44, 50
Scott, Stewart, 20, 22, 28, 253
Second Timothy (Bible), 74
Secular / Secularism, xi, 112, 229
Sefer Yetzirah / Book of Creation, 196
Self-defense, 93
Sellars, J., 253
Sex, x, 6, 9–11, 15, 42, 43, 48, 58, 64, 66, 156, 205, 215, 236
 Ritualized, 6
Sexism, 152
Shakers, 162
Shakespeare, 142, 253
Shaun of the Dead (film), 106, 146, 163
Shelley, Mary, 201, 202, 253
Shema Yisrael, 199

Index

S.H.I.E.L.D., 201
Shin / God, 199
Shtulman, 4, 17
Sholem the Golem (character), 204
Shtulman, Andrew, 17, 253
Shuster, Joe, 201
Sid and Nancy (characters), 39
Siegel, Carol, 214, 224, 225, 253
Siegel, Jerry, 201
Simpsons, The, 204, 208
Sin, xv, 154, 228–34, 238
Siouxsie and the Banshees, 214, 224, 253
Sisters of Mercy, 225, 253
Sixth commandment, 92
Skal, D. J., 163, 253
Skellington, Jack (character), 220
Skin Trade, 6, 17, 18
Slayer / slaying, 31, 34, 39, 40, 44, 45
Slayers and their Vampires, 31
Snow in August (1997) (book), 204, 208
Snow in August (2001) (film), 204, 208, 245
"Snowlem," 204
Snyder, Zack, 146
Society, 3, 4, 21, 56, 59, 101, 149, 150, 210, 212
    Religion in, 21, 59
Solidarity, xiii, 124, 135, 136, 138–41
Sophie (character), 184, 185
Soskice, Janet Martin, 123, 253
Soul / Soullessness, xi, xv, 47, 87–88, 93–94, 110, 112, 115, 117, 118, 186, 196, 198, 214, 227–30, 232, 235–37
    Human, 47, 87, 110, 186, 196
Soul Lite, 197
Spider-Man (character), 204, 207
Spike / William (character), xi, 35, 37–46, 48, 49, 51, 52
Spinoza, Baruch, 142

Spirit, 87
Spiritual, x, xii, 107–9, 111, 112, 116, 205, 236
Stackhouse, Sookie (character), 226
Stanley, John, 64, 74, 253
Star of David, 200
Steve (character), 152–56, 162
Stevens, Dr. (character), 180
Stewart, Ryan, 50, 52
Stigmata (film), 22
"St. James Infirmary," 96
St. Louis, 5
Stoke, Father Gabriel (character), 174, 187
Stoker, Bram, 23, 33, 35, 36, 50, 73, 182, 253
Stone, Bryan, 122, 253
Stonebrook, Marnie (character), 221, 222
Storm Thief (book), 206, 208
Stott, John, 58, 59, 61, 74, 254
Stovell, Beth, xiv
Stovell, Jon, 225
Strange Tales, 201
Stuart, Alasdair, 254
Subissati, Andrea, xiv, xv, 120, 121, 254
Suffering, 229, 232, 233
Suicide, 80, 83, 84, 94, 95, 130, 159, 186, 235
Superman (character), 201
Supernatural, xiv, 112, 149, 197
Survivalists, 104
SWAT, 150
Swoon (book), 206, 208
Symbolism, ix, 212, 223, 235, 237
"Sympathy for the Devil" (song), 64
Szerszynski, Bronislaw, 51, 254

Talmud, 196, 199, 203
Tancons, Clarie, 121, 254
Taste the Blood of Dracula (film), 64–67
Technology, 227, 237

Tempest, The, 142
Tertullian, 45
Temptation, xv
"Ten-The Empire" (song), 218
TEOTWAWKI / The End Of The World As We Know It, 80, 82, 97
Texas Chainsaw Massacre (film), 161
Their Satanic Majesties Request (album), 64
Thayer, Thomas B., 238, 254
Thomas (character), 173, 176, 177
Thomas, John Christopher, xii
Thomism, 25
Tiffany (character), 233
Thrill of Fear: 250 Years of Scary Entertainment, The, 107
Tibetan Book of Dead, 114
Times, The, 216
To Present an Eschatology of Hope, 118
Tolkien, J. R. R., 60
Toppe, Jana, 122, 254
Torah, the, 197
Tradition, ix, 113, 126, 237
Transcendence, 109, 110, 118, 119, 228
Trinity, 46
TrueBlood, 29, 168, 221, 222, 226
Turner, Alice K., 238, 254
Twentieth century, 4, 36, 55–57, 188, 202
Twenty-first century, 3, 11, 101, 116, 145, 206, 207, 237
Twilight (film), 19, 28, 145, 168
Tyreese (character), 172, 173, 178, 180, 184

Übermensch, 136
Un Homme de Dieu/ A Man of God, 134
Understanding Comics: The Invisible Art (book), 167
Underworld, 221
Uncyclopedia, 103
Undead, ix–xii, xiv, xv, 36, 38, 44, 49, 54, 80, 84, 85, 89, 91, 92, 94, 115, 140, 149, 170, 171, 189, 195, 198, 200, 201, 205, 206, 210, 216, 219, 222, 223
Union Theological Seminary, 120
United Nations, 86
United States of America, 55, 58, 61, 62, 63, 104–6, 113, 114, 145, 149, 150–51, 153, 201, 207, 213, 214, 218, 219, 223

Universal Pictures, 202
Upanishads, 114
Urban, Karl (actor), 20

Vampire as Numinous Experience, The, 4
Vampire Chronicles, 36
Vampire God: The Allure of the Undead in Western Culture, 4, 17
Vampire Hunter D (film), 23, 33
Vampire, The, 5
Vampires, ix–xi, 3–76, 147, 205, 221, 222
   Anti-vampire weapons, 5, 19, 23–25, 35, 36, 43, 50, 55, 56, 65, 67
   Stake, 67
   Appearance, 28
   As deified, 30, 31
   As diabolical, 4, 30, 37, 39, 40
   As disease, 3
   Attack, 147
   Attracted to light and sound, 80
   Attraction of, 4, 28
   Blood, 40, 66, 216
   Blood oath of, 7, 14
   Christian symbolism and, 5, 64
   Difference from humans, xi, 37, 47

Index

Vampires (cont.),
 Entropy and, 3–4
 Evil of, 6, 16, 40, 44
 Faith and, 5, 6, 13, 43, 65,
 Familiar of, 28, 29, 30, 33
 Feeding of, 40, 66
 Forming of, 39, 55
 Human qualities of, 4, 11, 19, 49
 Love and, 3, 4, 10–12, 43
 Lust and, 11–15, 40
 Morals of, 6, 8, 9, 16, 29, 41, 44
 Natural / supernatural, 5
 Otherness of, xi, 4, 28, 37
 Power and / of, 4, 7, 8, 11, 14, 15, 43
 Religion and, 3–5, 7, 19–22, 24, 64
 Sex and, 6, 9, 10, 11, 15, 42, 64
 Societal issues and, 3, 4, 67
 Soul / Soulless, xi, 7, 9, 10, 28, 35, 37, 38, 42–44, 47–49
 Spiritual transformation of, 5, 6, 8–11, 13, 14–15
 Superhuman qualities of, 4, 24, 28, 44, 147
 Symbolism of, 3–5, 14, 29, 64
  Religious, 64
  Native American, 29
  Throughout history, 23
  Tropes of, 4, 5
Vampirism: Literary Tropes, 17
Vampires Today, 67
"Vampyre, The," 11
Van Buren, Derek, 121, 254
Van Helsing (character), 24, 50, 56
Van Helsing(film), 24
Van Henten, Jan Willem, 254
Vatican, 120
Vatos,the (character), 133
Via Dolorosa, 41
Victor (character), 220
Victor, Jeffrey, 56–57, 73, 254
Vietnam, 160
Violence, xiii, xiv, 148, 165, 167–69, 173–76, 178, 179, 185, 186, 188, 189, 199, 227
Virgil, 230
Virginia, 168, 181
Visigoths, 26
Vltava, 198
Voltaire, 27, 214, 219, 224, 226, 254
Von Wachenfeldt, Jason, 123, 254
Voodoo / Voudoun, 146, 197
Vrita, 234

WAHBL / When All Hell Breaks Loose, 88
Walking Dead, The (comic), xiii, 79–81, 101, 124, 146, 166, 186, 189–91
Walking Dead, The (television show), xii–xiv, 97–99, 106, 111, 124–26, 132, 139, 141, 142, 146, 160, 167–69, 171, 172, 175, 176, 182, 183, 187–89
Wall Street, 157
Waller, G. A., 160–64, 254
Walliss, John, 121, 254
Walsh, Shane (character), 126, 131, 133, 134, 140
Walsh, Susan, 73
War, 23, 141, 234
Watterson, Bill, 208, 254
Weapon, 104
Wegener, Paul (actor), 200, 204
Weiner, Robert G., 254
Welker, Michael, 123
Wellington, David, 146
Werewolves, 6, 147
 Ritual of, 6
West, Dr. Herbert (character), 202
Western Civilization (or Culture), ix, xi, 55, 101, 105, 107–9, 111, 114, 115, 119, 160, 205, 214, 218, 222, 229, 233
Westminster Record, 59

Index

Wetmore, Kevin J., 121, 254
Whale, James, 63, 254
Whedon, Joss, 34, 50, 254
Wheen, Francis, 55, 73, 75, 76, 255
White House, the, 157
White Zombie (1932) (film), 145
Wicca, 6, 36, 37, 221, 222
Wiesel, Elie, 206, 255
Wilcox, Rhonda, 41, 52, 255
William of Newburgh, 99, 255
Wilson, Amelia, 239, 255
Wilson, F. Paul, 28
Wilson, Leah, 244, 245, 247, 252, 253
Wilson, Scott (actor), 126
Wisniewski, David, 206, 255
Wojcik, Daniel, 105, 121, 255
Wolfman, the (character), 63
Wood, Ed (character), 220
Wood, R., 161–63, 255
Woodbury, 174, 176, 177, 180
Wooding, Chris, 206, 255
Woods, Paul Anthony, 226
Word, 199
World of Warcraft, 202
World Interfaith Council, 86
World Trade Center (WTC, Two Towers), 219
World War Z (book), 146, 165, 166, 180
World War I, 55
World War II, 55, 58
Worley, Lloyd, 36, 50, 51, 255
Wright, Edgar, 98, 251
Writing Horror and the Body (book), 110

X-Files (television show), 200, 207
Xenophobia, 3

Yarbro, Chelsea Quinn, 4
YouTube, 103
Yuzna, Brian, 208, 255

Zen, 79
Zeus, 234
Zimmerman, Jens, 143, 255
Zizek, Slavoj, 76, 255
Zombie Strippers (film), 146
Zombiedefense.org, 165, 171
Zombies, ix, x, xiv, 77–191, 205, 217
    Anti-zombie weapons,
        Blade, 91
        Cold, 82, 95
        Crossbow, 83
        Crowbar, 83
        "Defusing," 83, 95, 96
        Decapitation, 146
        Disease, 147
        Disposing, 84, 95
        Fire, 83, 92
        Gun, 83, 91, 146
        Pick-axe, 83
        Trap, 81, 85, 92, 140, 184
        Water, 82
    Apocalypse, 79, 106, 179, 183
    Appearance, 90
    Attack, 147
    Denver Zombie Crawl, 103
    Difference from humans, 83, 86, 90
    Feeding of, 80, 124, 189
    Forming of, 89, 147
        Bacteria / contagion / infection / virus, 89, 91, 146
        Bite, 170
    Infection, 146, 147
    Humanization of, 81, 84
    Human qualities of, 79, 187
    Humans and coexisting with, 106
    Mob, 146
    Names for,
        Geeks, 82, 84, 85, 89, 90, 92, 94, 96
        Drones, 82
        Slugs, 82

Index

Zombies, Names for (cont.),
   Goons, 82
   Leeches, 82
   Living dead, 106, 115
   "Bob," 82
   Walker, 81, 82, 89, 92, 94,
      124, 126, 129, 133, 140
Outbreak, 79
Philly Zombie Crawl, 103, 121
Philosophical, xii, 79, 90, 91,
   93, 187
Rising of, 92, 112
Qualities of, 146–47
Re-animation of, 94, 197
Reaction to, 91, 140, 184
Religion and, 91, 187, 197
Rightness of killing of, 84, 85,
   88, 93, 94, 97, 140, 184
Romero rules of, 146
Symbolic of, 147
Zombie Jesus, xii, 103, 104, 106,
   109, 112, 113, 115, 120
Zombie Jesus Day, 103, 113
Zombie Walk, xii, xiii, 101–4,
   106–9, 111–19, 163
Zoroastrian / Zoroastrianism, 229

www.ingramcontent.com/pod-product-compliance
Lightning Source LLC
Chambersburg PA
CBHW071238230426
43668CB00011B/1491